PEARSON CUSTOM LIBRARY

COMMUNICATION

PUBLIC ORAL COMMUNICATION
Indiana University
2nd Edition

ISBN 10: 1-269-28791-5
ISBN 13: 978-1-269-28791-3

Table of Contents

Public Oral Communication

An Introduction to the Textbook

A course in public oral communication may be among the most valuable and most useful classes you will take.   It will help you to become more comfortable speaking before a group, something that you will almost certainly be required to do in any career you choose.   In survey after survey, employers emphasize the importance of oral communication skills, often ranking them at the very top of their list of the skills they desire most among their new employees.   Gaining the ability to organize and articulate your thoughts in an oral presentation also means that you will be able to participate more fully and more effectively in your civic life, as a neighbor, citizen, and advocate.   There will be times when you need to speak out on issues that are important to you — perhaps to protect your own interests or those of others, perhaps to articulate or defend your values, or perhaps to gain approval or support for a proposal — and this course will enhance your ability to do so effectively.   The skills that you learn in this course also will contribute to your success in most other courses that you take, enabling you to respond more successfully to questions and to contribute more confidently to class discussions. Your effectiveness as a communicator — whether as professional, citizen, or student — always is improved by thinking of your message as addressed to a specific audience and by practicing the art of tailoring your message to that specific audience.

Just as important as the skills that you will gain in speaking by taking this course are the skills that you will acquire in listening. The ability to attend carefully to an oral presentation is an extraordinarily useful skill that will serve you in all of the same ways as skill in speaking: it will make you more comfortable in situations in which information is being presented orally, it will enable you contribute more substantively in your work life and in your civic life, and of course listening skills are among the most important learning tools that you can cultivate. Developing your skills as a listener fosters your ability to put yourself in another's shoes, to see an issue, a problem, or a proposal — and of course also your own positions and values — from another's point of view. The two skills, speaking and listening, actually depend upon one another: almost all public oral communication is produced in response to some other public oral communication, so the more effectively you are able to listen to that other public speech, the more effective your own speech is likely to be.

The teaching of public speaking as a foundation to later success in both professional and civic life is associated with the art of *rhetoric*. As you will learn from reading some of the chapters of this textbook, the study of rhetoric goes back over 2500 years, to the beginning of democracy in ancient Athens. In order for a democracy to function, citizens must be able to make their points in public and also must be able to interpret, critique, and respond to the public communication of others. Simply put, a robust democratic culture cannot be sustained without a citizenry skilled in the art of rhetoric. So as you take this course, and as you read this textbook, you participate in a long tradition of people turning to the study of rhetoric as a vital component of their preparation for civic and professional life.

This textbook has been specially assembled for this class. The chapters have been selected from several different textbooks in order to best address the particular goals and objectives of this class. For that reason, some of the chapters may refer to ideas or concepts that appeared in other chapters in the textbooks from which those chapters were taken but that do not appear in this custom textbook, or in a few cases some of the chapters may use different terms to refer to similar concepts. I realize that this may cause some inconvenience and perhaps even some minor confusion from time to time, but it allows this textbook to draw from some excellent textbooks only those particular sections that are most specifically related to this class. However, as long as you follow the reading schedule as outlined in the Course Syllabus and attend or view all of the Lectures and Speech Workshops, you should have no trouble keeping on track.

- Robert E. Terrill, Course Director

- Cynthia D. Smith, Course Coordinator

Public Speaking and the Public Sphere

David Young-Wolff/PhotoEdit, Inc.

This chapter is intended to help you:

- See how public speaking benefits you in many areas of life
- Understand the public dimensions of public speaking
- Learn how public speaking is part of a communication process
- Identify how public speaking is connected to democracy
- Recognize the ethical challenges and opportunities of public speaking

Colleges and universities today are encouraging students to engage with public issues in a variety of ways. Inside the classroom, you may find yourself exploring daunting topics such as terrorism, globalization, climate change, and health care. Outside the classroom, students are engaging in diverse forms of service in their local communities and around the world. Traditional political activity has seen resurgence, too—through voter registration drives, face-to-face campaigning, and lobbying by and for students. Even getting involved with clubs, student government, or your residence hall are ways in which you can engage with issues that affect your campus community.

CASE SCENARIO

Carlos Serves His Community through Public Speaking

Carlos is in his last semester of college and is thinking about his future, but he is also thinking about how he got to this point in his life. In high school, his guidance counselor did not give Carlos much help in identifying colleges or careers that might suit him. His parents had not attended college and were unfamiliar with the details of the admissions process. Somehow, he managed to figure it out on his own, and he is now about to graduate with a degree in engineering. He just wished it could have been a little easier.

One day on campus, Carlos saw a flyer for a group called MEChA, or Movimiento Estudiantil Chicano de Aztlán. He read that the group was planning its annual youth conference, which brought Latino high school students to campus to inform them about their options after graduation, including college. Carlos thought this would be a great opportunity. He thought he could help out by reserving rooms or making the lunch arrangements. But by the end of the first planning meeting, he found himself on the list of potential speakers; he would be speaking about the rights of students from immigrant families. He was a little nervous but also excited by the prospect of contributing something to his community.

Indeed, the stereotypes of lazy or self-absorbed students no longer fit. No matter what their background, students are active participants in public life. Some of you may come with experience in such activities—volunteering for a soup kitchen or a political campaign, for example—while others of you may have little familiarity with or interest in them (CIRCLE, 2006). Ideally, during the course of your college career, each of you will find some opportunity for engagement. No matter when or where that happens, you can be more confident and more effective if you have training and practice in public speaking.

This text can give you guidance for becoming a better public speaker. Like other texts on public speaking, it will help you to understand the basic principles of effective speaking and will provide you with many techniques for crafting and delivering speeches. It also will show you how the principles and skills of public speaking are applicable to public life, as well as to your college classes, your job, and your personal life. Skill in public speaking can help you to thrive in all areas of your life.

This chapter is intended to orient you to a concept of public speaking that fits our times. After illustrating why a course in public speaking is such an important course for you to take, this chapter will define public speaking and illustrate three models for thinking about the process of public speaking. This part of the chapter introduces the idea of the public sphere. The next section of the chapter elaborates on this idea, showing how public speaking is related to democracy and public life. The chapter concludes by introducing you to some of the key ethical considerations of public speaking. ∎

Why Study Public Speaking?

For many of you, your public speaking course fulfills some sort of requirement. At some schools, public speaking is a required course for all students. At others, public speaking is required for certain majors. It is not only students majoring in the liberal arts or in communication who find it on their list of required courses. Professional programs in areas such as business, education, engineering, natural resources, and pharmacy often require public speaking for their students. Why is public speaking so often a required course?

Public speaking is a common requirement because it is a fundamental skill that has direct personal and social benefits. These benefits make public speaking a vitally important course for every college student. No matter how students feel about public speaking, by the end of the course, they consistently recognize and appreciate these benefits. Comments like these are typical on course evaluation forms:

> I wasn't looking forward to taking this course, but now I feel like I really improved during the semester.
>
> I have always been nervous about public speaking. Now I am a lot more confident. I might even take another speech course so I can keep practicing!
>
> This course really helped me figure out how to organize my thoughts and support my ideas. It has already helped me at my job—I persuaded my boss to give me a raise!
>
> I never used to feel comfortable expressing my opinions or taking a position on issues. But the skills we learned in class have helped me get over that. Thanks!

Indeed, the tangible benefits that come from public speaking are obvious to students as well as to the faculty members and administrators who make curriculum decisions at colleges. They see that public speaking courses teach foundational skills that help students to lead fulfilling and successful lives and contribute to their community. From a student's perspective, a public speaking course can enhance your development in three areas of life: achievement in the classroom, success in your job and personal life, and empowerment in public life.

Achievement in the Classroom

> Jeremy's sociology class had a group project at the end of the semester. His grade hinged on how well he and his group could pull the project off. He had confidence in his groupmates Sookoun and Kayla; all of them were doing well in the class. But the group presentation made him a little nervous. Fortunately, Sookoun was taking a public speaking class and had some great ideas about how to organize their presentation. Sookoun also encouraged the group to rehearse their presentation and offered Kayla and Jeremy some helpful tips for how to improve their delivery. This helped them to feel more confident about their presentation, and their instructor said that it was one of the clearest she had seen.

The most immediate payoff for taking this course is that public speaking can help you to do better in your other classes (Morreale, Osborn, and Pearson 7–9). No matter what your major, you will need to make oral presentations. If you are in the sciences, you need to be able to present data effectively and put it into context for your audience. If you are in the humanities, you need to offer clear interpretations that you can support with historical and textual evidence. In every discipline, group projects are common assignments that require presentations. The public speaking practice that you gain in this class can be directly and immediately transferred to improve your performance in other classes.

Public speaking courses also develop knowledge and skills beyond giving presentations. Knowing the principles of communication that are covered later in this chapter, as well as the skills of listening and giving feedback, can help you to be a better participant in classroom discussions. Research skills provide a solid foundation for doing research in a variety of disciplines. The ability to develop a compelling central idea, organize those ideas coherently, and support your ideas applies to writing papers as well as to speaking. In many ways, public speaking is an all-purpose course that focuses on many of the core skills that faculty members say college students need to succeed (Diamond).

Finally, public speaking can help you to build the confidence you need to thrive in college. Even if you feel somewhat nervous about public speaking right now, by the end of this course, you are likely to feel far more confident about yourself and in your speaking skills. The guidance that is provided in this text, the feedback and support from your instructor and classmates, and the extensive speaking practice you will get will all contribute to enhancing your confidence. You will likely find it easier to participate in class discussion, engage your instructors, and tackle challenging assignments.

Success in Your Job and Personal Life

Maria never thought of herself as a "people person." Ever since she was a little girl, she liked being outdoors and was fascinated by animals of all kinds. In college, she discovered the field of wildlife biology and knew that it was the right career path for her. Her courses took her out in the field and prepared her well for a job with her state's Department of Natural Resources. When she interviewed for the job, the interviewer was impressed by the fact that Maria had taken several classes in communication and public speaking. "A big part of this job is interacting with the public and giving interpretive talks at state parks," he said. Maria mentioned several of the skills she learned in these classes, but it was her performance in the interview—her confidence and ability to explain ideas clearly and concisely—that ultimately won her the job.

For many students, the big question about any college class is: Will it help me get a job? When it comes to public speaking, the answer is an absolute "Yes!"

Surveys of employers and scholarly research studies consistently show that communication skills in general—and oral communication skills in particular—are among the most desired competencies for workers (Pittenger, Miller, and Mot). The ability to interview effectively, deliver oral reports, and participate in meetings is crucial for success in your job and career. The renowned business-man Warren Buffett, when asked his opinion of the most valuable skill for college students entering the job market, said unequivocally: public speaking ("Buffett and Gates").

You might be surprised to learn that even technical fields or jobs that "crunch numbers" involve public speaking. One study of business students, for example, found that their expectations about the frequency of oral presen-tations and meetings are far too low (McPherson). Meetings and presenta-tions are a basic part of virtually every career, even if public speaking is not a primary part of your day-to-day work. It will be to your advantage to develop your public speaking skills now.

Public speaking skills also can help you to lead a fulfilling personal and social life. Everyone wants to be able to give a good toast at the wedding of a friend or family member. Similarly, giving a speech that praises a friend or co-worker, participating in a club meeting, and celebrating a group accom-plishment are among the many situations in which you can put your public

VIDEOCONFERENCING
Not even the explosion of elec-tronic forms of communication will replace the need for public speaking in the workplace.

Tom Merton/Alamy

speaking skills to good use. Speaking at rituals like these can go much more smoothly when thinking about your audience and purpose becomes second nature to you.

Empowerment in Public Life

Public speaking also prepares you for participation in public life. For instance, if you are concerned about parking on your campus, you might decide to speak to administrators or present your concerns to your student government. If you want to start a program to help teens who are at risk for suicide, you might need to enlist the help of your friends and discuss the idea with high school counselors or public health professionals. If you want to help out a political candidate, you might be asked to go door to door and answer questions about your candidate. Skill in public speaking can help you in all of these activities.

For some of you, participation in public life might seem distant or unrealistic. How can one college student have a real impact? The answer, as the examples above suggest, is that you can participate in public life in many different ways. This perspective on participation in public life emerges from a large study, the National Youth Civic Engagement Project Index, which recently examined citizen engagement in the United States and gave special attention to people under 40 years old (Zukin et al.). On the basis of data collected from focus groups, telephone and web-based surveys, and expert panels, researchers revealed four broad ways in which people in the United States participate in public life:

"Four Broad Ways That People in the U.S. Participate in Public Life from the National Civic Engagement Project Index" from *A New Engagement? Political Participation, Civic Life, and the Changing American Citizen* by Scott Keeter, Molly Andolina, Krista Jenkins, Michael Carpini. Copyright © 1987 by Oxford University Press. Reprinted with permission.

- *Civic engagement.* **Civic engagement** is hands-on work with others that seeks to achieve a public good. Addressing an important issue or concern in your community—for example, improving access to buildings for disabled people or raising awareness of public transportation—is at the heart of civic engagement. Volunteering for a community group or service organization is a common form of civic engagement.

- *Political engagement.* **Political engagement** focuses on government, and your participation aims to influence policy or the election of public officials. Voting, persuading others to support a candidate or legislation, and participating in a political organization fall into this category.

- *Cognitive engagement.* Simply paying attention to politics and public issues is another type of participation in public life. Following the news and discussing issues with other people are examples of **cognitive engagement**.

- *Public voice.* When you express your opinion or viewpoint on an issue that is important to you and others, you are exercising your **public voice**. Contacting public officials, signing petitions, publicizing your viewpoint in a letter to the editor or through social media, and raising awareness of issues via a rally or protest are some of the ways of using your public voice.

Public speaking skills certainly help you to exercise your public voice, but they also can help you in other forms of engagement. As the researchers point out, there is definitely some overlap between the categories: "Notably, the expression of public voice is characteristic of *both* political and civic activists" (Zukin et al. 54). Furthermore, people who are involved in both civic and political engagement are typically more vocal than other citizens are.

No matter how much or how little you are engaged in public life right now, the point is that developing your public speaking skills can empower you as well as your audience. Public speaking has long been associated with encouraging people to stand up for their own interests, make a difference in their society, and participate in the exercise of political power. As a result, public speaking is a crucial skill for everyone in a democracy, not just members of the elite or elected officials. As one scholar puts it, "The power of speech is not the power to command obedience by replacing argument with silence. It is the power to challenge silent obedience by opening arguments" (Billig 48). This connection between public speaking and empowerment is perhaps the most crucial reason to study public speaking. Skill in public speaking helps you to have a sense of power over the direction of your life.

What Is Public Speaking?

What comes to your mind when you think of public speaking? Do you think of yourself standing in front of a room full of people? Maybe you recall attending a meeting of a community organization at which a member of the group informed others about the group's activities? Perhaps you think of an activist inspiring a crowd on your campus, or you might envision the President giving the State of the Union address. Each of these events reveals some of the basic characteristics of public speaking and shows the diversity of situations that call for public speaking. To understand what public speaking is all about, let's take a closer look at both words in that phrase.

The "Speaking" in Public Speaking

Courses in public speaking are concerned not just with the physical act of speaking. Instead, speaking is understood as a type of **communication**: interaction that creates meaning through symbols. You may be taking this course within a department called "Communication Studies" or "Speech Communication," where scholars study and teach about different types of communication. When a speaker gives a speech to an audience, symbols such as words, voice changes, and gestures help the speaker and audience to create meaning.

To help you understand the unique aspects of public speaking, then, it can be useful to compare it to other forms of communication, such as interpersonal communication, group communication, and mass communication.

INTERPERSONAL COMMUNICATION
Compared to an interpersonal conversation, public speaking should be somewhat more formal and structured.

Monkey Business Images, 2009/Shutterstock

Interpersonal Communication Chatting with your roommate, having a heart-to-heart talk with a family member, and socializing with your co-workers are all examples of **interpersonal communication**: one-on-one conversations that are primarily about negotiating relationships. Like interpersonal communication, public speaking involves negotiating relationships with your listeners; but in public speaking, you are communicating with many listeners—an audience—not just one person. An important part of public speaking is learning how to adapt to audiences composed of a diverse range of people.

In addition, interpersonal communication is typically casual and unstructured. A conversation with your friends over dinner is probably informal and may cover a wide range of different topics in no particular order. You probably do not prepare notes or an outline for these conversations. In contrast, public speaking is almost always more formal than conversation. Although it is common advice for public speakers to have a "conversational" tone, be careful of taking this too far. Your language and your body should convey confidence, intelligence, and preparation in order to make a good impression on your audience. Effective public speaking also is more structured than a free-flowing conversation. Good speeches logically follow a set of points and are focused by a specific purpose.

Group Communication Classroom discussions, committee meetings, and work projects all involve **group communication**: interaction among multiple people for purposes such as mutual understanding, exploration of ideas, or coordination of action.

Like group communication, public speaking may try to achieve these purposes. You certainly want your audience to understand you. Some types of public speaking, such as informative speaking, may explore ideas, while persuasive speaking may encourage collective action among audience members.

The key difference between group communication and public speaking is where responsibility for communication lies. Even in groups that have a definite leader, people expect that most if not all group members should contribute to the discussion. The point of most group meetings is to encourage communication and involvement among members. In other words, each group member has an equal responsibility to participate.

But in public speaking, the primary responsibility for communication lies with the speaker. It is the speaker's job to take the lead: He or she must consider the audience, prepare material, and organize and deliver a speech. For example, imagine that you were excited to attend a speech by someone who had climbed Mount Everest. You probably would be disappointed if the speaker, someone with a wealth of knowledge and firsthand experience, didn't prepare a thing and simply said, "So, what do you want to talk about?" A group conversation might be nice, but you likely would learn much more if the speaker had fulfilled the responsibility of preparing in advance.

Mass Communication Television programs, radio shows, Internet sites, podcasts, and newspapers are just a few examples of **mass communication**: interaction between a source and large, impersonal audiences via mediated messages. Both mass communication and public speaking circulate messages to audience composed of many people. In that way, both types of communication involve the challenge of adapting a message so that it is compelling to a diverse range of people. What makes public speaking different from some forms of mass communication—such as television and newspapers—is the capacity for the audience to talk back to the speaker immediately and directly. Other forms of mass communication, however, have more interactive capabilities. Email, social media, and even radio can be used in ways that are nearly as interactive as face-to-face communication (see Figure 1).

Mass communication and public speaking also overlap when mass media transmit or circulate speeches. The speeches of Adolf Hitler and the fireside chats of Franklin Delano Roosevelt are two classic examples of how radio was used to create large audiences for public speaking. These days, television and YouTube allow both leaders and ordinary citizens to circulate the verbal and visual messages of public speaking. For speakers, this means that the audience for a public speech may be much bigger than just the people who are physically present. This makes audience adaptation all the more challenging.

The "Public" in Public Speaking

Think back to the examples at the beginning of this section. Whether you are speaking in front of a room full of people, listening to a speaker at a meeting of a campus or community organization, or watching a televised speech about important political issues, you are part of an event that is public in some way.

FIGURE 1 Comparing Public Speaking to Other Forms of Speech Communication

	How Public Speaking Is Similar	**How Public Speaking Is Different**
Interpersonal Communication	Both involve developing and maintaining relationships between participants.	Public speakers must adapt to multiple audience members, while interpersonal communication is between just two people.
	Both involve negotiating meaning and taking into account the beliefs, values, and attitudes of one another.	Public speakers typically speak with more formality and structure, while interpersonal communication is informal and conversations are rarely structured.
Group Communication	Both involve interaction among multiple people.	One public speaker has primary responsibility for communication. In a group, the responsibility is shared.
	Both occur in settings that usually have a clear purpose.	Public speakers usually give a predetermined speech and then take feedback. Group communication involves spontaneous dialogue and ongoing feedback.
Mass Communication	Both involve interaction among multiple people.	Audiences typically have the ability to interact directly and immediately with a public speaker.
	Both assume a model of one person communicating to many, some of whom may be strangers.	Most mass communication involves barriers between speaker and audience.

Using the word "public" to describe these varied speaking events suggests that speaking can be public for many different reasons.

On the most basic level, public speaking *addresses an audience*. As mentioned above, public speaking is not simply the physical act of using your voice. It involves using your voice to communicate with others. To do so effectively, you need to learn about your audience and adapt your message accordingly. You also need to practice speaking in front of audiences. Through practice, you can reduce your nervousness and become more comfortable in future speaking situations. A class in public speaking helps you with all of these things as it encourages you to think not only about speaking, but primarily about speaking to particular audiences.

Another way in which speaking can be public is if it *addresses common interests* (Hauser). Even if you are talking about a personal experience, reporting to a group about work you have done, or describing a private concern, effective public speaking connects those ideas to the interests of your audience. For example, a report at your job should show how your contribution helps the group to complete their project. In other situations, you might describe personal concerns in terms of broader public issues. If you had difficulty registering for classes, you might frame that personal experience as an instance of why many students are concerned about basic services on your campus. Making this connection between personal and common interests is a crucial aspect of public speaking.

Finally, speaking has a public dimension when it *addresses the exercise of power* (Habermas, Hove). In democratic societies, this is the key role that public speaking plays. In the United States, the First Amendment protects freedom of speech and assembly so that citizens can come together and freely discuss matters that affect their lives, especially matters of power and self-governance. Formally elected bodies, such as your student senate or city council, provide a space for this kind of public speaking, but civic associations, neighborhood groups, and clubs also give people opportunities to speak to others about things that matter in their community. Participating in these organizations helps you to have a say in the direction of your campus, your community, and your society.

These "public" dimensions reinforce how public speaking can be empowering. Public speaking connects you with others so that you can make a difference in your community. It helps you to contribute to civic life by influencing the interests and issues that should matter to everyone. Public speaking can help you to engage in issues of public significance, ones that are important for civic life and political decision making.

Three Models of Public Speaking

Visual models can further represent how public speaking works. One model, often called the transmission model, reflects many common beliefs about how communication works. Because this is such an easy way to think about communication, the first part of this section will look at this model and explain some of its shortcomings. Then we will turn to two better models: a speech communication model and a public sphere model.

The Transmission Model

The model of communication that is frequently used to visualize the public speaking process is not based on public speaking at all. Instead, engineers working on telephone systems generated this model to study how messages were

FIGURE 2 The Transmission Model of Communication

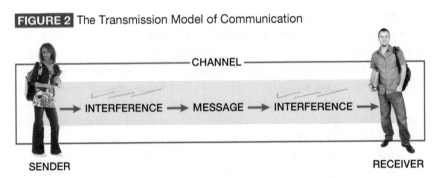

transmitted and where various problems could emerge (Shannon). It is commonly called the **transmission model** of communication because, for these researchers, effective communication meant the clear transmission of sound via the telephone. This model's elements are based on the idea that effective communication involves a *sender* who transmits a *message* through a *channel* to a *receiver* (see Figure 2). In addition, effective communication must minimize the amount of *interference* that might disrupt the transmission of the message.

This model translates easily to represent a public speaking situation:

- The sender is equivalent to the speaker.
- The message is the speech.
- The receiver is an audience member.
- The channel is the medium that carries the message. For the telephone researchers, the channel was the physical equipment—the handsets and wires that transmitted the message. In public speaking, the channels may be technologies such as television, radio, or the Internet. Speakers themselves have two main channels: the auditory channel, which carries the sound of words and voice changes, and the visual channel, which carries the appearance of the speaker, body movements, gestures, and visual aids.
- Interference is anything that disrupts the transmission of the message. On telephones, interference might be static or a bad connection. In public speaking, interference means the physical and psychological barriers that prevent an audience from hearing the message.

Take a few moments to think about this model. Does it accurately reflect how public speaking works? Are there significant differences between public speaking and communicating via telephone?

The limitations of the transmission model become apparent when you consider that the model encourages you to think about communication as if you were playing catch. The message is a ball. The sender throws the ball, and as long as there is no interference, it is up to the receiver to catch the ball. Either she catches it or she doesn't. (Our everyday language about public speaking often reflects the transmission model; we talk about "getting the message across" or "passing along information" to the audience.)

But why might this not be an adequate model for public speaking?

First, *the transmission model shows whether listeners receive a message but does not show how they understand and interpret that message.* While a telephone researcher merely wants receivers to hear the words, public speakers want audiences to *understand* words—what their meaning is, how they support an idea, and why they are relevant to the overall purpose of the speech. Because audience members bring their own beliefs, attitudes, opinions, and experiences to a public speaking situation, they are likely to interpret the message in ways that are different than the speaker intended.

In other words, the transmission model depicts listeners as passive recipients of messages. For example, consider the slogan "We must take back America!" It is not clear who is part of the "we" in that slogan and what specifically should be taken back. Those words probably would mean one thing to a group of immigration activists and something else to a group of Native Americans. A model based on simply hearing a message suggests little about how audiences understand and interpret messages.

Second, *the transmission model downplays the situation of the speech.* In the transmission model the speaker appears to convey a message to an audience member without any connection to time or place. But the situation is crucial to determining the meaning and effectiveness of a speech. For example, during the 2008 presidential campaign, Barack Obama gave a prominent speech about race shortly after some commentators raised concerns about remarks made by Rev. Jeremiah Wright, pastor of Obama's church. Although Obama had spoken about racial issues before, this speech took on added meaning in relation to the concerns about Rev. Wright's statements.

Third, the transmission model does not include feedback. The verbal and non-verbal responses that audience members give to speakers are a crucial part of the communication process. They show that communication is not really a one-way process of speakers sending messages to receivers, but rather a two-way process involving messages going back and forth between speakers and audiences. Think again about the metaphor of playing catch: What does it mean if your partner returns your throw with a fastball aimed at your head? A better understanding of communication process comes from examining the entire interaction and not just a single "transmission."

Taken together, these problems with the transmission model point to a clear conclusion: The transmission model provides little insight about *meaning*. Because the model depicts communication as simply transmitting information from the sender to a passive receiver without reference to particular situations, the model downplays the complex process of negotiating meaning. Other models are more useful in showing the factors you need to consider for effective public speaking.

The Speech Communication Model

The **speech communication model** displays a more dynamic view of the public speaking process. While the transmission model focused on the one-way action of sending a message, the speech communication model emphasizes the ongoing transaction between speaker and audience (see Figure 3). There are two important ways in which this dynamic model can help you to think more carefully about effective public speaking.

Most important, this model shows that *audiences are active participants in the communication process.* This is a central idea in contemporary communication theory (Ceccarelli, Fiske). Rather than being passive "receivers" or "targets," audience members bring their own beliefs, attitudes, opinions, and experiences into public speaking situations. Therefore, this model reminds speakers that their job is not one of "hitting the target" with their own viewpoints and lots of information. Rather, speakers should think of their audience as equal participants whose ideas must be examined during speech preparation if speakers want to be effective. Indeed, the audience will be participating even before the speaker begins to speak.

Audiences also participate by giving feedback. During a speech, audience members may nod, look puzzled, start reading the campus newspaper, or stare out the window. Rather than thinking of these as distractions, the speaker

FIGURE 3 The Speech Communication Model of Public Speaking

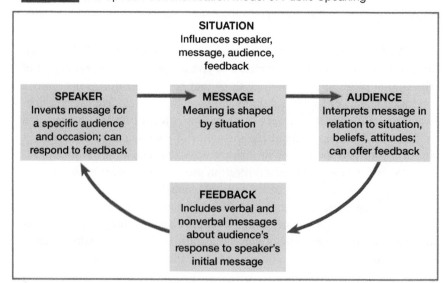

should think of them as messages. With practice and experience, speakers can pick up on this kind of feedback and adapt messages accordingly. By adding feedback into the mix, this model reminds speakers to attend to the messages that others are sending in addition to their own.

The speech communication model also shows that *the situation influences the entire communication process.* For now, think of situation as the setting or occasion for the speech. Like differences among audience members, differences between situations can greatly influence the meanings of a speech. One relevant aspect of the situation is the physical setting; for example, the President may give a speech in the Oval Office, in the White House Rose Garden, or at Camp David. These different backgrounds shape the message and can influence how audiences perceive the speech's meaning. Situation also includes the history or past events that led up to a speech. For example, in the workplace, even a simple factual announcement such as "Everyone gets a $1,000 bonus this year" means something different depending on how bonuses have been distributed in the past. It might not mean much if that is the standard bonus, but it will mean something different if the usual bonus is $3,000 or if only a few people have received the bonus in the past.

The Public Sphere Model

While the speech communication model focuses on the immediate speaking situation, the **public sphere model** (Figure 4) focuses on the role of public speaking in a democratic society. This model draws on recent scholarship about the public sphere in communication studies and other disciplines (Asen and Brouwer, Hauser, Loehwing and Motter). The public sphere model is not meant to replace the speech communication model. Instead, it adds another layer to our understanding of public speaking and shows how public speaking is connected to political and civic engagement—think of it as helping you see the "big picture."

You can begin to see the big picture by observing how a specific public speaking situation is part of the broader flow of messages in society:

> Scott had been hearing a lot about climate change. One day, he read an editorial that was discussing the connection between climate change and national security; another day, he was encouraged to become a Facebook "fan" of a climate action group that was forming on campus; the following day, he came across a flyer in a store touting the benefits of compact fluorescent light bulbs. As he got more interested in the issue, he gave speeches about it in his class and eventually joined the student group. Because of his speaking skills, other members of the group encouraged him to speak about climate change at a rally on campus.
>
> Scott's speech went over really well with the audience. The group gained some new members, and several signed a petition for the campus

FIGURE 4 The Public Sphere Model of Public Speaking

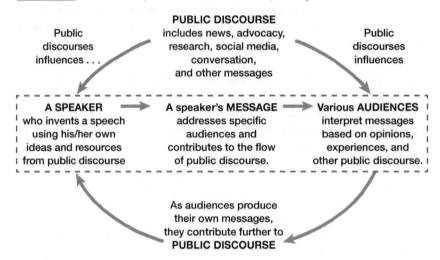

The constant flow of messages among diverse speakers and audiences can be thought of as CIRCULATION.

to become "carbon-neutral." One of new members mentioned that he had heard about the rally from a friend who was in Scott's public speaking class. The group also posted a video of Scott's speech on YouTube. He could hardly believe that it had over 500 views in just a couple of weeks! He later found out that similar organizations at other campuses had posted it on their websites, too.

Like those of most public speakers, Scott's ideas and interest in the topic did not come out of nowhere. Instead, messages that were available in his everyday experience helped to shape Scott's thinking and speaking. And in speaking, he was not only addressing his immediate audience; he also reached others who were not immediately present but had an interest in the topic. This constant and unpredictable flow of messages among diverse speakers and audiences—what scholars call **circulation**—is a defining feature of the contemporary public sphere (Warner). Circulation provides another metaphor for thinking about public speaking that is different from the ideas of transmission and communication in the previous two models.

The idea of circulation is crucial for understanding how your own speaking is connected to the public sphere. First, *a speaker's message is influenced by other messages that circulate in the public sphere.* As Scott's example suggests, speakers do not come up with ideas entirely on their own. Rather, the ideas of both speakers and audiences are shaped by the messages that are already circulating in the public sphere—what we will call **public discourse**, including conversations, news reports, and public advocacy. For public speaking, the research process is essentially a strategy for helping you to manage that flow of messages. After thinking critically about those messages, you are better prepared to create your own message for a particular audience.

Second, *a speaker's message contributes to the circulation of messages in the public sphere*. While communication is a useful concept for thinking about the goal with your immediate audience, circulation indicates how a message may reach beyond your immediate audience. In some instances, circulation is intentional; you might agree to have your speech recorded or transcribed so that others can have access to it. But in many cases, circulation happens unintentionally or indirectly. A classmate might talk about your speech with one of her friends. If you are speaking in a public meeting, a journalist might quote some of your words when reporting about the meeting. These words can then reach all kinds of people who may respond very differently from your immediate audience.

Finally, *the circulation of messages helps to create publics*. For our purpose, a **public** can be thought of as a group of people who are engaged in addressing issues of common interest. For example, the public that is involved in addressing climate change is not limited to Scott's audience but includes everyone who engages with the issue: ordinary citizens reading magazine articles about it, activists campaigning about it, church members discussing it, government officials debating it. Many of these people will never hear Scott's message, but they are still connected by other messages about the issue. This public is constantly changing as new messages circulate and different people pay attention to those messages (Warner).

What does all this have to do with your own public speaking? The public sphere model and the idea of circulation have at least two very concrete, practical implications for effective public speaking. *First, public speakers need to pay close attention to messages that are already circulating in the public sphere.* Because your audience may be familiar with some of these messages, you need to be familiar with them, too. This will enhance your credibility and help you to adapt how you explain your ideas to the beliefs and values that your audience holds.

Second, *public speakers need to encourage their audience members to see themselves as part of a public*. Your audience is not necessarily part of a public; publics emerge and develop only when messages get people's interest and attention. In the public sphere, your basic task as a speaker is to help your audience members engage with issues on a civic or political level.

Public Speaking and Democracy

The art of public speaking traditionally has been closely connected to effective citizenship and political decision making. But the public dimension of public speaking has not always had this focus. Both the theory and the practice of public speaking, in fact, have changed in relation to historical and political circumstances. In this section, we take a brief look at how the focus of public speaking has changed through history. Then we explore some of the distinctive features of contemporary public speaking.

Traditions of Public Speaking

The earliest teachings about public speaking in the Western world were very concerned with public impact and political engagement. The Sophists, the first teachers of rhetoric in ancient Greece, recognized that effective participation in political institutions, such as the courts and the Assembly, required skill in public speaking. Therefore, they trained aspiring leaders in public speaking techniques that could help them to gain power in the political arena (Herrick).

However, some people questioned the ethical basis of the Sophists' teachings. For example, Plato claimed that the Sophists and their students were more concerned with achieving success than with telling the truth. As a result, many later theorists of rhetoric, such as the Greek teacher Isocrates and the Roman orator Cicero, emphasized that ethical public speaking requires both eloquence and wisdom. The Roman educator Quintillian even defined the perfect orator as the "good man, speaking well."

Other historical eras further show how the public dimension of public speaking has changed over time. During the Middle Ages, the rise of the Christian church shifted the focus of public speaking away from preparation for debating in political institutions. Instead, public speaking was oriented toward preaching, defending the Scriptures, and using poetic language. During the Enlightenment period, theorists of rhetoric and public speaking tended to emphasize matters of style, language, and delivery more than the invention of arguments. Some people saw public speaking as "a path to personal refinement and an avenue into polite social circles," focusing on the possibilities for social advancement (Herrick).

In the United States, early theorists of rhetoric and public speaking advanced both of these traditions. The importance of freedom of religion during the colonial period meant that much public speaking training was concerned with preaching. At the same time, ideas of the Enlightenment influenced the conception of public speaking as a means for cultural refinement among elites. But theorists also incorporated the idea of speaking for the public good. For example, John Quincy Adams—who was not only the second President of the United States but also the first professor of rhetoric at Harvard University—revived the Ciceronian ideal of public speaking as the unity of eloquence and wisdom embodied in the political orator, whose main role was to unite the community. However, Adams suggested that civic elites, not ordinary citizens, were the ones who could play this role (Potkay).

As you can see, ideas about public speaking in previous eras have some similarities with the vision of public speaking that has been emphasized so far. As in the ancient world, contemporary public speaking has a connection with effective citizenship and political decision making. People also remain concerned about the ethics of public speaking. And public speaking has long been viewed as a means of personal advancement in one's society. But other ideas about public speaking have changed, especially in relation to the practice of democracy. Recognizing these differences can help you to become a more effective speaker in the contemporary public sphere.

Contemporary Public Speaking and Diversity

The differences that are most important for speaking in the public sphere today can be summed up in a single word: diversity. While attention to diversity on college campuses often involves celebrating cultural differences, our reason for focusing on diversity is to help you see how cultural differences raise both challenges and opportunities for effective speaking and listening in the public sphere.

Diversity of Speakers As you have seen, even in democratic societies, the public sphere has not always been welcoming or open to everyone. But people have long struggled to gain access to the public sphere and have used public speaking to persuade others to move toward a more democratic and inclusive society. In the United States, nineteenth-century speakers such as Frederick Douglass, Sojourner Truth, and Elizabeth Cady Stanton paved the way for African-Americans and women to be recognized as equal participants whose voices deserved to be heard.

As a result, public speaking is no longer a skill that is reserved for elites. The emergence of the public sphere as a space for participation by everyone means that public speaking is important for everyone. Even if you do not aspire to being active in traditional politics, public speaking is a crucial skill that helps you to participate in your society.

Diversity of Speaking Styles The wide range of speakers in the contemporary public sphere leads to a diversity of speaking styles. Traditionally, training in public speaking has reinforced the norms of "manly speech" that were attributed to men from elite backgrounds (Jamieson). Speech that was factual, analytical, and impersonal was presumed to be an inherently superior style of speech.

But the practice of public speaking has increasingly involved people from diverse backgrounds whose speaking styles have often diverged from those norms. For example, many women speakers in the nineteenth and twentieth centuries adopted a "feminine style" of speaking that placed greater emphasis on concrete examples, audience participation, domestic concerns, and personal experience (Campbell). In African-American cultural traditions, public speaking has often involved a form of interaction between speaker and audience known as call and response. And many Native American tribes share a cultural perception of time that differs from the dominant perception of time in the United States that affects both Native and Euro-American public speech (Lake).

Awareness of diversity in speaking styles is extremely important for both speakers and audiences. For example, the dominant culture's expectations about appropriate speaking style can cause other speaking styles to be judged as inadequate or inferior. As many speakers know from experience, there is no clear answer about how one should negotiate these tensions between cultural expectations and one's preferred speaking style. In turn, audiences need to be attentive to how their assumptions about the "best" form of speech may prevent them from appreciating different speaking styles.

Diversity of Issues Although public speaking has historically been connected with decision making in government institutions, the public sphere involves a much wider range of issues (Asen and Brouwer). It provides a space

AUDIENCE DIVERSITY
Diverse backgrounds and experiences among audience members often leads to different interpretations of a speaker's message.

Paul Conklin/PhotoEdit, Inc.

for ordinary citizens to discuss what matters to them. These discussions may address issues of power, social needs, and common interests. But these issues do not necessarily intersect with official government action. In other words, speaking in the public sphere is not limited to speaking about traditional politics. For example, speaking in your community about ways to reduce your carbon footprint might focus on personal habits or neighborhood initiatives.

Similarly, an apparently private or personal matter can be an appropriate topic for speaking in the public sphere. For example, abuse within marriage was once considered a strictly private matter; now domestic violence is an important public issue. Likewise, some troubles at work are not merely personal; concerns about equal pay and working conditions affect others and therefore have a public dimension, too.

The lack of a clear dividing line between private and public issues presents a wonderful opportunity for you as a public speaker. The concerns of elected officials and the interests of dominant groups in society are not the only legitimate subjects for discussion. The sheer number of magazines, websites, blogs, and social media outlets that circulate messages about issues and interests means that virtually no issue is off limits for discussion. Through effective public speaking, you can bring to light the issues that matter to you.

Diversity of Publics Perhaps the most important impact of public speaking is that it enables free people to engage one another in discussion about the direction of their society. But because there are so many issues and concerns that merit discussion, the public sphere allows for many publics that may overlap, intersect, or collide with one another. Indeed, it would be impossible to make a list of publics, since they are not the same as formal organizations.

The diversity of publics is important for public speakers because it pushes speakers to think carefully about the audience they are trying to reach. For most public speakers, it is rarely useful to think about the audience as a single, monolithic group called "the public" or "the general public." Even if you are trying to reach a diverse group of people, think less about speaking to "the public" and more about inspiring listeners to actively engage with a particular issue. The real power of public speaking lies in its capacity to create groups of engaged people who were not engaged before.

Ethical Dimensions of Public Speaking

As you have already seen, ethical concerns have been a persistent part of the theory and practice of public speaking. And for good reason: public speaking is like any other type of human conduct. It can be performed appropriately or inappropriately. Lying, promoting violence, and manipulating emotions are some of the most egregious ethical violations in public speaking, but there are other tactics that raise ethical issues. In the remaining chapters in this book, you will learn about several ethical issues related to public speaking in a feature called "The Ethical Dimension."

There are many different traditions or ways of thinking about ethics. Some traditions conceive of ethics as a set of virtues that one aspires to follow, while others frame ethics as applying absolute principles to specific situations and yet others focus on the consequences of one's actions. Classes in philosophy and ethics can teach you about these different traditions. For the purposes of introductory public speaking, however, the differences between ethical traditions are less important than the overarching idea that **ethics** are guides for personal conduct in relation to one's community.

In this view, ethical public speaking has both personal and social dimensions. It involves making sound personal choices while constructing speeches *and* supporting broadly shared commitments in your society. Democratic participation, social justice, and sustainable natural and social systems are some of the shared commitments that orient this book's approach to the ethics of public speaking. Because communities are strengthened through these commitments and because each of us is dependent on the communities that surround us, ethical public speaking requires attention to both personal and social concerns.

Ethics and the Speaker

On the personal level, you can observe some of the most important ethical issues in public speaking by thinking about the three broad ways in which individual speakers appeal to audiences. The ancient Greek theorist Aristotle identified these appeals as follows:

- **Ethos**, the character and credibility of the speaker
- **Pathos**, the emotions that can be evoked in the audience
- **Logos**, the reasoning that is offered in the speech

Each of these appeals can be used to speak ethically. But each can also be deformed or used inappropriately by speakers. Understanding the basic pitfalls of each of these appeals can help you to identify some of the fundamental challenges of ethical public speaking.

Your ethos as a speaker is a complex mix of factors as perceived by your audience. Your *knowledge or expertise* on the topic, your *honesty and trustworthiness*, and your *appearance of goodwill toward others* all play a part in shaping the audience's perception of you as a speaker. In turn, each of these factors raises ethical issues and principles:

- *Knowledge.* Have you become adequately knowledgeable about your topic? To what extent are you truthful in describing your expertise rather than exaggerating or misrepresenting it?

- *Honesty.* To what extent are you honest with the audience about your motives and purpose for speaking? Can they trust that you have researched your topic adequately? To what extent have you ignored or misrepresented competing ideas?

- *Goodwill.* How respectful are you of other points of view? Why should the audience trust that you have their best interests in mind as you speak?

At its core, the ethical use of appeals to ethos requires two things of you simultaneously. It involves both being a good person and appearing to be a good person. Being ethical and being effective, then, are not opposed to one another; in fact, being ethical can enhance your effectiveness.

The appeal of pathos always raises ethical concerns, in part because this appeal is misunderstood. Emotion is often viewed as being opposed to reason and therefore as an unethical influence on an audience's judgment. But emotions are better understood as judgments—as responses to a situation that may or may not be appropriate depending on the circumstances and our values. For example, if racial slurs have been painted on the door of a fellow student's dorm room, it would be appropriate to feel sympathy for the student and to feel angry about racism. Conversely, it would be inappropriate to appeal to joy if you were advocating for punishment for the student who painted the slurs.

Ethical public speaking, then, does not mean eliminating emotional appeals. Instead, your goal should be to use emotional appeals in a way that promotes fair judgment in relation to your topic, the situation, and shared values. Ask yourself: *Will my audience recognize these emotional appeals as fair judgments about my topic?* Also ask yourself about consistency: *Are my emotional appeals consistent with reasonable arguments, or do they undermine reasonable thinking?* For example, imagine a speech that tells a sad story about victims of a natural disaster and then blames the federal government for not providing enough support for those victims. Such an emotional appeal is ethically questionable. Although the story may be appropriate for generating sympathy for victims, it would be inappropriate for generating anger at the federal government if the speech does not include evidence about what the government has done or what it should reasonably be expected to do. The ethical concern is that the emotional appeal substitutes for supporting material and sound reasoning.

Finally, appeals to logos might not seem to harbor any ethical concerns. Most of us would appreciate appeals to reason in a speech. But both the supporting material in a speech and the patterns of reasoning in a speech are susceptible to being used in unethical ways. One crucial ethical question about supporting material asks: *Has the supporting material been accurately and fairly represented?*

For example, it is generally considered unethical to take a quotation or statistic out of context and make it mean something that the original author did not intend. Unfortunately, many political speakers violate this rule when they quote one part of an opponent's statement and leave out other parts that would make that opponent's position appear more reasonable or more complex.

Some appeals to logos might appear to be reasonable, but critical inspection could show that these are **fallacies**, or faulty patterns of reasoning. For now, be aware that one of the fundamental ethical questions related to reasoning and fallacies is: *Does this reasoning cut off a fair examination of alternatives?* It is easy to make it appear as if you are giving your audience choices and then using reason to identify the best choice. But if your speech presents a distorted or extreme picture of one alternative or suggests that there are two and only two choices, then your speech is prematurely cutting off discussion of alternatives. This fails to empower your audience to make sound decisions.

Ethics and Society

While ethical public speaking concerns the personal choices you make as a speaker, it also involves how your speech relates to the rest of your society. Because each of us is a member of various communities of interdependent parts, each of us has an obligation to support and sustain those communities. Thus, ethical public speaking should be shaped by the values and commitments of the communities that surround us. Fortunately, this does not mean that everyone must have exactly the same beliefs; we can disagree about the meaning of these values and the best ways to put those commitments into practice. But acknowledging these values and commitments gives us a common ground for speaking to one another. Consider the following three values.

Democratic Participation No matter what our differences, we must acknowledge that in a democratic society, all people should be able to participate freely in public discussion, community problem solving, and decision making. Consequently, public speakers have an obligation to avoid speech that degrades individuals or groups, that intimidates or coerces others, or that attempts to stifle disagreement or dissent. The principles of freedom of speech and freedom of association, enshrined in the First Amendment to the U.S. Constitution, is central to the commitment to democratic participation.

Many individuals and groups work to improve and ensure democratic participation specifically among college students. For example, the organization Rock the Vote has been active in getting young people to register and vote in elections. A key part of their efforts has involved assisting students who are challenged when trying to vote where they attend college. Another organization, Campus Compact, has helped more than 20 million college students engage in service opportunities such as tutoring, building homes, and volunteering at nonprofit agencies, and it has helped students to articulate the connection between community service and politics as a new form of civic engagement known as "service politics" (Long).

Social Justice While differences and inequalities persist in all societies, most nations and religious traditions also acknowledge the existence of basic human rights and the principle of social justice. Fair treatment, equal opportunity, and equal access to the benefits of living in the society are fundamental commitments in societies that are concerned about human rights and social justice. In turn, ethical public speakers need to be mindful of how their positions may promote or undermine these commitments.

For example, for more than ten years, college students have partnered with immigrant tomato pickers in the Student/Farmworker Alliance. Since 2009, their "Dine with Dignity" campaign has pressured campus food service providers such as Aramark and Sodexo to improve pay and working conditions as well as to give workers a greater voice in the company (Student/Farmworker Alliance). Speaking out on these issues has included raising awareness among students and soliciting more than 80,000 signatures on a petition. Dominique Aulisio, a student leader at the University of Central Florida, told her campus newspaper that students should consider the issue as a topic for their speech classes (Fortis).

Sustainable Natural and Social Systems As an ethical guide, the idea of sustainability encourages human activity that "meets the needs of the present without compromising the ability of future generations to meet their own needs" (World Commission on Environment and Development 43). Under this ethic, current decisions need to take into account long-term impacts on the environment as well as on society and human institutions. For public speakers, the ethic of sustainability entails an obligation to consider how our messages are constructive or destructive in relation to future generations, not just our own.

Many college students are actively involved in speaking out about issues of sustainability. For example, a group of thirty students met with elected officials in Washington, D.C., to share the Evangelical Youth Climate Initiative, a declaration signed by more than 1,500 Christian college students. Their declaration emphasized the need to address climate change in relation to the long-term needs of natural and social systems: "We seek a secure nation that is economically and environmentally sound for generations to come" (Evangelical Youth Climate Initiative). Ben Lowe, a student at Wheaton College who was part of the delegation to Washington, also appealed to the ethic of stewardship in explaining his support for the Initiative: "Making the world safer for our generation, and for their grandchildren, is not exclusively Republican or Democratic; it is a moral issue, and the faithful expression of God's people" ("Cooling Our Future").

CASE CONCLUSION

Carlos Serves His Community through Public Speaking

As the speaking event approached, Carlos thought about what he was going to try to accomplish in his speech. He decided that the central theme would be to help his listeners understand how their immigration status might affect college admission, financial aid, and other opportunities.

Carlos found connections with issues surrounding immigration on many levels of communication. The more he focused on the issue, the more he found himself in interpersonal conversations with friends outside of class. He also was regularly engaged in group communication at his MEChA meetings. And it seemed that every time he picked up a newspaper or turned on the television, immigration issues immediately grabbed his attention through those forms of mass communication.

It was not surprising that immigration was a prominent topic in the news, since it has important public dimensions. Especially in his state of California, speakers were addressing audiences about immigration all the time—during electoral campaigns, rallies for ballot initiatives, and even on campus. In addition, all the personal stories involving legal and illegal immigrants could easily be connected to broader public concerns about social services, taxes, and race relations. And since much of the discussion about immigration was directly related to official action—legislation, law enforcement, university policies—the exercise of power was always involved in those discussions.

Carlos had to think carefully about how best to communicate with his audience. He recognized that his own interests in immigration issues and the things that were important to him about college probably would not intersect with the interests and needs of most members of his audience. So he contacted his college's admissions office to find out what kinds of information prospective students might be interested in hearing. Carlos also learned about the questions that these students and their parents usually asked so that he could anticipate how they would be active listeners to his speech.

He also started reading newspaper and magazine articles about immigration and got materials about his school's admissions and financial aid process. Not only did this give him a sense of what might be on his audience's mind, it also gave him the knowledge he needed to assemble an effective speech.

Carlos's speech went well. His audience seemed to have a great deal of respect for him, not only because he was well-informed about his topic but also because he displayed true concern for his audience and their success. He shared his own story about struggling to get to college and how he wanted to give something back to his community. And rather than using the event to generate anger that would do little to help these students, he inspired them with his own success story and the experiences of successful Latino alumni. In the end, Carlos was not only empowering these students; he was helping to make his society more democratic and more just.

Summary

WHY STUDY PUBLIC SPEAKING?

- Public speaking can strengthen your performance in other classes.
- Public speaking can help you to achieve success at work.
- Public speaking can enhance important moments in your personal life.
- Public speaking empowers you as a citizen, allowing you to effectively engage with your community and address political issues.

WHAT IS PUBLIC SPEAKING?

- Public speaking involves developing and maintaining positive relationships and negotiating meaning with others.

- Public speaking is typically more formal and structured than interpersonal communication, more speaker-centered than group communication, and more interactive than mass communication.

- Public speaking gains its public character as it addresses audiences, common interests, and the exercise of power.

THREE MODELS OF PUBLIC SPEAKING

- The transmission model depicts public speaking as a form of one-way communication from the speaker to the audience.

- The speech communication model emphasizes the ongoing transaction between speaker and audience; audiences are active participants in the communication process.

- The public sphere model contributes to the ongoing circulation of discourse in the public sphere and helps to create publics around issues of common interest.

PUBLIC SPEAKING AND DEMOCRACY

- While public speaking traditionally has been connected to political decision making, the theories and the practices of effective public speaking have constantly shifted between an elite focus and a more democratic focus.

- The contemporary public sphere exhibits increasing diversity in speakers, speaking styles, issues, and publics.

ETHICAL DIMENSIONS OF PUBLIC SPEAKING

- Ethical speaking focuses on your character and credibility as a speaker by relying on sound knowledge, being honest about your evidence and your motives, and keeping the audience's interests at the forefront of your thinking.

- Be attentive to whether your emotional appeals represent fair judgments and are consistent with reasonable arguments.

- Use supporting materials accurately and fairly, and avoid patterns of reasoning that undermine your audience's ability to make rational choices among alternatives.

- Ethical public speaking should be consistent with fundamental social commitments, such as democratic participation, social justice, and sustainable natural and social systems.

Key Terms

civic engagement
political engagement
cognitive engagement
public voice
communication
interpersonal communication
group communication
mass communication
transmission model
speech communication model

public sphere model
circulation
public discourse
public
ethics
ethos
pathos
logos
fallacies

Comprehension

1. Identify three ways in which public speaking can help you in other classes.

2. What is the difference between political and civic engagement?

3. How does public speaking differ from group communication?

4. What are three ways in which public speaking can have a public dimension?

5. What are the problems with the transmission model of communication?

6. What practical implications can public speakers draw from the public sphere model and the idea of circulation?

7. In what ways is diversity exhibited in the contemporary public sphere?

8. What are the three basic appeals that are used in public speaking?

9. Are emotional appeals inherently unethical? Why or why not?

Application

1. Ask your instructor or alumni office to get you into contact with some alumni of your school. Interview them about the importance of public speaking and communication skills in their work, their personal life, and their public life. Share your results with your class.

2. Using a copy of your local or campus newspaper, identify articles that have the clearest "public" dimensions and those that are the least publicly relevant. Discuss your conclusions with your classmates.

3. Identify a prominent speech by an elected official or spokesperson for an organization. Working with your classmates, see whether you

can produce a public sphere model of messages circulating around that speech. Identify some prior public messages that may have influenced the speech and subsequent messages that were influenced by the speech.

4. Examine a list of your state's legislators and/or the issues they addressed during their last session. Discuss the extent to which these speakers and issues exhibit diversity.

5. Go to a public speech on your campus or in your community. Identify all the ways in which the speaker appeals to his or her ethos. Also, see whether there are other messages—newspaper articles, flyers, or the introduction of the speaker—that contribute to the speakers' ethos.

References

Asen, Robert, and Daniel C. Brouwer. *Counterpublics and the State*. Albany: SUNY Press, 2001.

Billig, Michael. *Arguing and Thinking*. New York: Cambridge UP, 1996.

Buffett and Gates go Back to School. PBS Home Video. Lincoln: Net Foundation for Television, 2006.

Campbell, Karlyn Kohrs. *Man Cannot Speak for Her*. Vols. I and II. Westport: Praeger, 1989.

Ceccarelli, Leah. "Polysemy: Multiple Meanings in Rhetorical Criticism." *Quarterly Journal of Speech* 84 (1998): 394–414.

CIRCLE *The 2006 Civic and Political Health of the Nation*. College Park: Center for Information and Research on Civic Learning and Engagement, 2006.

"Cooling Our Future: Young Evangelicals Take Powerful Message to U.S. Congress." *Creation Care Magazine* (Winter 2007). Accessed May 25, 2008. Available at http://www.creationcare.org/magazine/winter07.php#congress

Diamond, Robert M. "Curriculum Reform Needed If Students Are to Master Core Skills." *The Chronicle of Higher Education*, August 1, 1997: B7.

Evangelical Youth Climate Initiative. "Cooling Our Future: A Declaration by Young Evangelicals on Climate Change." May 2006. Accessed May 25, 2008. Available at http://www.christiansandclimate.org/pub/eyci.pdf

Fiske, John. *Understanding Popular Culture*. London: Unwin Hyman, 1989.

Fortis, Bianca. "Students, Workers Protest Burger King." *Central Florida Future*. April 25, 2008. Accessed May 27, 2008. Available at http://www.centralfloridafuture.com/home/index.cfm?event=displayArticlePrinterFriendly&uStory_id=0db5dba1-c856-47af-85fe-73ed4d9f10de

Habermas, Jurgen. "The Public Sphere." *Rethinking Popular Culture: Contemporary Perspectives in Cultural Studies*. Ed. Chandra Mukerji and Michael Schudson. Berkeley: U of California P, 1991. 398–404.

Hauser, Gerard. *Vernacular Voices: The Rhetoric of Publics and Public Spheres*. Columbia: U of South Carolina P, 1999.

Herrick, James A. *The History and Theory of Rhetoric: An Introduction*. 3rd ed. Boston: Pearson Allyn & Bacon, 2005.

Hove, Thomas. "The Filter, the Alarm System, and the Sounding Board: Critical and Warning Functions of the Public Sphere." *Communication and Critical/Cultural Studies* 6.1 (2009): 19–38.

Jamieson, Kathleen Hall. *Eloquence in an Electronic Age: The Transformation of Political Speechmaking*. New York: Oxford UP, 1990.

Lake, Randall A. "Between Myth and History: Enacting Time in Native American Protest Rhetoric." *Quarterly Journal of Speech* 77 (1991): 123–51.

Loehwing, Melanie, and Jeff Motter. "Publics, Counterpublics, and the Promise of Democracy." *Philosophy and Rhetoric* 42.3 (2009): 220–41.

Long, Sarah E. *The New Student Politics: The Wingspread Statement on Student Civic Engagement*, 2nd ed. Providence, RI: Campus Compact, 2002.

McPherson, Bill. "Student Perceptions about Business Communication in Their Careers." *Business Communication Quarterly* 61.2 (1998): 68–79

Morreale, Sherwyn P., Michael M. Osborn, and Judy C. Pearson. "Why Communication Is Important: A Rationale for the Centrality of the Study of Communication." *Journal of the Association for Communication Administration* 29 (1998): 1–25.

Pittenger, Khushwant K. S., Mary C. Miller, and Joshua Mot. "Using Real-World Standards to Enhance Students' Presentation Skills." *Business Communication Quarterly* 67 (September 2004): 327–36.

Potkay, Adam S. "Theorizing Civic Eloquence in the Early Republic: The Road from David Hume to John Quincy Adams." *Early American Literature* 34 (1999): 147–70.

Shannon, Claude. "A Mathematical Theory of Communication." *Bell System Technical Journal* 27 (1948): 379–423.

Student/Farmworker Alliance. "Dine with Dignity Campaign Headquarters." Accessed December 23, 2010. Available at http://www.sfalliance.org/foodservice.html

Warner, Michael. *Publics and Counterpublics*. Cambridge: Zone Books, 2002.

World Commission on Environment and Development. *Our Common Future*. Oxford: Oxford University Press, 1987.

Zukin, Cliff, Scott Keeter, Molly Andolina, Krista Jenkins, and Michael X. Delli Carpini. *A New Engagement?: Political Participation, Civic Life, and the Changing American Citizen*. New York: Oxford UP, 2006.

Organizing the Speech: The Body

From Chapter 9 of *Public Speaking: Strategies for Success*, Seventh Edition. David Zarefsky.

Organizing the Speech: The Body

Listen to the
Audio Chapter at
MyCommunicationLab

After studying this chapter, you should be able to:

Objective 1	Explain why the organization of a speech is important for both the speaker and the audience.
Objective 2	Identify criteria for selecting the main ideas to include in your speech and the characteristics that a main idea should have.
Objective 3	Arrange the main ideas into recognizable patterns and decide what patterns of arrangement to use.
Objective 4	Decide how much and which kinds of supporting material you need and how to arrange the support for each idea.

OUTLINE

You now should have a better understanding of the issues that are implicit in your thesis. You also should have located a variety of supporting materials for your ideas—examples, statistics, testimony, and so forth. You have probably investigated many more ideas than you can discuss in the time available, and you very likely have located far more supporting materials than you can use, even after applying the tests of reasoning. For all this effort, your ideas and materials may show no evident pattern and may not seem to fit together well. What, then, do you do with all the ideas you have explored and all the evidence you have gathered?

Identifying and locating material for the speech is not enough; you also need to organize it in strategic ways that advance your purpose. **Organization** is the selection of ideas and materials and their arrangement into a discernible and effective pattern. Here, we will focus exclusively on the body of the speech.

OBJECTIVE 1

Why Is Organization Important?

To help orient new students to the college, the counseling office offers a program in which seniors give speeches about how to develop good study habits. The first speaker, Burt Wilson, maintained that "good habits depend on several important factors. For one thing, you have to avoid procrastination. Good reading skills are also helpful to college students. Oh yes, and by the way, you also need to be self-motivated." The incoming students looked puzzled and unconvinced; they stopped taking notes, and no one asked questions. The very next speaker, Laura Simmons, covered the same ground, but she said: "Good study habits depend on a balance of skills plus motivation. On the one hand, you have to develop good reading skills; on the other hand, you need to overcome procrastination. You can do both if you focus on the priorities that motivate you to study." The audience responded very differently to Laura's speech; they took notes and asked a number of questions when she finished.

This example illustrates that audiences will understand, remember, and be influenced by an organized message more than by a disorganized one. The reason is obvious. Careful listening is difficult under any circumstances, and it is even more difficult when listeners cannot tell where the speaker is going or how the parts of the speech relate to one another. An idea or example that is not connected to anything else is easy to forget.[1] The mental energy that listeners use in reconstructing a confused or disorganized speech is not available for absorbing and reflecting on its main points.[2] Moreover, even critical listeners may resent this additional work of listening to a disorganized speech and may express their resentment by resisting the message.[3]

Beyond such basic considerations about the audience, a speaker should recognize that form itself is persuasive. The ability to follow a speaker's organizational pattern is important for several reasons:

- *Recall.* An audience can better remember the main ideas of a speech when the speaker presents them in a recognizable pattern. For example, the past/present/future pattern encourages listeners to remember the first idea if they can connect it mentally to the heading "past."

organization
The selection of ideas and materials and their arrangement into a discernible and effective pattern.

- *Active listening.* Effective organization engages listeners' attention and helps them to ignore or override distractions.
- *Personal satisfaction.* Being able to anticipate what's coming next makes listeners feel that they are "in the know." If the speaker has just discussed recent issues in intercollegiate athletics, for example, they may believe that the next natural step is to discuss the merits of a playoff system for college football. If that indeed is the next main idea, they are likely to feel personal satisfaction at having "called it right."[4]

For a political candidate to hold the attention of students in an informal setting, it's especially important that the speech be well organized and easy to follow.

Organization is important for the speaker as well. In any rhetorical situation, the goal is to respond to your constraints and to take advantage of your opportunities to achieve your purpose. Organization is a major strategic resource as you make decisions about the number and order of ideas, how you group them, what you call them, and how you relate them to the audience.

Moreover, in planning your speech, organization can be a guide to check that you haven't accidentally left anything out. For example, noticing that your speech covers both the past and the present of your topic, you recognize that the audience will be likely to think, "But what about the future?" During your presentation, too, keeping the organization in mind can prevent the embarrassment of suddenly forgetting about the next point.[5]

Organization has two basic components: *selection* and *arrangement.* We will discuss each component with respect both to the main ideas of the speech and to the supporting materials.

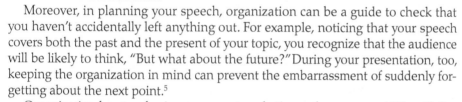

Selecting the Main Ideas

OBJECTIVE
2

The thesis statement is the principal claim of your speech, the statement you want listeners to accept. When you ask questions about your thesis statement, you identify the issues that you must address in order to establish the thesis. **Main ideas** are the claims that address the issues in your thesis statement, and they are the major divisions of the speech.

Identifying Your Main Ideas

The first step is to identify the main ideas in your speech. To do that, you must determine the possible main ideas from which you could choose. You can do so either (1) from your thesis or specific purpose or (2) from patterns in your research.

In either case, your answers will be affected by the current status of the topic in the public forum: what aspects or issues people generally are considering, which matters are accepted and uncontested and which are in dispute, which questions seem central and which seem peripheral.

> **main ideas**
> Claims that address the issues in the thesis statement; the primary divisions of the speech.

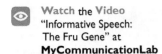
Watch the Video "Informative Speech: The Fru Gene" at **MyCommunicationLab**

From Your Thesis or Specific Purpose.

Stuart Kim used this approach to identify his main ideas in a speech seeking to persuade the audience to contribute to the United Way. Like many college students, Stuart was a community-service volunteer; he tutored reading and math at an after-school center for children from low-income families who had no parent at home during the day. Stuart enjoyed the work and felt that he was really helping the children, but toward the end of the year he was startled to learn that the center would have to close. It was funded by the United Way, and contributions were down. Appalled that "his" children would have nowhere to go, Stuart decided to speak to community groups and urge them to support the United Way. He used his public speaking classmates as a test audience to practice the speech.

Because Stuart's purpose was to persuade the audience to contribute to the United Way, he thought immediately of several ideas that he needed to address. He would have to tell listeners what the United Way is, that the agencies it supports (such as Stuart's after-school center) were important and valuable, that other sources of funding were not readily available, and that the United Way needed and merited *their* support. If the speech failed to address any of these elements, the audience was unlikely to be persuaded to donate money. Stuart regarded these as the main ideas, and he divided the speech into corresponding sections:

I. The United Way is a federation of health, recreational, and social service agencies.

II. The activities of these agencies are important and valuable to our community.

III. These activities cannot be continued unless we support the United Way.

In this example, Stuart was able immediately to see the main ideas that derived from his thesis and purpose. But sometimes the connection is not so obvious. If Stuart had not identified his main ideas at once, he might have worked them out by quizzing his thesis statement:

TOPIC:	The United Way.
GENERAL PURPOSE:	Inducing a specific action.
SPECIFIC PURPOSE:	Convincing listeners to give money to the United Way.
THESIS:	Everyone should contribute to the United Way.
ISSUES:	1. Everyone → Why me?
	2. Should contribute → Why? What does it do?
	3. The United Way → What is it?
MAIN IDEAS:	1. The United Way needs and merits your support.
	2. The United Way supports important and valuable programs.
	3. The United Way is an umbrella organization to raise money for social service programs.

Looking over this list, Stuart would probably decide to put main idea 3 first in the speech and to end with main idea 1. Why? Because listeners need to know what the United Way is before they can decide whether to support it and because the direct appeal in main idea 1 provides a strong conclusion. Applying these analytical steps, Stuart would derive the same main ideas that he was able to recognize instinctively.

Checklist 1 contains some of the standard questions to ask about a thesis statement in order to identify your main ideas.

From Patterns in Your Research.   Another approach to identifying main ideas is to observe patterns in the research that you have completed. If the people you interview and the literature you read repeatedly mention certain subjects, those may well be the main ideas about your topic.

For example, suppose that almost everything Stuart Kim read about the United Way mentioned its low administrative costs and suggested that its reliance on volunteers meant that most of the money raised can be spent directly on providing services. This idea may not have emerged from Stuart's initial conception of a strategy, and yet it may be very important to include the idea in the speech. It suggests that it is better for people to contribute to the United Way than to support a host of individual charities that do not use their funds as efficiently.

> **CHECKLIST 1**
>
> ## Questions to Help Identify Main Ideas
>
> ❏ What does it mean?
> ❏ How to describe it?
> ❏ What are the facts?
> ❏ What are the reasons?
> ❏ How often does it occur?
> ❏ What are the parts?
> ❏ What is the reasoning?
> ❏ Why is it strange?
> ❏ What are the objections?
> ❏ Compared with what?

Choosing Among Main Ideas

Whichever method you use to identify main ideas, you are likely to have more ideas than you have time or energy to pursue—and more than your audience will be willing and able to consider.

Suppose, for example, that Stuart's research suggested all the following points:

- The administrative costs of the United Way are low.
- Organizations in the United Way must be nondiscriminatory.
- The United Way had its origins in charitable organizations of the late nineteenth century.
- Some groups within the public object to the programs of certain United Way organizations.
- The United Way is staffed largely by volunteers.
- It is not clear whether someone who lives in one community but works in another should support the United Way at home or at work.
- The United Way substitutes a single annual campaign for what otherwise would be continuous solicitation for each of the member agencies.
- The alternative to supporting the United Way is to expand the government's social welfare programs.

Each of these topics could be discussed at length, and each might be supported by a variety of materials. Yet no speech of reasonable length could address them all. Therefore, like most speakers, Stuart will need to select from among the possible main ideas which ones to use in his speech.

Criteria for Selecting the Main Ideas

Most speeches cover between two and five main ideas. Although there is no magic to these numbers, they do generally represent what an audience expects and can likely follow and remember.

If you have derived more than five main ideas from your thesis and purpose and from your research, you can reduce their number and select which ideas to include by asking two questions:

- Is this idea really essential to the speech?
- Can a more general statement combine several ideas?

Is This Idea Essential?   In researching a speech, you may discover many interesting things about your subject that are, frankly, sidelights. Although they may be fascinating to you, they distract from your specific purpose. For example, knowing that the United Way developed from nineteenth-century charitable organizations may reveal quite a bit about American attitudes toward charity or about how organizations evolve. But remember that Stuart Kim's purpose is to persuade audience members to donate money. Most people don't need to know about the United Way's origins and history in order to decide whether to contribute. Likewise, if Stuart's goal is only to persuade people to give, it may not matter whether they do so at work or at home.

This first criterion is often difficult to apply. Speakers are reluctant to omit ideas that interest them, and valuable research time seems wasted if the results do not find their way into the speech. Material that does not directly relate to your topic and purpose is nonessential. Including nonessential material may distract the audience and prevent you from achieving your ultimate purpose. It is necessary, then, to be hard-nosed and to subject all potential main ideas to this rigorous test: If an idea—no matter how interesting—is not essential to your specific purpose, it does not qualify as a main idea and should be excluded.

Can Several Ideas Be Combined?   When you find yourself considering a large number of main ideas, consider whether some of them are not main ideas at all but illustrations of, or support for, more general statements. You may be able to combine what you thought were distinct main ideas into one general statement, thereby reducing the number. Your thesis should suggest these more general statements into which you could combine elements.

In the United Way example, the low administrative costs, the nondiscriminatory policies, and the convenience of a single annual campaign might turn out not to be separate main ideas but examples to support a general statement such as "The United Way is the best way to contribute to charity." The three statements all answer the question "Once I've decided that it's important to make a charitable contribution, why should I do so through the United Way?" That question is a longer form of "Why me?" which was derived from the thesis statement. All these examples could support the main idea, "The United Way merits *your* support."

Audience members listen attentively to a presentation that is well organized and easy to follow.

Characteristics of the Main Ideas

Unfortunately, just cutting the number of main ideas—as difficult as that is—may still result in a speech that does not seem complete, coherent, or persuasive. It is also important that the selected main ideas have the following characteristics.

Simplicity.   Because the main ideas serve as memory aids for both speaker and audience, they should be stated simply and succinctly so that they can be remembered. "The United Way is efficient" is a better statement of a main idea than is "The United Way has low administrative costs, economies of scale from combining campaigns, and simple distribution mechanisms." As a general rule, a main idea should be stated in a single short sentence.

Discreteness.   Each main idea should be separate from the others. When main ideas overlap, the structure of the speech becomes confusing, and it is difficult to remember what was said under each main heading. For example, if one main idea is "The United Way supports agencies that meet social needs" and another main idea is "The United Way supports health and recreational agencies," the two ideas overlap; they are not discrete. After all, health and recreation are also among our social needs. Such a structure will not be clear to listeners, and the speaker will not know where to put supporting material.

Parallel Structure.   When possible, main ideas should be stated in similar fashion. Sentences should have the same grammatical structure and should be of approximately the same length. This principle, known as **parallel structure**, makes the pattern easy to follow and to remember. For example, Stuart Kim might use this pattern:

> The United Way is effective.
>
> The United Way is efficient.
>
> The United Way is humane.

In this example, *effective, efficient*, and *humane* are the key terms that listeners are asked to remember.

Balance.   Taken together, the main ideas should not be loaded toward one particular aspect of the subject. Rather, they should add up to a balanced perspective. In the preceding list, each of the three key terms refers to a different aspect of the United Way: what it accomplishes, what it costs, and what values it represents. These are three different factors that would affect the decision to contribute, and together they offer a balanced perspective. If, on the other hand, three or four main ideas related to the United Way's finances and only one dealt with its underlying values, the organization of the speech would appear unbalanced. Finances would be covered in detail, but other important aspects of the topic would be treated superficially or ignored.

Coherence.   **Coherence** means that the separate main ideas have a clear relationship and hang together; listeners can see why they appear in the same speech. If Stuart Kim wished to persuade listeners to contribute to the United Way but offered one main idea about the origins of charitable organizations, another about efforts to extend the United Way to Eastern Europe, another about controversial agencies that the United Way supports, and another about accounting procedures, it is

parallel structure
Structure in which phrases are of similar syntax and length.

coherence
Clear relationships among ideas and topics so that the speech appears to hang together as a natural whole.

CHECKLIST 2

Characteristics of Main Ideas

- ❒ Are my main ideas **simple** and succinct?
- ❒ Is each main idea **discrete,** or separate from the others?
- ❒ Are the main ideas stated in a **parallel structure**?
- ❒ Are the main ideas **balanced** in perspective?
- ❒ Are the main ideas **coherent** and clear?
- ❒ Do the main ideas, taken together, offer a **complete** view of my topic?

hard to imagine how the speech could be coherent. These topics are not clearly related to each other (except that they all involve the United Way), and they do not come together to support any conclusion—certainly not the ultimate claim that "you should contribute to the United Way."

Completeness.   Finally, the main ideas taken together should present a complete view of the subject, omitting nothing of major importance. If Stuart wants to convince the audience to contribute to the United Way but fails to explain what the organization does with the money it receives, the pattern of main ideas would not be complete. Most people who make charitable gifts want to know how their contributions are used.

Arranging the Main Ideas

After selecting the main ideas for your speech, the next step is deciding upon their order—which ideas to put first, last, or in the middle. We'll look at the factors you should consider in arranging your main ideas and then at a variety of organizational patterns that you can use.

Factors Affecting Arrangement

Are the Main Ideas Dependent?   Ideas can be arranged in a pattern that makes them either *dependent* or *independent*.

Logically dependent ideas are like links in a chain, because the strength of each depends on all the others. If one link is broken, the chain is destroyed. Here is such a chain of logically dependent main ideas:

1. If we develop regulations for campus speech, they will necessarily be vague.
2. If regulations are vague, people will not know whether or not the regulations apply to them.
3. If people are unsure whether regulations apply to them, they will hesitate to speak out about controversial issues.
4. If people do not speak out about controversial issues, intellectual debate is undermined.

The links in this chain need to be arranged precisely as shown if the audience is to follow the speaker's reasoning.

Logical dependence is common in telling a story. With obvious exceptions (such as flashbacks), you should relate events in the order in which they occurred so that listeners can follow the plot. Likewise, if you arrange ideas in a spatial pattern—talking, for example, about colleges in different regions of the country—then you need to maintain that pattern of geographical movement. You might move from east to west or from west to east, but you would not want to zigzag from New England to the Southwest and then to the mid-Atlantic states.

In contrast, **logically independent ideas** stand alone, and the truth of each in no way rests on the others. Again, using the example of a proposed code to regulate campus speech, here is a logically independent pattern of reasoning:

Campus speech codes are unacceptably vague.

Campus speech codes discourage the airing of controversial issues.

Campus speech codes bring bad publicity to the college.

 Watch the Video "Demonstration Speech: Baking a Cake" at **MyCommunicationLab**

logically dependent idea
Cannot stand on its own but requires that another claim or statement be true.

logically independent idea
Does not require the truth of any other claim or statement as a condition for its own truth.

This speaker also wishes to oppose campus speech codes, but notice the difference in the structure of main ideas. In this case, each idea bears *independently* on the conclusion. Any one of these claims by itself could give the audience good reason to oppose speech codes, regardless of the other claims. Speech codes are undesirable if they are too vague, *or* if they chill the discussion of controversial issues, *or* if they bring unfavorable publicity.

A dependent pattern of reasoning can be risky, because the defeat of any one link will cause the chain to break. But a dependent pattern also offers advantages. It is highly coherent and easy to follow. And if each link is established successfully, the force of the overall pattern may cause the whole chain to seem even stronger than the sum of its links.

The choice of a dependent or an independent pattern is influenced most strongly by your thesis statement. Use whichever pattern is more effective in establishing your claim for your audience. But one thing is certain: If your main ideas are dependent on each other, their arrangement is virtually decided. You can begin at either end of the chain, but you must connect the ideas in order, link by link. With an independent pattern, however, you do not have to present the main ideas in any particular order. In that case, additional questions will arise.

Are Some Main Ideas Relatively Unfamiliar?
Because most people comprehend unfamiliar ideas by linking them to familiar ideas, you may wish to begin your speech with a main idea that is already familiar to listeners. This will attract their interest and get them thinking about your topic. Then you can move to the less familiar ideas, knowing that the audience is working with you.

Your audience analysis may suggest that most people realize that campus speech codes attract adverse publicity but that they may not be familiar with the vagueness of such codes and may not have thought about their effect on the airing of controversial issues. You therefore might begin with the familiar idea that campus speech codes attract negative publicity, making the point that this is just the tip of the iceberg. Speech codes also have two less obvious problems: They are too vague to be administered fairly, and—even worse—they stifle discussion of controversial issues. If your audience analysis is correct, you have succeeded in arranging the ideas from most familiar to least familiar.

There is another reason to begin with the familiar. If your first main idea were completely unfamiliar to the audience, it would be much more difficult for listeners to grasp. You might distract them by making them stop to think about what you mean by "the inherent vagueness of speech codes," and they might miss your next point. On the other hand, discussion of a familiar main idea can be used to explain a less familiar idea. For example, knowing that listeners might quickly recognize that campus speech codes cause adverse publicity, you might ask why the publicity is so adverse. This question would provide a natural transition into your second, less familiar idea.

When you have a strong idea that you plan to present emphatically, as this speaker does, should it be placed first or last in your speech?

Should the Strongest Idea Come First or Last?
This question comes into play when two conditions are met: when the main ideas are independent and when they are not equally strong.

A "strong" idea is one that will seem compelling to an audience of critical listeners. An idea is not considered strong if it does not make much difference to listeners—even if it is true and well supported.

Should you present your strongest main idea first in order to make a strong first impression on the audience? Or should you present it last, to end with a bang and leave the audience on a positive note? Many researchers have studied the relative merits of a **primacy effect** (strongest idea first) versus a **recency effect** (strongest idea last), but the results are inconclusive because too many other factors also influence the impact of arrangement.[6] However, if one idea seems weaker than the others, you should present it in a middle position rather than either toward the beginning or toward the end.

Often, the strength of an idea depends not on any inherent feature of the idea itself, but on how well the idea sits with the audience. Therefore, your audience analysis is not finished when you first select a topic, purpose, thesis, and strategy; the audience affects all major decisions about speech preparation and delivery.

Patterns for Arranging Main Ideas

In theory, you can arrange main ideas in an infinite number of patterns, but several common patterns are easy for an audience to follow, and they work well for a variety of topics. You first should focus on these general patterns, which are described next. Then, if your topic, purpose, or audience seems to call for a different pattern, you can develop your own.

Chronological.
The passage of time is the organizing principle in the chronological approach. The units of time (most often the past, the present, and the future) become the main ideas. For example, in discussing the topic of "Discrimination Against Female Sports Reporters," student Jordan Breal organized her speech this way:

   I. Female sports reporters received little credit for their work until the 1930s.
   II. Female sports reporters were not allowed into press rooms until the 1970s.
   III. Female sports reporters were not allowed into locker rooms until the late 1970s.
   IV. Treatment of female sports reporters leaves much room for improvement in the future.

This example proceeds in normal chronological order, beginning with the past and ending with the future. But you can start at any point in the chronology. For example, you might decide that a speech about AIDS should begin with a discussion of the current crisis in Africa, then move backwards in time to examine the origins of AIDS, and conclude with a discussion of the future of AIDS research and possible cures.

Spatial.
Whereas chronological order organizes main ideas according to time, spatial order arranges them according to place or position. A speech might begin with the aspects of the topic that are nearest and then proceed to the aspects that are farther away. This pattern might work well for a speech about the effects of a strong national economy, in which the main points include the following:

   I. A booming economy increases the individual's spending power.
   II. A booming economy supports state and local projects.
   III. A booming economy improves the federal budget.

Watch the Video "Informative Speech/ Self-Introduction: Martha Margaret Clark Cherry Gaines" at **MyCommunicationLab**

primacy effect
A tendency for what is presented first to be best remembered.

recency effect
A tendency for what is presented last to be best remembered.

Another common spatial arrangement would be to present ideas literally in geographic order:

I.   A booming economy helps farmers in the South.

II. A booming economy helps manufacturing in the Midwest.

III. A booming economy helps the oil industry in the Southwest.

IV. A booming economy helps technology industries in the Northwest.

Categorical (Topical).

In the categorical pattern, each main idea that you identified in analyzing your topic becomes a major division of the speech. For example, in researching the Hindu religion, student Anuj Vedak learned that Hindus hold many distinct beliefs, including a belief in karma as a guide to treating others ethically, a belief in reincarnation for those who have died, and a belief in Nirvana as the soul's act of attaining salvation. Each of these topics can become a major heading in a speech. Because a categorical pattern has no required order (e.g., from past to present or from left to right), it is important that main ideas be stated in parallel fashion and that they be easy to recognize and remember. The major headings for a speech on Hinduism might be the following:

I.   Hindus believe in karma as a guide to ethical behavior.

II. Hindus believe in reincarnation as the process of rebirth for the deceased.

III. Hindus believe in Nirvana as the soul's act of attaining salvation.

This pattern is also called *topical* because it derives from the *topoi*. These are obvious or typical categories for organizing subject matter. They usually will have an obvious or standard structure. "People, places, and events" is an example of a set of *topoi*, as is "economic, military, and political aspects."

Cause–Effect.

Cause–effect is also an organizational pattern, and it can proceed in either direction. You can focus on causes and then identify their effects, or you can first identify effects and then try to determine their causes. For example, a speech about global warming might proceed like as follows:

I.   Factories, refineries, power plants, and cars emit vast amounts of carbon into the Earth's atmosphere.

II. Industrialized societies generate so much atmospheric carbon that they are effectively wrapping the Earth in a heating blanket.

III. As the Earth's surface temperatures rise, fundamental and irreversible shifts in our planet's climate patterns are occurring.

Or, rather than moving from cause to effect, you might proceed from effect to cause:

I.   We are becoming more vulnerable to the effects of global warming and climate change.

II. This effect results from the release of carbon into the atmosphere from the world's factories, refineries, power plants, and cars.

III. Widespread use of carbon-based fossil fuels is a major source of the problem.

The choice between these two arrangements would be governed by which topics you wanted to present first and last, not by anything intrinsic to the cause–effect organizational pattern.

A Question of Ethics

Ethics and Organization

The desire to organize our thoughts and make them easily memorable for our audiences is natural. But what if our organizational patterns distort the subject matter of our speech? Suppose we would like to deliver a speech in a chronological pattern, explaining the historical development of the topic, but that history would not allow for some of the more critical information that might show up in a categorical pattern. For example, the history of the civil rights movement often focuses on major achievements since the 1960s rather than on the internal tensions within the movement or the extent and ferocity of resistance to it. Or suppose we select a categorical pattern but the categories are not really separate from one another. What are our ethical responsibilities to our subject, and how can these be reconciled with our strategic interest in effective organization? How do we negotiate these tensions?

Watch the Video
"Persuasive Speech:
Living Wills" at
MyCommunicationLab

Problem–Solution.

A variation of the cause–effect pattern is one that focuses on problems and their solutions. A speech using this pattern first lays out the dimensions of the problem and shows why it is serious; then it considers one or more potential solutions. It may simply report on the various possible solutions or it may proceed to explain why a particular solution is best. For example, a speech about the difficulties of the campus parking system might be structured like as follows:

I. There is a shortage of parking spaces near the main classroom buildings.

II. As a result, many students must walk almost a mile from their cars to their classes.

III. In the short term, expanding the campus bus service, and in the long term, building a central parking garage would solve the problem.

The development of the first two major headings would establish that there is a problem, perhaps by claiming that the current situation is unsafe for students attending evening classes. Possibly after considering other solutions, the speaker would claim in the third main idea that these problems can be overcome by a combination of expanded bus service and construction of a parking garage.

Often, problems are not self-evident to an audience. A speaker has to motivate listeners to feel that some important need is not being met before they will regard a situation as a problem. A variation on the problem–solution pattern, then, is to emphasize *psychological order*. The speaker first motivates listeners to perceive a problem and then provides the means to satisfy that feeling by identifying a solution. If Stuart Kim had chosen this approach in speaking about the United Way, his speech might have been organized as follows:

I. We all have a responsibility to others.

II. This responsibility includes financial support for the social service organizations that help others.

III. Giving to the United Way helps us to meet our responsibilities.

In this example, the first step is to arouse an attitude, motive, or desire among the audience members. Subsequent steps then refine that motivation and show how it can be satisfied by a particular action.

Comparison and Contrast.   Sometimes it is easiest to examine a topic by demonstrating its similarities to, and differences from, other topics with which the audience is likely to be familiar. From your studies of American history, for example, you know that women and racial and ethnic minorities have sometimes been subjected to prejudice and discrimination in the workplace. Your speech might be organized to compare the experiences among these groups:

I. Women often are not promoted to senior positions because executives do not think they will remain on the job while raising children.

II. Mexican Americans, in many parts of the country, are hired only for the most menial jobs.

III. Earlier, German Americans and Japanese Americans were fired from their jobs because employers thought they were unpatriotic.

IV. Today, immigrants from the Middle East are denied access to some jobs because they are categorically suspected of involvement in terrorist activities.

V. African Americans have been limited in work opportunities because many whites believe that they do not want to work.

Rhetorical Workout

Shape and Organize Main Ideas

You are working on an informative speech about zero waste and are ready to choose and arrange your main ideas. Your *general purpose* is to provide new information, and your *specific purpose* is to inform listeners of what zero waste means and what initiatives have been successful. You write this thesis: "Zero waste initiatives are making a difference for a better environment."

1. Use the criteria for selecting main ideas to assess the points below. Which ideas seem essential to your speech? Which can be combined into fewer general statements?

   • Zero waste initiatives have proven to reduce pollution.

   • Zero waste means eliminating waste in all stages of a product's life.

   • Initiatives are under way in nearly 20 countries.

   • Not creating waste is more environmentally friendly than recycling it.

   • The quantity of garbage in landfills has gone down in areas using zero waste initiatives.

   • At least five U.S. states have adopted zero waste initiatives.

   • A zero waste economy is based on recovering resources and can create jobs.

2. Using the principle of parallel structure, create three main ideas out of the above list. Is the grammatical structure of each main idea the same? Are the three main ideas approximately the same length? If not, revise the sentences to fit these requirements.

3. Does each of your three main ideas stand alone, as a *logically independent idea*, or are all three like links in a chain, as *logically dependent ideas*? Explain. If they are logically dependent, write them down in the order they need to appear in your speech.

4. Which organizational pattern would be best suited to your three main ideas: chronological, spatial, categorical (topical), cause–effect, problem-solution, comparison and contrast, or residues? Why? Apply the pattern to your three main ideas. Is the result logical and effective? Why or why not?

Now the question is whether you want to highlight the differences or the similarities among these groups. You might select either of the following as your last main idea:

VI. Although some groups have managed to overcome the effects of discrimination and have succeeded in the workplace, others have not been so lucky.

or

VI. Although the experiences of these groups are very different, they have one factor in common: Society's prejudice places an artificial ceiling on their economic opportunities.

In either case, the earlier main ideas are brought together in the last one, which shows either how differences outweigh similarities or the reverse.

Residues. A final organizational pattern is to arrange the speech by process of elimination. This pattern works well when there are a finite number of possibilities, none particularly desirable, and you want to argue that one of them represents "the least among the evils." For example, in a political campaign in which you find no candidate particularly appealing, you could use this pattern to rule out all but one candidate, whom you then support as being the least objectionable.

Student speaker Jennifer Aiello used organization by residues to get her classmates to consider seriously the proposal that gun manufacturers should be required to install locks on guns. She arranged her main ideas to rule out the other options available to society:

No one wants freedom infringed upon. And no one wants to have to pay more for a gun. But let's consider the alternatives. Does anyone want more children to have access to guns that take virtually no effort to use? Does anyone want to attend more funerals of children shot dead while at school? Does anyone want to see more six-year-olds lying in critical condition in hospital beds because they thought their parents' handgun was a toy? Does anyone want to see parents, friends, and family mourning another unnecessary death?

By ruling out each of these other alternatives, Jennifer was able to convince many of her audience members that putting locks on guns was a proposal worthy of their reflection.

Choosing the Organizational Pattern

The organizational patterns described here do not exhaust all the possibilities, but they illustrate that you have many options from which to choose.[7] How should you decide which organizational pattern to use in your speech? Does it matter, for example, whether you use a cause–effect pattern or a comparison and contrast pattern? How do you know whether, say, the costs and benefits of voting are more important than the convenience of voting? Questions like these require you to think strategically. The answers are complex and must take into account your subject, your purpose, your audience, and your culture.

CHECKLIST 3

Basic Organizational Patterns

☐ **Chronological:** Can my topic be broken down into units of time?

☐ **Spatial:** Can my topic be organized according to place or position?

☐ **Categorical (topical):** Is my topic best organized according to my existing main ideas? If so, are my main ideas in parallel form?

☐ **Cause–effect:** Can my topic be organized around causes and effects?

☐ **Problem–solution:** Does my topic suggest a problem that can be organized around its possible solutions?

☐ **Comparison and contrast:** Can I examine my topic by showing similarities to or differences from other topics?

☐ **Residues:** Does my topic lend itself to a process-of-elimination pattern?

Based on Your Subject. Certain subjects lend themselves to particular organizational patterns. For example, because the collapse of communism in Eastern Europe is a historical event, it has a dramatic structure that would be emphasized by telling a story in chronological order. However, a speech about the components of air pollution would more likely suggest a topical pattern—unless, perhaps, it was being delivered to an audience of environmental historians who would be more interested in understanding when and how these components became serious national problems.

Based on Your Purpose. Your purpose or strategy also influences the selection of an organizational pattern. For instance, if you want to urge the audience to lobby for updated privacy laws that better protect consumers against online identity theft, an analytical pattern that emphasizes the problems and solutions will be especially appropriate because it will focus attention on the specific proposal for which you want listeners to lobby. In contrast, if your purpose is to show that the protection of a person's online identity is very different from the traditional practice of maintaining personal privacy, a comparison and contrast pattern probably would make more sense.

Based on Your Audience. Your audience is another influence on the arrangement of your speech. For example, listeners who have paid little attention to developments in relations between Russia and Ukraine probably would be more interested in an overview of events since the fall of the Soviet Union than in a detailed analysis of oil and gas supply agreements between the two countries. But an audience composed mostly of people with family origins in either Russia or

Strategies for Speaking to Diverse Audiences

Respecting Diversity Through the Organization of the Body of Your Speech

A sense of form is achieved in different ways for different cultures. Here are strategies to respect the diversity of the audience when organizing the body of the speech.

1. Acknowledge the presuppositions of your audience members. Analyze your audience, but be careful not to stereotype cultures by assuming that one's culture completely determines one's response to your speech.

2. Organize your ideas according to what you believe will appeal to the majority of your audience, but do not rely heavily on a structure that might alienate parts of your audience.

3. Consider whether cultures differ in their approach to space; for example, Hebrew and Arabic texts read from right to left. If you use spatial order in your speech, do not automatically move from left to right.

4. Consider whether cultures differ in their approach to time. For example, tradition remains an important source of authority for many, giving greater weight to the past, while some regard tradition as a hindrance to progress and give greater weight to the present.

5. Consider whether cultures differ in their approach to consistency. For example, Taoism celebrates *wu wei* ("action without action"), a concept that seems impossible to understand in the world of science, embracing opposites rather than regarding inconsistency as a logical error. You may not be able to assume that by identifying an inconsistency you have discredited an opposing argument.

6. Consider whether cultures differ in their dominant mode of reasoning; for example, prizing cause–effect thinking or prizing narrative and myth.

Ukraine might be strongly interested in hearing about developments in their "old countries." And listeners who are involved in foreign policy issues probably would be most interested in the implications of changes since the Orange Revolution and the political ascent of Vladimir Putin. These differences can help you decide which points to put first and last.

Based on the Culture.   Finally, the culture will affect your organizational pattern. For example, mainstream American culture is strongly oriented toward pragmatism, and so a pattern that focuses on problems and solutions would resonate well for many listeners. But other cultures and subcultures have a much greater concern for ideology, for myth and ritual, for narrative, or for authority; the preference for these values would affect the pattern of analysis.

Joanna Watkins was about to address an audience with a high proportion of Asian students. She had studied some Roper Poll surveys about dominant values among various cultural groups in the United States and had learned that many Asians value family and group loyalty and mutual support more than such mainstream American values as competitiveness and individual achievement. Because Joanna's topic was about how to get ahead in college, she needed to arrange her speech carefully. In this case, a highly pragmatic cause–effect pattern—which might be just right in other situations—would probably be inappropriate.

Joanna chose to include material about the value of close friendships and the sense of community that often develops among Asian college students. At the same time, she was careful not to stereotype her audience or to assume that "all Asians think alike." She did not say, "Since most of you are Asian, let me talk about group loyalty," and she was careful also to include at least some appeals based on pragmatic values, too.

Clearly, no organizational pattern is automatically "right" for any given speech. You need to think critically about the implications and effects of any pattern and choose an arrangement that suits your strategy. Moreover, although we have considered these basic patterns as though they were mutually exclusive, you obviously can combine them. For instance, you could use a chronological pattern, but at each step in the chronology you might examine developments topically or by reference to causes and effects. Or you could organize your speech using both a topical pattern and comparison and contrast. In theory, the potential combinations of patterns are limitless. Particularly when audience members have different cultural backgrounds, value systems, and priorities, a creative combination may be most effective.

Explore the **Exercise** "Organization" at **MyCommunicationLab**

OBJECTIVE
4

Selecting and Arranging Supporting Materials

subheadings
Ideas that are components of or support for the main ideas in the speech.

Most main ideas are sufficiently complex that they involve several supporting ideas or **subheadings**. The supporting material that you located will usually support these subheadings, which in turn will support the main ideas. Subheadings are chosen and arranged using the same methods that we have described for main ideas. Moreover, many of the same considerations also apply to the materials you will use to support your main ideas and subpoints. Now, you should consider which materials to select and how to arrange them.

Selection of Supporting Materials

Watch the **Video** "Persuasive Speech: Secondhand Smoke" at **MyCommunicationLab**

How Much? Probably the most important question, and the hardest to answer, is "How much support is enough?" You need to offer enough evidence to establish your claims but not so much that the speech becomes repetitive and boring. But how do you know what is the right balance?

The only all-purpose answer to this question is, "It depends."[8] It depends, most of all, on your audience analysis. In examining listeners' prior understanding of your topic, you may find that your main idea is one with which they are likely to agree. If so, a relatively modest amount of support will be enough. But if the audience is likely to find your main idea controversial, you will need more support to convince doubters.

For example, a speaker who tells a college audience that the legal drinking age should be lowered to 18 is probably "preaching to the choir." These listeners have likely already accepted the claim, and so the speaker needs only a few pieces of reliable supporting material. But a speaker who tells the same audience that the legal drinking age should be kept at 21 will probably need to supply much more evidence to convince listeners that the disadvantages of change would outweigh the benefits. In contrast, if the audience were composed of older people, the reverse would likely be true: The speaker who wants to raise the drinking age might need less supporting material than the speaker who wants to lower it.

Besides listeners' beliefs about the specific topic, their common knowledge and experience will affect how much supporting material you need. Also, if they are skeptical by nature, you will want to add more support. If they are impatient or are not good listeners, you will want to keep the speech short and the supporting materials simple. If they are accustomed to asking questions after a speech, you will want to anticipate their major questions and to incorporate supporting material that prepares you to answer them.

The general principle to follow is: The greater the distance between the audience's current views and the position you wish listeners to adopt, the more supporting material will be required. Yet you also must be careful not to stereotype or to assume that all listeners would identify their position on an issue in the same way.

CHOOSE A STRATEGY: Organizing Your Speech

The Situation

You and a number of other students are dismayed by your university's decision to limit Internet access to certain sites on campus. You've been attending rallies against the policy and have been invited to speak at the next student government meeting about your objections.

Making Choices

1. How should you decide what main points you want to relay to your audience, and in what order should you present them?

2. What do you know about the school board's position that would affect your organizational choices?

3. What kind of supporting material would be important to include—and where in the speech should you include it?

What If...

How would your organizational decisions change if the following were true?

1. There was evidence of illegal Internet activity among the student population.

2. The university had asked for student feedback before making the decision to limit Internet access.

In any case, supporting material should not be redundant; each piece of evidence should add something new to the speech as a whole. The testimony of three different people who say exactly the same thing is not likely to be higher in value than one person's testimony. Nor will you strengthen the speech by citing the same example from multiple sources.

What Kind?   Regarding the types of supporting materials to use, the general goal is to aim for variety. The speech should not depend entirely on statistics, on testimony, on examples, or on primary documents. The reasons are simple. First, you are more likely to hold the audience's interest by varying the types of evidence you offer. Although it is important that the audience be able to anticipate your general pattern, too much repetition induces boredom. Second, different listeners will be persuaded by different kinds of evidence. If your audience is heterogeneous, then using a variety of support helps you to strike a responsive chord among many different listeners.

What Criteria?   Having decided how much and what types of support you need, you still face other choices. For example, you may have decided that testimony is the form of support you need and that one quotation from an expert will be enough. But your research may have accumulated the testimony of four or five experts. How do you decide which one to use? Similarly, you may have found multiple examples, various statistical measures, or more primary documents than you might need.

What criteria can you use to assess these supporting materials?

1. *Apply the criteria for strength of supporting.* For instance, with regard to testimony, you should ask which authority has the greatest expertise on the subject, which statement is most recent (if timeliness is a factor), and so on. With respect to examples, you want to use a case that is representative. And if you are choosing among pieces of statistical evidence, consider the reliability and validity of each.

2. *Select the supporting material that is easiest to understand.* If listeners have to work hard to understand and remember your supporting material, they will be distracted from the focus of your speech.

   This can be a special concern with respect to statistical evidence. Complicated or overly precise statistics may be hard to comprehend orally, and using them may require some minor editing. For example, rather than reporting that the federal budget deficit is projected to be $4,267,153,697,000 over a 10-year period, you might report the projection as "more than $4 trillion." Rather than "significant at the 0.001 level," you might say, "These are results we would get by chance only one one-thousandth of the time."

3. *Select vivid or interesting supporting material when you can.* Less interesting material requires the audience to give it greater concentration, which again will distract from your main ideas.

4. *Select supporting material that is consistent with other things you know.* If you use material that challenges commonly held beliefs, you should be prepared to defend it and explain why the audience should not reject it out of hand.

CHECKLIST 4

Selecting Supporting Materials

- ❑ Does the supporting material meet tests of strength for its type?
- ❑ Will the supporting material be easily understood?
- ❑ Is the supporting material vivid and interesting?
- ❑ Is the supporting material consistent with other things you know?
- ❑ Will the supporting material be efficient to present?
- ❑ Can the supporting material be easily cited in the speech?

5. *Select supporting material that will be efficient to present.* In general, a short anecdote is better than a long narrative, if they make the same point. And a statistical measure with categories that are clear is more useful than one that needs lengthy explanations.

6. *Select supporting material that can be cited easily in the speech.* Unlike a written mode, you cannot supply a full bibliographic citation orally. But you do want to give enough information so that a listener knows where you got the material. An "oral footnote" that refers to "Secretary of State Clinton in last January's issue of *Foreign Affairs*" is a good example provides more guidance on creating oral citations to include in your presentation outline.

Arrangement of Supporting Materials

Just as the main ideas of a speech can be arranged according to a variety of patterns, so, too, can the supporting materials that establish each main idea. The same considerations—your purpose and your strategy—govern the arrangement of main ideas and of supporting materials.

Suppose, for example, that for a main idea you want to demonstrate that the percentage of deaths from car crashes linked to alcohol use declined over a certain period of time. Because your objective is to demonstrate a rate and direction of change, a chronological pattern might serve best. It would enable you to "take a snapshot" of how many crash fatalities were linked to alcohol at different points in

	Total Killed in Alcohol-Related Crashes		Total Killed in All Traffic Crashes	
Calendar Year	Number	Percent	Number	Percent
1990	22,587	51	44,599	100
1991	20,159	49	41,508	100
1992	18,290	47	39,250	100
1993	17,908	45	40,150	100
1994	17,308	43	40,716	100
1995	17,732	42	41,817	100
1996	17,749	42	42,065	100
1997	16,711	40	42,013	100
1998	16,673	40	41,501	100
1999	16,572	40	41,717	100
2000	17,380	41	41,945	100
2001	17,400	41	42,196	100
2002	17,524	41	43,005	100
2003	17,105	40	42,884	100
2004	16,694	39	42,836	100

Table 1 Total traffic fatalities versus alcohol-related traffic fatalities, 1990–2004

Source: National Highway Traffic Safety Administration FARS data.

time. You could show your audience that in 1990, 51 percent of accident fatalities were linked to alcohol; that it was down to 43 percent by 1994; and that by 2004 it was 39 percent (see Table 1). By arranging these "snapshots" in chronological order, you can convey the message of ongoing progress.

For another example, suppose you want to establish that alienation from politics is a nationwide occurrence. You might use a spatial pattern, drawing on examples from the East, the Midwest, the South, and the West. In yet another speech, you might want to emphasize trends in the training and preparation of popular music singers. You could use a topical pattern to focus on each singer you want to discuss or a comparison and contrast pattern that would let you demonstrate important similarities and differences among the singers.

You also can combine the patterns of arrangement in a single speech. In discussing the apathy of American voters, you might use both a chronological and a spatial pattern, as follows:

I. Voter apathy has become a growing concern.
   A. During the years before World War I, voter turnout was high.
   B. In the modern age, the height of voter participation came in 1960.
   C. Since 1960, there has been a slow but steady decline in political participation.
   D. By 1996, voter turnout was at the lowest level since 1924.
   E. Even in the razor-thin election of 2000, turnout rose only slightly.
   F. Even in 2008, although turnout among younger voters rose, the overall voter turnout remained a full 10 percentage points below its 1960 peak.
II. Voter apathy is widespread.
   A. It can be found in the East.
   B. It can be found in the Midwest.
   C. It can be found in the South.
   D. It can be found in the West.

Such a combination, aside from clarifying each main idea in the most appropriate way, also brings variety to the speech—a desirable objective in itself.

What Have You Learned?

Objective 1: Explain why the organization of the speech is important for both the speaker and the audience.

Organizing the body of the speech involves two sets of choices regarding main ideas as well as supporting materials:

- What to include
- What pattern of arrangement to use

Organization helps both the audience and the speaker, because

- Form itself is persuasive.
- A recognizable form makes content easier to remember.
- Listeners can anticipate what is coming next and feel satisfied when they are right.
- Structure is an aid in preparing the speech and in remembering what comes next.

Objective 2: Identify criteria for selecting the main ideas to include in your speech and the characteristics that a main idea should have.

Main ideas are chosen by reference to

- The speaker's strategy and purpose
- The themes most frequently identified in research

Main ideas should have these characteristics:

- Few in number
- Simple in phrasing
- Parallel in structure
- Coherent
- Complete in their treatment of the topic

Objective 3: Arrange the main ideas into recognizable patterns and decide what patterns of arrangement to use.

Arranging the main ideas raises questions such as the following:

- Their dependence on one another
- The value of beginning with the familiar
- The importance of first and last impressions
- The nature of the audience

Several of the most common organizational patterns are as follows:

- Chronological
- Spatial
- Categorical (topical)
- Cause–effect
- Problem–solution
- Comparison and contrast
- Residues

Objective 4: Decide how much and which kinds of supporting material you need and how to arrange the support for each idea.

Guided by audience analysis, speakers should select supporting material that is

- Tested for strength
- Easy to understand
- Vivid and interesting
- Consistent with what already is known
- Efficient to present
- Easy to cite in the speech

The same factors that govern arrangement of main ideas also affect arrangement of the supporting material.

 Listen to the **Audio Chapter Summary** at **MyCommunicationLab**

Discussion Questions

1. In this chapter, we examined Stuart Kim's strategic plan to select and organize main ideas for a speech to convince listeners to donate to the United Way. But what would Stuart's speech be like if he faced a different rhetorical situation? Imagine that he is planning to speak to fellow volunteers at a year-end gathering to celebrate the United Way. Using the list of ideas that Stuart developed in his research, and drawing on your own imagination, discuss the selection and arrangement of appropriate main ideas for such a speech.

2. Which organizational pattern would you recommend for each of the following rhetorical situations? Why?

   To inform an audience of high school students about their college options

   To explain the history of your state capital to a group of German tourists

   To teach a group of coworkers how to use a new computer program

   To strengthen the commitment of fellow party members to a candidate's campaign

   To persuade an audience of restaurant and bar owners that smoking should be banned in public spaces

   To introduce an award-winning journalist who is about to give a lecture at a school assembly

3. What is the best organizational strategy for your next speech in this class? Gather in groups of four or five, and discuss your strategic plan with your classmates. Answer the following questions about each group member's strategy:

   a. Do the main ideas satisfy the criteria of simplicity, discreteness, parallel structure, balance, coherence, and completeness?

   b. Which other organizational patterns might be more suitable for the purpose and audience of this speech?

   c. Which type of supporting material is needed to develop each main idea in the speech?

4. Identify the basic organizational pattern used in a speech shown or presented in class. In small groups, discuss the benefit of a particular organizational pattern for this speech, and also think about alternative organizational patterns that might have worked well for that speech.

Activities

1. Select the main ideas for your next speech.

   a. Use Checklist 1 to generate a list of potential main ideas.

   b. Subject each idea in the list to the tests described in this chapter: Is the idea essential? Can a more general statement combine several main ideas?

2. Arrange the main ideas for your next speech.

   a. Choose an organizational pattern and explain why it is more fitting than the other patterns discussed in this chapter.

   b. Write a paragraph or two to justify the pattern that you have selected. In doing so, ask yourself the following questions:

   Are the ideas dependent on or independent of one another?

   Are you beginning with the familiar or with the unfamiliar?

   Are the first and the last ideas strongest?

   Why is this pattern most appropriate for your audience and purpose?

3. Select the supporting material for your next speech.

   a. Apply the general principle described to determine how much supporting material you need.

   b. Choose the supporting material that you will use to develop each main idea in the speech.

   c. Using the criteria in Checklist 4, write a sentence or two to explain why you have chosen each piece of supporting material.

4. Using the presentation note cards from one of your previous speeches for this course, design a new organizational pattern. Since the content of your speech has remained the same, but the order is different, decide whether this reorganization affected the meaning or effectiveness of the speech. Try to imagine other audiences and situations in which your new organizational pattern might be desirable.

Key Terms

coherence	main ideas	primacy effect
logically dependent idea	organization	recency effect
logically independent idea	parallel structure	subheadings

 Study and **Review** the **Flashcards** at **MyCommunicationLab**

Notes

1 Experiments show that an audience retains more of a message that is organized than of one that is not. See Ernest C. Thompson, "An Experimental Investigation of the Relative Effectiveness of Organizational Structure in Oral Communication," *Southern Speech Communication Journal* 26 (Fall 1960): 59–69.

2 Research confirms that organized speeches are comprehended more fully than unorganized speeches. See Arlee Johnson, "A Preliminary Investigation of the Relationship between Message Organization and Listener Comprehension," *Communication Studies* 21 (Summer 1970): 104–107.

3 One study suggests that an unorganized persuasive message may actually produce an effect that is opposite to what the speaker intended. See Raymond G. Smith, "An Experimental Study of the Effects of Speech Organization

upon Attitudes of College Students," *Communication Monographs* 18 (November 1951): 292–301. Another study simply concludes that an extremely unorganized speech is not very persuasive. See James C. McCroskey and R. Samuel Mehrley, "The Effects of Disorganization and Nonfluency on Attitude Change and Source Credibility," *Communication Monographs* 36 (March 1969): 13–21.

4 Rhetorical theorist Kenneth Burke envisions form as "the creation of an appetite in the mind of the auditor, and the adequate satisfying of that appetite." See "Psychology and Form," *Counter-Statement*, Berkeley: University of California Press, 1931.

5 One study demonstrated that speakers who have a plan and practice that plan have fewer pauses in their speeches. See John O. Greene, "Speech Preparation and Verbal Fluency," *Human Communication Research* 11 (Fall 1984): 61–84.

6   See Howard Gilkinson, Stanley F. Paulson, and Donald
    E. Sikkink, "Effects of Order and Authority in an
    Argumentative Speech," *Quarterly Journal of Speech*
    40 (April 1954): 183–92; and Halbert E. Gulley and
    David K. Berlo, "Effect of Intercellular and Intracellular
    Speech Structure on Attitude Change and Learning,"
    Communication Monographs 23 (November 1956): 288–97.
    For a more recent look at how these questions affect
    other aspects of our lives, see Jaime Murphy, Charles
    Hofacker, and Richard Mizerski, "Primacy and Recency
    Effects on Clicking Behavior," *Journal of Computer-Mediated
    Communcation*, 11 (January 2006), 522–35.

7   For a few more ideas, see James A. Benson,
    "Extemporaneous Speaking: Organization Which Inheres,"
    Argumentation and Advocacy 14 (Winter 1978): 150–55.

8   Some researchers who have tried to determine
    experimentally the place of evidence in a speech have
    concluded that there are just too many variables (such as
    the prior beliefs of the audience members, the credibility
    of the speaker, and the different types of evidence) to draw
    deterministic conclusions. See Kathy Kellermann, "The
    Concept of Evidence: A Critical Review," *Argumentation
    and Advocacy* 16 (Winter 1980): 159–72; and Richard B.
    Gregg, "The Rhetoric of Evidence," *Western Journal of Speech
    Communication* 31 (Summer 1967): 180–89.

Photo Credits

Credits are listed in order of appearance.

Rhetoric as Symbolic Action

Human beings make sense of their interactions with the world and with each other through the symbols (the words and images) they attach to their experiences. Words (language) and images (icons, pictures, photos, bodies, architectural structures) are not merely a means to transmit information, they are the grounds for the judgments people make about things, events, and other people. Quite simply, symbols matter.

How many people you know ever went home from grade school crying because of something another person said or a mean picture another person drew? Even if some children shouted, "Sticks and stones may break my bones, but words will never hurt me" through tear-stained faces, they recognized the immense power of words and symbols to hurt.

Columnist Kathleen Parker wrote a column called "Google Bombs Can Ruin Your Reputation,"[1] demonstrating how the words of one person in the many-to-many space of the Internet can have real effects on the reputations and livelihoods of other persons. The things people say (and the photos they post on social networking sites) matter.

Symbols matter. Your professional self-image is influenced by how others describe you. If you have received a positive job review, you know the power of words to make you feel better about yourself. People's symbol use makes a difference in interpersonal relationships, too. If you grew up in the United States and have ever been in a serious relationship, you know the power of the words "I love you" or the symbolic significance of a gold band worn on the ring finger. Most people do not speak the words lightly. The symbolism of a ring extends far beyond the typical meaning of an expensive gift of jewelry. People's symbol use also makes a difference in public communication. The words of public figures and symbols of citizenship possess the power to inspire, calm, reassure, enrage, provoke, challenge, and change the world.

Words inspired a nation to reach for the stars when, in 1962, President John F. Kennedy said: "We choose to go to the moon in this decade and do the other things, not because they are easy, but because they are hard, because that goal will serve to organize and measure the best of our energies and skills."[2]

---

[1]Kathleen Parker, "Google Bombs Can Ruin your Reputation," *The (Waterloo/Cedar Falls) Courier*, September 6, 2009, F3.

[2]John F. Kennedy, "Address at Rice University on the Nation's Space Program," September 12, 1962, Rice Stadium, Houston, Texas, http://www.americanrhetoric.com/speeches/jfkriceuniversity.htm (accessed August 26, 2009).

Words calmed a nation faced with uncertainties when, from 1933 to the 1940s, President Franklin Delano Roosevelt delivered "fireside chats" to a nation buffeted by the Great Depression.

Words reassured the country of a person's fitness to serve when, in 1984, seventy-three-year-old President Ronald Reagan was running for reelection against the fifty-six-year-old former vice-president, Walter Mondale. When age became a campaign issue, President Reagan said, during a debate with Mondale, "I want you to know that also I will not make age an issue of this campaign. I am not going to exploit for political purposes my opponent's youth and inexperience."[3]

Visual symbols can enrage and provoke, as when leaders are burned in effigy, the US flag is burned in protest, or crosses are burned on homeowners' lawns to terrorize them out of living in a community.

Words and images also can be used to challenge, as when antiwar and free speech protestors at the 1968 Democratic Convention challenged Chicago police's repressive tactics by yelling at the cameras, "The whole world is watching."[4]

Because symbols matter, people debate the appropriateness of visual representations. After Olympic alpine skier Lindsey Vonn appeared on the cover of *Sports Illustrated*,[5] commentators discussed whether the image of her in a skiing tuck was sexist or sporty.[6] Given that women appear on only 4 percent of *SI* covers (including the yearly swimsuit edition), people began to consider what perception of women in general, and women athletes in particular, the cover generated.

What people communicate, and how they communicate it, has real effects on others and their perceptions. People cannot know what things or events mean until they have the symbols to attach meaning to them.

Because symbols have power, people can use them to induce others to take ethical, as well as unethical, actions. During World War II, Winston Churchill, considered one of the greatest English-speaking orators, delivered speeches to the British people to rally them to defend democracy and to US audiences to encourage them to become involved in the war. In the wake of British Prime Minister Neville Chamberlain's appeasement of Adolf Hitler on September 30, 1938, and German troops' occupation of the Sudetenland on October 15, Churchill, who at that time served no official role in the British government, sought to persuade the United States to defend democracy. On October 16 he warned, "The lights are going out.... We need the swift gathering of forces to confront not only military but moral aggression." He appealed to "English-speaking peoples" and "all the nations, great and small, who wish to walk with them. Their faithful and zealous comradeship would almost between night and morning clear the path of progress and banish from all our lives

[3]"Debating Our Destiny: The Second 1984 Presidential Debate," *PBS NewsHour*, http://www.pbs.org/newshour/debatingourdestiny/84debates/2prez2.html (accessed August 27, 2007).

[4]Todd Gitlin, *The Whole World Is Watching: Mass Media in the Making and Unmaking of the New Left*, 2nd ed. (Berkeley: University of California Press, 2003).

[5]*Sports Illustrated*, February 8, 2010.

[6]Kate Dailey, "Lindsey Vonn's *Sports Illustrated* Cover: Sexist or Sporty? Two *Newsweek* Writers Discuss," February 8, 2010, http://www.thedailybeast.com/newsweek/blogs/the-human-condition/2010/02/08/lindsey-vonn-s-sports-illustrated-cover-sexist-or-sporty-two-newsweek-writers-discuss.html (accessed October 12, 2011).

the fear which already darkens the sunlight to hundreds of millions of men."[7] He painted Hitler's forces as a darkness, smothering the lights of freedom; only the help of the United States could guarantee that Europeans would again see the sunlight of living in a free land. Churchill's speeches would help frame understandings of what the war in Europe meant to people living in the United States.

At the same time, Adolph Hitler was deftly persuading the German people to engage in horrific crimes aganist humanity and to wage total war. Using the metaphor of disease, Hitler explained on April 1, 1939: "Only when this Jewish bacillus infecting the life of peoples has been removed can one hope to establish a cooperation amongst the nations which shall be built up on a lasting understanding."[8] The vileness of this metaphor becomes clear in Hitler's call for an absolute eradication of the "Jewish bacillus" in order to save the German fatherland from disease. Infection can only be stopped when all the infection is removed. His use of language was dastardly as it sought the "perfection" of an Aryan nation. For Hitler, the Aryan race could only be saved if all Jewish people were eradicated.

These examples illustrate why rhetoric is profoundly important to civic society. **Rhetoric** is *the use of symbolic action by human beings to share ideas, enabling them to work together to make decisions about matters of common concern and to construct social reality*. Rhetoric is the means by which people make meaning of and affect the world in which they live.

Rhetoric can enlighten and confuse, reveal and hide. Churchill and Hitler both used rhetoric, but for very different purposes. Accordingly, the study of rhetoric involves not only an assessment of its effectiveness (both Churchill and Hitler were effective) but also of its ethics. (Churchill sought to defend freedom; Hitler sought the genocidal destruction of an entire people.)

We introduce you to concepts that will help you understand rhetoric and civic life. This chapter offers a foundational vocabulary you will need to understand, analyze, and creatively and ethically use rhetoric. We began by defining rhetoric as symbolic action that constructs reality. We will now explore rhetoric as the central means by which you engage in action in civil society, where you participate in public decision-making and culture formation. Finally, we will outline some constraints on and resources for rhetoric.

SYMBOLIC ACTION AND SOCIAL REALITY

To break down our definition of rhetoric, we look at each of its component parts: symbols and action. We then discuss how rhetoric actively constructs social reality.

Symbols

A symbol is *an arbitrary representation of something else, a word or an image that represents a thing, thought, or action*. The symbol $ represents the US dollar, although the symbol ∂ could just have easily been used. The symbol π represents

---

[7]Winston S. Churchill, "The Lights Are Going Out," *Never Give In: The Best of Winston Churchill's Speeches* (New York: Hyperion, 2003), 182–185.

[8] Adolf Hitler, *The speeches of Adolf Hitler,* vol. 1, ed. N. H. Baynes (Oxford, UK: Oxford University Press, 1942), 743.

pi, the ratio of any circle's circumference to its diameter, which roughly equals 3.141593. The US flag represents the nation and its values; a cross belief in a Christian faith; a Star of David in Judaism; and a crescent moon in Islam.

Symbols can be either verbal or visual. **Verbal symbols** are *symbols found in language* (whether spoken or written). Every word is a symbol insofar as it stands for something other than itself. When you use the term "dog," the word stands for an animal in the canine family. Other languages also have words for "dog" (perro/perra, suka, **псина**, 狗, chien, cane, hund, سگ), so symbols are by nature human constructions rather than innate to the things symbolized. Although people often think of symbols as abstractions, they may not think of words as symbolic. Yet, language is inherently a symbol system, both with written languages' use of alphabets and spoken languages' use of sounds to name and represents things, ideas, and people. Every word you use is a symbol.

Visual symbols are *symbols such as pictures, images, objects, and actions.* Examples of visual symbols include religious icons, photographs, tattoos, desktop icons, statues, flags, bodies, movies, and the act of bowing or saluting. For example, the US flag is just three colors of cloth sewn together, yet when people look at it, they think of it as the symbol of a nation. US citizens often have an emotional response to the flag because of what it symbolizes: such as democratic values. The key function of any symbol is that it conveys meaning. Although scholars for many years confined the study of rhetoric to the study of verbal symbols, they have recently recognized the importance of visual symbols.[9]

The meaning of a symbol is not the same for everyone. The fluidity of meaning is clear even when you consider language-based symbols. For example, "cat" refers to the scientific classification of the small carnivorous mammal *Felis catus or F. domesticus.* However, if a particular cat prowls around your life, the symbol "cat" may trigger thoughts of that particular cat, who symbolizes a warm, comforting, companion animal. On the other hand, if you have been scratched by a cat, you might have a different emotional response to the word. You might feel fear or distaste.

Although we describe verbal and visual symbols separately, almost all symbolic action is a mix of verbal and visual symbols. People listen to —and watch—speeches. People read— and look at—magazines and websites. People hear—and gaze at—movies.

Symbolic Action

When people use symbols, they engage in action. Our definition of rhetoric as symbolic action makes clear that humans use symbols to engage in actions with consequences. For example, when people exchange marriage vows and rings in a wedding ceremony, their actions create a new social relationship. The symbolic actions that compose a marriage ceremony (clothing, ring, vows, witnesses) create meaning beyond the wedding license the couple signs.

---

[9]Charles A. Hill and Marguerite Helmers, eds., *Defining Visual Rhetorics* (Mahwah, NJ: Lawrence Erlbaum Associates, 2004); Diane S. Hope, ed., *Visual Communication: Perception, Rhetoric, and Technology* (Cresskill, NJ: Hampton, 2006); Lawrence J. Prelli, ed., *Rhetorics of Display* (Columbia: University of South Carolina Press, 2006).

Things around you engage in motion: trees are moved by the wind, water by the tide, and earth by quakes. What distinguishes human action from these motions is that human action involves some level of intent and can be communicated about and reflected upon.[10] Human beings act on their environment in a variety of ways, such as walking, driving, planting a garden, and eating food. All these actions are instrumental—specific actions taken in order to cause an effect. Human action almost always is more than instrumental, however; it also is expressive and meaning-making.

Symbolic action is *expressive human action, the rhetorical mobilization of symbols to act in the world*. Symbolic actions include, but are not limited to, speeches, silent marches, movies, documentaries, plays, newspaper articles, advertisements, photographs, sit-ins, personal testimony, monuments, YouTube videos, and street theatre. People act in the world through symbol use that induces cooperation, generates identification, produces division, enables persuasion, and constitutes identity.

Rhetoric is constitutive, not just a tool of persuasion. Literary and legal scholar James Boyd White defines **constitutive rhetoric** as the *"art of constituting character, community, and culture in language."*[11] Rhetorical acts constitute character, community, and culture, as James Jasinski writes, by "invit[ing] their audience to experience the world in certain ways."[12] This understanding of symbolic action encourages thinking about how rhetoric constitutes people's understanding of themselves, their relations to each other, and the world; on the effects of rhetoric "beyond a narrow causal model of influence."[13]

The power of rhetoric to shape people's ideas of themselves, each other, and the world around them inspired rhetorical critic Kenneth Burke, an influential twentieth-century US scholar, to define human beings as the "symbol-using (symbol-making, symbol-misusing) animal."[14] Thus, the study of rhetoric provides insights into what it means to be human. For Burke, rhetoric is rooted in *"the use of language as a symbolic means of inducing cooperation in beings that by nature respond to symbols."*[15] Humans use symbols to interact with one another in order to work together to make decisions about matters of common concern.

Identification. For Burke, the primary aspect of rhetoric as symbolic action is **identification**, *a communicative process through which people are unified on the basis of common interests or characteristics.*[16] To make decisions about matters of common concern, people need to be able to identify what they have in common. Although attention to persuasion long dominated studies of rhetoric, "identifica-

---

[10]Kenneth Burke, "Dramatism," in *International Encyclopedia of the Social Sciences*, vol.7, ed. David L. Sills, 445–452 (New York: Macmillan and Free Press, 1968), 447.

[11] James Boyd White, *Heracles' Bow: Essays on the Rhetoric and Poetics of Law* (Madison: University of Wisconsin Press, 1989), x.

[12]James Jasinski, "A Constitutive Framework for Rhetorical Historiography: Toward an Understanding of the Discursive (Re)Constitution of 'Constitution' in *The Federalist Papers*," in *Doing Rhetorical History: Cases and Concepts*, ed. Kathleen J. Turner (Tuscaloosa: University of Alabama Press, 1998), 74–75.

[13] James Jasinski, *Sourcebook on Rhetoric* (Thousand Oaks, CA: Sage, 2001), 106.

[14] Kenneth Burke, *Language as Symbolic Action* (Berkeley: University of California Press, 1966), 16. Original is in italics.

[15] Kenneth Burke, *A Rhetoric of Motives* (Berkeley: University of California Press, 1969), 43.

[16]Burke, *A Rhetoric*, 20.

tion" now functions as a key term for what is known as "the new rhetoric."[17] With identification, the focus is less on how one person can "deliberate[ly] design" symbolic action to persuade other people, and more on how symbolic actions "spontaneously, intuitively, and often unconsciously act upon" people to create a sense of collective identity between them.[18] Identification does not automatically exist; it is created through symbolic action.

Identification can be created on the basis of characteristics over which a person has limited control (such as sex, race, class, sexual orientation, or nationality) or common interests (such as improving elementary and secondary education, lowering college tuition, or ending discrimination; or political party affiliation). Although Burke notes that "in forming ideas of our personal identity, we spontaneously identify ourselves with family, nation, political or cultural cause, church and so on," he also recognizes that rhetors induce listeners to feel identification with them;[19] the rhetor and audience become "consubstantial," or symbolically one.[20]

For Burke, the creation of identification is an essential characteristic of rhetoric and an integral element of persuasion. He writes: "there is no chance of keeping apart the meaning of persuasion, identification ('consubstantiality') and communication (the nature of rhetoric as 'addressed')."[21]

Rhetors can most effectively communicate and persuade when their audiences identify with them. For example, nineteenth-century abolitionist Angelina Grimké Weld used identification when she faced mob violence in Philadelphia on May 16, 1838, as she delivered a speech to an antislavery convention. Her challenge to the audience was to consider whether they wanted to identify with her and the slaves, or with the angry mob outside. Historian Gerda Lerner reports that while Grimké Weld was being introduced to the audience of three thousand men and women, "bricks crashed through the windows and glass fell to the floor."[22] As she spoke, the mob outside Pennsylvania Hall grew increasingly agitated, throwing stones and screaming during her hour-long speech. Although the people inside the hall were receptive to her message because they already opposed slavery, the mob outside the hall felt threatened by her argument that slavery was not an objective fact, but an immoral choice. Not wanting the mob to weaken her audience's resolve, Grimké Weld artistically turned the mob response into proof of the need to oppose slavery. She challenged the audience to use their fear of the mob as a basis for identifying with slaves' fear of violence from their masters:

> What is a mob? What would the breaking of every window be? What would the levelling of this Hall be? Any evidence that we are wrong, or that slavery is a good and wholesome institution? What if the mob should now burst in upon us, break up our meeting and commit violence upon our persons—would this be anything compared with what the slaves endure? No, no: and we do not remember them" as bound with them" [Heb. 13:3], if we shrink in the time of

---

[17]Jasinski, *Sourcebook*, 305.
[18]Kenneth Burke, *Development and Design* (Worcester, MA: Clark University Press, 1972), 27–28.
[19]Burke, *Language*, 301.
[20]Burke, *A Rhetoric*, 21.
[21]Burke, *A Rhetoric*, 46.
[22] Gerda Lerner, *The Grimké Sisters from South Carolina* (New York: Schocken, 1967), 245.

peril, or feel unwilling to sacrifice ourselves, if need be, for their sake. (*Great noise.*) I thank the Lord that there is yet life left enough to feel the truth, even though it rages at it—that conscience is not so completely seared as to be unmoved by the truth of the living God.[23]

She compared the threat of mob violence to the constant threat of violence under which slaves lived. She used the moment to induce her audience to identify with the slaves.[24]

Identification can bring people together to address and solve common concerns. Identification can also separate people by constructing "us" versus "them" social realities. For instance, Adolf Hitler induced non-Jewish German people to identify themselves as members of a superior race, an Aryan nation, which divided them from Jewish people. Identification can function for good or ill, unity or division. It can be used to recognize common concerns or disguise them, to solve common concerns or create new concerns.

Agency. Because rhetoric is an action, people exert some control over their messages. People possess rhetorical agency. Communication scholar Karlyn Kohrs Campbell explains that **rhetorical agency** is *"the capacity to act, that is, to have the competence to speak or write in a way that will be recognized or heeded by others in one's community."*[25] Because rhetoric involves both verbal and visual symbols, we extend her definition to include competence in visual rhetoric. Regardless of the medium, "agency" does not mean a person totally controls the meaning of a message. Instead, the term indicates some degree of control is available, that an individual is capable of symbolic action, not just motion.

In an autocratic or closed society, rhetoric plays a limited role because people lack agency. They have minimal control over what is said; people have to speak the party line or face punishment. In a democratic or open society, rhetoric plays a more significant role. People can form their opinions through the process of communication, and they have some degree of agency over what they communicate.

Social Reality

Rhetoric is more than a means to transmit information or persuade. When people engage in symbolic action, they participate in the construction of social reality. Saying that rhetoric "constructs social reality" does not mean that people and things do not pre-exist human symbolic action. Rather, we are saying that the *meaning* people ascribe to the things in their world is not predetermined, but created by symbolic action. Although people may know things exist apart from their symbol systems, they cannot know what those things mean or how to react to them except

---

[23] Angelina Grimké [Weld], "Address at Pennsylvania Hall," 1838, in Karlyn Kohrs Campbell, ed., *Man Cannot Speak for Her*, vol. 2 (New York: Praeger, 1989), 27.

[24] Karlyn Kohrs Campbell, *Man Cannot Speak for Her*, vol. 1 (New York: Praeger, 1989) 30. See also Stephen H. Browne, "Encountering Angelina Grimké: Violence, Identity, and the Creation of Radical Community," *Quarterly Journal of Speech* 82, no. 1 (February 1996), 55–73, for a discussion of how Grimké saw in violent reactions to abolitionists "not the repression of public discourse but an opportunity for it" (p. 70).

[25] Karlyn Kohrs Campbell, "Agency: Promiscuous and Protean," *Communication and Critical/Cultural Studies* 2 (2005): 3, italics added.

through the symbol system. Thus, reality is constructed—meaning that it is made and not given. It is social—meaning that it is created interactively.

Sociologist Peter Berger explains how, through language, humans impose order on reality.[26] People have individual experiences, but they classify those experiences in social terms. For example, a culture might have a sacred tree. The physical reality is that a plant exists, but the sacredness of the tree is socially constructed; members of the society agree that the tree is sacred and, through the use of symbols, communicate the importance of the tree to others in that society. The use of language orders (makes sense of) the physical reality.

Social reality is *reality as understood through the symbols humans use to represent it*. People create social reality as they name objects, actions, and each other. Although a material world exists from which human beings receive sensory data, they do not know how to interact with that world until symbolic action gives meaning to their sense data. Human beings' only access to reality is through symbols. Communication scholar Barry Brummett argues that "experience is sensation plus meaning" and "reality is meaning."[27] For example, the way you react to a dog named Cujo likely will be different from how you react to a dog named Puddles, even though they are the same breed.

Visual communication scholar Kevin DeLuca argues that people should understand rhetoric as "discerning [studying] and deploying [using] the available contingent means of constructing, maintaining, and transforming social reality in a particular context."[28] In other words, symbolic action—words and images—construct, maintain, and transform social reality. Imagine if you lived in a world devoid of symbolic action. You could not speak, take photos, upload video on YouTube, draw, pray, or engage in any action with symbolic importance. You also could not read, listen to music, watch videos, or receive others' symbolic actions. This world would not be total sensory deprivation, but it would be deprivation of all stimuli related to communication. Would you still feel human? Would you still possess the characteristics that make you human? Would you know how to act in the world or react to others? Symbolic action is not just an instrumental means to transmit information, it is central to making meaning of, and in, the world.

RHETORIC AS CIVIC ENGAGEMENT

Our definition of rhetoric focuses on the use of symbolic action to identify and solve issues of common concern and to construct social reality. A key aspect of that definition is that rhetoric is a social activity, meaning that it occurs among people. Thus, rhetoric has always been linked to social action and civic engagement.

---

[26]Peter L. Berger, *The Sacred Canopy: Elements of a Sociological Theory of Religion* (New York: Anchor, 1967); 20.

[27]Barry Brummett, "Some Implications of 'Process' or 'Intersubjectivity': Postmodern Rhetoric," *Philosophy and Rhetoric* 9, no. 1 (1976): 21–53, 28–29.

[28]Kevin Michael DeLuca, "The Speed of Immanent Images: The Dangers of Reading Photographs," in Hope, *Visual Communication*, 79–90, 81.

CLASSICAL ORIGINS

The word "rhetoric" comes from the ancient Greek word *rhetor*, which meant "public speaker." Thus, historically the term "rhetoric" referred to the art of public speaking.[29] Classicist George A. Kennedy explains that rhetoric was a civic art in ancient Greece and is a phenomenon of all human cultures; and that every communicative act is rhetorical in that it attempts to persuade someone.[30] Expanding on the original Greek definition, we use the term **rhetor** to mean *anyone or any institution that uses symbolic action.*

The academic study of rhetoric can be traced back to ancient Athens, where many of the most prominent thinkers and educators focused on it because citizens (adult males who were not slaves and whose parents were both Athenian) needed to know rhetoric to participate in political, economic, social, and legal structures. Athens's political system of direct democracy allowed male citizens the right to engage in civic discussion. When the Assembly met to discuss laws or issues of war, every citizen who had completed his military training was a voting member and had the right to speak and vote. All male citizens needed to be prepared to speak as members of the legislative body. Economically, business relied on a system of negotiation and bartering. Socially, male citizens spent leisurely afternoons at the gymnasium, a facility devoted not only to athletics, but also to discussions of art, poetry, politics, and gossip. Citizens spent evenings at dinner parties called *symposia*, where a man could be selected by lot to serve as the toastmaster for the evening, or be called on to deliver toasts or tell stories.

The legal system of Athens required rhetorical skill because it used juries, usually comprised of 201 to 501 citizens (but sometimes up to 2,001), depending on the importance of the case.[31] The legal system did not include lawyers; if someone was wronged or accused of wrongdoing, he spoke to the jury directly. (If a female of the citizen class was accused of wrongdoing, her closest male relative spoke for her.)[32] All citizens had to be able to speak effectively in front of the court.

The prominent role that rhetoric played in Athens generated disagreement, as represented by two groups: the Sophists and the Platonists. Sophists defended rhetoric, while Platonists were extremely skeptical of it.

Given the centrality of public speaking to Athenian politics and culture, when a man prepared to speak in public he either hired a speechwriter and then memorized the speech for presentation, or sought training in the art of rhetoric from Sophists.[33] In assessing the Sophistic tradition, communication scholar John Poulakos summarizes their definition of rhetoric: "Rhetoric is the art which *seeks* to capture in opportune moments that which is appropriate and attempts to suggest that

---

[29]George A. Kennedy, *A New History of Classical Rhetoric* (Princeton, NJ: Princeton University Press, 1994), 7.

[30]George A. Kennedy, *Classical Rhetoric and Its Christian and Secular Tradition,* 2nd ed. (Chapel Hill: University of North Carolina Press, 1999), 1–2, George A. Kennedy, *Comparative Rhetoric: A Historical and Cross–Cultural Introduction* (New York: Oxford University Press, 1998), 1–28.

[31]David Phillips, *Athenian Political Oratory: Sixteen Key Speeches* (New York: Routledge, 2004), 6.

[32]Eric W. Robinson, *Ancient Greek Democracy: Readings and Sources* (Malden, MA: Wiley–Blackwell, 2004).

[33]Kennedy, *Classical Rhetoric,* 1–5, 29–30.

which is possible."[34] Sophists, such as Protagoras and Isocrates, believed rhetoric was an art that could both delight and induce belief. The right thing spoken at the right time could entertain, even as it formed people's knowledge.

In contrast, Plato and Socrates believed knowledge could not be determined with the exchange of ideas, through rhetoric, but could only be known through philosophically understanding the existence of true and unchanging forms. Socrates argued that the Sophists' teaching of rhetoric made the weaker argument seem the stronger and, thus, worked against the truth. Plato used the trial of Socrates, who was convicted and sentenced to death for corrupting Athenian youth and not believing in the gods of the state, to demonstrate how rhetoric can be abused when it appeals to the baser instincts of majority rule.[35] In response to the injustice of this trial, Plato wrote several dialogues attacking rhetoric as a false art and a dangerous form of manipulation.

In one of these dialogues, the *Gorgias*, Plato recounted a debate between Socrates and the Sophist Gorgias about the ethics of rhetoric. Socrates warned that rhetoric is flattery and that people would misuse rhetoric for selfish or corrupt ends. In response, Gorgias argued that rhetoric was not to blame for these problems, any more than the maker of a knife or the knife itself was to blame for someone stabbing another person. Unconvinced by the Sophists, Plato distrusted rhetoric as a means of facilitating decision making, leading him to argue that democracy was not the best form of government. Good ideas were known only by the wisest, and not through public deliberations. He maintained that rhetoric could be used to deceive the masses within a democracy, and that it failed to teach virtue.

Despite Plato's criticisms, the study of rhetoric flourished in ancient Athens because of its role in legal, political, and social institutions. History demonstrates that where democracy is strong, the study of rhetoric is vibrant. Where nondemocratic government prevails, the study of rhetoric either disappears or is taught as merely a form of entertainment.

The disagreement between the Sophists and Platonists persists. Even in contemporary times, you probably have heard someone refer to an argument as "sophistry" or "mere rhetoric." Although Plato's dismissal gave Sophists a bad name, contemporary understandings of rhetoric are closer to the Sophistic tradition than to the Platonic tradition. We find ourselves more aligned with the Sophistic definition of rhetoric as the art of capturing the right thing to say in the right moment, of determining what is appropriate and possible; and opposed to the Platonic belief in fixed and immutable big-T Truths.

Because rhetoric had utility, Aristotle, a student of Plato's, systematized it. Aristotle, an extremely influential philosopher and scientist, is considered one of the founders of Western philosophy. One of the most influential writings on rhetoric in ancient Greece was his fourth-century BCE treatise, *On Rhetoric*.[36]

---

[34]John Poulakos, "Toward a Sophistic Definition of Rhetoric," *Philosophy and Rhetoric* 16, no. 1 (1983): 35–48, 37.

[35]I. F. Stone, *The Trial of Socrates* (New York: Anchor, 1989); Plato, *The Apology of Socrates*.

[36]Aristotle, *On Rhetoric*, trans. George A. Kennedy (New York: Oxford University Press, 1991). See Kennedy's "Prooemion," x–xi.

Aristotle defined rhetoric as "an ability in each [particular] case, to see the available means of persuasion."[37] Notice that the definition says that rhetoric is an *ability to see*. Thus, the use of rhetoric requires analysis of a situation in order to determine how to persuade. For Aristotle, a rhetorical situation "consists of three things: a speaker and a subject on which he [or she] speaks and someone addressed, and the objective of the speech relates to the last."[38] Rhetoric is addressed to particular people, on particular occasions, in particular times and cultures, about particular issues. Because rhetoric is specific to each particular situation, it is distinct from philosophy, which studies universals.

Persuasion plays a prominent role in Aristotle's definition insofar as a rhetor uses rhetorical proofs to persuade an audience. Aristotle identified three types of artistic proofs used in persuasion: **ethos**—*that which is "in the character of the speaker"*; **pathos**—*that which leads the audience "to feel emotion"*; and **logos**—*that which relies on "argument itself, by showing or seeming to show something."*[39] Although Aristotle noted the importance of the reasoned appeals of logos, he also made clear the importance of ethos and pathos. He argued that ethos was the most effective form of proof because an audience who trusted the rhetor would be more receptive to her or his message. Conversely, if an audience did not trust the rhetor, then the rhetor's use of logos and pathos would be ineffective. Aristotle also pointed out that audiences make decisions based on their state of mind, not only on the basis of reasoned appeals. Because emotions play a significant role in the human experience, pathos appeals are an important part of rhetoric. Many decisions people make are based on emotions, taste, and individual preferences. These decisions are not necessarily irrational. A person's favorite color is based on personal preference. All the logical arguments in the world may not change that preference, but that does not make the preference wrong.

Much has changed since Aristotle wrote—for example, photography, mass media, the Internet, and changing societal norms have altered the ways rhetoric is understood—but his concepts remain useful to understanding contemporary rhetoric. A recent newswire story about online product testimonials explains their power as stemming from "easy anonymity and participatory, peer-to-peer ethos."[40] A recent news article quotes political communication professor Joseph Tuman on the 2010 California gubernatorial primary candidates: "So they're waging classic pathos arguments. They're not designed to make you think; they're designed to make you feel."[41] A *Washington Post* article, shortly before Barack Obama's inaugural address, commented that Obama "hasn't needed logos much because he's usually preaching to the choir."[42] People still use Aristotle's terms to make sense of rhetoric.

---

[37]Aristotle, *On Rhetoric*, 1.2.1 [1355].

[38]Aristotle, *On Rhetoric*, 1.3 [1358b].

[39]Aristotle, *On Rhetoric*, 1.2 [1356a–60], italics added.

[40]Jennifer Peltz, "Whose 5 Stars? Online 'User' Reviews Get Scrutiny," *The Associated Press*, July 29, 2009.

[41]Quoted in Steven Harmon, "GOP Candidates Polluting Airwaves," *San Jose Mercury News*, May 23, 2010.

[42]Henry Allen, "His Way with Words: Cadence and Credibility," *The Washington Post*, January 20, 2009, AA23.

Rhetoric as Addressed

For Aristotle, the audience determines the objective of rhetoric. For Burke, rhetoric's "nature as addressed" to others is one of its definitive characteristics (in addition to identification).[43] Humans engage in symbolic action in order to communicate with one another. Rhetoric always involves an audience, even if that audience is not immediately present. Thus, the making of meaning is interactive and intersubjective. To construct, maintain, and transform reality requires the existence of others, of audiences.

Given that rhetors and audiences coproduce meaning, agency belongs not only to rhetors, but also to audiences. Agency includes the ability to construct and interpret symbolic actions, and to take action in response to those interpretations. Campbell describes agency as "communal, social, cooperative, and participatory and, simultaneously, constituted and constrained by the material and symbolic elements of context and culture."[44] In other words, we make meaning through a social, and not just individual, process. When you interpret messages or decode images you do not do so only with resources you alone innately possess. Instead, you rely on a complex set of contextual and cultural symbols.

Rhetoric is an action that creates meaning, informing how human beings understand and react to the world. It is not merely a mechanism of information transmission, but a means by which human beings construct social reality. The political, personal, and meaning-creating functions highlight how rhetoric affects what laws are passed, how people see themselves, and what people think they know. Rhetoric is essential to a democratic society.

Civic Engagement

Civic engagement is *people's participation in individual or collective action to develop solutions to social, economic, and political challenges in their communities, states, nations, and world.* Examples of how people engage in civic engagement include talking with others about ballot initiatives or pending legislation, using social networking sites for activism, volunteering with community organizations, participating in parades (whether celebratory or protest), working for electoral campaigns, signing petitions, voting, writing letters to the editor, and posting to blogs. Change (and maintenance) of social, political, and economic structures is accomplished through civic engagement, and civic engagement is accomplished through rhetoric.

Rhetoric scholar Gerard A. Hauser reviewed the scholarly research on why citizens engage in civic action in their communities, and concluded that the absolutely necessary requirement for "a well-functioning civic community is engagement in the ... rhetoric of civil society."[45] In any democracy, whether it is direct (like Athens) or representative (like the United States), rhetors must understand

---

[43]Burke, *A Rhetoric*, 37–46.
[44]Campbell, "Agency," 3.
[45]Gerard A. Hauser, "Rhetorical Democracy and Civic Engagement," in *Rhetorical Democracy: Discursive Practices of Civic Engagement*, ed. Gerard A. Hauser and Amy Grim, 1–16 (Mahwah, NJ: Lawrence Erlbaum Associates, 2004), 11.

how to frame ethical and effective appeals, and audiences need to understand how to see through manipulative appeals.

The use of rhetoric is not confined to people campaigning for office; nor are citizens' roles in rhetorical action confined to membership in audiences. Civic engagement helps each person understand who she or he is. Rhetoric scholar Bruce Gronbeck argues that "Civic engagement. . . is as much a matter of understanding the building and maintenance of political identity. . . as it is about getting legislation passed."[46] People use rhetoric as they develop identity (as individuals and citizens) and determine what should be done (by them as individuals and for them through legislation). They use rhetoric as they develop conceptions of themselves as individuals, group members, and citizens, all of whom can make a claim on others and on the government to act legislatively.

Rhetoric scholar Robert Asen points out that civic engagement was long defined in terms of what people did when participating in civil society. Citizenship was defined narrowly in terms of the specific acts of voting and civic organization membership.[47] Research using this *what* approach tends to see civic engagement as on the decline, as fewer people vote or belong to civic organizations. Asen is not so pessimistic. He advocates a different perspective, arguing that analysis of citizenship should focus on the *how*—not on citizenship as an act, but as a process of action. Thus, the question is: how do people enact citizenship and civic engagement? The answer is: through rhetoric. Civic engagement as a process, a "mode of public engagement," means participation in society has many different forms, all of which involve symbolic action.[48]

Asen argues that rhetoric is central to civic engagement because, in addressing other people in ways that seek identification, it is an act of interacting and engaging with others: "Engagement positions people as rhetorical agents hoping to persuade and/or seek recognition from others of their views, even as it recognizes that others hope to do the same. Commitment thus extends to a commitment to interaction itself."[49] When you engage in rhetoric, you necessarily commit yourself to an interaction, Thus, to understand citizenship, Asen examines the processes by which people engage and interact with each other. He explores how people come to understand themselves—through rhetoric—as members of groups and as individuals, and how "actions that begin on a small scale may spread across social, cultural, and political sites."[50] For Asen, engagement occurs when human communication generates new areas for discussion, when people are willing to accept the risk of being wrong (and accept correction of their views), when people affirm a commitment to engage one another in discourse, and when creative forms of communication create social connections among individuals.

Rhetorical citizenship in a democratic society is essential to the process of decision making in situations as mundane as a group of people deciding where to

---

[46]Bruce Gronbeck, "Citizen Voices in Cyberpolitical Culture," in Hauser and Grim, *Rhetorical Democracy*, 17–32, 28.

[47] Robert Asen, "A Discourse Theory of Citizenship," *Quarterly Journal of Speech* 90, no. 2 (2004): 189–211.

[48]Asen, "A Discourse Theory," 191.

[49]Asen, "A Discourse Theory," 201.

[50]Asen, "A Discourse Theory," 195.

eat dinner (at a national chain or at a restaurant that supports local farmers) to situations as serious as you determining whether you want to join a national service organization (the armed services, Americorp, or the Peace Corps). Although people's reasons for doing things can be personal, those reasons can be expressed and contested. To truly enter the realm of rhetoric, people must be open to having their minds changed and to providing the reasons for their beliefs. They must be willing to continually provide reasons, listen, and modify their positions. This process of interaction and modification of positions is essential to decision making in an open society.

For example, if members of a campus group disagreed about how to spend a thousand dollars, it would not be productive if each person simply stated: I want the money spent *this* way, period. Instead, for the group to decide collectively what to do, each person would have to articulate the reason the money should be spent as she or he wanted. As people gave their reasons, some shared interests might become clear, at which point each person could see the merits in others' ideas. As the discussion proceeded, agreement might emerge. Or, it might become clear that the group members had totally competing interests, so that agreement could never be reached. At that point, they may find that the disagreement is less about what to do with the money (policy) and more about what it means to be a member of the group (identity).

Unfortunately, modern society increasingly allows people to refuse such interactions. The fragmentation of media enables you to seek out and listen only to those with whom you agree. When exchanges of diverse opinions do occur, it is becoming more common to hear people refuse to participate. You probably have heard comments such as "we'll just have to agree to disagree," or "it works for me," or "I don't have time to get involved," or even just "whatever." These comments are a way of ending discussion about differing opinions and ideas, rather than actually engaging people in discussion. They are antithetical to decision making based on the principles of rhetoric. Agreeing to disagree is not always a viable option. Oftentimes, decisions must be made between competing options and ideas.

What differentiates an open and free society from a closed, fascist, and dictatorial society is its willingness to tolerate the open expression of differing ideas and beliefs. In an open society, communication serves personal, epistemological, and political functions. It serves a personal function when it enables people to express themselves, both communicating and developing their sense of self. It serves an epistemological function when it enables people to test their ideas and to develop knowledge. It serves a political function when it enables people to participate in the processes of governance. President Abraham Lincoln's ideal of a "government of the people, by the people, for the people" cannot be realized if the people do not participate in those processes.[51] Additionally, a free press and its ability to report on public issues fulfills a political function when it serves as a check on government abuses. Your own rhetoric and your ability to listen to the rhetoric of others are essential to an open society.

---

[51]Abraham Lincoln, "Gettysburg Address," November 19, 1863, http://www.americanrhetoric.com/speeches/gettysburgaddress.htm (accessed September 1, 2009).

For these reasons, the United States has a long tradition of protecting open communication, which it codified in the First Amendment to the Constitution. Supreme Court Justice Holmes articulated this trust in freely exchanged ideas in 1919:

> [T]he ultimate good desired is better reached by free trade in ideas—that the best test of truth is the power of the thought to get itself accepted in the competition of the market, and that truth is the only ground upon which their wishes safely can be carried out. That, at any rate, is the theory of our Constitution. It is an experiment, as all life is an experiment. Every year, if not every day, we have to wager our salvation upon some prophecy based upon imperfect knowledge. While that experiment is part of our system, I think that we should be eternally vigilant against attempts to check the expression of opinions that we loathe and believe to be fraught with death, unless they so imminently threaten immediate interference with the lawful and pressing purposes of the law that an immediate check is required to save the country.[52]

Open communication is not to be feared. Ideas with which you disagree should not be avoided or suppressed. Instead, all people should develop the critical faculties that enable them to judge which ideas in the marketplace they should "buy," which expressions are worthy of assent, and which ideas should define their characters. People not only need the right to express their opinions, but also the skills and knowledge with which to do so, as well as a government and society willing to consider and respond to those opinions.

CONSTRAINTS ON AND RESOURCES FOR SYMBOLIC ACTION

When you engage in rhetorical action, you are constrained by social factors. Not every symbolic action will be completely and immediately understood by everyone hearing or seeing it, or accepted even if it is understood. You also possess resources for rhetorical action: stories, images, memories, and cultural values that are generally shared and can be used to communicate your message. In this section we discuss some of the limits on and resources for rhetoric: (1) the persuasive continuum, (2) culture, (3) public memory, and (4) power, ideology, and hegemony. This list is not exhaustive; other resources and constraints will be discussed throughout the text. However, this list constitutes overarching constraints and resources that influence most aspects of rhetorical engagement in civic life.

Persuasive Continuum

Because of limits on persuasion stemming from an audience, a topic, or even the rhetor, seldom is persuasion absolutely achieved or arguments completely dismissed. An audience is not totally persuaded or completely unconvinced by a single

---

[52]Justice Oliver Wendell Holmes, *Abrams v. United States* 250 US 616, argued October 21–22, 1919, decided November 10, 1919, http://www.bc.edu/bc_org/avp/cas/comm/free_speech/abrams.html (accessed August 26, 2009).

rhetorical action. When people think of persuasion, they often think of it as intentionally trying to change another person's actions or beliefs (sometimes against the other person's will), but such goals are not descriptive of all rhetoric.

Communication scholar Karlyn Kohrs Campbell describes persuasive purposes in terms of a persuasive continuum:[53]

| create virtual experience | alter perception | explain | formulate belief | initiate action | maintain action |

←——→

In many cases, changing a person's mind is not possible. Beliefs can be so deeply ingrained that an audience may not even recognize alternative meanings are possible. For this reason, a rhetor's goal may be to create a virtual experience for the audience members, so they come to feel they have experienced something they never thought possible. For example, when African-American activist Mary Church Terrell spoke about the effect of Jim Crow segregation laws in her 1906 speech "What It Means to Be Colored in the Capital of the United States,"[54] she *created a virtual experience*. When speaking to her primarily white, Northern audience, she had to make clear the effects of segregation. She provided example after example of the segregation African Americans faced in what was thought to be the cradle of liberty and equality: Washington, DC. Moving from finding shelter; to finding food; to finding a place to worship, work, and be entertained and educated, her speech created for her white audience the virtual experience of being "colored in the capital of the United States" and enabled them to identify with African Americans.

If a rhetor can create a virtual experience for audience members, s/he might be able to *alter their perception*, or at least introduce them to a new perspective. Ida B. Wells, journalist and long-time activist for African-American rights, fought against lynching. In her 1892 essay (also delivered as a speech), "Southern Horrors: Lynch Law in All Its Phases," she attempted to alter audience members' perception that black men were lynched because they were accused of raping white women.[55] She made clear that, as reported by white sources, the real reason that white people lynched black people was economic. White business people resented black people's economic success. She also pointed out that black children and black women had been murdered by white lynch mobs, but no white man had ever been lynched for raping a black woman, or even a black eight-year-old child, making clear that the fear of rape was an inadequate explanation for lynching. Although she may not have been able to convince her audience that all lynching was wrong, she at least opened their minds to an alternative perspective on lynching—that it was an economically and racially motivated crime of hate, rather than an act defending fragile white women's honor. Wells sought to create divisions between white people who lynched and those who would oppose lynching, and to foster identification between white people and black people.

---

[53]Karlyn Kohrs Campbell, *The Rhetorical Act*, 2nd ed. (Belmont, CA: Wadsworth, 1996), 9–17.

[54]Mary Church Terrell, "What It Means To Be Colored in the Capital of the United States," in Campbell, *Man Cannot*, vol. 2, 421–432.

[55]Ida B. Wells, "Southern Horrors: Lynch Law in All Its Phases," in Campbell, *Man Cannot*, vol. 2, 385–420.

If audience members are willing to entertain the possibility of an alternative perception, a speaker can then *explain* reasons behind that perception. Wells explained the reasons for her opposition to lynching, her demand that northerners condemn the act, and her call to African Americans to arm themselves in self-defense. She ended by explaining: "Of the many inhuman outrages of this present year, the only case where the proposed lynching did *not* occur, was where the men armed themselves in Jacksonville, Fla., and Paducah, Ky[*sic*], and prevented it. The only times an Afro-American who was assaulted got away has been when he had a gun and used it in self-defense."[56]

A more recent illustration of explanation is found in a speech George W. Bush delivered to the National Association for the Advancement of Colored People (NAACP) Convention when he was running for president in 2000. Going into the speech, he was aware that members of the NAACP tended to support Democratic candidates. Instead of going into the convention to tell them they were wrong, he took the approach of simply explaining his policies and why they would benefit the communities for which the organization worked. He opened the speech by recognizing that the relationship between the Republican Party and the NAACP had "not been one of regular partnership," so he asked them simply to give him "the chance to tell you what is in my heart." He sought to explain his own position, rather than to change the NAACP's. He described the central part of his education agenda as being "to challenge and change Title I, to make sure we close the achievement gap, to make sure that children are not forgotten and simply shuffled through the system." He explained that testing would be used to identify low-performing schools, which would then have three years to improve. If they failed to improve, he explained, "the resources must go to the parents so the parents can make a different choice."[57]

Once audience members are willing to alter their perception of an issue and listen to an alternative explanation, a rhetor might be able to *formulate beliefs*. As a result of speeches and essays such as Ida B. Wells's, she and other rhetors were able to begin formulating a belief in audience members' minds that lynching was a criminal act that violated black people's rights and that lynchers should face the most severe legal punishments possible. It took time to formulate that belief: a federal antilynching law was not even proposed until 1900 (and then received only three votes), and lynching persisted well into the 1950s. In fact, no federal antilynching law was ever passed, an oversight for which the US Senate apologized in 2005.[58]

Formulating belief is not the only possible goal for a rhetorician. In many cases, audience members seek out speakers in order to reaffirm their own beliefs. For example, people attend religious services to have their beliefs reaffirmed and attend political rallies for candidates they already support in order to maintain (and

---

[56]Wells, "Self Help," 1892, http://www.gutenberg.org/files/14975/14975-h/14975-h.htm (accessed June 10, 2010).

[57]George W. Bush, speech to the NAACP Annual Convention, Baltimore, Maryland, July 10, 2000, http://www.pbs.org/newshour/bb/politics/july-dec00/bush_7-10.html (accessed June 10, 2010).

[58]Avis Thomas-Lester, "A Senate Apology for History on Lynching," *Washington Post*, June 14, 2005, http://www.washingtonpost.com/wp-dyn/content/article/2005/06/13/AR2005061301720.html (accessed June 9, 2010).

demonstrate) their belief in a candidate. In such cases, persuasion can maintain belief as well as formulate it.

Having a belief does not necessarily mean one acts on it. People often have good intentions but fail to turn those beliefs into lived realities. Most public service announcements (PSAs) attempt to *initiate action*. People may know that smoking is bad and that reading is good, but PSAs reminding people of these beliefs encourage them to turn those beliefs into action. The Rock the Vote campaign seeks to initiate action each election, as do on-campus alcohol awareness campaigns each term.

Social movements also employ rhetoric aimed at initiating or *maintaining action*. When a movement or campaign achieves success, members must be reminded that more work is yet to come. Thus, in the wake of the passage of the Civil Rights Act of 1964, which outlawed racial segregation in schools, public places, and employment, the civil rights movement did not stop. Instead, it maintained its members' actions for social equality, leading to the Civil Rights Act of 1968, which sought to end discrimination in housing. Conversely, when a movement faces a defeat, the members must be rallied in order to keep the movement going. During the struggle for women's right to vote, which lasted from the 1848 Seneca Falls Convention until the 1920 ratification of the Nineteenth Amendment, woman suffrage advocates had to work to maintain the activism of the movement's members. The period from 1896 to 1907 came to be known as "the doldrums" because of the number of defeats the activists faced: a total of 164 referendum defeats, an average of one every 27 days. In response, movement leaders had to develop rhetorical appeals that maintained the activists' prosuffrage activities.[59]

Culture

Rhetoric and civic engagement occur within particular cultures. According to anthropologist Clifford Geertz, **culture** is the *"historically transmitted pattern of meanings embodied in symbols, a system of inherited conceptions expressed in symbolic forms by means of which men [and women] communicate, perpetuate, and develop their knowledge, about and attitudes toward life."*[60] Culture is composed of knowledge, experiences, beliefs, values, attitudes, meanings, hierarchies, religions, conceptions of time, social roles, worldviews, myths, and even the material possessions or artifacts acquired by a group of people, the meanings of which are transmitted through symbols. Your culture frames how you interpret rhetorical messages.

For example, in an individualist culture, appeals to each person's individual rights may carry more weight than in a more communitarian culture that places the concerns of the group ahead of individuals' rights.[61] In their study of the famous image of the man standing in front of the tank during the 1989 Tiananmen Square protests, communication scholars Robert Hariman and John L. Lucaites argue that Western media sources made that image emblematic of the event, rather than

---

[59]Campbell, *Man Cannot*, vol. 1, 157–179.
[60]Clifford Geertz, *The Interpretation of Cultures* (New York: Basic Books, 1973), 89, italics added.
[61]William B. Gudykunst, "Individualistic and Collectivistic Perspectives on Communication: An Introduction," *International Journal of Intercultural Relations*, 22 (1998): 107–134.

images of massive crowds, because the lone individual confronting the power of the state made sense to Western cultures that emphasize liberal individualism.[62]

Geertz uses the metaphor of a spider's web to explain the complex relationship between culture and symbol use: he says that humans are "suspended in webs of significance" they themselves "have spun."[63] For Geertz, symbols do not literally bring something into existence but locate a thing within systems of meaning. Patriotism, the love of or devotion to a country, is an example of a cultural system of meaning. In the US patriotic web of signification, key words such as "freedom," "equality," and "liberty;" visual symbols such as the US flag; and icons such as Uncle Sam and the Statue of Liberty have come to symbolize the country. People who are citizens come to understand who they are because of their relationship to the United States, and pledge allegiance to it. Expressions of patriotism (as in Lee Greenwood's 1984 song "God Bless the USA," which played at the Republican National Convention that year, increased in popularity during Operation Desert Storm in 1991, and then regained popularity in the wake of the 9/11 attacks) create a sense of identification among many citizens. As that sense of belonging develops so, too, does a sense of differentiation and exclusion. Even as one creates identification (a sense of "us"), one also creates division (a sense of "them"). Identification is meant to counteract the feeling of division, but even as it does so it tends to recreate divisions along new lines. Patriotism normalizes the idea that some people deserve rights in a country because they "belong" while others do not because they do not belong. Patriotism also normalizes the idea that the loss of life of a fellow countryperson counts more than the death of an other.[64] Patriotism gives a particular meaning to being a citizen of a country. The words and symbols interweave so that to attack one (freedom) means you have attacked all (attacking freedom means you are attacking all the United States stands for). Sometimes dissent is called unpatriotic because it means one does not support the country unconditionally. Patriotism is a web of significance in which people are suspended and which they, themselves, have spun.

Geertz's definition of culture includes "a system of inherited conceptions expressed in symbolic forms,"[65] which means that the web of significance is learned. Communication scholars Judith Martin and Thomas Nakayama state that culture is comprised of "learned patterns of behavior and attitudes shared by a group of people."[66] The primary functions of culture are to teach shared meanings, shared views of the world, and a group identity. Through these functions, cultures also help reduce uncertainty and chaos, largely by socializing their members to behave in prescribed ways. Even as you are enmeshed in the web, however, you also help spin it.

---

[62]Robert Hariman and John Louis Lucaites, "Liberal Representation and Global Order: The Iconic Photograph from Tiananmen Square," in Prelli *Rhetorics of Display*, 121–138. Image at http://www.sbs.com.au/news/article/1171447/-Tank-man-photo-on-Google-China.

[63]Geertz, *Interpretation*, 5.

[64]Judith Butler, *Precarious Life: The Power of Mourning and Violence* (New York: Verso, 2004) and Steven Johnston, *The Truth about Patriotism* (Durham, NC: Duke University Press, 2007).

[65]Geertz, *Interpretation*, 89.

[66]Judith N. Martin and Thomas K. Nakayama, *Intercultural Communication in Contexts*, 3rd ed., (Boston: McGraw-Hill, 2004), 3.

Rhetoric is constrained by culture, but also constructs culture. Rhetoric is constrained by culture because people's interpretations of symbolic action depend on the culture in which they participate. What is persuasive to a rural, midwestern, US audience might not be persuasive to an audience in another nation, or even another part of the United States. Yet, rhetoric can be used to change culture. US culture has changed over time because of rhetoric. For example, women were once considered inferior and thus were systematically denied the right to vote. This state of affairs was considered "normal" in eighteenth-and nineteenth-century United States. Yet, in twenty-first-century United States, if someone advocated not allowing women the right to vote, you would probably think that person was crazy. Women achieved their current role through rhetoric and civic engagement that altered the culture.

Public and Collective Memory

Geertz points to the link between culture and memory, to the existence of cultural memory that resides in the web of significance, when he refers to historically transmitted meanings. If culture is learned patterns, where does one learn those patterns? People do not inherit a chest of drawers that contains their culture. Instead, people develop their culture as they inherit symbol systems that contain memories.

Memories are maintained through symbolic actions. Sociologist Barry Schwartz makes clear how memory requires symbolic action: "Recollection of the past is an active, constructive process, not a simple matter of retrieving information. To remember is to place a part of the past in the service of conceptions and needs of the present."[67] Memories do not just exist; instead, to remember requires human symbols to re–present memory. Communication scholar Carole Blair explains: "memory is based on the capacity to *re-present* an event, a place, a person, or an idea that one has already encountered."[68] People engage in the act of remembering, and in doing so develop a sense of collective identity. Remembering requires symbolic action on the part of people.

Memory can exist at the personal level, as when family members recall past experiences with each other. It can also exist at the cultural level, when the members of a culture engage in the memory work that sustains them as a culture. **Public memory** is *a particular type of collective memory that combines the memories of the dominant culture and fragments of marginalized groups' memories, and enables a public to make sense of the past, present, and future.*[69] Public memory is a particular type of **collective memory**, *memory that is not simply an individualized process, but a shared and constructed creation of a group.*[70] Memory is the product of rhetorical action even as it constrains the rhetorical actions of those who would challenge the dominant memory.

[67]Barry Schwartz, "The Social Context of Commemoration: A Study of Collective Memory," *Social Forces* 61 (1982): 374–402, 374.

[68]Carole Blair, "Communication as Collective Memory," in *Communication as . . . Perspectives on Theory*, ed. Gregory J. Shepherd, Jeffrey St. John, and Ted Striphas, 51–59 (Thousand Oaks, CA: Sage, 2006), 52.

[69]Richard Morris, *Sinners, Lovers, and Heroes* (Albany: State University of New York Press, 1997), 26, italics added.

[70]Maurice Halbwachs, *On Collective Memory* (Chicago, University of Chicago Press, 1992).

For example, citizens of a nation maintain and construct public memory though the monuments and memorials they choose to erect, and in the process construct an identity for themselves. In the United States, the Lincoln Memorial, Washington Monument, Vietnam Veterans Memorial, National World War II Memorial, and Korean War Veterans Memorial all construct particular memories of the nation's past. Memorials and monuments are examples of shared resources, collective memory made public.

Although a person may have particular memories and families may have group memories, public memories are those memories that give identity to a particular society. You personally have no memory of national events such as the American Revolution, but through your education and your participation in Fourth of July celebrations, through national monuments and speeches, you participate in a public memory of the events of the American Revolution, memories the Tea Party movement seeks to revivify. Thus, an individual's memories do not really make sense unless situated within a larger collective. Communication scholar Iwona Irwin-Zarecka writes, "'Collective memory'—as a set of ideas, images, feelings about the past—is best located not in the minds of individuals, but in the resources they share."[71]

However, remembering always involves forgetting. Collective memory may be controversial. It can be a point of contestation, in part because collective remembering is always intimately linked to collective forgetting. No single version of the past exists, and dominant interpretations of past events can "wip[e] out many of the others."[72] Thus, the subject of rhetoric can be which things to remember and how to remember them. For example, memorial depictions of Christopher Columbus illustrate both the amount of work done to maintain collective memory and the way memory also always induces forgetting.

Symbols in the form of statues and images, poems, stories, and named holidays all sought to fix collective memory of Columbus as definitive of the US identity as a nation of explorers. He has been celebrated as an American mythic hero since the genesis of the nation. His emergence as one of the pantheon of heroes was due, in part, to the revolutionary leaders' reluctance to ascend the pedestal in a country that ostensibly was built on democratic principles.[73] Into this void people placed Columbus. In the years during and immediately following the Revolutionary War, a number of poetic histories and references to Columbus emerged, including Phillis Wheatley's 1775 innovation of the poetic device "Columbia" as a symbol of both Columbus and America.[74] In 1792, the new capitol in Washington was subtitled the District of Columbia. These are acts of rhetoric that participate in the creation and maintenance of public memory.

---

[71]Iwona Irwin-Zarecka, *Frames of Remembrance: The Dynamics of Collective Memory* (New Brunswick, NJ: Transaction, 1994), 4.

[72]Irwin-Zarecka, *Frames*, 217.

[73] Michael Kammen, *The Mystic Chords of Memory: The Transformation of Tradition in American Culture* (New York: Alfred A. Knopf, 1991), 27.

[74] Thomas J. Steele, S.J., "The Figure of Columbia: Phillis Wheatley Plus George Washington," *The New England Quarterly: A Historical Review of New England Life and Letters* 54, no. 2 (1981): 264–266.

The original narrative of Columbus-the-discoverer was woven into and stabilized US public memory without opposition for many years, if not centuries. Regardless of whether he was the first to land in the Americas, his is the day celebrated, his is the image immortalized in the US capitol, and his is the story told in textbooks and movies. In other words, all available anchoring devices for collective memory have been used to fix Columbus-the-discoverer in US public memory. However, in the process of commemorating Columbus, much was forgotten.

The Columbian quincentenary in 1992 provided a unique moment to highlight the way collective forgetting was connected to collective remembering. Native American protests against Columbus Day parades offered a way to materialize grievances. Native Americans engaged in rhetorical action in order to challenge collective memory and public memorializing practices. A leading scholar on indigenous peoples of Latin America, José Barreiro, introduced the special issue of the *Northeast Indian Quarterly* that was dedicated to "American Indian Perspectives on the Quincentenary." He explained the rhetorical significance of the quincentenary: "To the degree that the Quincentenary spectacle exalts Columbus as a metaphor for the expansion of Western materialist culture[,] a debate is joined that focuses issues of cultural values survival, environmental ethics and practice and sustainability in economic activity."[75] The celebration of Columbus's memory provided a focal point through which to reframe the nation's understanding of discovery and settlement. The reframing was not to be achieved by a single protest or a single text. For Native Americans, the issue was not the accurate chronicling of history, although that was a part of it, but the effects of commemorative holidays and parades on memory of what was done to Native Americans as a result of Columbus's landfall. The point was that Columbus did not "discover" an empty land, but claimed a land populated by a number of different peoples. The memory of Columbus is rhetorical insofar as it exhorts people in the United States to perceive their identity as explorers. Native Americans countered that rhetorical exhortation by depicting Columbus not as an explorer but as a colonizer.

Memories, even those enshrined in memorials, monuments, parades, and holidays, do not proceed uncontested. Memory can be a site of rhetorical conflict precisely because of the necessary relationship between remembering and forgetting. Those with power tend to shape public memory; those with less power tend to shape public memory; those with less power must contest the forgetfulness caused by the partial memory of the powerful.

Power, Ideology, and Hegemony

Power, as defined by feminist scholars Cheris Kramarae and Paula A. Triechler, is *"the ability to get things done."*[76] The concept is not innately troublesome. However, because power is a social phenomenon, people have power in relationship to

---

[75] José Barreiro, ed., *Northeast Indian Quarterly: View from the Shore: American Indian Perspectives on the Quincentenary* 7 (Fall 1990), 2. See also José Barreiro, "What 1992 Means to American Indians," in *Without Discovery: A Native Response to Columbus*, ed. Ray Gonzales (Seattle: Broken Moon, 1992): 57–60.

[76] Cheris Kramarae and Paula A. Triechler, *Amazons, Bluestockings and Crones: A Feminist Dictionary,* 2nd ed. (London: Pandora, 1992), 351, italics added.

others. Social power is embedded in the communicative negotiations of gender/sex, race, class, sexual orientation and other identity ingredients. Differences are rarely constructed equally. Rather, the groups with more say about the construction are privileged over others.

Power is central to the study of rhetoric because it delimits the agency of rhetors. Communication scholars John L. Lucaites and Celeste M. Condit point out that people who study rhetoric need to consider the "systems of social conditions and their impact on public discourse."[77] Not all people have equal access to the public podium, because rhetorical actions occur in culturally and historically specific contexts in which power is apportioned unequally. Class, sex, race, citizenship, political affiliation, education, sexuality, and religion all influence the cultural resources that rhetors may access. Thus, Lucaites and Condit posit a refined definition of rhetoric that "portrays significant rhetors as those able to realign material life experiences and cultural symbols through the artful use of the available means of persuasion."[78] When you study rhetoric, you need to judge the skill of a rhetor, not against some abstract list of available persuasive means, but within the range of means available at a time, in a culture, and to a person given the social barriers she or he may face. The means of persuasion available to a US president differ from those available to an unemployed steel–worker or to an immigrant living and working in the United States illegally. When you are in an audience, you need to consider these things before you judge a rhetor to be a failure or success.

Power is also central to the study of rhetoric because rhetoric is, itself, a form of power. Philosopher Michel Foucault, who has written extensively about power, notes that "as history constantly teaches us, discourse is not simply that which translates struggles or systems of domination, but is the thing for which and by which there is struggle, discourse is the power which is to be seized."[79] Rhetoric is both the object of power over which people struggle and the means by which people engage in a struggle for power. This becomes clearer as you explore the way in which ideology is rhetorical.

Power manifests itself rhetorically through the creation of a dominant **ideology**, which can be defined as *the ideas, values, beliefs, perceptions, and understandings that are known to members of a society and that guide their behaviors. In Making Sense of Political Ideology*, communication scholars Bernard L. Brock, Mark E. Huglen, James F. Klumpp, and Sharon Howell define ideology as "typical ways of thinking about the world [that] help shape human action"[80] because it normalizes "day-to-day social, political, economic, and cultural structures" by making them appear natural and inevitable.[81] It is composed of a group's socially accepted knowledge that explains, justifies, and interprets the social order. In short, ideol-

---

[77] John Louis Lucaites and Celeste Michelle Condit, "Reconstructing <Equality>: Culturetypal and Counter-Cultural Rhetorics in the Martyred Black Vision," *Communication Monographs* 57 (March 1990): 21n3.

[78] Lucaites and Condit, "Reconstructing," 6.

[79] Michel Foucault, "The Order of Discourse," in *Language and Politics*, ed. Michael J. Shapiro, 108–138 (New York: New York University Press, 1984), 110.

[80] Bernard L. Brock, Mark E. Huglen, James F. Klumpp, and Sharon Howell, *Making Sense of Political Ideology: The Power of Language in Democracy* (New York: Rowman and Littlefield, 2005), 39.

[81] Brock, et al., *Making Sense*, 39.

ogy is a symbol system that explains why society is the way it is. Geertz identifies ideology as one example of a web of significance, because "the inherent elusiveness of ideological thought" is "expressed as it is in intricate symbolic webs as vaguely defined as they are emotionally charged."[82] Ideology is created and maintained through symbol use, but the ideological content of symbols is often difficult to track.

Ideology becomes most powerful when humans forget it is socially constructed and give it "the status of objective reality."[83] For example, marriage ceremonies are socially constructed rituals, but people forget these ceremonies are choices and begin to think they must be performed a particular way in order to be real. Cultural ideology about marriage ceremonies explains why the average cost of a US wedding tops $21,000, a hefty sum for a couple starting out, which might be better spent to make a down payment on a house or to pay off debts. You might even hear someone complain at a nontraditional (or less expensive) wedding that it was "not right" or "unnatural." Such comments indicate the existence of cultural ideology.

British cultural studies scholar Stuart Hall argues that dominant cultural ideology influences how people come to perceive reality.[84] For example, capitalism is not only an economic system, but also a dominant ideology in the United States that undergirds the values and behaviors that support competition, individualism, and consumerism, and that enables money to determine status and power. This does not mean that every person in US culture embraces the ideology unquestioningly, but it does explain the predominant US culture.

Burke offers a metaphorical description of how words operate together to constitute an ideology, and how that ideology induces people to act in certain ways: "An 'ideology' is like a spirit taking up its abode in a body: it makes that body hop around in certain ways; and that same body would have hopped around in different ways had a different ideology [or set of terms] happened to inhabit it."[85] In the case of the mob violence targeted at abolitionists, white supremacist ideology made the mob hop in a particularly violent way, legitimating the violence of slavery and the violence targeted at those who would challenge slavery. Ideology is not neutral, but tends to normalize the possession of power by the "haves" and the denial of power to the "have-nots."

Ideology guides the way people evaluate (attach meaning and valuations to) the world. It makes sense of social knowledge and order, helps people in a culture explain the reasons for good and ill, and offers direction for social action.[86] Like culture, ideology is resistant to change, but, also like culture, it is not unchangeable.

---

[82] Geèrtz, *Interpretation*, 195.

[83] Peter Berger defines legitimation in this way. We see ideology as legitimizing the social order. See Berger, *The Sacred Canopy*, 4, 9, 29.

[84] Stuart Hall, "Ideology and Communication Theory," in *Rethinking Communication Theory*, vol. 1, ed. Brenda Dervin, Larry Grossberg, Barbara O'Keefe, and Ellen Wartella, 40–52 (Newbury Park, CA: Sage, 1989).

[85] Burke, *Language*, 6.

[86] V. William Balthrop, "Culture, Myth, and Ideology as Public Argument: An Interpretation of the Ascent and Demise of 'Southern Culture,' " *Communication Monographs* 51 (December 1984), 343–344.

Because it is constructed and maintained by symbols, ideology can be challenged and altered through symbolic action.

Not all ideologies carry equal power. Some become dominant. **Hegemony** is *the dominant ideology of a society, exerting social control over people without the use of force.*[87] Philosopher Rosemary Hennessy explains that hegemony is not a form of power that controls through overt violence; rather, it subtly controls by determining what makes sense: "Hegemony is the process whereby the interests of a ruling group come to dominate by establishing the common sense, that is, those values, beliefs, and knowledges that go without saying."[88]

Hegemony is constructed and maintained by rhetorical actions. Communication scholars draw on Italian political theorist Antonio Gramsci's concept of hegemonic ideology.[89] Gramsci argues that social control is primarily accomplished through the control of ideas. People are encouraged to see an idea as common sense, even if it conflicts with their own experiences. By following the cultural norms that guide behaviors, members of the culture uphold the ideology. People willingly belong to cultures for the protection and order they provide, even though (and because) hegemonic cultural ideology may control (or strongly influence) their beliefs.

Hegemony reduces one's agency because it limits the choices that make sense to a rhetor or audience. For example, because capitalism is the hegemonic US ideology, most people in the United States believe in free and open markets and in the freedom of consumers to choose where to shop and what to buy. Recently, in a small town where two locally owned restaurants were located next to a park, a multinational fast-food restaurant offered to buy the park land and pay to relocate the park so it could build a restaurant on that location. The town council held an open meeting to discuss the proposal. Some members of the community opposed the fast-food restaurant, arguing that it would put the locally owned restaurants out of business and destroy the community by taking away a valuable central public meeting place. These community members were accused of being "antidevelopment" and "against the free enterprise system." One council member said, "If you do not like fast food, then don't eat there. The other restaurants need to learn to compete. It's a free country." These statements did not really answer the opponents' arguments, but sought to silence the opposition by making them seem un-American, opposed to competition and freedom.

Because hegemony is embedded within symbolic actions, rhetorical critics need to learn how to read through it. Media scholar Stuart Hall identifies three positions from which audiences can decode a text: dominant or preferred (hegemonic) reading, negotiated reading, and oppositional (counterhegemonic) reading.[90] Different

---

[87] Antonio Gramsci, Raymond Rosenthal, and Frank Rosengarten, *Letters from Prison* (New York: Columbia University Press, 1993).

[88] Rosemary Hennessy, "Subjects, Knowledges, ... and All the Rest: Speaking for What," *Who Can Speak? Authority and Critical Identity*, ed. Judith Roof and Robyn Weigman, 137–150 (Urbana: University of Illinois Press, 1995), 145–146.

[89] Joseph P. Zompetti, "Toward a Gramscian Critical Rhetoric," *Western Journal of Communication* 61, no. 1 (Winter 1997), 66–86, and John M. Murphy, "Domesticating Dissent: The Kennedys and the Freedom Rides," *Communication Monographs* 59, no. 1 (March 1992), 61–78.

[90] Stuart Hall, "Encoding, Decoding," *The Cultural Studies Reader*, ed. Simon During, 90–103 (London: Routledge, 1993), 98–102.

people in any given time have different resources available for oppositional readings, and have to expend more or less effort to construct them. Communication scholar Bonnie Dow observes that it is easy to "acquire the codes necessary for preferred readings" while "the acquisition of codes for negotiated or oppositional readings is more difficult and less common."[91] This text should provide you with the code, or vocabulary, with which to critically and oppositionally understand rhetoric.

CONCLUSION

Rhetoric is the use of symbolic action by human beings to share ideas, enabling them to work together to make decisions about matters of common concern and to construct social reality. What this definition makes clear, and Aristotle's does not, is that rhetoric is much more than a tool of information transmission or persuasion. Through rhetoric, people constitute identity, construct culture, maintain and challenge memory, and develop and sustain ideology; and are able to identify, maintain, and counter hegemonic power.

Our goal in this book is to introduce you to some of the joys and responsibilities of rhetorical action. Democracy is not a spectator sport, nor is life. To be able to participate, you need to understand how rhetoric works, and that it is at work in a variety of places: politics, religion, family, sports, entertainment, small town life, and workplaces. The ability to self-reflexively attach meaning to the world and to make sense of what the world means requires an understanding of rhetoric.

When studying rhetoric, scholars do not really use a single approach or a preset step-by-step method. Instead, they use what communication scholars William L. Nothstine, Carole Blair, and Gary A. Copeland refer to as "conceptual heuristics or vocabularies."[92] Throughout the chapters that follow, we present a vocabulary that describes the forms, components, and functions of rhetoric, and that should enable you to explain rhetoric's power to liberate *and* subordinate. We introduce you to diverse forms of symbolic action, including language, visual rhetoric, argument, and narrative. We show you ways to analyze how rhetorical action is composed of rhetors, audiences, and situations that constrain rhetoric even as they, themselves, are rhetorically constructed. We end with a discussion of public rhetoric that shows how you can identify yourself as an agent of civic action.

Rhetoric is essential to the functioning of civic culture. Civic engagement in open societies exists so that citizens can challenge the actions of those in power and engage each other in discussions and debates over what is right—for individuals, communities, the nation, and the world. Civic engagement is much more than the act of voting. It necessitates that you engage with other people and participate in symbolic actions that constitute your identity as a person, a group member, and a citizen. An understanding of how culture, memory, power, and ideology are rhetorical is integral to a complete understanding of the full power of rhetoric and of the constraints on rhetorical action.

---

[91] Bonnie J. Dow, *Prime-Time Feminism* (Philadelphia: University of Pennsylvania Press, 1996), 13.

[92] William L. Nothstine, Carole Blair, and Gary A. Copeland, *Critical Questions: Invention, Creativity, and the Criticism of Discourse and Media* (New York: St. Martin's, 1994), 40.

KEY CONCEPTS

civic engagement

collective memory

constitutive rhetoric

culture

ethos

hegemony

identification

ideology

logos

pathos

power

public memory

rhetor

rhetoric

rhetorical agency

social reality

symbol

symbolic action

verbal symbols

visual symbols

DISCUSSION QUESTIONS

1. The authors suggest that the study of rhetoric is tied to democratic societies. Think about how the study of rhetoric may have been helpful in the years preceding the rise of Hitler. How might a society with a stronger emphasis on rhetoric have better understood Hitler and the Nazis?
2. Can you provide examples of the power of rhetoric in politics, the law, and your own daily life?
3. What is your position on the debate between Socrates and the Sophists? Is rhetoric morally neutral, or is it to blame for human failures?
4. The text suggested some constraints and resources for rhetoric and civic engagement. Can you identify others?

RECOMMENDED READINGS

Aristotle. *On Rhetoric*. Translated by George A. Kennedy. New York: Oxford University Press, 1991.

Asen, Robert. "A Discourse Theory of Citizenship." *Quarterly Journal of Speech* 90, no.2 (2004): 189–211.

Hauser, Gerard A. "Rhetorical Democracy and Civic Engagement." In *Rhetorical Democracy: Discursive Practices of Civic Engagement*. Edited by Gerard A. Hauser and Amy Grim, 1–16 (Mahwah, NJ: Lawrence Erlbaum Associates, 2004).

Kennedy, George A. *A New History of Classical Rhetoric*. Princeton, NJ: Princeton University Press, 1994.

Poulakos, John. "Toward a Sophistic Definition of Rhetoric." *Philosophy and Rhetoric* 16, no. 1 (1983): 35–48.

Delivering Your Speech Effectively

From Chapter 11 of *Public Speaking and Civic Engagement*, Third Edition. J. Michael Hogan, Patricia Hayes Andrews, James R. Andrews, Glen Williams. Copyright © 2014 by Pearson Education, Inc. All rights reserved.

Delivering Your Speech Effectively

In 1847, a young woman graduated from Oberlin College and began a career as a reformer, lecturing throughout the country. She first spoke in support of the abolition of slavery and then took up the cause of women's suffrage. In a time when women who dared to speak in public were often subjected to ridicule and abuse, it took conviction, courage, and a commanding presence to appear before such hostile audiences. Her supporters, however, frequently praised her logic and command of the facts. According to one listener, her message was "wholly irresistible to every person who cares for reason or justice." Yet she probably would have failed without a powerful delivery—and that Lucy Stone had. She was, one observer wrote, "small in stature but large of soul…her bearing modest and dignified, her face radiant with feeling, and speaking all over, as it were, in eloquent accord with her earnest voice."[1]

You are not likely to confront the kind of challenges faced by Lucy Stone, and most of us would have a hard time standing up to such challenges. But whenever you speak in public—in the classroom, in a business meeting, or at a town hall meeting—your delivery will play a significant part in your success. Delivery is one of the most obvious aspects of public speaking, and it shapes your listeners' first impressions of your skills as a speaker. Yet you should never count on an engaging delivery to compensate for a speech that is poorly structured or lacking in substance.

SOUNDING GOOD VERSUS BEING SOUND

Preview.   One of your ethical obligations as a speaker is to present a message of substance. Good delivery, though important, is no substitute for sound ideas. Having an ethical and effective delivery means remaining audience-centered, avoiding behaviors that distract from the message, and promoting the listeners' understanding.

1 Explain the ethical issues involved in delivering your speech.

Sometimes you may find yourself thinking that a speaker sounded good but did not have anything important to say. On another occasion, a speaker's delivery may be so dramatic that it actually distracts from the content of the speech. Whether intentional or not, a distracting delivery is not good delivery.

Beyond Delivery: Listening to the Message

As listeners, we sometimes give too much weight to how a speech is delivered. A speaker who is poised and articulate, has a good voice, and appears confident and friendly may impress us. However, such a speaker might be merely facile—he or she can speak easily but may not have much to say. It is important to distinguish between a speaker who *is* sound and a speaker who just *sounds* good.

A sound speaker's ideas pass the tests of evidence and reasoning. As much as we might admire the ease and grace of some speakers, we need to be on our guard against the slick, superficial speaker who tries to manipulate or deceive us rather than engage us in a discussion of important ideas.

The Foundation of Ethical Delivery

Ethical delivery grows out of a collaborative, transactional model of communication. It means communicating with respect for your listeners, never seeking to manipulate them, but aiming instead for a mutually beneficial outcome. The ethical speaker does not put on an "act" but speaks sincerely and authentically—always mindful of the needs, values, and priorities of those assembled to listen.

Ethical delivery does not distract from the content or meaning of the speech. It is appropriate to the situation, including the size and makeup of the audience. By contrast, an unethical speaker may intentionally use overly dramatic gestures, striking movement, or exaggerated vocal patterns to distract the audience from the speech's content. Not only is this kind of delivery ethically questionable, it can also backfire. Effective and ethical delivery should *reinforce* rather than distract attention from the speaker's ideas.

Finally, ethical delivery promotes the listeners' trust and comprehension. When you make a speech, your body, voice, and gestures must be in tune with the mood and nature of your message. Never forget that your audience will form impressions of you and your ideas based, in some measure, on how you deliver your speech. A speaker may have some compelling ideas, but if that speaker seems dull and lifeless—if the speaker does not seem to care—the message may be lost.

PRINCIPLES OF GOOD DELIVERY

2 Describe the basic principles of effective delivery.

Explore the Concept "Speech Delivery" at **MyCommunicationLab**

Preview. *Certain basic principles of effective delivery apply to a wide variety of public speaking situations. You will want to adapt your delivery to the specific situation and to audience expectations. In general, effective delivery is associated with proper attire, good eye contact, appropriate gestures and movement, and facial expressions that reinforce your message. Good delivery also means a dynamic yet conversational speaking voice.*

Most of us recognize the importance of delivery, yet we may become apprehensive at the thought of standing in front of a group of people and delivering a speech.[2] As you prepare to deliver a speech, you will confront many questions: Should I use a podium? Should I move around during my speech? Will everybody be able to hear me? There are no absolute answers to any of these questions. You will need to adjust your style of delivery to the demands of each situation.

In your classroom, these questions are relatively easy to answer; they become more problematic when giving a speech in a different setting. In that case, the person who invited you to speak should be able to offer you guidance concerning the formality of the occasion and the expectations of the audience. It is wise to find out as much as you can about the situation before you begin planning your speech. Above all, you need to think about what sort of delivery style will best help you connect with your audience.

Watch the Video "Martin Cox Discusses Tips for Speech Delivery" at **MyCommunicationLab**

Understand the Situation and Audience Expectations

What is appropriate in one speaking situation may be inappropriate in another. The more you learn about audience members' needs, norms, and preferences, the more likely you will deliver your speech effectively. Do these listeners expect a formal presentation, or do they like to sit in a circle and have the speaker "chat" with them? Is this an after-dinner speech, to be delivered in a hotel conference room equipped with a podium and technological support? If so, will the listeners expect you to speak from behind the podium and make use of that technology?

How you dress when you deliver a speech can also be important. Your appearance can influence how your audience judges your ethos or credibility. Although there are no fixed rules for attire, listeners generally expect an invited speaker to be well groomed and nicely dressed.[3] How the audience itself will be dressed may provide one clue. You do not want to be wearing jeans and a T-shirt if your audience will be dressed in suits and ties.

In your public speaking class, casual attire may be appropriate, but you still want to feel confident and comfortable with the way you look. Avoid shoes that are too tight or clothes that are too snug. Also avoid any attire that detracts from your speech, such as a flamboyant blouse, a T-shirt with written or visual content, or a baseball cap.

Establish Eye Contact

Have you ever talked with someone who did not look you in the eye? Did you feel that the person was uncomfortable? Nervous? Ashamed? Preoccupied? Dishonest? In most cultures, a communicator who does not look us in the eye makes us suspicious.[4] The same is true in formal public speaking. As listeners, we respond more positively to speakers who make eye contact with us.

Of course, there are cultural variations in practices and reactions to eye contact. The *Highlighting Eye Contact* feature provides examples of some of these cultural differences.

Watch the Video
"Student Scholarships and Awards Ceremony" at **MyCommunicationLab**

HIGHLIGHTING EYE CONTACT | Acknowledging Cultural Differences in Eye Contact and Gaze

- In Japan, meeting participants often look down or close their eyes while others are talking. By doing so, they show their attentiveness to and even agreement with the speaker.
- African Americans, Native Americans, Chicanos, and Puerto Ricans often avoid eye contact as a nonverbal sign of recognition and respect for an authority-subordinate relationship.
- In some Far Eastern cultures, it is considered rude to look into another person's eyes while talking to him or her.
- For Arabs, the eyes are considered a key to a person's being; looking deeply into another person's eyes allows one to see another's soul.
- In U.S. culture, establishing eye contact with others conveys a sense of directness, openness, and candor.

Sources: Edward T. Hall and Mildred Reed Hall, *Understanding Cultural Differences* (Yarmouth, ME: Intercultural Press, 1990); Carolyn Calloway-Thomas, Pamela J. Cooper, and Cecil Blake, *Intercultural Communication: Roots and Routes* (Boston: Allyn & Bacon, 1999); and Michelle Le Baron, *Bridging Cultural Conflicts: A New Approach for a Changing World* (San Francisco: Jossey-Bass, 2003).

Whatever our cultural differences, our eyes can be very expressive. As we squint, smile, laugh, frown, or scowl, we communicate many emotions: concern, commitment, joy, or anger. When we fail to establish eye contact, we must rely solely on our words, voice, gestures, or facial expressions to convey emotions. In U.S. culture, we clearly place ourselves at a disadvantage if we do not use our eyes to communicate.[5]

Good eye contact also conveys sincerity. We are more likely to believe a speaker who looks us in the eye while speaking.[6] When we establish eye contact with our listeners, we come across as more truthful, candid, open, and trustworthy.

Finally, looking at the members of the audience gives us a chance to observe their reactions to our speech. How can we clarify what we are saying if we have not even noticed that our listeners look confused? How can we benefit from appreciative smiles and nods of encouragement if we are not looking? With the exception of comments or questions after the speech, the feedback you get from your audience will consist of nonverbal signs, such as nods, smiles, or expressions of excitement or boredom. If you "close your eyes" to such feedback, you will miss out on an important chance to adjust your speech and to engage in more of a dialogue with your audience. When you *do* respond to audience reactions, you show sensitivity and respect.

As you establish eye contact with your listeners, remember to share your attention with everyone. Figure 1 highlights several patterns of eye contact to avoid. Of all the principles of effective delivery, maintaining good eye contact with your listeners is among the most important.

FIGURE 1

Ineffective Eye Patterns

When you deliver your speech, seek to avoid all of the following:

- *Staring at one or two listeners—excluding others and creating discomfort for those who are the focus of your excessive gaze*
- *Directing your gaze to those of particular interest—an attractive classmate, the instructor, the boss, a key competitor, or an elected official*
- *Directing your gaze only to those who are smiling and appear to agree with what you are saying*
- *Looking at one side of the room as if listeners on that side are magnetized*
- *Staring at the floor while speaking and failing to connect with the audience altogether*
- *Looking over listeners' heads and speaking to the back wall*
- *Talking mostly to your speaking notes and only occasionally bobbing up to look briefly at listeners as if making sure they haven't left the room*
- *Directing your eye contact to your presentational aids—speaking directly to a screen, a flip chart, or a handout while losing contact with the audience*
- *Rolling your eyes during audience questions and thus expressing your low regard for the question or the questioner*

Reinforce Ideas through Gestures, Movement, and Facial Expressions

Explore the Concept "Nonverbal Communication" at **MyCommunicationLab**

Most of us use several physical gestures in ordinary conversation. We wave our hands, point, or pound on the table to emphasize a point. How we hold or move our bodies can also communicate information to others, intentionally or unintentionally.[7] If we pace or slouch in our chair, we may imply we are nervous or disinterested. We might move closer to someone to express affection or intimacy, or we might move farther away to create distance or convey aloofness. We communicate a great deal with our faces, too.[8] We might smile broadly, scowl, raise an eyebrow, or clench our teeth to communicate our determination, anger, or stubbornness. Through facial expressions, we can "say" a lot.

Your words and physical actions should be mutually reinforcing.[9] If you were talking to a friend about something that really mattered to you, you might say, "I *really* want you to consider doing this!" At the same time, you might lean forward, look into her or his eyes, and nod your head. In public speaking, you can use similar nonverbal signals to reinforce your message, perhaps gesturing to emphasize a point or moving laterally to reinforce a transition. If, on the other hand, you contradict your words with your nonverbal actions—say, you smile when discussing a serious matter or appear uninterested when claiming to be excited—your audience is likely to give more weight to your nonverbal cues.[10]

Perhaps you are uncertain about whether your movement, gestures, and facial expressions are appropriate. If so, you might ask someone to watch you practice your speech and give you feedback. Here are some questions you may want to consider:

- Does my movement seem to reinforce the flow of the speech?
- Are my gestures distracting in any way?
- Do I rely too much on any one gesture?
- Does my face seem to convey sincerity and reinforce the meaning of my speech?
- Are there different gestures, movements, or facial expressions that might better communicate my intended meaning?
- Does my nonverbal communication consistently convey a respectful attitude toward the audience?[11]

Although you may plan a few basic gestures and movements in advance, *most* should occur spontaneously as you interact with your audience. Your nonverbal delivery will vary as you give your speech at different times, in different rooms, and to different audiences. For instance, the same gestures that you use in ordinary conversation may work well if you are speaking to an audience of 25 or fewer. But if you are speaking to 150 people assembled in an auditorium, you may want to enlarge your gestures so that everyone can see them.

Finally, you should work at avoiding nonverbal behaviors that may come across as nervous or distracting. Figure 2 lists some specific gestures and movements to avoid while delivering a speech.

Whenever a gesture calls attention to itself, eliminate it. Gesture and movement can reinforce your ideas, but they can also distract from the message you hope to convey.

FIGURE 2

Nonverbal Behaviors to Avoid

Like all other "rules," some nonverbal behaviors will appropriately vary with the speaking situation. In general, however, you should seek to eliminate the following behaviors:

- *Pacing nervously while you speak*
- *Moving to a different spot in the room for no apparent reason*
- *Pointing your finger at the audience while making an important point*
- *Wagging your finger back and forth as if saying, "That's a no-no!"*
- *Using the same gesture repeatedly*
- *Using large, expansive gestures in a small room*
- *Using tiny gestures in a large room*
- *Stroking your face or hair*
- *Biting your lip*
- *Fiddling with your glasses or jewelry*
- *Leaning on or gripping the podium*
- *Smiling throughout the speech*
- *Frowning throughout the speech*
- *Chewing on your nails while listening to audience questions or comments*

Strive for an Effective Speaking Voice

One of the most obvious aspects of your delivery is your voice. Have you ever listened to a speaker whose voice really bothered you? Perhaps she or he spoke in a monotone, stumbled over words, or inserted *you know* at every pause. Or maybe the speaker's voice sounded too high and squeaky or too low and unvarying. Clearly, our voices can get us into trouble as public speakers. But they can also be used effectively to enhance our messages. When you use your voice effectively, you can add extra emphasis to key ideas, display a variety of emotions, demonstrate your commitment, and enhance your credibility.

How can you improve the vocal aspects of your delivery? You might try speaking into an audio recorder and playing it back to see what your voice sounds like to others. Obtaining feedback from friends can also be helpful. You can modify some features of your voice by recognizing their importance, paying attention to them as you practice your speech out loud, and monitoring them as you speak. The features that you can control and perhaps improve include volume, rate, pitch, and clarity.

Volume   If listeners cannot hear you, they obviously cannot benefit from your message. Nor will they be able to concentrate on your message if you speak so loudly that they feel uncomfortable.

The volume of your delivery should be determined by the setting in which you speak. Naturally, a small room calls for a quieter voice than does a large lecture hall or an outdoor setting. If you are concerned that you cannot be heard, you could simply ask your audience as you begin to speak. Doing so shows your respect for your listeners, and they will be glad to give you feedback.

In some situations, you may need a microphone to amplify your voice. Some microphones clip to your clothing, while others are handheld or attached to a podium. If you use a microphone, make sure it is working properly before you start your speech. If the microphone is attached to a podium, you may need to adjust its height so that you can speak directly into it.

Rate   It is not uncommon for a beginning speaker to sit down after giving a speech, look at the clock, and be amazed to find that the planned ten-minute speech took only seven or eight minutes. Several miscalculations could account for this, but often the problem is that the speaker rushed through the speech. Keep in mind that your audience needs time to absorb and process your speech—especially if you are addressing a complex or thought-provoking issue.

The needs of the listeners should be paramount. Just as they cannot keep up with a speaker who is talking too quickly, they may lose interest in one who speaks too slowly. In most speaking situations, about 125–150 words per minute is considered an appropriate rate of speaking,[12] but you may choose to speak more quickly or slowly, depending on the complexity and novelty of the information you are presenting. Some research suggests that listeners may perceive speakers who speak quickly (though not *too* fast) as more knowledgeable,[13] but you should speak at a rate that fits your own personal style and that allows the audience to process the information you present.

Finally, your speaking rate can be used to emphasize key ideas. The effective use of pauses can give your audience the opportunity to absorb information and ideas. Some speakers even use pauses or silence to reinforce a compelling statistic, quotation, or narrative, in effect saying, "Let's stop to think about this for a moment. This is important." Similarly, you may slow down or use repetition to emphasize an important idea. When you *vary* your rate—by pausing, slowing down, or using restatement or repetition at critical and strategic moments—you enhance your chances of getting your message across.

Pitch   Sometimes a speaker's voice is simply unpleasant to listen to. It may be squeaky or raspy, or it may be pitched so low that you can hardly distinguish one word from the next. *Pitch* refers to the highness or lowness of your voice on a musical scale. It is the voice's upward or downward inflection. A speaker's vocal pitch can be too high, too low, or too unvarying. When the pitch is too high, listeners tend to cringe. When the pitch is too low, listeners may be unable to hear what the speaker is saying. An unvarying pitch is called a monotone—a vocal quality guaranteed to put your audience to sleep.

Rightly or wrongly, listeners often draw conclusions about speakers whose pitch seems inappropriate. A high pitch may be associated with immaturity, inexperience, tension, or excitability. A low pitch or a monotone may cause listeners to view the speaker as bored or disengaged. By contrast, a richer pitch, one with depth and variety, can communicate a sense of authority and competence.[14]

What can you do about the pitch of your voice? Start by audio-recording your voice and listening to how you sound. If you are not satisfied, you may want to use some vocal exercises to improve your pitch. In extreme cases, you may want to seek assistance from someone trained in voice therapy. Here are a few pointers to keep in mind:

- Your pitch will vary throughout your life. It will be higher when you are younger and lower later in life. Working with the pitch of your voice is an on-going process.
- If you are tense, your pitch tends to rise. Use relaxation techniques to help you manage communication apprehension.
- Strive for variety in your pitch. Avoid repetitive pitch patterns, such as *uptalking* (in which your pitch rises as you seem to question the statement you have just made).[15] You want your voice to be interesting, and you want to use all aspects of your voice to emphasize your most important points.

Clarity To be effective as a speaker, you must be understood. Although speaking at an appropriate speed can help you communicate more clearly, vocal clarity is also important. A clear vocal style depends on several things: First, strive for distinctness in *articulation*. Dropping the endings off words, slurring sounds, and running words together can interfere with the clarity of your message. For example, if you say "locked out" but you sound like you said "lucked out," you did not articulate clearly. Articulation especially becomes a problem when a speaker rushes through a speech, failing to take the time to articulate each word carefully.

Second, strive for correct pronunciation of the words you use. Whereas articulation refers to the clarity with which we say words, *pronunciation* involves saying words correctly. If you are unsure of the correct pronunciation of an uncommon or unfamiliar word, look it up in a dictionary. Practice aloud so that you are comfortable saying the words you are using, and especially check the pronunciation of words used in quoted material.

Finally, avoid *vocal mannerisms*. It is pointless and distracting to keep saying *you know* every time you pause during speaking. Some speakers also have a habit

HIGHLIGHTING THE IMPORTANCE OF A GOOD VOICE | The Practices of Demosthenes

One of the greatest orators of ancient Greece was Demosthenes. According to historians, Demosthenes had difficulties speaking clearly, but he recognized the importance of good articulation, so he did all he could to improve. Plutarch writes the following:

His inarticulate and stammering pronunciation he overcame and rendered more distinct by speaking with pebbles in his mouth; his voice he disciplined by declaiming and reciting speeches or verses when he was out of breath, while running or going up steep places; and in his house he had a large looking-glass, before which he would stand and go through his exercises.

It is told that someone once came to request assistance as a pleader, and related how he had been assaulted and beaten. "Certainly" said Demosthenes, "nothing of the kind can have happened to you." Upon which the other, raising his voice, exclaimed loudly, "What, Demosthenes, nothing has been done to me?" "Ah," replied Demosthenes, "now I hear the voice of one that has been injured and beaten." Of so great consequence towards the gaining of belief did he esteem the tone and action of the speaker.

Source: From Plutarch, "The Practices of Demosthenes," *Plutarch's Lives, vol. 12.* Published 1909 by P.F. Collier & Son.

of concluding almost every statement with the unnecessary question, "Right?" Also, some regional mannerisms clutter speech and thus reduce clarity, for example, "Ya know?" Other speakers seem to end every sentence with an *at*, as in "He didn't know where I was *at*." These vocal mannerisms often are distracting to listeners.[16]

Remain Flexible

No matter how carefully you plan and practice in advance, some speaking situations will surprise you. Flexibility is the key to responding successfully to these situations. You might find that the podium is missing or the microphone is not working. You might be told at the last minute that you have less time to speak than originally planned and that you will have to cut your speech short. Or, imagine that you expected to deliver a formal speech to a large audience, but when you arrived, only five or six people were present. Rather than standing behind a podium and speaking formally, you might want to adapt to the situation by sitting on the edge of a table and informally "chatting" with the group.

The foundation of flexibility is spontaneity and open-mindedness—a willingness to recognize that there are many different ways to deliver a good speech and an ability to discover a "better" way whenever a situation seems to demand it. Speakers

---

HIGHLIGHTING FLEXIBILITY | A Dramatic Example

Perhaps the most extraordinary—and certainly unique—example of adapting to the situation came during the presidential campaign of 1912. Former president Theodore Roosevelt, who had failed to secure his own party's nomination, was running for president as a candidate of a third party, the Progressive or "Bull Moose" Party. With scarcely three weeks to go before the election, Roosevelt's campaign pulled into Milwaukee, where he was scheduled to speak before a huge rally of supporters. As Roosevelt left his hotel, a man stepped up to him and fired a gun at point-blank range. The bullet passed through the copy of Roosevelt's speech, which was 50 pages, folded over—long speeches were typical in those days—and his glasses case before lodging in the candidate's chest. Feeling as if he had been "kicked by a mule" but determined to continue, TR refused to go to a hospital, insisting instead that he go on and give his speech. Usually a dynamic speaker with a robust, energetic style, Roosevelt quieted the cheering crowd that greeted him. Raising his arm, he said quietly, "I shall ask you

to be as quiet as possible. I don't know whether you fully understand that I have just been shot; but it takes more than that to kill a bull moose." Opening his coat, revealing the bloodstained shirt, Roosevelt showed the crowd the speech text with the bullet hole. Because "the bullet is in me now," Roosevelt explained, he would not give a very long speech. "But," he said, "I will try my best." Speaking without the bullet-torn manuscript, Roosevelt spoke extemporaneously for a very painful hour and a half before his anxious aides were able to get him off the platform and to a hospital.

This example is, of course, dramatic and makes the loss of a note card or facing a larger audience than you anticipated seem like a small thing. You may never experience such an extreme challenge, but you *will* have times when you will have to deliver your speech under difficult circumstances, and you will need to be flexible.

Sources: See H. W. Brands, *TR: The Last Romantic* (New York: Basic Books, 1997), 720–22; and Nathan Miller, *Theodore Roosevelt: A Life* (New York: Morrow, 1992), 530–31. ◢

need not always stand or use a podium, and they *can* engage the audience in dialogue if doing so seems fitting and consistent with the audience's norms and expectations.

Practice Your Speech

Sometimes speakers think that once they have carefully researched their topic, organized their thoughts, and prepared their outline, all they need to do is read through the outline silently a few times—and they will be ready to go. Nothing could be further from the truth. If you have not practiced your speech aloud several times, chances are you are not prepared to speak.[17]

Here are a few guidelines for practicing your speech:

- *Practice delivering your speech aloud with your keyword outline.* But first read through your notes silently several times until you feel ready to begin.
- *Practice your speech all the way through—noting sections that are rough, re-reading and revising your notes, and then practicing again.*
- *Break the speech into parts and practice major sections, such as the introduction, several times in a row.*
- *Always take breaks.* Avoid practicing so much at one time that you begin to lose your energy, voice, or concentration.
- *Practice in front of friends and ask for their constructive feedback.* Over a period of time, practice your speech again several times, all the way through, but do not try to memorize your speech.
- *Incorporate your visual aids into your practice sessions.* If possible, visit the room where you will speak and practice using the equipment there. If you are going to deliver your speech using computer support, such as PowerPoint or Prezi slides, prepare those slides in advance and incorporate them into your practice sessions. Remember that when you deliver the speech, you want to avoid talking to the screen, standing where you might block any projected image, or reading every word appearing on each slide. At the same time, you will want to point to key features of maps or other visuals to direct the audience's attention to key elements of your speech.
- *Time yourself several times.* If your speech is too long, make appropriate cuts. For instance, you may cut a section that is less important, use fewer examples, or edit long quotations. It is important to remember that practicing your speech is something you do *before* the beginning of class or *before* you are seated in front of your audience. Sometimes speakers read through their notes while others are speaking. Do not fall into this trap. Practice sufficiently beforehand so that you will be able to listen to other speakers. Not only do they deserve your respectful attention, but you might even learn something you can refer to in your own speech.

Seek Out Opportunities to Speak

As you gain experience and confidence as a speaker, you will naturally deliver your speeches more effectively. This is especially true if you ask for listener feedback and strive to improve by addressing whatever weaknesses they identify. In addition, you will speak with more confidence and credibility if you speak about topics that genuinely concern you. When you deliver your remarks with personal conviction, you tend to speak with more force, clarity, directness, and spontaneity—all hallmarks of effective delivery.

Look for opportunities to speak inside *and* outside the classroom. You may join your college's student speakers bureau, run for political office on campus, or volunteer with a local service or nonprofit organization and join *their* speakers bureau. You can also use your volunteer work as a foundation for bringing your life's passions into the classroom. When you take courses with an emphasis on service learning or civic engagement, you will have more opportunities to make these kinds of connections between your life experiences and the classroom.

Speakers with deep personal conviction tend to deliver their speeches more effectively.

SPEAKING EXTEMPORANEOUSLY

Preview. *Extemporaneous speaking requires careful preparation. Using this delivery style and speaking from a keyword outline allows you to be completely involved in your speech. At the same time, you can maintain the flexibility you need to adapt to differing situations.*

Depending on the occasion, listener expectations, and other demands of the situation, speakers may choose to use different styles of delivery. Some of these styles are more informal and spontaneous, whereas others are more formal and scripted. In *most* speaking situations, however, you will probably want to deliver your speech in an *extemporaneous* style.

Extemporaneous speaking should not be confused with *impromptu* speaking, or speaking with no preparation at all. Extemporaneous speaking still requires careful preparation. In preparing an extemporaneous speech, you will thoroughly research your topic, decide how to best organize your ideas, carefully prepare your outline, and practice delivering the speech from notes. An extemporaneous speech is not memorized word for word. Yet neither is it completely spontaneous or delivered "off the cuff."

When delivering a speech extemporaneously, you may commit some key ideas to memory, but your specific words, phrases, and examples may vary both as you practice the speech and during its final delivery. With the extemporaneous style of

3 Explain the advantages of delivering your speech extemporaneously.

Watch the Video "Whatever Happened to Sisqo?" at **MyCommunicationLab**

delivery, you have the advantage of being well prepared, yet you can also adapt to changing circumstances if necessary.

Advantages of Speaking from a Keyword Outline

When you deliver a speech extemporaneously, you will typically use speaking notes with a keyword outline. This outline keeps you on track and reminds you of your main ideas, but it does not lay out the speech word for word. A keyword outline is not something you can use as a crutch. It will keep you on track, reminding you of your main points and perhaps some of your key examples, statistics, or other forms of evidence. But you will still need to think on your feet and interact with your audience. When delivering your speech extemporaneously, you can speak more directly with your audience, watching for their responses, and making any changes in the content or delivery of your speech that may seem necessary.

On occasion, circumstances before your speech may dictate last-minute changes in your own presentation. In your speech class, for example, another student may speak before you and refer to an event or a piece of information that you had planned to discuss. Would you go ahead as planned and just pretend that the other speaker had not already mentioned the matter? Or would you have the flexibility to build on what the other speaker said without just repeating the same information? When you deliver your speech from a keyword outline, you have the flexibility to adapt to changing circumstances. Of course, to take advantage of that flexibility, you need to listen closely to those other speakers and quickly come up with ideas for building on their remarks.

Whenever you do some last-minute fine-tuning on your speech, you demonstrate respect for your fellow speakers and your audience. You show that you have been paying attention to what others have said, and you demonstrate a commitment to dialogue, not just to having your say. In doing so, you help build a sense of community among speakers and listeners. Delivering your speech extemporaneously will not guarantee that it will be a success, but it will give you that flexibility you need to adapt to changing circumstances. In the *Focus on Civic Engagement* feature, we provide a sample of a keyword outline that a speaker might use to deliver a speech about Habitat for Humanity.

Keep in mind that there are no hard-and-fast rules for constructing your keyword outline. You may choose to record only a few main ideas to jog your memory, or you may elect to write out the speech in more detail, recording both main ideas and more detailed information, such as statistics, quotations, or particular phrasings that you want to use. In either case, practicing with your notes (as well as revising and refining them as you practice) is essential.

Why Use Extemporaneous Delivery?

With an extemporaneous delivery, you can more easily adapt to the audience and the situation. You can make changes, clarify or elaborate with examples or illustrations, omit a minor point if time is running short, and more effectively involve the audience in your speech.

FOCUS ON CIVIC ENGAGEMENT | A Keyword Outline for a Speech about Habitat for Humanity

INTRODUCTION

SHARE STORY—Single-parent domestic abuse survivor

SHARE PERSONAL BACKGROUND WITH HABITAT

IMPORTANCE OF HH—Providing thousands with decent, affordable housing

THESIS

Becoming actively involved with Habitat is an excellent way of making a difference in others' lives.

PREVIEW

- Habitat—mission and background
- International impact
- The Habitat selection system
- How to get involved

TRANSITION: First, I'd like to give you a little background on Habitat.   Speak fairly quickly

BODY

I. Habitat—a terrific organization
  - Nonprofit Christian housing ministry (Habitat Web site)
  - Started in the U.S. in 1976
  - Eliminates substandard housing worldwide
  - Adequate housing—a matter of conscience and action

TRANSITION: Habitat has had a huge impact all over the world.   Point to slide with Habitat map

II. HH has gained a large following in its 36 years.
  - All 50 states in the U.S.
  - Nearly 100 other countries
  - More than 2,000 total affiliates
  - Local Habitat building 115th house (2012 newsletter)

TRANSITION: How are families chosen to become HH homeowners?   Point to slide—keep eye contact!

III. Habitat—developed fair and efficient selection system
  - Selection criteria for homeowners (local Habitat ED, Thomson)
  - Need
  - Ability to repay no-interest mortgage
  - Willingness to put in 300–500 "sweat equity" hours
  - Builds modest homes
  - About 1,100 square feet
  - Low mortgage payments—less than $300 per month
  - Money reverts to a "Fund for Humanity"—supports future projects

TRANSITION: If you agree with me that Habitat is a wonderful organization, you may be wondering, "How can I get involved?"   Move closer to audience—direct eye contact

IV. Getting involved is easy!   Show slides of each program
  - Find local affiliate
  - Gifts from the heart (financial and food donations)
  - Global village—Habitat volunteer vacation
  - Women Build
  - Campus chapters and programs
  - Jimmy Carter's Work Project (distribute handouts)

CONCLUSION

Revisit personal story—*working with great people, community building.*

(Continued)

Summary

We've looked closely at Habitat—what it is, where it operates, how it works, and how you can get involved.

Appeal for Action

Sign up today!

Final slide—contact information

Share quote from HH homeowner: "This is the first time my three children have had a real home. They will be able to attend the same school and live in a safe neighborhood. Without HH, this *never* would have been possible."

Pause for questions

Extemporaneous speaking, however, demands focused concentration. When delivering a speech extemporaneously, you cannot just read from a manuscript or rely on a detailed outline if you lose your train of thought. You cannot just "zone out" or "wing it." Speaking extemporaneously demands careful preparation, good notes, and a clear mind as you speak.

An extemporaneous style works best when you have a genuine passion for your topic. As you speak extemporaneously, you can interject spontaneous comments or include personal observations that reflect your own interests and experiences. If *you* are intellectually and emotionally engaged, you are better able to speak in the moment and communicate the conviction and passion that you feel to your audience. When well done, an extemporaneous style also contributes to your ethos as a committed and effective advocate.[18] For example, former president Bill Clinton, who was well known for connecting personally with his audiences, was at his best when speaking extemporaneously. One journalist writing on Clinton's presidency pointed out that he was at his very best when he spoke, without a manuscript, at political rallies or from the pulpit of host churches.[19]

ALTERNATIVE STYLES OF DELIVERY

4 Compare and contrast different styles of delivery, listing strengths and weaknesses of each.

Explore the Concept "Methods of Delivery" at **MyCommunicationLab**

Preview. *Besides the extemporaneous style of delivery, speakers can choose from several other presentation styles that range from very informal to quite formal. The style you choose will depend on your preference, the demands of the speaking situation, and audience expectations.*

Successful speakers develop the ability to use a variety of different styles of delivery because different topics and occasions may call for different approaches to presenting your speech. You would not want to speak to a large, formal meeting with a casual, off-the-cuff style; nor would you want to speak to your classmates about getting involved in student government by writing out and reading a speech word for word. It is important to fit the delivery style to the situation.

In addition to the extemporaneous style, you may want to consider three other styles of delivery: impromptu, manuscript, and memorized speaking. Although the extemporaneous style is appropriate in most situations, one of these alternative approaches may be called for on certain occasions.

The Impromptu Speech

Watch the Video "Martin Cox Discusses Types of Delivery" at **MyCommunicationLab**

Impromptu speaking is off-the-cuff and casual, delivered with little or no preparation. In general, you should never choose to make an impromptu speech if you have time to prepare in advance. There may be occasions, however, when you find yourself in a situation where impromptu speaking is the only option.

Imagine that you are attending a community forum on heath care, for example, and you feel the need to respond to what some of the speakers have said. Perhaps you want to share a hair-raising experience you once had in the local hospital's emergency room, or maybe you want to argue for a new health care facility for low-income citizens. At your place of work, you may be called on to articulate your point of view, make a brief report, or explain some rule or procedure. Requests for these spontaneous "speeches" are more common than you may think in business and professional settings. As a student, you may be called on to make brief, impromptu speeches during discussions or debates in your classes. It is important to learn how to respond effectively to these demanding situations, even if you have little or no time to prepare.

If your instructor assigns an impromptu speech in your speech class, take advantage of this opportunity to get accustomed to standing up and speaking in front of your classmates without advance preparation. Your impromptu speech does not have to be perfect. Your instructor and classmates will understand that you had no time to prepare, and they won't expect the same polished performance they might expect in a formal speech. So relax! You may even enjoy this opportunity to "think on your feet" and fashion a speech "off the top of your head."

Guidelines for Giving Impromptu Speeches When giving an impromptu speech, you have limited time to organize your thoughts. Even so, here are a few things you can do to succeed:

- *Anticipate the possibility that you may be called on to speak and be thinking about what you might say.* Every class, conference, business meeting, or community forum will have an agenda. When you attend one of these, become as well versed as possible on issues to be discussed and reflect on what ideas or experiences you might like to share. You may want to jot down a few notes and have them ready if, in fact, you have the opportunity or are called upon to speak.
- *Practice active listening.* During a meeting, be sure to follow the flow of the discussion. You don't want to be daydreaming and then suddenly hear someone say, "Kevin, does this plan make sense to you?" If you are listening to formal presentations by others, you likewise will want to listen actively.
- *Increase your feelings of confidence by reminding yourself that no one expects perfection from impromptu remarks.* Listener expectations are always higher when the speaker is delivering a planned presentation. In impromptu speaking, however, listeners expect less fluent delivery.
- *Use even limited preparation time to your advantage.* At community forums or in professional conferences, you can take notes while listening to a panel or symposium. These notes will help you recall more accurately what others have said and can serve as the foundation for your own impromptu remarks.

- *Use basic principles of speech organization.* Even an impromptu speech should have an introduction, a body, and a conclusion. Within the body, you can still organize your main points in some basic strategic order. You may briefly introduce your remarks, make two or three main points, and perhaps summarize or appeal to listeners. However limited the time you have to prepare, it is always a good idea to sketch out at least a rough outline of the main ideas you want to cover.
- *Speak briefly and concisely.* Regardless of the situation, impromptu speeches should not consume too much time. Nobody appreciates a speaker who tries to dominate the meeting. If you are given the chance to speak, keep your comments brief and on-issue. Always assume that others will want to speak as well, and be respectful of their right to do so.
- *Think of impromptu speaking as an opportunity to practice and improve your delivery skills.* When you speak without notes or with limited notes, you have an opportunity to focus even more on your vocal and physical delivery. Take advantage of that to practice and more closely observe how listeners react to your style of speaking.

The Manuscript Speech

When former president Clinton speaks from a manuscript, he still connects with his audience and preserves his engaging style.

At the other end of the continuum is manuscript speaking. Manuscript speeches are carefully prepared formal speeches. They are speeches designed to be delivered exactly as written, such as a speech on a controversial issue that might be covered by the news media, or a ceremonial address with language carefully crafted to sound eloquent or even poetic. In these situations, the manuscript not only allows you to say precisely what you planned to say but also provides a written transcript of your remarks.

Some settings may call for manuscript speeches because of their formal nature. The president of the United States delivers many important speeches from manuscript, such as the State of the Union address. Commencement addresses are also typically delivered from manuscript. If you were called on to make formal remarks upon the installation of new officers at a civic or fraternal organization, a manuscript speech again may be most appropriate. Using a manuscript allows you to time your speech precisely, choose your words carefully, and decide exactly how to phrase your most important ideas. The underlying principles of good public speaking still apply to the manuscript speech: even though you may be reading from a manuscript, you should pay attention to audience reactions and be responsive to feedback. And it's important that you prepare a copy of the manuscript that you can read easily while speaking.[20]

Guidelines for Giving Manuscript Speeches Delivering a manuscript speech presents special challenges relating to eye contact, movement, the use of your voice, and flexibility. Here are some guidelines to follow:

- *Use a manuscript for the right reasons.* Use a manuscript when it is important to choose your words carefully and say exactly what you mean. Do not use it as a crutch to hide behind or as a way to manage your anxieties.
- *Use good oral style.* Even though you are speaking from a manuscript, you should still use language that is appropriate for oral presentation. This means that you will choose words and construct your sentences in ways that are easily spoken and more readily understood by listeners.
- *Practice extensively.* You need to know the speech well enough to look at the audience and get back to the manuscript without losing your place. If you're going to deliver the speech from a written manuscript, prepare a clean, double-spaced copy printed in an easily readable font (14, 16, or even 18 points). If you use a more advanced technology to deliver your manuscript speech, such as a laptop or teleprompter, be sure to practice your speech using that technology. And it's always a good idea to prepare a backup manuscript in case the technology fails.
- *Look for opportunities to move and gesture.* When you speak from a manuscript, you will normally be speaking from behind a podium. As a result, you may feel compelled to stand in one place or be tempted to lean on the podium. Resist these temptations. With planning and practice, you can deliver a manuscript speech and still move, use appropriate gestures, and engage your audience through eye contact and facial expressions.
- *Use your voice effectively.* Some speakers sound artificial or flat when delivering a manuscript speech. Their inflection may be less animated than normal, or they may sound monotonous or singsong, as if they were doing a poor job reading a poem. To speak effectively, concentrate on adding variety, color, and emphasis to your voice—just as you do when speaking extemporaneously. You may want to write delivery reminders on the manuscript itself, such as *Slow down*, *Pause for emphasis*, or *Repeat this*. You can also underline or boldface key words or phrases in the manuscript that you want to emphasize with your voice.
- *Maintain flexibility.* Rather than adapting to the moment or reacting to audience feedback, some speakers feel compelled to read from their manuscript word for word, never deviating, no matter what. Yet your manuscript need not be a straitjacket. Although the idea behind speaking from a manuscript may be to deliver the speech exactly as written, that does not mean you should *never* change a single word or improvise in response to audience

reactions. A manuscript speech *can* be changed if circumstances warrant it. You *can* (and often should) elaborate on a point with some spontaneous remarks. When you speak from manuscript, you *can* be flexible, remain connected to your listeners, and respond to their feedback.

The Memorized Speech

You will rarely find yourself in a situation where you will want to give a memorized speech. Some students participate in speaking contests, such as the American Legion Oratorical Contest, where they deliver memorized speeches. Some formal or ceremonial occasions may also call for a short memorized speech, such as a wedding toast or a brief tribute to a colleague at a retirement dinner. In extemporaneous speaking, you may want to memorize key parts of a longer speech, such as the attention-getter, the concluding appeal or challenge, or an especially important quotation or passage from a literary work. Generally, however, memorized speeches are a thing of the past—a form of delivery quite common 100 or 150 years ago but increasingly rare today.

Guidelines for Giving Memorized Speeches If you *do* find yourself in a situation where you want to speak from memory, keep these pointers in mind:

- *Stay focused on your specific purpose and the key ideas you want to convey.* When you memorize, you may be tempted to focus on the specific language you want to use. You may try to memorize your speech word for word, but don't forget that it's more important to remember your main ideas than your exact phrasing.
- *Speak in the moment.* When speakers deliver a speech from memory, they risk going on "automatic pilot." If this happens, the speech becomes a ritualistic performance rather than a communicative exchange with an audience. Remember: Even if speaking from memory, you should stay focused on your listeners and remember your specific purpose. If you lose yourself in your own thoughts and fail to speak in the moment, you may say all the words you planned, but you will not really be *communicating*.
- *Practice, practice, practice.* To be effective, all speakers must practice, regardless of their method of delivery. The memorized speech, however, may require even more practice. If your speech is long, you may want to read through it several times and practice it in sections before trying to memorize all of it. Practice sessions should be spaced out over time rather than crammed into a few hours to help you resist fatigue and commit the speech to your long-term memory.

Each method of delivery, as we have noted, has its benefits and potential liabilities. Table 1 compares the four styles of delivery.

Over time, you will discover your own preferences, and you may even develop a style of delivery that is uniquely your own. Experiment with different speaking styles. Discover the techniques that make you most comfortable and allow you to speak with confidence and conviction. Whatever style you choose, remember that the purpose of public speaking is to communicate with an audience. So however you deliver your speech, it's crucial that you remain connected to your listeners.

TABLE 1

Comparing Styles of Delivery

Extemporaneous

- Carefully prepared with thorough research, strategic organization of ideas, and practiced delivery
- Delivered from speaking notes, typically using a keyword outline
- Offers the opportunity to deliver the speech with flexibility, spontaneity, and directness
- Encourages audience adaptation
- Works best when the speaker cares deeply about the topic and can speak with passion and commitment

Impromptu

- Off-the-cuff, casual style that deemphasizes preparation
- Often called for in business, community, and classroom settings
- Delivery and organization are helped by informally jotting down notes as impromptu occasions arise
- Should be seen as an opportunity to practice and improve delivery skills

Manuscript

- Carefully prepared formal speeches, usually delivered precisely as written
- Sometimes delivered using a teleprompter, often delivered from behind a podium
- Typically used in important political speeches or on ceremonial occasions
- Allows for precise, eloquent language and control of speaking time
- Requires easily readable manuscript and extensive practice for a more natural style of speaking

Memorized

- Delivered from memory without the aid of speaking notes or manuscript
- Sometimes used by students in speaking contests or by citizens delivering toasts or other short tributes
- Requires extensive practice and concentration on key ideas

RESPONDING TO AUDIENCE QUESTIONS

Preview. *After you speak, you may be expected to entertain questions. The question-and-answer period is important because it allows you to interact informally with the audience, to provide additional information, to enhance your credibility, and to participate in a mutually beneficial dialogue.*

5 Anticipate audience questions and explain appropriate ways of responding to them.

Some speakers give little thought to the question-and-answer period that often follows a formal address. Instead, they focus all their attention on the preparation and delivery of the speech itself. Yet if you don't respond effectively to questions, you can damage your credibility and undermine the success of your speech. You don't want to give a good speech and then appear defensive, ignorant about related issues, or insensitive to your audience's concerns or questions about your speech.

The question-and-answer period is a potentially decisive moment in the audience's ultimate judgment of your speech. It gives your listeners a chance to ask for clarification or elaboration of the points that most interested them. As such, it provides a good barometer of how well your speech came across, as well as one last opportunity

The question-and-answer period following a speech is a time for respectful and mutually influential dialogue.

to address any confusion or skepticism left by the speech itself. You should listen carefully to the questions posed by your audience and strive to engage your listeners in a genuine dialogue.

Preparing for the Question-and-Answer Period

Although you cannot anticipate everything listeners may ask, you certainly can make some educated guesses about their potential questions and concerns. You should expect questions about any controversial issues you may bring up during your speech, and you should give some thought in advance to how you might respond to questions about those matters. Try to anticipate arguments that listeners may use to challenge your ideas, and make sure you have a good command of your sources. A questioner may well ask you to provide additional information or evidence for your claims, and you should be prepared to do so. Consider which parts of your speech may prove most difficult to understand, and be prepared to elaborate on those matters. Try to have additional examples, statistics, and other sorts of evidence "in reserve," ready to use in response to audience questions. When it seems that you *could* have said much more about your topic, you come across as more credible. The more you know about your topic, of course, the better prepared you will be to deal with questions.

Show Respect for Your Listeners   In addition to anticipating questions about the content of your speech, you should think about the sort of attitude you convey as you respond to questions. Will you seem defensive and closed-minded? Or will you strike your listeners as somebody who genuinely respects their opinions and wants to engage in a productive dialogue? Listeners occasionally will challenge you or openly disagree with you. Sometimes they may even do so in ways that you consider disrespectful, abrasive, or even rude. Although being challenged in this way can be unpleasant, you should keep your cool! Always try to respond with class and civility. As the speaker, *you* have a lot of control over the tone of the exchange, and you can refuse to respond in kind to a rude or disrespectful questioner. Should you get a hostile question, it is often best to respond only briefly, and then move on to the next question.

Conducting the Question-and-Answer Period

Decide where you will stand as you receive audience questions. One option is to remain behind the podium. This conveys a sense of formality, maintaining some distance between you and the audience. Another option is to stand at the side or in front of the podium, where you can interact more directly with the audience. Finally, in informal settings, you may sit on a table or a stool and engage in more of a "chat" with your audience. Any of these options may work well, depending on the situation, the audience's expectations, and your own preferences.

The following guidelines will help you conduct the question-and-answer period more effectively.

- *Listen carefully to each question.* If you can't hear a question very well, ask the questioner to stand and repeat it. Or move away from the podium and stand closer to the audience. As you listen, provide a few nonverbal cues, such as nodding your head, to let the questioner know that you understand the question. Generally, you should avoid interrupting audience members while they are asking their questions. Occasionally, however, an audience member will abuse the right to ask a question by making a long, perhaps even belligerent statement. In that case, you may intervene in the interest of allowing others to ask questions. Elizabeth Warren, a candidate for the United States Senate from Massachusetts, faced a hostile questioner who addressed her with a rude epithet. As supporters began to boo, Ms. Warren quieted them and calmly responded to the questioner before moving quickly on to another question. This exchange was recorded on YouTube.[21]

- *If appropriate, repeat each question so that everyone can hear it and keep track of what is happening.* In repeating the question, you may want to rephrase it because audience members sometimes ask poorly phrased or rambling questions.

- *Do not allow one person to dominate.* If many people raise their hands at once, make sure you call on people who have not already spoken. If someone who already asked a question raises his or her hand again, you might ask, "Is there anyone else who has a question?" Occasionally, a persistent questioner may try to engage you for an extended period of time. If that happens, you may invite that person to speak with you later, and then move on to the next question.

- *Do not try to fake your way through a response.* If you do not know the answer to a question or are not familiar with some topic raised by a questioner, it is best to admit it. Perhaps a questioner will ask if you have read a particular book or whether you know about some incident or event. Admitting that you do not know everything will not hurt your credibility. Indeed, we tend to be more suspicious of speakers who pretend to "know it all."

  If a listener poses a difficult question that you can't answer, you can always offer to investigate the matter and get back to the person. It is easy to get a listener's e-mail address following your talk—and then do your research and follow through with a thoughtful response. When you do this, you are showing respect for the listener. At the same time, you are learning more about your topic—and will be better prepared to answer questions the next time you speak.

- *Respect time limits.* Question-and-answer periods should not go on forever. Like speeches, they have time constraints. Sometimes you will be asked to speak briefly and leave plenty of time for audience questions. Other times, you will have only a little time left for interaction with the audience. Ask in advance what the audience expects or desires, and then follow through, limiting the question-and-answer period to the agreed-upon time.[22]

■ *Anticipate the possibility of no audience questions.* On occasion, you may conclude your speech and ask for questions but get no response from the audience. If you have used most of the time available for speaking and responding to questions, you may choose simply to thank them and take your seat. However, if time permits, you may also consider sharing some additional information or experiences that you didn't have the chance to address during your speech. Sometimes listeners need extra time to formulate good questions. By talking just a bit longer (but not too long), you give them the time to think. As a result, they may offer more thoughtful or interesting questions.

 Study and Review materials for this chapter are at **MyCommunicationLab**

SUMMARY

 Listen to the Audio Chapter Summary at **MyCommunicationLab**

Sounding Good versus Being Sound

1 Explain the ethical issues involved in delivering your speech.

■ Ethical delivery grows from a collaborative, transactional approach to public speaking:
  ■ Good speakers try never to distract the audience with their delivery.
  ■ They do all they can to promote audience comprehension and understanding.
  ■ They know that good, ethical delivery not only sounds good, it also grows from a solid foundation—a carefully constructed, thoughtfully reasoned, and well-supported speech.

Principles of Good Delivery

2 Describe the basic principles of effective delivery.

■ Underlying principles of good delivery apply across public speaking situations:
  ■ Understand the speaking context and audience expectations.
  ■ Establish eye contact with listeners.
  ■ Reinforce ideas through gestures, movement, and facial expressions.
  ■ Strive for an effective speaking voice.

Speaking Extemporaneously

3 Explain the advantages of delivering your speech extemporaneously.

■ For most public speaking situations, you will likely want to use the extemporaneous style, which involves meticulous preparation and is typically delivered from a keyword outline:
  ■ When you speak extemporaneously, you are encouraged to speak with flexibility, adapting to audience expectations and to the context.
  ■ As you speak, you are able to establish eye contact with audience members, use appropriate gestures, and make effective use of your voice.
  ■ Extemporaneous delivery also encourages you to speak with passion and conviction.
  ■ Practicing your speech aloud and seeking out opportunities to speak can help you develop an effective extemporaneous style of delivery.

Alternative Styles of Delivery

4 Compare and contrast different styles of delivery, listing the strengths and weaknesses of each.

■ Other styles of delivery may be appropriate on certain occasions, but each presents some special challenges:
  ■ Even impromptu speaking requires some preparation and organization.
  ■ Manuscript speaking demands a special focus on using good oral style, incorporating gestures and movement, and using your voice effectively.
  ■ Speaking from memory requires extensive practice; it challenges you to speak "in the moment" and to stay focused on the ideas you are conveying.

Responding to Audience Questions

5 Anticipate audience questions and explain appropriate ways of responding to them.

- The question-and-answer period is an important part of most formal speeches:
  - As you respond to audience questions, you have the chance to show listeners how well informed you are and how quickly you can think on your feet.
  - You can also demonstrate how carefully you listen, how open you are to others' ideas, and how honest you are in responding to difficult questions.
- Anticipate and prepare for possible questions from your audience, and do all you can to establish a climate of respectful and mutually beneficial dialogue.

QUESTIONS FOR REVIEW AND REFLECTION

Sounding Good versus Being Sound

1 Explain the ethical issues involved in delivering your speech.

1. Describe the difference between "sounding good" and "being sound."

Principles of Good Delivery

2 Describe the basic principles of effective delivery.

2. Your friend has to make an important presentation at a fund-raising event for the local Boys and Girls Club. He comes to you and asks you for advice on how to deliver his speech. What three things would you stress? Why are they important?
3. To what extent may cultural differences influence the way listeners respond to a speaker's delivery?
4. You have heard many people give speeches (classroom speeches, lectures, political speeches, after-dinner speeches, speeches at memorial services). Given your experience as an audience member, what things most annoy you about some speakers' delivery habits or styles? What delivery characteristics do you especially admire?

Speaking Extemporaneously

3 Explain the advantages of delivering a speech extemporaneously.

5. How would you describe extemporaneous delivery? Why is this style most appropriate in most public speaking situations?

6. Why is a keyword outline useful in delivering a speech? Can you think of any potential disadvantages to using such an outline? What might you do to minimize any potential disadvantages?

Alternative Styles of Delivery

4 Compare and contrast different styles of delivery, listing the strengths and weaknesses of each.

7. Some situations may call for a style of delivery other than extemporaneous. Describe each of these alternative delivery styles:
   a. Impromptu
   b. Manuscript
   c. Memorized
8. Compare and contrast the advantages and disadvantages of each.

Responding to Audience Questions

5 Anticipate audience questions and explain appropriate ways of responding to them.

9. You have given a speech, and now it is time for audience questions. How would you deal with each of these situations?
   a. An audience member is hostile.
   b. An audience member asks three questions in a row.
   c. Someone asks you a question and you do not know the answer.
   d. No one asks you a question.

✓ Study and Review the Flashcards at **MyCommunicationLab**

PHOTO CREDITS

Credits are listed in order of appearance.
Photo 1: Time & Life Pictures/Getty Images
Photo 2: © Realistic Reflections/Alamy

Photo 3: Franklin II/AP Photo
Photo 4: Darren Staples/AP Photo

GLOSSARY

ethical delivery Speaking authentically, with respect for one's listeners and concern for their well-being.

extemporaneous speaking The presentation of a thoroughly prepared speech using an abbreviated set of speaking notes, often in the form of a keyword outline.

impromptu speaking Casual, off-the-cuff delivery used when a speaker has little or no time for preparation.

manuscript speaking Presenting a speech from a prepared text, often in formal ceremonial settings.

memorized speech A prepared speech presented from memory, without the assistance of speaking notes.

monotone Use of the same vocal pitch without variation.

NOTES

1. Doris G. Yoakam, "Women's Introduction to the American Platform," *History and Criticism of American Public Address*, vol. 1, ed. William Norwood Brigance (New York: McGraw-Hill, 1943), 74–76.

2. See, as examples, Joe Ayres, "Speech Preparation Processes and Speech Apprehension," *Communication Education* 45 (1996): 228–35; Joe Ayres and Tim Hopf, *Coping with Speech Anxiety* (Norwood, NJ: Ablex, 1993); Ralph R. Behnke and Chris R. Sawyer, "Anticipatory Anxiety Patterns for Male and Female Speakers," *Communication Education* 49 (2000): 187–95; and Thomas Robinson II, "Communication Apprehension and the Basic Public Speaking Course: A National Survey of In-Class Treatment Techniques," *Communication Education* 46 (1997): 188–97.

3. See John T. Molloy, *Dress for Success* (New York: Warner Books, 1975), one of the first books to address the importance of appearance in the professional world. For a more recent work, see Molloy's *New Women's Dress for Success* (New York: Warner Books, 1996).

4. For a classic work on nonverbal communication, see Edward T. Hall, *The Silent Language* (Garden City, NY: Doubleday, 1959). More recent works include Edward T. Hall, *The Dance of Life* (New York: Doubleday, 1983); and Mark Knapp and Judith Hall, *Nonverbal Communication in Human Interaction* (Philadelphia: Harcourt Brace Jovanovich, 1997).

5. You can learn more about these differences by enrolling in a course in intercultural communication.

6. Virginia P. Richmond and James C. McCroskey, *Nonverbal Behavior in Interpersonal Relations*, 3rd ed. (Boston: Allyn & Bacon, 1995).

7. Nathan Bierma, "Hand Gestures May Expand, Express Unspoken Thoughts," *Chicago Tribune*, August 5, 2004, sec. 5, 2.

8. Paul Ekman, *Emotions Revealed: Recognizing Faces and Feelings to Improve Communications and Emotional Life* (New York: Holt, 2004), 84–112.

9. Knapp and Hall, *Nonverbal Communication in Human Interaction*, 58–74.

10. Albert Mehrabian, *Silent Messages: Implicit Communication of Emotions and Attitudes,* 2nd ed. (Belmont, CA: Wadsworth, 1982); Paul Ekman and Erika Rosenberg, *What the Face Reveals* (New York: Oxford University Press, 1998).

11. For an excellent collection of readings on all aspects of nonverbal communication, see Laura K. Guerrero, Joseph A. DeVito, and Michael L. Hecht, eds., *The Nonverbal Communication Reader: Classic and Contemporary Readings*, 2nd ed. (Prospect Heights, IL: Waveland Press, 1999).

12. PBS Home Programs, www.pbs.org/standard-deviantstv/transcript_public.html#rate (accessed March 13, 2012).

13. Richmond and McCroskey, *Nonverbal Behavior in Interpersonal Relations,* 68–70.

14. "A Powerful Tool: Your Voice," *Costa Connection,* June 2004, 9.

15. See, for example, Deborah Tannen, *You Just Don't Understand: Men and Women in Conversation* (New York: Quill, 2001). Tannen and other linguists have noted that men and women often exhibit different speech patterns, with women more inclined to use inflectional patterns that appear to seek validation from listeners. When using a rising inflection at the end of a statement (as in, "We really have to find a permanent home for the new shelter, don't you think?"), the speaker suggests an attitude of uncertainty. Especially if used often, this kind of vocal pattern can undermine a speaker's credibility.

16. For an extensive guide on vocal communication, see Jeffrey C. Hahner, Martin A. Sokoloff, and Sandra L. Salisch, *Speaking Clearly: Improving Voice and Diction*, 5th ed. (New York: McGraw-Hill, 1996).

17. John O. Greene, Marianne S. Sassi, Terri L. Malek-Madani, and Christopher N. Edwards, "Adult Acquisition of Message-Production Skills," *Communication Monographs* 64 (1997): 181–200. This article emphasizes the importance of practicing speech delivery.

18. See Herbert W. Hildebrandt and Walter W. Stevens, "Manuscript and Extemporaneous Modes of Delivery in Communicating Information," *Communication Monographs* 30 (1963): 369–72.

19. John F. Harris, *The Survivor: Bill Clinton in the White House* (New York: Random House, 2005), 10.

20. For one of the best guides on the techniques of manuscript speaking, see James C. Humes, *Talk Your Way to the Top* (New York: McGraw-Hill, 1980), 125–35.

21. Elizabeth Warren, www.youtube.com/watch?v=vQ3zt3YlNSU (accessed March 13, 2012).

22. For additional advice on managing question-and-answer sessions, see Thomas K. Mira, Speak Smart (New York: Random House, 1997), 115–23.

The Rhetorical Situation

This chapter introduces rhetoric as a situated discursive act within a larger public context of deliberation about controversial and pressing issues. It expands the notion of "public speaking" beyond the walls of the classroom to encompass one's larger social and historical environment. The rhetorical situation is divided into rhetorical background, which provides the broader historical and social context of the speech and its audience, and rhetorical foreground, which represents those aspects that stand out significantly to specific audiences in the immediate present. The rhetorical background includes components such as the public, public opinion, public memory, social knowledge, counterpublics, and the state; while the rhetorical foreground includes the components of exigence, audience, constraints, motive, practical judgment, and occasion. The most important of these concepts for rhetorical public speaking is attention to exigence, which focuses rhetorical public speaking on the shared problems that an audience wishes will be addressed in a timely manner.

In much of our daily lives, we take most of the aspects of our environment for granted. Like fish in water, we are rarely aware of the medium through which we are moving—and rightly so. If a fish was always dwelling on the water, it would undoubtedly have little energy left for eating and finding shelter. Our "critical" spirit usually arises whenever some **contingency**—some unexpected obstacle, perplexity, or problem—arises out of that environment, stands out concretely before us, and threatens to disrupt our lives in some way. The appearance of contingency makes us look critically at our previous choices in the assumption that the path we had earlier chosen may not, in fact, be the best way forward. According to John Dewey, this process of reflection, judgment, and valuation "takes place only when there is something the matter; when there is some trouble to be done away with, some need, lack, or privation to be made good, some conflict of tendencies to be resolved by means of changing conditions."[1]

Rhetoric is the creature of shared contingency. Thus, a **rhetorical situation** is one that occurs when public contingencies generate concern and uncertainty within a public audience and give force and effectiveness to persuasive discourse that encourages collective

---

[1]John Dewey, "Theory of Valuation," in *John Dewey: The Later Works*, vol. 13, ed. Jo Ann Boydston (Carbondale: Southern Illinois UP, 1988), 34.

action.[2] In rhetorical situations, contingencies are problematic aspects of a situation shared by a group of people who must collectively deliberate about which actions to take to resolve their common problem. Contingencies are experienced this way whenever people encounter shared obstacles without knowing for sure the nature of the problem or the way to proceed effectively. Aristotle summed this up best:

> The duty of rhetoric is to deal with such matters as we deliberate upon without arts or systems to guide us. . . . The subjects of our deliberation are such as seem to present us with alternative possibilities: about things that could not have been, and cannot now or in the future be, other than they are, nobody who takes them to be of this nature wastes his time in deliberation.[3]

Of course, not all contingencies require rhetorical resolution. Many contingencies already have pre-established means of resolution that are generally accepted as effective. In such cases, we have a **technical situation**, which exists when we confront problems with a proven discourse and method to guide us. A technical situation does not guarantee a positive result, but it does resolve the uncertainty about how to proceed. For example, a person diagnosed with cancer faces a contingency—his or her health might go this way or that way. But most people treat cancer by following the advice of established medical authorities and pursue some combination of chemotherapy or radiation treatment. Although they do not know their fate, they know the course to pursue. Yet the same applies for one who might choose alternative methods of healing, such as prayer or herbal medicine. What makes a situation "technical" is not the prudence of the response, but the assurance that one knows the way forward. A situation only becomes "rhetorical" when the way forward is in doubt and multiple parties engage in symbolic persuasion to motivate cooperative action.

There are two major components to the rhetorical situation. The first is the **rhetorical background**, which represents the larger environment that defines the historical and social context for any particular rhetorical event.

Knowing the rhetorical background provides a speaker with a broader perspective to more efficiently identify resources from which to draw when creating the speech and to better anticipate the possible long-term consequences after speaking. Public memory, social knowledge, and maxims are the basic building blocks of what holds any public together. This

---

[2]The literature on the rhetorical situation includes Lloyd Bitzer, "The Rhetorical Situation," *Philosophy and Rhetoric* 1 (1969), 13–14; Richard E. Vatz, "The Myth of the Rhetorical Situation," *Philosophy and Rhetoric* 6 (1973), 154–161; Barbara A. Biesecker, "Rethinking the Rhetorical Situation from Within the Thematic of Difference," *Philosophy and Rhetoric* 22 (1989), 110–130; Alan Brinton, "Situation in the Theory of Rhetoric," *Philosophy and Rhetoric* 14 (1981), 234–248; Scott Consigny, "Rhetoric and Its Situations," *Philosophy and Rhetoric* 7 (1974), 175–186; Kathleen Hall Jamieson, "Generic Constraints and the Rhetorical Situation," *Philosophy and Rhetoric* 6 (1968), 162–170; John H. Patton, "Causation and Creativity in Rhetorical Situations: Distinctions and Implications," *Quarterly Journal of Speech* 65 (1979), 36–55.
[3]Aristotle, *Rhetoric*, 1357a.

"public," then, forms the rhetorical background for any rhetorical speech act. In common interpretation, the public is thought to represent the total population of any national culture. However, a "public" is more than just a "mass." A **public** is a complex interaction of individuals that constitutes a political culture. Defined in a functional way, a public is a group of citizens who recognize each other's interests and have developed habits of settling disputes, coordinating actions, and addressing shared concerns through common communication media. Therefore, what ultimately characterizes the American public in general is common participation within a political process. A public, then, comes about when a group of strangers comes together for a common purpose that affects them all directly or indirectly. The **state** is thus distinct from the public insofar as it represents the instrument that the public uses to address consequences that it deems important enough to manage. In this sense, democracy is defined in terms of a state developed as a means for the public to regulate itself.[4]

However, if a state (in the name of one clearly defined public) formally excludes other publics, then **counterpublics** develop outside of and counter to the established mechanisms of the state. As Michael Warner writes, the discourse that constitutes a counterpublic "is not merely a different or alternative idiom, but one that in other contexts would be regarded with hostility, or with a sense of indecorousness."[5] Consequently, their rhetoric tends to be directed internally, toward group cohesion, rather than externally, at social persuasion. Yet the goal of a counterpublic is usually to form a genuine public able to express its will through legitimate public institutions and governing bodies. They exist as counterpublics only when this access is denied and they are forced to organize through alternative channels of communication. Once democratic reforms are initiated, they reclaim their status as one public among many.

The idea of the public influences rhetorical invention in three ways. First, rhetorical persuasion can produce visible and concrete changes in reality only if there is an audience capable of acting on its beliefs through organized channels. Speaking to people who had opted out of collective social life may produce persuasion, but those persuaded people will have few means of acting upon that new belief in collaboration with others—unless they have been persuaded to participate in the public. Second, a functional definition of the public encourages a speaker to think of people as something other than a stereotyped group of generic individuals who all think and feel the same thing. A functional definition of the public helps us realize that what binds people together is common interests in regulating social affairs and resolving common problems for the benefit of everyone *despite* their obvious differences. Third, it reminds a speaker that there is almost always a plurality of "publics" that exists within any more generic "public." It is a relatively straightforward matter to adapt to the specific group of people who might be arranged in a room. It is quite another to interpret that specific group as an amalgam of overlapping publics joined together in a common space.

---

[4]This notion of the public comes from John Dewey, *The Public and Its Problems* (Athens: Ohio University Press, 1927).
[5]Michael Warner, "Publics and Counterpublics," *Public Culture* 14, no. 1 (2002), 49–90 (86).

What is most important in constructing a speech with respect to knowledge of the public is the current state of public opinion. **Public opinion** thus represents the percentage of people who hold certain views to be true. Often we see this portrayed in "opinion polls" that represent public opinion with a series of bar graphs and pie charts. Although there are many flaws to such polls, not the least of which is the assumption that opinions are discrete entities that can be discerned by narrow questioning, they are nonetheless valuable to the extent that they show general trends of opinion.[6] Walter Lippmann defines public opinion this way:

> Those features of the world outside which have to do with the behavior of other human beings, insofar as that behavior crosses ours, is dependent upon us, or is interesting to us, we call roughly *public affairs*. The pictures inside the heads of these human beings, the pictures of themselves, of others, of their needs, purposes, and relationship, are their public opinions. Those pictures which are acted upon by groups of people, or by individuals acting in the name of groups, are Public Opinion with capital letters.[7]

The important thing about public opinion from a rhetorical perspective is the fact that it represents the collective *opinions* of a public audience. An **opinion** is a conscious personal belief expressed as a commitment to a certain matter of fact or value. We might have opinions that television is a wasteland, that our neighbor's yard is a mess, that America's foreign policy is too isolationist, or that gay marriage is a sin. Public opinion is thus valuable for rhetoric in that it provides a starting point to approach an audience. It lets rhetors know what truths they can take for granted, which ones they need to challenge, and which ones they need to promote.

The rhetorical background, as represented by the current state of the public and of public opinion, is important to consider, in order to provide a broader perspective on how to understand a specific speech act. One encounters extensive explanations of a speaker's rhetorical background in any biographical account of famous orators. Here, for instance, is biographer Douglas L. Wilson providing a bit of the rhetorical background to Abraham Lincoln's Gettysburg address:

> Lincoln had a theory about public opinion. He told a meeting of his fellow Republicans in 1856 that public opinion "always has a *'central idea'* from which all its minor thoughts radiate. That central idea in our political public opinion, at the beginning was, and until very recently has continued to be, 'the equality of all men.' And although it has always submitted patiently to whatever of inequality there seem to be as a matter of actual necessity, its constant working has been a steady progress toward the practical equality of all men." What had changed by 1856 was that the defenders of slavery had begun either to deny that this assertion from the Declaration of Independence was meant to apply to blacks, as Stephen A. Douglas would do in his debates with Lincoln, or to disparage it as a "self-evident lie." Lincoln had discovered in his campaigning

---

[6] For an exploration of public opinion, see Carroll J. Glynn, Susan Herbst, Garrett O'Keefe, and Robert Shapiro, *Public Opinion* (Boulder, CO: Westview Press, 1999).

[7] Walter Lippmann, *Public Opinion* (New York: Simon & Schuster, 1922), 18.

in the 1850s, if not previously, that the declarations theme of the equality of all men had an especially powerful effect on ordinary citizens, appealing, it would seem, to something deeper than parties or policies, something, perhaps, having to do with ordinary people's sense of themselves.[8]

As this account demonstrates, considering the rhetorical background of any particular rhetorical situation provides a speaker added resources from which to draw upon, namely, the general values, maxims, conventions, memories, attitudes, and aspirations that hold together publics over time and provide good reasons for particular judgments, in this case embodied in the language of the Declaration of Independence. Without acknowledging the rhetorical background, a speaker will have tunnel vision that risks either ignoring or even offending the core beliefs of an audience, thereby making even the most well-defended position fall flat.

By contrast, the **rhetorical foreground** represents the specific and salient aspects of a common situation as it affects or interests some audience at a particular moment in time, including the motives of the audience itself. The rhetorical foreground represents those aspects of a situation that "stand out" from the background. These aspects include not only the problem or contingency at hand, but also the components of the specific speech situation in its relative immediacy. Expanding on the model initially posed by Lloyd Bitzer, these include exigence, audience, constraints, motive, practical judgment, and occasion. Although each of these aspects emerges out of the rhetorical background, the nature of the contingency gives each a distinct individuality that demands our focused attention. Importantly, every rhetorical speech begins with an understanding of the rhetorical situation; it does not begin with the desires or ideas of the speaker. What the speaker initially wants to say is merely a stimulus to learn about a specific rhetorical situation. But it is knowledge and acquaintance with the situation that is the ground on which any worthwhile speech is constructed.

Discussion: Consider the relationships between publics, public opinion, and the state in a democracy. In theory, the actions of a democratic state are guided by the dominant public opinion expressed by various publics about matters of public concern. In this system, rhetoric becomes the way that public opinion is formed during large-scale rhetorical situations. In your experience, do you feel that the democratic governance actually works this way? If so, when have you actually felt that your opinion (outside of the act of voting) has actually influenced the actions of a state?

EXIGENCE

What dominates the foreground of any rhetorical situation is the presence of an exigence that requires an act of persuasion to resolve. An **exigence**, in a general sense, is any outstanding aspect of our environment that makes us feel a combination of *concern*, *uncertainty*, and *urgency*. Not all exigencies are rhetorical. During our everyday lives, we encounter numerous exigencies, both large and small, that

---

[8]Douglas L. Wilson, *Lincoln's Sword: The Presidency and the Power of Words* (New York: Alfred A. Knopf, 2007), 202.

require on exertion of energy to deal with and possibly overcome but that may not call out for any particular rhetorical response. For instance, you may have woken up too late to get to work on time, you might have forgotten your spouse's anniversary, you may be at risk of losing your home to foreclosure, or you may be anxious about an oncoming hurricane. In each of these situations, you are concerned because they each have the possibility of impacting your life negatively or positively, you are uncertain because you are not sure what to do about it, and you feel a sense of urgency because you must act soon if you are to change the outcome. But you may be able to deal with these situations by non-rhetorical action, such as not taking a shower and running red lights to get work on time, buying an extra-special gift for your spouse and pretending it is a surprise, taking out a loan to cover a mortgage payment to avoid foreclosure, or packing things in a car and driving north, out of the hurricane's path.

A specifically *rhetorical* exigence is more than just the existence of a pressing problem; a **rhetorical exigence** must be an issue that generates concern and uncertainty for some organized or semi-organized group that can be resolved, in whole or in part, by persuading an audience to act in a way that is actually capable of addressing the situation. For instance, each of the four examples just given can become rhetorical under certain circumstances. If you discover that lateness to work is a constant problem in the office due to more structural problems such as pervasive road construction or cuts to public transportation, you can make a case to management of the need for flex time. If you decide that you forgot the anniversary because both you and your spouse have been working too many hours and not seeing each other enough, you can persuade your spouse that you should both quit your jobs and hitchhike around Europe for year. If your home foreclosure is a result of what you think to be a systematic policy of unethical loan practices, you can form a network with other homeowners to petition Congress to alter financial policy. And if you have no resources with which to use to escape the hurricane, you can make public demands that the state provide adequate shelter for you and your family. In each of these cases, what makes the situation rhetorical is a practical problem, or contingency, experienced by a large number of people, a shared desire to address that problem, and a realization that certain significant parties need to be persuaded to act in a certain way in order to solve it.

The concept of a rhetorical exigence can be difficult to grasp because there is often no agreement about the nature or even the existence of a particular problem. Indeed, convincing people that there *is* an exigence is often one of the most significant challenges to any speaker. Consequently, it is helpful to distinguish between two kinds of rhetorical exigence relative to the different nature of consensus and uncertainty. With a **contested exigence**, not everyone agrees that a problem exists. Sometimes people disagree whether certain things exist or not, such as whether or not Saddam Hussein of Iraq actually possessed weapons of mass destruction that threatened the United States. Others acknowledge the existence of things but question whether we should consider them a problem, such as those who might argue that even if Hussein did possess such weapons, he would never use them. In these cases, speakers have to work to persuade people of the nature of the exigence itself before ever getting to proposing a solution. By contrast, an **uncontested exigence** is one that everyone acknowledges to be a pressing problem that demands to be addressed; the issue is not to acknowledge the problem but to come up with an adequate solution. In such cases, a speaker concentrates on advocating some solutions over others, such as the preference for sanctions over war or for war instead of appeasement.

Patrick Henry: "Suffer not yourselves to be betrayed with a kiss."

Following the Boston Tea Party of December 16, 1773, the British Parliament passed a series of acts intended to suppress the rebellion in Massachusetts. In May of 1774, General Thomas Gage arrived in Boston with four regiments of British troops. For the next two years, uncertainty spread as to whether Britain was preparing for a full-scale war on the colonies or whether tensions could be resolved through political petition and deliberation. When the Virginia Convention met in 1775, many delegates clung to the hope that the British government would rely on sensible reasoning instead of force and therefore remained skeptical that a pending war was a genuine exigence that required urgent action.

However, Patrick Henry firmly believed that war was imminent, and in his famous speech "Liberty or Death," he set out to resolve any doubt about the reality of the contested exigence even while acknowledging the limits of his own knowledge. For Henry, one had to act on the best available knowledge to avoid disastrous consequences, and his knowledge led him to the conclusion that the British were about to attack. To convince more skeptical "gentlemen," he attempted to undermine the feeling of "solace" that many American diplomats felt when their petition of grievances to the British Crown was given a friendly reception. But Henry then points to the contrary evidence that shows how, despite conciliatory remarks by the British, they were, in fact, preparing for war. He continues:

> Is it that insidious smile with which our petition has been lately received? Trust it not, sir; it will prove a snare to your feet. Suffer not yourselves to be betrayed with a kiss. Ask yourselves how this gracious reception of our petition comports with these warlike preparations which cover our waters and darken our land. Are fleets and armies necessary to a work of love and reconciliation? Have we shown ourselves so unwilling to be reconciled that force must be called in to win back our love? Let us not deceive ourselves, sir. These are the implements of war and subjugation—the last arguments to which kings resort. I ask gentlemen, sir, what means this martial array, if its purpose be not to force us to submission? Can gentlemen assign any other possible motives for it? Has Great Britain any enemy, in this quarter of the world, to call for all this accumulation of navies and armies? No, sir, she has none. They are meant for us; they can be meant for no other. They are sent over to bind and rivet upon us those chains which the British ministry has been so long forging.[9]

Henry's powerful oral performance combined attention to factual detail with passionate argumentation that accused those not willing to recognize the "reality" of

---

[9]Patrick Henry, available from <http://www.bartleby.com/268/8/13.html> (accessed 6 September 2012).

being dupes, cowards, and ultimately slaves. With Thomas Jefferson and George Washington both in attendance, the result of his speech was said to be a unified cheer, "Give me liberty or give me death!" The contested exigence was contested no more and the audience had become a unified public body prepared to act in the face of uncertainty. [10]

Discussion: One way of thinking about a rhetorical situation is to consider situations in which you simply have a problem that forces you to call upon reluctant others for help. Oftentimes, then, one of the obstacles to effective rhetorical action is the stubbornness that comes from the reluctance to ask for that help. Do you think that this fear of appearing "weak" is one of the obstacles to effective rhetorical action in a problematic situation?

AUDIENCE

In its most general sense, an audience represents any person, or group of people, who hears, reads, or witnesses any communicative event. However, there are always multiple audiences to consider in any speech act, some existing in other places, some existing at other times. In an age of reality television, for instance, navigating multiple audiences simultaneously has become something of an art form. One contestant, for instance, might conspire with a second with the pretense of knocking a third out of the game. Yet the first one does this with the knowledge that the second contestant will tell a fourth contestant (at a later time) about their conversation, and therefore influence the actions of the fourth contestant from a distance. Meanwhile, all of the contestants are well aware of the television audience, with individuals watching simultaneously (in different places) all across the country. And many of them hope that their performance will be so engaging that it will persuade other television producers (in a different place at a later time) to cast them for exciting roles once their current show has ended. Only those unfamiliar with the genre interpret the on-screen characters to be the "real" audience; similarly, only those unfamiliar with rhetoric believe that an audience consists only of those immediately listening to a speech at a particular place and time.

We can break down audience into three categories: the primary audience, secondary audience, and the target audience. The **primary audience** for rhetorical public speaking consists of those people actually assembled together to hear the speech as it is delivered in person by the speaker—for instance, the delegates at the Virginia convention for Patrick Henry. **Secondary audiences** represent all those people who encounter the speech either through some another media or secondhand through the spoken word of another person; in the case of Henry's speech, this would include not only the King of England and the American colonists but also readers of this chapter. Finally, **target audiences** are those individuals or groups in either the primary or secondary audiences who are able to be persuaded and are capable of acting in such a way to help resolve the exigence. For Henry, the

---

[10]For more on Henry's speech, see Judy Hample, "The Textual and Cultural Authenticity of Patrick Henry's 'Liberty or Death' Speech," *Quarterly Journal of Speech* 63, no. 3 (1977), 298–310.

target audiences included not only the Virginia delegates but also the opinion leaders throughout the colonies who would read his words as they were reprinted and distributed through the printing press. For he understood that even if the Virginia delegation voted to support a war policy, actually raising an army would require the full support of the majority of the property-owning class, those who held all of the resources necessary for an extended campaign.

As indicated by the discussion on speeches of advocacy, the relationship between the primary and secondary audiences is actually very significant. Even though secondary audiences may only receive transcripts of the speech (as we do with Henry), knowing that his actual speech brought the entire delegation to its feet chanting "give me liberty or give me death!" has a direct impact on how we receive and interpret his words. We are naturally drawn to read speeches that we know had a very powerful effect on the primary audience, for we interpret their reaction as we do the reviews of a movie critic. Their excitement is a sign to us that the speech contains something significant, particularly when the crowd in attendance is of a significant size. Bringing thousands of people to their feet, as Martin Luther King Jr. did on the Washington Mall with his "I have a dream" speech, draws the attention of the news media and these days becomes a candidate for a viral video or an e-mail distribution campaign. Consequently, even if the primary audience has only minimal significance as a target audience (as many audiences do during presidential campaigns in which candidates deliver major policy addresses in front of select organizations), they cannot be ignored. With only rare exceptions (and those usually for unflattering reasons), nobody wants to read a speech that was a complete dud during its actual delivery. Almost any successful public speech must therefore satisfy the expectations and desires of the primary audience even if the target audience is a secondary audience watching from a distance.

Maria Stewart: "Let us make a mighty effort and arise!"

Shockingly, before September 1832, no African-American woman had ever delivered a "public" lecture in the sense of being authorized by the state. They were a **marginalized** group, denied access to the **public sphere** by the norms of convention and the **social knowledge** concerning matters of race and gender. So it must have been a surprise to her diverse audience, including men and women, both black and white, when Maria Stewart stood up in Boston's Franklin Hall to give a speech (despite the fact that the meeting was being sponsored by the women of the African-American Female Intelligence Society!). What made her speech even more provocative is that she spoke directly to the black women in her audience, targeting them (rather than men) as the primary agents of social change because of their power as mothers to influence and educate their children. Her strategy of speaking directly to women, in their roles as mothers, is announced early on in the speech. Challenging their sense of despair and resignation, she appeals to them:

> Oh, do not say you cannot make anything of your children; but say, with the help and assistance of God, we will try. Perhaps you will say that you cannot send them to high schools and academies. You can have them taught in the first rudiments of useful knowledge, and then you can have private teachers,

who will instruct them in the higher branches. It is of no use for us to sit with our hands folded, hanging our heads like bulrushes lamenting our wretched condition; but let us make a mighty effort and arise...Did the pilgrims, when they first landed on these shores, quietly compose themselves, and say, "The Britons have all the money and all the power, and we must continue their servants forever?" Did they sigh and say, "Our lot is hard; the Indians own the soil, and we cannot cultivate it?" No, they first made powerful efforts to raise themselves. And, my brethren have you made a powerful effort? Have you prayed the legislature for mercy's sake to grant you all the rights and privileges of free citizens, that your daughters may rise to that degree of respectability which true merit deserves, and your sons above the servile situations which most of them fill?[11]

The combination of criticism, challenge, and plea is indicative of Stewart's belief that her audience had the capability to change and the power to alter the situation for the better.[12] The fact of her speaking at all at this event, and with such eloquence and passion, probably had a significant impact on her primary audience, including both men and women. Yet her message remained powerful to secondary audiences who heard of it in print or by word of mouth, particularly because of her use of historical analogy that made the motive of former slaves identical with the motive of the pilgrims and the founders of the nation. In her speech, she addresses her target audience of African-American women and tells them, in effect, that they are the new founders of a new nation based in equality rather than in servitude.

Discussion: The easiest way to understand the importance of identifying the right target audience is to consider moments of failure. Oftentimes in comedy, part of the humor comes from cases of mistaken identity in which one person targets another for persuasion or manipulation only to find out that it is the wrong person. Can you think of any movie plots that failed in identifying target audiences for part of the narrative? And have you ever experienced similar failures in your own professional life?

CONSTRAINTS

Almost nothing that we do in life happens without resistance. Only in the realm of fantasy or dream does a wish become a reality by a word and a snap of the fingers. And even our most simple tasks often require an exertion of physical and mental effort, as we have all experienced on mornings when we simply cannot get out of bed for one reason or another. Every single reason why we cannot accomplish a task is a **constraint**, which represents any counterforce that stands between us and the attainment of our interests. Sometimes these constraints are physical things,

---

[11]Maria Stewart, "Speech at Boston's Franklin Hall." Available at <http://sankofareadinggroup .blogspot.com/2011/02/maria-stewart.html> (accessed 15 July 2012).
[12]For more on Maria Stewart's role in abolitionism, see Jacquiline Bacon, "'God and a Woman': Women Abolitionists, Biblical Authority, and Social Activism," *Journal of Communication & Religion* 22, no. 1 (1999), 1–39.

such as when the car doesn't start or when we hit traffic on the road. Sometimes they are emotional things, such as when we dislike our job so much that it is hard to perform up to our potential. And sometimes they are other people, such as when our co-workers resist our suggestions about how to streamline an office's business practices. Anything that restrains or inhibits movement toward a desired end functions as a constraint.

In rhetoric, constraints are defined in relationship to interests or ends that require rhetorical persuasion to achieve. **Rhetorical constraints** are those obstacles that must be overcome in order to facilitate both the persuasive and practical effects desired by the speaker. By "persuasive" effects, we mean those effects that make people think and act differently than they did before the speech. Constraints relating to persuasive effects are thus called **internal constraints**, referring to the beliefs, attitudes, and values of an audience that must be changed if persuasion is to occur. For example, convincing a population to support a tax on junk foods to cut down on child obesity may require challenging the **belief** that obesity is not a social problem, changing the pervading attitude of resisting higher taxes, and dissociating the eating of junk food from the value of personal choice and freedom. Unless these internal constraints can be modified, they will lead to the rejection of the proposal. However, a public speaker who actually desires to make a lasting change in actual conditions must also consider **external constraints**, which are the people, objects, processes, and events that may physically obstruct any productive action even if persuasion of an audience has occurred. A *person* acting as a constraint is someone who cannot be persuaded and who possesses the power to obstruct your goal, such as the governor who threatens a veto of your bill. An *object* is defined here as any tangible and enduring thing that tends to resist change while having constant influence on an environment, such as the presence of vending machines in schools (a "physical" object) or the laws that give schools financial incentives to place them in schools (a "legal" object). An *event* that is a constraint is a tangible but ephemeral thing that occurs at a specific point and time and has a distinct beginning and end, such as a sudden downturn in the economy that makes new taxes unpopular. Last, a *process* represents a sequence of events that must be followed in order to bring something to conclusion. As a constraint, such a process might be a lengthy and burdensome petition process by which any changes in tax laws require years of persistent effort.

Any of these external constraints may impede successful social action even *after* an audience has been persuaded to act. Consequently, public speakers who fail to account for external constraints may recommend a course of action, only to find it to be impossible to implement later, thereby wasting everyone's time and energy. Successful speakers should always consider all possible constraints before creating and delivering rhetorical discourse. Ignoring constraints often ruins any possibility of instigating effective social action. On the one hand, if external constraints are ignored, a speaker risks appearing ignorant about the "realities" of the situation. On the other hand, ignoring internal constraints is the common flaw of all "technical" discourse believing that the only things needed for persuasion are accurate facts and reasonable solutions. The most effective speaker combines elements of both types of discourse by adapting his or her language to both types of constraints.

Gen. George S. Patton: "You are not all going to die."

If any one governmental institution understands the logic of constraints, external and internal, it is the military. In wartime, for instance, there is an obvious external constraint to attaining one's goal—the enemy. But there are also significant internal constraints that have to do with "morale," meaning the state of mind of the soldiers. Perhaps the most famous administrative speech ever given during World War II was by Gen. George S. Patton to the U.S. 3rd Army on June 5, 1944, the day before D-Day. On June 6, U.S. forces would storm the heavily defended beaches of Normandy and begin the ground assault against Germany. Knowing that many of the soldiers would be facing battle for the first time and had already heard stories about the ferocity of the battle-hardened German military, Patton knew he had to confront their fears head-on and provide them the courage and motivation to fight as a team despite the horrors around them. He said:

> Men, this stuff some sources sling around about America wanting to stay out of the war and not wanting to fight is a lot of baloney! Americans love to fight, traditionally. All real Americans love the sting and clash of battle. America loves a winner. America will not tolerate a loser. Americans despise a coward; Americans play to win. That's why America has never lost and never will lose a war.
>
> You are not all going to die. Only two percent of you, right here today, would be killed in a major battle. Death must not be feared. Death, in time, comes to all of us. And every man is scared in his first action. If he says he's not, he's a goddamn liar. Some men are cowards, yes, but they fight just the same, or get the hell slammed out of them. The real hero is the man who fights even though he's scared. Some get over their fright in a minute, under fire; others take an hour; for some it takes days; but a real man will never let the fear of death overpower his honour, his sense of duty, to his country and to his manhood.[13]

Given the fact that he was giving an administrative speech, Patton could have simply told the soldiers that they had no choice but to follow orders or else be court-martialed. However, administrative speaking is not simply about laying down the law; it is about justifying the law and motivating the audience to embrace it by helping them overcome their internal constraints. The soldiers had no choice but to fight, but Patton gives them the motive to fight as a team with honor and duty, and therefore hopefully survive, or to give in to the internal constraint of fear and be killed more easily by the external constraints resisting their invasion.

Discussion: Consider the notion of providing universal health care for all Americans. What are the external and internal constraints to instituting such a policy? And what is the relationship between these two types of constraints? How is it sometimes difficult to tell the difference between an internal and external constraint in such complicated matters of policy?

---

[13]<http://www.famousquotes.me.uk/speeches/General_George_Patton/index.htm.>

MOTIVE

As indicated by the discussion of internal constraints, the psychological state of the audience is a crucial component of a rhetorical situation. Following Burke, we can describe this psychological state as a structure of motives. A **motive** refers to any conscious psychological or physiological incitement to action within a particular situation.[14] A motive is not to be confused with a mere "wish," however. Wishes merely exist in the abstract realm of fantasy and need not relate to anything actual; a motive only exists within a situation in which successful attainment of a goal is possible. For instance, a child may wish to fly to Mars and take great pleasure in imagining a fantastic voyage; this wish only becomes a motive when it stimulates the child to earn a degree in astrophysics while training to be a pilot. In other words, the number of wishes we might have at any one time is nearly infinite, which of course means they are all equally powerless to alter our actual behavior at any one time. By contrast, motives only occur in particular situations when a single desire or goal moves us to action and judgment.

The study of rhetoric in many ways is equivalent to the study of how to influence human motivation through conscious symbolic appeals. For Aristotle, audiences were motivated by respect for the speaker (**ethos**), by emotional affection or dislike (**pathos**), and by the strength of reason and evidence (**logos**). This study of motivation then took a "scientific" leap during the Age of Enlightenment when the new study of psychology was used to explain the phenomenon of persuasion. Rhetorician George Campbell, for example, wrote that the function of rhetoric is "to enlighten the Understanding, to please the Imagination, to move the Passions, or to influence the Will." The novelty behind this definition was the application of the recently discovered mental "faculties" to the study of rhetoric. Much like different departments within a modern corporation, these faculties were explained as existing in our minds as discrete units, each with its own unique process and function. So when we wanted to think about ideas, we called on the Understanding (sometimes called Thought or Reason); when we felt like stimulating our bodies, we sought out the Passions (sometimes called Emotions or Feeling); when we pondered the unknown, we appealed to the Imagination; and when we wanted to act, we rallied the Will. The most successful rhetoric engaged all the faculties at once. We argued logic to the Understanding, aroused the Passions through visual examples, used fantastic possibilities to excite the Imagination, and moved the Will through imperatives to action.

Today, we tend not to think in terms of discrete "faculties" that exist as separate entities in our minds. We simply talk about having beliefs, feelings, emotions, habits, desires, and values. However, the basic model of crafting language that is imaginative, thoughtful, and passionate in order to redirect human motivation remains effectively the same. The specific concern for rhetoric is those motives that arise in the context of the exigence as a means of resolving the situation in accordance with the needs and desires of an audience. The following concepts are therefore useful in

---

[14]For an explanation of Burke's theory of motive, see Andrew King, "Motive," *American Communication Journal* 1, no. 3 (1998).

understanding the structure of motivation of an audience. Each of these components represent one of three things for the speaker: (a) *a preexisting resource* to draw upon in support of judgments, (b) *a constraint* to overcome because its presence in the audience obstructs a course of action, or (c) *a possibility* to create as a means to encourage people to think, feel, or act a certain way as a means to resolve a situation.

1. **Belief:** A belief is a statement of fact on which a person is prepared to act. Beliefs can be stated as propositions, such as "the earth goes around the sun" or "all men are created equal" or "cutting taxes increases economic growth" or "people shouldn't smoke." Each of these beliefs only acts *as* a belief for a person if he or she actually acts in accordance with its content. When someone says one thing but does another, we do not attribute belief but accuse that person of hypocrisy. Rhetorically, beliefs are the building blocks of judgments, for they provide a concrete place to stand so that we know we are acting on a firm basis of understanding of reality (e.g., "Clean water is an essential component of a healthy nation.")

2. **Value:** A value is an abstract ideal quality that guides our behavior across a variety of situations. Whereas beliefs are propositions, values are usually stated as single virtue terms, such as "love" or "justice" or "liberty" or "equality." A value is a "quality" because it is something that we feel to be present in certain situations and that we treasure and wish to preserve for as long as possible. Usually values are things that almost everybody agrees are valuable; contention arises only in the clash between two competing values and their relative importance. "Love" and "justice" are in competition when a parent must decide whether to turn in a child who has committed a crime, and "liberty" and "equality" are in competition in economic debates that weigh the balance between the unregulated pursuit of individual wealth and the regulated distribution of resources to all. Rhetorically, values guide the speaker by investing the speech with an overall quality that resonates with the treasured values of the audience (e.g., "Our rivers should be as free and pure as the day the *Mayflower* landed.")

3. **Feeling:** A feeling is a sensory response to some environmental stimulation or physical state. Feelings make up the substance of our perceptual world, and represent the basic elements that physically connect us with the world around us. However, each audience comes to a situation being acquainted with a unique set of feelings based on that audience's particular experiences in an environment. For instance, people who live in a busy metropolis know the feelings associated with traffic, crowds, skyscrapers, construction, and city parks, whereas those who live in a rural farming community know the feelings associated with quiet landscapes, isolation, farmhouses, animals, and swaying fields of grain. Rhetorically, the familiar feelings (both negative and positive) of an audience can be effectively re-activated through language by calling forth familiar senses and by incorporating them into metaphor (e.g., "Many of us here remember the first time we walked with our bare feet through the cool, rocky streams during a sultry August day.")

4. **Emotion:** An emotion is a dramatized feeling that attracts or repels us to certain objects because of their specific character and qualities. An emotion is a

kind of "feeling" because it is usually a reaction to sense perception and also is attached to feelings of pleasure or pain; but it is a "dramatized" feeling because emotions carry with them narrative elements in which we play out scenarios in our minds of what will happen. It is the difference between simply perceiving the color red (as in feeling) and seeing a blinking red warning light on a console (as in emotion). Our emotional response to the red light is based on our narrative sense of whether the light signifies a danger that brings about a state of fear and urgency. Consequently, emotions are always related in some form or another to the "things" that surround us and are never simply "in our heads." Rhetorically, emotions are powerful tools to direct people toward or away from certain actions or judgments by connecting them to the people, objects, and events that bring about powerful emotions (e.g., "The month after a chemical spill in a nearby town, a thousand dead, stinking fish washed ashore and the water was covered with a frothy yellow scum.")

Despite their incredible variety, all emotions can be characterized by two things—orientation and salience. An **orientation** represents how we stand in relationship to a thing, whether we are attracted to (+) or repulsed by (–) it. A *neutral* orientation in which we have no stance thus represents the absence of emotion. For instance, I might have a positive orientation toward my family, a negative orientation to the fire ants in my back yard, and a neutral orientation to my neighbor's mailbox. **Salience** represents how strongly this emotion is felt within a particular situation. When I go on a long business trip I might miss my family terribly (high salience), whereas I like to look at the picture of my family during my lunch break at work (low salience).[15]

5. **Habit:** A habit is a learned sequence of behavior in which mental and physical energies work relatively effortlessly together to accomplish a familiar task. Habits are what Aristotle called "second nature" because once acquired they take almost the same form as instinct, guiding our thoughts and actions in familiar groups without the requirement of deliberative choice or reflective thought. Habits therefore include more than simply ordinary tasks such as tying shoes or waking up early or cleaning up after oneself; they also include complex tasks such as writing depositions and painting landscapes and fly fishing. Any type of group, no matter how large or small, has common goals and common activities and shares a core group of habits. There are habits of being a carpenter, an engineer, a bachelor, or a U.S. citizen. Rhetorically, habits can be problems ("we are careless with our waterways"), resources ("let us apply the habits of housekeeping to our rivers"), or goals ("we need good habits of water conservation").

6. **Desire:** A desire is a concrete energetic ideal that propels people to action in pursuit of some value or pleasure. Desires are products of either *imagination*

---

[15]For an exploration of the situational characteristic of emotional response, see Phoebe C. Ellsworth, "Some Reasons to Expect Universal Antecedents of Emotion," *The Nature of Emotion: Fundamental Questions,* ed. Paul Ekman and Richard J. Davidson (Oxford, UK: Oxford University Press, 1994), 150–154.

or *memory*—imagination when they are products of novel creations of the mind and memory when they are recollections of the past that a person aspires to re-experience. Like a motive, a desire is not simply a "wish" that exists in an ideal and impossible realm of fantasy; it is something that we invest energy in seeking and that guides our decisions in actual situations of choice. Our desires are based on how clearly we can envision a future state of affairs and how powerful the subsequently produced emotions are. Rhetorically, similar to habits, desires can be problems ("We dream too much of big houses and fast cars"), resources ("Don't you all want to bring your kids to the same clean streams?"), or created products ("Let us imagine a whole nation of clean waterways where humans and nature care for one another.")

The motives of the audience are thus a product of how all of these components interact. An audience enters into a situation holding to a specific set of beliefs; treasuring certain values over others; being acquainted with a general sphere of feelings; associating specific emotions with types of events, objects, and people; having developed a nexus of habits that helps them deal with their environment; and harboring certain desires for which they will sacrifice time and energy to attain. A speaker must then decide which of these things to draw from in support of the position, which represent problems that prevent an audience from attaining their goals, and which need to be created in an audience in order for them to accomplish something new.

Lucy Stone: "I have been a disappointed woman."

Because speeches of advocacy have as one of their primary functions the capacity to mobilize a group around a common cause, many of the most influential of these types of speeches have occurred at conventions organized for this explicit purpose. One of these was the National Women's Rights Convention first held in 1850, initiated in part by American suffragist and abolitionist Lucy Stone. As the first woman from Massachusetts to earn a college degree in 1847, Stone dedicated her life to the cause of women's rights so that more women could challenge the often oppressive social norms that kept women in their "place"—the home. Organization of the convention was thus designed to unify the movement and give individual women a collective voice and purpose. At the convention in Cincinnati, Ohio, in 1855, she delivered one of her most famous speeches of advocacy that addressed the motives of her audience:

> The last speaker alluded to this movement as being that of a few disappointed women. From the first years to which my memory stretches, I have been a disappointed woman. When, with my brothers, I reached forth after the sources of knowledge, I was reproved with "It isn't fit for you; it doesn't belong to women." Then there was but one college in the world where women were admitted, and that was in Brazil. I would have found my way there, but by the time I was prepared to go, one was opened in the young state of Ohio—the first in the United States where women and Negroes could enjoy opportunities with white men. I was disappointed when I came to seek a profession worthy of an immortal being—every employment was close to me, except that of the

teacher, the seamstress, and the housekeeper. In education, in marriage, in religion, in everything, disappointment is the lot of woman. It shall be the business of my life to deepen this disappointment in every woman's heart until she bows down to it no longer. I wish that women, instead of being walking showcases, instead of begging of their fathers and brothers the latest and gayest new bonnet, would ask them of their rights.[16]

As Stone appeals to the motive of the audience, one can also see demonstrated here three common characteristics of speeches of advocacy. First, Stone clearly identifies her audience as fellow women who share her experience. Second, she attempts to motivate this audience by rousing emotions of dissatisfaction and frustration with their situation and also their own failure to act. Last, she points out exactly what she wants them to do—demand their rights rather than ask for a new bonnet. At each point, she touches on aspects of motive. Challenging belief: "It isn't fit for you; it doesn't belong to women." Praising values: courage, integrity, honesty. Arousing emotion: disappointment. Cultivating habits: assertiveness instead of passivity. And arousing desire: ask for your rights. Only by transforming the motives of the audience is change possible.

Discussion: Think of a situation of a master and slave relationship, in which two individuals with two competing motivations are nonetheless acting together despite their differences. How do we account for this apparent "cooperation" by understanding each person's motives in terms of belief, value, feeling, emotion, habit, and desire? What would have to change in the situation for cooperation to come to an end?

PRACTICAL JUDGMENT

Once an exigence becomes universally recognized, the immediate question becomes "What do we do?" The answer to this question always involves a **practical judgment**, which is the act of defining a particular person, object, or event for the purposes of making a practical decision. In other words, practical judgment tells us both *what things are* and *what we should do about them.* The mere giving of commands—such as "Go!" or "Halt!—is therefore *not* a practical judgment because it does not satisfy the first criterion of the definition. A practical judgment demands action but only after an act of cognition that explains to our minds the relationship among a *thing,* an *idea,* and an *action.* For example, I wake up at night and hear a tapping sound (thing). Fearful that it is a burglar (hypothetical idea), I get up and discover it is just the rattling of the air conditioner (conclusive idea). I then decide to go back to sleep (action). As indicated by this example, usually our practical judgments are absorbed into the habits and **conventions** (or shared, normative habits) of our everyday lives. We do not need to think consciously about whether we should respond to a stop sign (thing), by associating it with the command to stop

---

[16]Lucy Stone, "A Disappointed Woman." Available at <http://www.dupage88.net/aths/resources/AT%20MCweb02/Pathfinders/AmSpeeches/stone.htm> (accessed 3 September 2012).

(idea), and then stopping (action). We just stop. But when we are learning to drive, all of these practical judgments must be consciously taught and enforced through instruction.

As indicated by the discussion of exigence, practical judgment takes on rhetorical qualities when we are unsure about what *to do* because we are unsure about what things *are*. Are British soldiers in Boston "peacekeepers" or "oppressors"? Should we view the violence in Darfur as "genocide" or "civil war"? In each case, rhetorical conflict involves the struggle to properly name things in such a way as to advance one judgment over another and thereby encourage forms of action on the basis of that judgment. The question of practical judgment thus centers around the matter of naming and therefore of meaning. We must be very careful of the words we use to describe our environment, because every word is loaded with particular denotations and connotations and associations that inevitably lead people to act in a certain ways instead of other ways. One of the central challenges of any rhetorical public speaker is to promote his or her version of practical judgment and thereby provide the correct "names" for any contingency that will make an audience prefer certain options over others.

Frederick Douglass: "Must I argue that a system thus marked with blood is wrong?"

It was not until the nineteenth century that a concerted movement to abolish slavery finally took hold in the United States. Previously, the majority of Americans made the practical judgment that slavery was a necessary (if at times grotesque) means to the advancement of the nation's economic growth and political power. Although Thomas Jefferson had originally included a long condemnation of the slave trade in the Declaration of Independence, it had been struck out by the representatives of the Southern colonies. It took several generations following the American Revolution for slavery to become the dominant question of practical judgment in the United States. What is interesting, then, about the speech given by Frederick Douglass, a former slave turned writer and abolitionist, to the Rochester Ladies' Anti-Slavery Society on July 4, 1852, is that Douglass addressed the matter of slavery as if the matter of practical judgment had already been decided, and that the only thing that remained was to act upon it:

> What, am I to argue that it is wrong to make men brutes, to rob them of their liberty, to work them without wages, to keep them ignorant of their relations to their fellow men, to beat them with sticks, to flay their flesh with the lash, to load their limbs with irons, to hunt them with dogs, to sell them at auction, to sunder their families, to knock out their teeth, to burn their flesh, to starve them into obedience and submission to their masters? Must I argue that a system thus marked with blood, and stained with pollution, is wrong? No! I will not. I have better employment for my time and strength than such arguments would imply.
>
> What, then, remains to be argued? Is it that slavery is not divine; that God did not establish it; that our doctors of divinity are mistaken? There is blasphemy in the thought. That which is inhuman, cannot be divine! Who can reason on such a proposition? They that can, may; I cannot. The time for such

argument is passed. At a time like this, scorching irony, not convincing argument, is needed. O! had I the ability, and could reach the nation's ear, I would, to-day, pour out a fiery stream of biting ridicule, blasting reproach, withering sarcasm, and stern rebuke. For it is not light that is needed, but fire; it is not the gentle shower, but thunder. We need the storm, the whirlwind, and the earthquake. The feeling of the nation must be quickened; the conscience of the nation must be roused; the propriety of the nation must be startled; the hypocrisy of the nation must be exposed; and its crimes against God and man must be proclaimed and denounced.[17]

According to Douglas, slavery by its very existence calls forth the practical judgment that it is an expression of barbarism rather than some divine order of things. What is required, rather, is a thunderous judgment upon the nation for its tolerance of this inhumane institution. Douglas therefore does not waste his time persuading us to make a radical judgment about slavery; rather, he directs the nation's attention to making a practical judgment upon itself.[18]

Discussion: Although we might not intuitively associate practical judgment with leisure, it is in our social relationships and choices of pleasure that we often make the most important practical judgments—whom we should associate with, where we should go, what we should consume, how we should act. What was the worst practical judgment you made while at a social gathering? Did it have lasting negative consequences? How did it affect your future judgments?

OCCASION

Rhetoric as a form of public speaking specifically refers to rhetoric that occurs at a specific time and place shared by both speaker and audience. In other words, occasion represents all of those elements that characterize a particular rhetorical act as a distinctly *oral* performance. The **occasion** is the specific setting shared by speaker and audience whose circumstances determine the genre, the purpose, and the standards of appropriateness of what is said. Examples of different types of occasions include a wedding ceremony, a political rally in front of City Hall, a Thanksgiving dinner, a graduation ceremony, or murder prosecution at a law court. The power of occasion is its tendency to focus attention and interest on a single subject, a tendency that on the one hand significantly constrains the freedom of a speaker but on the other hand allows him or her to more powerfully use language to unify the audience's emotional, intellectual, creative, and physical capacities around a single theme. Consequently, it is not unusual for speakers to provide two rhetorical responses to any rhetorical situation, one using the spoken word to address people at a specific occasion, and the other using writing or electronic media to communicate to secondary audiences without the constraints of occasion.

---

[17]<http://www.pbs.org/wgbh/aia/part4/4h2927t.html>.

[18]For more on Douglass, see Kevin McClure, "Frederick Douglass' Use of Comparison in His Fourth of July Oration: A Textual Criticism," *Western Journal of Communication* 64, no. 4 (2000), 425–444.

The most important function of occasion is to establish a common purpose for bringing speaker and audience together in the same place. The **purpose** for rhetorical public speech represents the reason for and circumstances under which an occasion occurs. To be clear, the purpose is not the purpose of the *speaker;* it is the purpose for the *event.* Purpose establishes common expectations among members of a diverse public that help direct their attention and focus. This is obvious for most conventional occasions. The occasion of the wedding establishes the purpose of the best man's speech, regardless of who is chosen for that role, just as the purpose of a defense attorney's speech is not up to the whim of the lawyer. In these cases, the occasion came first, and the speaker was selected based on his or her ability to fill its purpose. However, many times the speaker's intent and the occasion's purpose coincide. These are situations in which an individual creates an occasion explicitly for the purpose of speaking his or her mind and generates an audience on that basis alone. These types of speeches are usually given by well-known celebrities or political figures capable of attracting an audience based on the strength of their *ethos* alone, although one cannot rule out the proverbial "soapbox" oratory of the anonymous citizen standing up on a street corner. However, once these speeches begin, they nonetheless take on a purpose of their own that still constrains what can be said.

In addition to purpose, the occasion determines the genre and standards of appropriateness of the speech. Speech genres are literally infinite. Speeches of commemoration alone can be broken down into endless subgenres, such as wedding speeches, graduation speeches, award ceremony speeches, Veteran's Day speeches, coronation speeches, and so on. The important thing is simply to keep in mind that any occasion creates generic expectations in an audience for what they will hear and how they will hear it based on tradition and on past experiences. Finally, occasion determines **appropriateness**, or how "fitting" the speech is to all of the particular elements and unique circumstances of the speech.[19] An appropriate speaker considers the audience's needs and desires before composing the speech, whereas an inappropriate speaker thinks first of his or her own self-interest and only afterward makes minor accommodations to the audience. For instance, the speech by a best man at a bachelor party has norms of appropriateness vastly different from a speech given in front of grandparents and grandchildren. More than one movie has used a best man's ignorance of standards of appropriateness as a source of comedy.

It is important to note, however, that the constraints of appropriateness are not fixed rules or absolute responsibilities. They are norms of behavior usually established through cultural tradition and social habit. In everyday life, following the dictates of appropriateness as determined by the purposes of the occasion is the easiest way to get our voices heard. Anyone preparing for a job interview quickly realizes the importance of saying the right thing in the right way in order to get what one wants. Yet sometimes norms of appropriateness are so narrow as

---

[19]For the Sophistical view of appropriateness, see John Poulakos, "Toward a Sophistic Definition of Rhetoric," in *Contemporary Rhetorical Theory: A Reader,* ed. John Louis Lucaites, Celeste Michelle Condit, and Sally Caudill (New York: The Guilford Press, 1999).

to be oppressive. What is considered appropriate might not equate with what we consider ethical or moral. It is simply what is expected. It is up to rhetors to judge whether their conformity to or violation of these constraints helps enable the productive resolution of some larger problem.

Susan B. Anthony: "Resistance to tyranny is obedience to God."

The power of occasion is demonstrated in the testimony of Susan B. Anthony before a court of law. Anthony still appears on the face of some dollar coins, but it is not as well known that she also was convicted of a crime—the crime of casting a ballot in the 1872 presidential election, which happened during a time when women could not vote. On June 19, 1873, after having been denied the opportunity to say a word in her defense, she stood before Judge Ward Hunt after her lawyer appealed the guilty verdict. This excerpt from her interaction with the judge demonstrates how occasion and appropriateness influence the performance of situated rhetorical discourse. The fact that her words were spoken in resistance to the formal requirements of a defendant and the direct commands of the judge make her words much more powerful. Imagine, for instance, the courage it must have taken to respond to the judge as she does in this exchange:

JUDGE HUNT (Ordering the defendant to stand up) Has the prisoner anything to say why sentence shall not be pronounced?

MISS ANTHONY Yes, your honor, I have many things to say; for in your ordered verdict of guilty, you have trampled under foot every vital principle of our government. My natural rights, my civil rights, my political rights, my judicial rights, are all alike ignored. Robbed of the fundamental privilege of citizenship, I am degraded from the status of a citizen to that of a subject; and not only myself individually, but all of my sex, are, by your honor's verdict, doomed to political subjection under this, so-called, form of government.

JUDGE HUNT The Court cannot listen to a rehearsal of arguments the prisoner's counsel has already consumed three hours in presenting.

MISS ANTHONY May it please your honor, I am not arguing the question, but simply stating the reasons why sentence cannot, in justice, be pronounced against me. Your denial of my citizen's right to vote, is the denial of my right of consent as one of the governed, the denial of my right of representation as one of the taxed, the denial of my right to a trial by a jury of my peers as an offender against law, therefore, the denial of my sacred rights to life, liberty, property and . . .

JUDGE HUNT The Court cannot allow the prisoner to go on . . . . The Court must insist the prisoner has been tried according to the established forms of law.

MISS ANTHONY Yes, your honor, but by forms of law all made by men, interpreted by men, administered by men, in favor of men, and against women; and hence, your honor's ordered verdict of guilty, against a United States citizen for the exercise of "*that citizen's right to vote,"* simply because that citizen was a woman and not a man. As then, the slaves who got their freedom must take it over, or under, or through the unjust forms of law, precisely so, now, must women, to get their right to a voice in this government, take it; and I have taken mine, and mean to take it at every possible opportunity.

JUDGE HUNT   The Court orders the prisoner to sit down. It will not allow another word. . . . (Here the prisoner sat down.)

JUDGE Hunt   The prisoner will stand up. (Here Miss Anthony arose again.) The sentence of the Court is that you pay a fine of one hundred dollars and the costs of the prosecution.

MISS Anthony   May it please your honor, I shall never pay a dollar of your unjust penalty. All the stock in trade I possess is a $10,000 debt, incurred by publishing my paper—The Revolution—four years ago, the sole object of which was to educate all women to do precisely as I have done, rebel against your man-made, unjust, unconstitutional forms of law, that tax, fine, imprison and hang women, while they deny them the right of representation in the government; and I shall work on with might and main to pay every dollar of that honest debt, but not a penny shall go to this unjust claim. And I shall earnestly and persistently continue to urge all women to the practical recognition of the old revolutionary maxim, that "Resistance to tyranny is obedience to God."[20]

The power of occasion, in this case, was to focus attention on Anthony's testimony, which was then recorded and distributed in subsequent newspapers and pamphlets. Without the trial, public attention would not have been focused on her protest or the courage it took to speak her mind in the context of education in which she was told to be silent. The fact that she was not allowed even to defend herself (it being considered inappropriate at that time for a woman to speak during the formal proceedings) made her act of speaking all the more powerful, an effect magnified by her appeal to the legacy of the American Revolution to justify her own resistance to American law. Because she consciously attends to the rhetorical background, she is able to speak beyond the immediate particulars of her exigence and occasion. She speaks to a broader public, including the public of today.[21]

Discussion: The spread of social media has altered the way we think of occasions. "Flash mobs," for instance, are spontaneous gatherings by strangers at a particular point in time to perform some random activity, such as having a pillow fight in a subway station or square dancing in a mall. Do you think that rhetoric can exploit this new type of occasion?

---

[20]Susan B. Anthony, available from <http://law2.umkc.edu/faculty/projects/ftrials/anthony/sbaaccount.html> (accessed 6 September 2012).

[21]For more on Anthony's significance as a public speaker, see Elaine E. McDavitt, "Susan B. Anthony, Reformer and Speaker," *Quarterly Journal of Speech* 30, no. 2 (1944), 173–180.

KEY WORDS

Appropriateness
Belief
Constraints
Contested exigence
Contingency
Conventions
Counterpublics
Ethos
Exigence
External constraints
Internal constraints
Logos

Marginalized
Motive
Occasion
Opinion
Orientation
Pathos
Practical judgment
Primary audience
Public
Public opinion
Public sphere
Purpose

Rhetorical background
Rhetorical constraints
Rhetorical exigence
Rhetorical foreground
Rhetorical situation
Salience
Secondary audience
Social knowledge
State
Target audience
Technical situation
Uncontested exigence

SUMMARY

Considering the rhetorical background that frames any rhetorical public speech provides a speaker with the broader perspective that is necessary for any sustained effort at persuasion. This perspective not only expands the spatial horizon beyond the immediate physical context, but it also extends the temporal horizon so that it speaks to the past and looks toward the future. For example, simply thinking in terms of a larger "public" makes even one's immediate audience representatives of a larger social group with a shared history. One must simply remember that the qualities of the rhetorical background should never be taken to represent anything more than convenient and pragmatic shorthand that ultimately proves the worth of those qualities within the successful act of rhetorical persuasion. In the end, all groups and individuals are unique and exceed the capacity for such broad generalizations. But these generalizations are necessary starting points nonetheless, for they help us look beyond the immediate moment and give us perspective. As Roman orator Cicero observed long ago, audience adaptation requires a great deal of labor beyond just adapting to what the members of an audience might be thinking, feeling, and saying in the present:

> We must also read the poets, acquaints ourselves with histories, study and peruse the masters and authors in every excellent art, and by way of practice praise, expound, emend, criticize, and confute them; we must argue every question on both sides, and bring out on every topic whatever points can be deemed plausible; besides this we must become learned in the common law and familiar with the statutes, and must contemplate all the olden time, and investigate the ways of the senate, political philosophy, the rights of allies, the treaties and conventions, and the policy of empire; and last we have to cull, from all the forms of pleasantry, a certain charm of humor, with which to give a sprinkle of salt, as it were, to all of our discourse.[22]

Although we are far from ancient Rome, the same principles apply. The best public speakers always think beyond the scope of their immediate situation and audience, thinking not only in terms of the past and the future but also the larger publics that might encounter their speeches in various mediated contexts. The more one knows about the complexities of history and culture, the richer and more durable one's speech becomes.

However, no speech is successful without first and foremost being able to address the *unique* and *pressing* character of the problem in the *present*.

---

[22]Cicero, 221.

The considerations of the rhetorical foreground thus link us to the concrete characteristics of our present surroundings that help balance the more universal characteristics of our larger social and historical environment. Attention to exigence, practical judgment, audience, constraints, speaker, and occasion gives a speech its energy and life. Whereas the rhetorical background helps to identify the general aspects of a somewhat generic American audience, the rhetorical foreground puts us in a specific place and time. It tells us what stands out from a background environment and strikes us as being something urgent and important.

Each of the concepts within the rhetorical foreground distinguishes different parts of a rhetorical situation to help focus attention on specific aspects before addressing the whole situation. The *exigence* defines the immediate problem at hand rather than some vague moral abstraction or political maxim. The *constraints* represent the known obstacles to resolving this problem, whether they be physical constraints in a situation or emotional and psychological constraints within an audience. The *audience*, in turn, identifies that particular group, often a subset of some public, whose members are capable of resolving that problem if they act in a specific way. The *motives* represent all of those characteristics of an audience (actual or potential) that influence their decision in that particular moment. *Practical judgment* represents the specific action they are called upon to make by the speaker, in this case a judgment upon a certain event, person, or object that affects the course of future events. Finally, the *occasion* stands for the actual context of the speech situation, including the place and time of the event, the purpose for the occasion, and the expectations of the audience in attendance.

EXERCISES

1. Select a speech on americanrhetoric.com that you will explore. This will be called your "rhetorical artifact." No two students should have the same speech. Analyze your rhetorical artifact according to the table provided in the summary.

2. Identify a convention in your immediate environment that annoys you. Explain why it bothers you in terms of its consequences. Then violate this convention. Explain what happens and how you feel.

3. As a class, select a major historical event in the nation's history. Have everyone privately draw a historical lesson from this event and present it as a brief commemorative speech. How are these lessons the same or different?

4. Find an actual written text or speech created by someone whom you would consider as belonging to a "marginal" group. Read this text out loud in class and discuss how that group's marginalization may have affected certain aspects of the speech—for example, consider constraints and occasion. Can you think of any situations in which the marginalization of a group might be justified?

5. Bring in a common object that has no mysterious or controversial aspects (e.g., a fork, a rock, a hat). Then make a new practical judgment about this object (however hypothetical or fanciful) in front of the class in order to make this audience approach it differently in the future.

6. Remember a time you experienced a "contingency" as a child. (This does not have to be rhetorical.) Tell the story of your experience, trying to make it as vivid as possible so that your audience feels what you felt. The purpose here is to try to embody the *feeling* of contingency.

7. Find a print advertisement for some product. Who do you think is the target audience? What cues point you to this conclusion?

8. As in the examples presented in this chapter, think of an exigence that can take different forms according to the situation. Describe your exigence as a personal problem, a public problem, or a rhetorical problem. What factors determine it to be that specific type of problem?

10. Invent a new "crisis" that might face your community or the country as a rhetorical exigence. What would be the constraints to resolving this exigence rhetorically? Then create a short impromptu speech proposing a solution.

11. Think of an "occasion" with which you are very familiar and that recurs frequently. What are the rules and expectations (in terms of communication) at such an occasion? Can you think of a time when such expectations were violated? What were the consequences?

Understanding Audiences

Understanding Audiences

Jeff Greenberg/Alamy

This chapter is intended to help you:

- Understand demographic characteristics of your audience
- Identify your audience's opinions
- Gather useful information about your audience
- Implement general tips for using audience analysis in your speeches

Attention to your audience's opinions and concerns is crucial for effective speaking in the public sphere. A focus on the audience distinguishes the social act of *public* speaking from the mere physical act of speaking. Even with excellent delivery skills and powerful supporting evidence, a speech will not be effective if it fails to engage its audience. This chapter is devoted to helping you understand your audience so that you can adapt your ideas to them as well as encourage them to become a rhetorical audience. **Audience adaptation** is the term for this process of modifying both your message and your audience's identity to achieve a message that resonates with your audience.

Han's Uncertainty about His Audience

Han was interested in speaking to his audience about U.S. foreign policy, but he wasn't quite sure how his audience might respond to such a speech. As a new student at his university, Han knew little about the student body and their culture. He did not know whether the students tended to hold liberal or conservative opinions or how much they knew about current issues. Han also was unsure how his audience felt about him.

From the first few days in class, he could not tell whether his predominantly white audience would be especially interested in or especially skeptical of someone whose voice and skin suggested that he might be from a different culture. He also wasn't sure how they would respond to his religious identity as a Muslim. He knew that he would have to overcome some cultural obstacles with at least a few people in his audience.

This chapter goes into detail on the topic of audience and gives you several tools for analyzing your audience. An initial assessment of audience members should determine whether they are neutrals, partisans, or opponents with regard to your topic. In this chapter, you will learn about several other categories that facilitate audience analysis, and you will be shown practical strategies for obtaining this information. This chapter will also discuss how audience analysis can be used to adapt your speech as a whole.

Ultimately, the goal of this chapter is for you to become an **audience-centered** speaker—one who considers the needs of the audience during both speech preparation and delivery. By learning how to better understand your audience and by gaining tools that will help you to gather information from audiences, you will be well on your way to becoming an audience-centered speaker. ∎

Identifying Audience Demographics

Pete had had enough of all the bicyclists. Nearly every day, he encountered multiple bicycles whizzing by him on the way to class, and while driving around town, he saw many bicyclists riding on the wrong side of the street and ignoring stop signs. After one of his best friends got hit by a bicyclist, Pete decided to give a speech that would call attention to the problem of bicyclists in his community. He figured he would have a sympathetic audience, since he had seen a few letters to the editor in the campus newspaper complaining about biker behavior.

"You're probably as sick of the bikers as I am," Pete started. "They obviously don't care about anyone but themselves. They don't care about the rules of the road, and most of them have run over someone on campus.

Since it's only the hippies and a few old fogeys who ride bikes anyway, I think our campus should ban bikes, and my speech will tell you why."

Pete started to feel a little uneasy when he got a few dirty looks during the rest of his speech. During feedback, he discovered that many of his listeners were bicyclists who felt that they followed the laws. None of them had had an accident with a pedestrian. Most objected to being called hippies, and one of the middle-aged students asked Pete whether he thought she was an "old fogey." Even the non-cyclists were put off by Pete's attitude toward cyclists.

By forgetting to engage in audience analysis, Pete missed a golden opportunity to intervene in the public sphere. Pete assumed that everyone in the audience was like him and saw the world in the same way that he did. Even if he had important observations and criticisms of bicyclists' behavior, his expression of those ideas failed to resonate with his audience.

Audience demographics, or information about relatively stable characteristics of audience members, are a good starting point for thinking about constraints and opportunities for your speech. Especially if you are asked to speak before an audience of people with whom you are not familiar, inquiring about demographic characteristics is essential to avoid significant failures of adaptation.

When used properly, audience demographics can help you to avoid several tendencies that can hurt your effectiveness and interfere with building positive relationships with your audience:

- First, speakers need to guard against **egocentrism**, the habit of privileging their own knowledge and interests above all others. As Pete's example shows, egocentrism can manifest itself by assuming that everyone has the same experiences and attitudes as you do. By acknowledging demographic differences between yourself and your audience members, you can identify specific areas in which audience analysis is needed.

- A similar tendency is **ethnocentrism**, the habit of assuming that your own cultural standards are, or ought to be, shared by others. Customs and value judgments that you might take for granted are not necessarily shared if you are speaking to a culturally diverse audience. Assuming that all audience members celebrate Easter and believing that support for women's equality is universal are examples of projecting one's own culture onto the audience.

- Finally, careless use of audience demographics can lead to **stereotyping**, or the habit of overgeneralizing about the characteristics of a group. Assumptions that all bicyclists are hippies, all women are feminists, and all computer enthusiasts are socially inept are examples of stereotypes. Stereotyping is dangerous because it denies individual differences and because it often reinforces negative images of particular groups of people.

The challenge for effective and ethical audience analysis is to draw conclusions that aid the process of audience adaptation without unfairly stereotyping your audience. By thinking of demographic factors as simply the starting points for your audience analysis, you are reminded that several factors can influence audience identity and attitudes. This can check the tendency to draw stereotypical conclusions about your audience. In the last section of this chapter, we'll examine ways to apply this demographic information as you prepare your speeches.

Age

Age differences among audience members pose one of the first challenges for speaking in the public sphere. Your audience's knowledge base is one constraint that is likely to vary according to age. For example, most college-aged students are familiar with technologies such as iPods, MP3 players, and Xbox videogames and have used social networking sites such as Facebook, whereas at least some of those technologies may be less familiar to older listeners. As a result, you might need to explain references in more detail if some people in your audience are unfamiliar with those terms.

Your audience members' interests often will shift as they age. If your topic is loans, younger listeners might be most interested in the availability of loans for college costs, while older students might be more interested in mortgages and home equity loans. Remember, though, that this constraint is not always negative; it could also present an opportunity to enrich your invention of a topic. For example, a speech on college loans could easily address current college students as well as parents of high school students and grandparents. Similarly, younger audiences might be interested to learn how employers use social networking sites to research job candidates, while older audiences might be interested in how those sites facilitate unwanted interaction involving their children.

Sex, Gender, and Sexual Orientation

The differences between sex, gender, and sexual orientation point to areas that are rich with possibilities for audience adaptation but also with potential for stereotyping. In this context, **sex** refers to one's identity as male, female, or intersexed based on biological and physical characteristics. **Gender** refers to a person's enactment of his or her sex in relation to cultural norms and expectations, often described with words such as "masculine" or "feminine." In other words, sex is determined by biology, while gender is a cultural performance, in which individuals interact in ways that are more or less acceptable within particular cultures (Butler). **Sexual orientation** refers to one's romantic and erotic desires, most often as heterosexual, gay or lesbian, or bisexual. Because these categories do not overlap perfectly and involve human choice as well as biology, they create great potential for misunderstanding and stereotyping; as a result, it is necessary to pay close attention to the differences between them.

Recognizing the difference between gender and sex will help you to avoid making hasty assumptions about your audience. For example, the interests of an all-female audience are not limited to the contents of either *Cosmopolitan* or *Ms.* magazines, just as the interests of an all-male audience are not necessarily football and motorcycles. Because people perform their gender differently, speakers need to look beyond sex alone to determine their audience's attitudes and interests; other demographic factors must be taken into account as well.

Sexual orientation also creates potential for stereotyping. Just as members of a single-sex audience will not all share the same gender patterns, they also might not share the same sexual orientation. As a result, be on the lookout for **heterosexism**—the assumption that all people desire an opposite-sex romantic partner—and the use of **heteronormative language**—words and phrases that assume that everyone's romantic partner is of the opposite sex (Cooper). For example, if you are a woman speaking to other members of your same-sex residence hall, the term "partner" rather than "boyfriend" or "future husband" will avoid stereotyping and be more inclusive of listener perspectives.

As knowledge and attitudes have changed over time, it is increasingly inaccurate and inappropriate to assume that there are simple equations between sex, gender, and sexual orientation. Sensitivity to the differences between these categories will help you greatly in the process of audience adaptation.

Race and Ethnicity

Race and ethnicity are fundamental aspects of most people's identity. In part, that is because many people identify strongly with their heritage. It is also because those categories have often functioned to rationalize unequal treatment and discrimination. As a result, one's race and ethnicity are particularly powerful components of one's identity.

Multiracial and multiethnic audiences pose challenges and present opportunities in public speaking. Differences mean that you cannot presume that your audience members all have the same attitudes, interests, and experiences. But differences also can encourage you to examine issues from multiple perspectives and give these perspectives broader circulation. For example, a speech on immigration that gives voice to a recent Hispanic or Filipino migrant's perspective can circulate that perspective among audience members who might not have heard or understood that point of view.

Religion

Your audience members' religious beliefs contribute another dimension to their identity and attitudes. Religion is likely to influence their perspective not

RACIAL AND ETHNIC DIVERSITY

As college campuses increasingly show racial and ethnic diversity, public speaking classes can be an important site for exploring public issues from multiple perspectives.

Monkey Business Images/Shutterstock

only on issues such as prayer in school and public funding of faith organizations but also on issues such as poverty, media regulation, and environmental protection. As a result, religion is important to consider during audience analysis even when you are addressing issues that are not explicitly about religious practices.

As with other demographic categories, be wary of stereotyping based on religious identity. For example, since September 11, 2001, much public discourse has equated Muslims with terrorists, which stereotypes Muslim people and implies a distorted understanding of Islam as a religion (Morey and Yaqin). Although this is a particularly extreme form of stereotyping, it reflects what can happen if we draw conclusions too quickly from one aspect of identity. We can see this on other issues in the public sphere; not all Catholics oppose birth control, not all Christians are politically conservative, and not all atheists hate religion. These differences stem from personal decisions as well as the fact that religious traditions have long histories of internal disagreements over their meaning and application to public life.

Rather than making assumptions about specific beliefs and positions that your audience members might hold on the basis of religion, consider appealing to broader values and principles that can help you bridge differences across religious identities—even with those who do not affiliate with a faith tradition. For example, many religions have some version of the Golden Rule as an ethical guideline that incorporates notions of justice, equality, and compassion. A precept like that can help you to appeal to religious values while also establishing common ground.

Class and Economic Standing

The class position and economic standing of your audience members are probably some of the more difficult demographic factors to analyze. In the United States, there is less attention to class than there is in many other countries; consequently, many of your audience members might not think about their own identity or their beliefs and values in terms of class. In addition, class is a complicated mix of family history, income, and job status. For example, how would you describe the class and economic status of a plumber who makes $80,000 a year and those of a college professor who makes $50,000 a year? Does it make a difference if the plumber came from a family full of doctors and lawyers or if the college professor's father was a mechanic?

Still, the status of your audience members plays a significant role in the experiences, the knowledge, and the interests that they have. That can and should influence how you choose your topics and how you discuss those topics. For example, the economic standing of your audience members may affect their interest in the topic of the alternative minimum tax, since that tax has more direct effect on more affluent families. However, changes in those taxes could have an impact on public services or the taxes on lower-income families. As with other aspects of audience adaptation, use class position and economic standing as categories to brainstorm ways to show the relevance of your topic to your audience.

Place

An often-overlooked demographic factor is the place where people live (Kemmis; Snyder). Is your campus in a large urban area or in a small rural town? Is your environment dominated by mountains, prairie, desert, or ocean? Do most students commute to their classes, or do they live and study and work mostly on campus? These and other questions can spur you to think about how your audience's physical environment shapes their daily life, their interests, their concerns, and their desires.

One of the easiest ways to adapt your speech to your audience's place is by discussing local issues. Campus and city matters that directly affect your audience are perfect topics for classroom speeches. Conversely, you can make broader issues come alive by connecting those issues to the specific places where you and your audience live. For example, the topic of skin cancer could be introduced by talking about a popular lake, river, or beach that is known by your audience as a summer recreation spot.

In addition, consider your audience's sense of place, that is, the feelings that they have toward the natural and social environments that surround them. The mood of a place—the hustle and bustle of a big city or the serenity of a small coastal village—is recognized in people's everyday talk about where they live. Tapping into this sense of place can promote identification among your audience members, and it can direct their attention to the things that they most value. For example, if you are discussing the pros and cons of a new Walmart, your audience's sense of place will affect whether they are disposed to see the new store as a needed boost to a town with a flagging economy or as a threat to family businesses in a close-knit community.

Identifying Audience Opinions

In addition to broad demographic categories, it is helpful to learn what your audience thinks and feels about the topic of your speech. Analysis of **audience opinions**—their beliefs, attitudes, and values related to your topic—gives you details about your audience's engagement with the topic and the possibilities for inventing your speech. Identifying opinions helps you to learn the composition of your audience as partisans, opponents, and neutrals. More important, opinions indicate *why* some members of your audience are partisan, *for what reasons* they might oppose your position, or *what prevents them* from committing to a particular position on an issue. Understanding these opinions can help you to find the most effective ways to inform and persuade your audience.

Beliefs

A **belief** is a statement that expresses what an individual thinks is true or probable. Whatever an individual *thinks* is factually correct about the past, present, or future counts as a belief, even if that belief actually is incorrect. What was the primary cause of the Civil War? Does capital punishment deter crime? How much is the global mean temperature likely to increase in the next fifty years? Your audience's answers to these types of questions constitute their beliefs about these issues.

A speaker needs to understand an audience's beliefs, whether or not those beliefs are actually true. That is because incorrect beliefs can be a major barrier to an audience's reception of your message. If you were trying to inform an audience of young people about Social Security, for example, it would be crucial to know whether they believe that Social Security has no impact on them right now. In fact, that belief is false; Social Security directly affects them through their paycheck, and it indirectly affects them if it influences their grandparents' quality of life. As a speaker, you probably need to address that belief if you want your audience to sit up and listen to your speech.

While almost any idea can be made to sound like a belief by adding the words "I believe that ...," for our purposes, the category of belief is limited to factual matters. Your audience might believe that "abortion is wrong," that "the Red Sox are the best team in baseball," or that "the United States should invade Canada." However, none of these statements are factual beliefs. They might be based on facts, but they are not assertions about facts alone. To describe these more complicated opinions, it is necessary to talk about values and attitudes.

Values

A **value** is a relatively stable commitment about the quality or merit of objects, actions, or ultimate goals (Inch, Warnick, and Endres). Commitments about what is morally appropriate, aesthetically pleasing, or desirable for individuals or groups fall into the category of values. Often, a value can be summarized in a word such as "equality," "justice," "stability," or "consistency." The meanings that listeners attribute to these words form the basis of value judgments about specific things or practices. For example, someone who values "fairness" is likely to evaluate a campus policy or a school bond proposal on the basis of how fairly the costs and benefits of those actions are distributed.

Compared to beliefs, values are difficult to change. Because values develop over a long period of time and are grounded in personal experience as well as instruction from parents, churches, schools, and other social institutions, they are constantly reinforced as a relatively coherent value system (Rieke, Sillars, and Peterson). For example, people who value "fairness" probably learned that value early in life, when they were taught to share with others, and were probably reminded of that value as they experienced unfair situations throughout their life, such as losing the big game after a referee's call or not having the same opportunities as their friends.

Because values tend to be stable and enduring, they are a significant constraint in any rhetorical situation. On one hand, the stability of values means that no single speech is likely to produce a major shift in a person's values. On the other hand, deeply held values present great opportunities for a public speaker. Because values are central to people's identities—both who they are and the kind of person they hope to be—tapping into those values can show your audience the significance and relevance of your speech for their own lives.

One way to understand your audience's values is to identify their **value hierarchy**, which is the relative importance of different values within an individual or group's value system. In particular situations, specific values may come into conflict, pushing people to make difficult choices based on which values have greater importance or higher priority. For example, initiatives to enhance national security—such as surveillance of telephone conversations and screening procedures at airports—have sparked public controversy because they appear to violate our assumptions of privacy. People's judgments about the initiatives may be rooted in how they prioritize values. Supporters of the initiatives might place a higher value on "security" than on "privacy" in these situations, while opponents might reverse that priority. Whenever possible, adapt your message to listeners' values, and show the relevance that different values may have in a particular context.

Attitudes

An **attitude** is an expression of an individual's preferences. Like beliefs, attitudes express someone's opinion, but these opinions are not about facts alone. They include an implicit or explicit value judgment. As a result, you can think of an attitude as a preference that is based on an individual's beliefs and values. Attitudes are usually stated in a way that expresses a *favorable or unfavorable* disposition toward an object or idea or that evaluates a policy or practice as *desirable or undesirable*. For example, consider these attitudes:

> I don't like taking the bus.
> Our university does an excellent job of helping students find internships.
> Stem cell research is a good thing.
> I think the United States needs to cap immigration at current levels.

All of these statements express an attitude about some object, idea, policy, or practice. The first two statements express a personal opinion about whether something is favorable or not, while the latter two share judgments about policies or practices that are desirable.

Learning your audience's attitudes about your topic is one of the primary goals for audience analysis. You need to know whether your audience favors capping immigration levels if you want to give an effective speech on the topic. In turn, because attitudes are based on beliefs and values, you might need to determine those underlying beliefs and values to discover why someone holds a particular attitude. An unfavorable attitude about taking the bus might be based on beliefs (whether accurate or inaccurate) about the bus system: The bus is dirty; it doesn't arrive on time; it's crowded. But that attitude also might be related to the person's values, such as convenience, affordability, and flexibility.

Investigating the beliefs and values that underlie attitudes can help you to pinpoint opportunities for informative and persuasive speaking that will resonate with your audience. If your audience perceives that the bus is usually late or has limited routes, an informative speech might help to alter some of those beliefs. A persuasive speech might encourage the audience to value the affordability of taking the bus over any minor inconveniences it might pose.

Taken together, attention to audience demographics and attention to audience opinions related to your topic are absolutely necessary for effective public speaking. The next section offers some practical tools for gathering this information about your audience.

THE ETHICAL DIMENSION

Pandering

Especially for beginning speakers, it can be very enticing to tell your audience what they want to hear. If you are anxious about speaking, you might want to do whatever it takes to get the audience on your side. In a classroom setting, you might feel that a positive response from your classmates will lead to a good grade from your instructor. The more general desires to be liked and to avoid conflicts might also push you to embrace whatever opinions your audience holds.

Agreeing with one's audience on all issues or merely telling them what they want to hear has come to be known as **pandering**. This ethical issue related to audience adaptation has concerned rhetoricians for thousands of years. In his dialogue *Gorgias*, the ancient Greek philosopher Plato criticized teachers of public speaking for encouraging their students to merely reinforce their audiences' opinions rather than showing audiences what is in their best interest. Today, political candidates often get accused of pandering when they tell every interest group that they share the group's concerns and will make these a top priority if elected. Some political commentators pander to particular viewpoints to keep a loyal fan base rather than promoting effective deliberation.

The ethical problem with pandering is that it creates an inauthentic relationship between speaker and audience. Rather than honestly acknowledging differences of opinion, a speaker hides his or her opinions in order to appear in complete agreement with the audience. You can imagine what happens once the speaker's actual opinions surface. What if a classmate were to campaign for student body president on a platform of opposing tuition hikes but in fact believes that some tuition increases are beneficial and actually supports some increases while in office? People who voted for the candidate might feel that they were used to gain votes. They and others probably would find the president untrustworthy and might not be willing to support his or her other initiatives. Paradoxically, pandering can create barriers between speakers and audiences rather than bringing them closer together.

WHAT DO YOU THINK?

1. Can you think of a prominent speaker who has gone out of his or her way not to pander to the audience?
2. How does pandering inhibit the full range of voices from being heard in the public sphere?

Analyzing Your Audience

Gathering information about your audience can be more or less systematic depending on the availability of two things: time and access to your audience. If your preparation time is limited, you might not be able to gather in-depth information about the basis of your audience's attitudes. Likewise, if you are not able to interact with your audience while you are preparing your speech—typical for most speeches in the public sphere—then you might not even know the demographic composition of your audience until you begin to speak.

However, you can still make some educated guesses about your audience in these situations. Your method for audience analysis will be *indirect*. Instead of asking your audience directly about their demographic characteristics and their opinions on your topic, you will infer as much as you can from observations and external sources that provide clues about your audience.

Indirect Methods

First, *examine past statements* by your audience members. In the classroom, for example, you have probably learned some audience demographics if classmates have talked about growing up in a poor neighborhood, the importance of their synagogue, or their experiences of discrimination. Beyond the classroom, established organizations—such as a group that assists teenage mothers, the Republican Party in your county, or a nearby branch of the Sierra Club—usually have made statements or taken positions in the past that might provide clues about their opinions.

Second, you can *talk with third parties* who know something about your audience. If you are invited to speak before a group, you could have a conversation with the person who invited you to gain insight into the people who are likely to attend your speech and why they are interested in your topic. Similarly, you might speak with a representative of the group who serves as a stand-in for the type of people who are likely to attend your speech. Or you might seek out other people who have spoken to this audience to learn about their experiences and the audience's reactions.

Third, *explore mass media and social media* that are connected to your audience. In particular, popular magazines tend to target very specific groups. For example, *Essence* aims to reach black women, and *AARP The Magazine* goes to older people who are members of the American Association of Retired Persons. Both *Commentary* and *Tikkun* address Jewish readers, but they do so from contrasting political perspectives. Magazines like these succeed in part because their staffs do intensive market research about the interests, desires, and opinions of their target audience. Essentially, these sources have already done a significant amount of audience research for you. Websites and Facebook pages that serve organizations also can be useful indicators of the topics and issues that concern your audience.

Keep in mind that indirect strategies will never represent the exact demographics and opinions of your particular audience, so use them with caution. When you have the opportunity, supplement these strategies with more formal and direct methods of audience analysis.

Interviews

When you have easy access to your audience, such as with your public speaking class, use direct methods such as *interviews* and *surveys*. These methods can yield more focused and specific information than indirect methods can. The rest of this section will use examples related to the topic of organic food to illustrate how to use direct methods.

Interviews can reveal audience opinions that are not apparent through observation. For example, if you observe someone eating what you think is unhealthy food, that does not necessarily tell you anything about the person's opinions about organic food. To adapt a speech on this topic effectively, you need to discover your audience members' beliefs and attitudes about organic food as well as underlying values that might be relevant to their food choices (e.g., health, affordability, concern for the environment). Therefore, try to generate questions that explore each of these categories:

Beliefs: Do you think that organic food is more healthy than nonorganic food?

What does the "USDA Organic" label mean to you? What does it tell you about your food?

Attitudes: If the federal government were to propose more subsidies for organic food production, would you be likely to support it, oppose it, or be neutral?

Values: What are your top three considerations when buying food?

Interviews give you the flexibility to engage in dialogue to elicit underlying opinions. For example, you could ask interviewees why they hold a particular position on subsidies in order to elicit additional beliefs (e.g., "The government can't afford it"), attitudes (e.g., "I think small farmers deserve more support"), or values (e.g., "The free market is superior to government action"). The main disadvantage of interviews is that they take a lot of time. For most speeches, it is probably not feasible to interview every audience member. You might try to interview just a few members of your audience, but be mindful of whether they are representative of your audience as a whole. If you do consider interviewing, look ahead to the next chapter to find out more about preparing and conducting an interview.

Surveys and Questionnaires

A more efficient method of direct audience analysis is a **survey**, a systematic attempt to gather information about a particular population. The tool for demographic and opinion surveys is called a **questionnaire**. Think of the survey as the overall effort and the questionnaire as the actual document of questions that each individual will answer. To make a questionnaire worth your time and your audience's time, think carefully about what you need to know in order to construct and improve your speech.

Planning the Questionnaire First, *determine the relevant demographic characteristics*. Some demographic items might not be related to your topic. Your audience's economic standing probably would not matter much to a speech on illegal steroid use among Olympic athletes, but it might significantly affect their perception of issues surrounding work and careers, trade, and taxation.

Demographics also can help you think about the perspectives and voices to include in your speech. A largely male audience might need to hear from a well-respected male about the prevalence of domestic violence or might need to hear the voices of women who have experienced violence. Rather than just producing a laundry list of demographic questions, figure out which ones can tell you something meaningful about your audience's relationship to your topic.

Second, *determine the audience opinions you want to understand.* For an informative speech, questions about beliefs and attitudes can illuminate areas in which additional information could be useful for your audience. In effect, questions about beliefs are like questions on classroom tests. For example, you might ask one or more true/false questions to get at basic knowledge: "The USDA Organic label means that there are no genetically modified organisms in the product. True or false?" Knowing whether your audience holds true or false beliefs can help you to determine the amount of time and supporting material you will need to address a particular aspect of your topic.

To get at attitudes, ask a series of questions that first identify an attitude and then elicit underlying beliefs and values. For example, you might first ask whether respondents prefer to buy organic food. Additional questions could inquire about beliefs (such as cost or availability) or values (such as health or safety) that ground their attitudes.

Values can be evoked in multiple ways. As was shown above, a question that probes the reasons behind an attitude may elicit audience values. You also can access values directly by asking respondents to rank a set of value terms that are relevant to the topic. On the topic of organic food, you might ask, "What are the three most important factors in your food purchasing decisions?" and provide a list that includes items such as health, taste, affordability, and proximity. These values can then be used to generate appeals that will be persuasive to your audience rather than ones that you yourself find to be persuasive.

Third, *determine a reasonable length for your questionnaire.* This might seem minor, but you get the benefits of a questionnaire only if respondents are willing to fill it out. People are bombarded with survey research—online, through the mail, over the telephone, and in shopping malls—so they might not be enthusiastic about filling out a questionnaire. Even if it is required for your class, respect your classmates' time, and keep the questionnaire to a one-page document that takes no more than ten minutes to complete.

Composing Good Questions Writing a clear question is more difficult than it might seem. Ambiguous wording, leading questions, and inflexible choices all can distort the actual opinions of your audience. Professional survey

USING A QUESTIONNAIRE
Questionnaires are extremely useful for learning about your audience's demographics and opinions. Plan ahead to determine exactly the information you need to know so that you can keep the questionnaire at a reasonable length.

Diego Cervo/Shutterstock

researchers have developed standard types of questions and have noted several pitfalls; awareness of these pitfalls that can help beginners to come up with good questions. For starters, try to compose questions that fit the following categories.

Closed Questions Closed questions yield definite answers within a predetermined set of choices. These are sometimes called forced-choice questions, since they force the respondent to answer only from the alternatives that are listed. You are probably familiar with true/false and multiple-choice questions, but others are extremely useful for learning about your audience.

- *Demographic questions.* These are easily written as closed questions.

  Where You Live:

  On-campus   **City**   **Suburb**   **Rural**

- *True/false or yes/no questions.* These are useful for testing basic beliefs, gauging familiarity with an issue, and evoking simple attitudes and preferences.

  The average food product travels 1,500 miles to get to your table.

  True   **False**

  Do you know who decides which foods can be labeled "organic"?

  Yes   **No**

  Would you favor your local supermarket carrying more organic food?

  Yes   **No**   **Undecided**

- *Multiple-choice questions.* These give respondents a wider range of options than yes/no questions and provide a more detailed understanding of beliefs and attitudes.

  Which statement do you think describes the relationship between organic food producers and industrial agriculture most accurately?

  a. Organic producers and industrial agriculture are mostly separate entities.
  b. Organic producers and industrial agriculture are relatively equal competitors in the market.
  c. Many of the main organic producers are owned by industrial agriculture companies.

  Which statement most closely reflects your opinion about industrial agriculture? You may circle more than one answer.

  a. Industrial agriculture is positive because it provides a wide range of food choices.
  b. Industrial agriculture is positive because it provides food at affordable prices.
  c. Industrial agriculture is negative because it harms our environment in the long term.
  d. Industrial agriculture is negative because it tends to produce less nutritious food.
  e. Overall, the benefits and harms of industrial agriculture are about equal.

- *Scale questions.* These questions can reveal the intensity of an opinion or the relationship between different items, such as with a ranking.

> Identify your level of agreement with the following statement:
> "It is easy to purchase locally grown food in my community."
> **Strongly agree   Mildly agree   Neutral   Mildly disagree   Strongly disagree**
>
> On a scale of 1 to 5, rank where you are most likely to shop for food. Use 1 for most likely and 5 for least likely.
>
> __National supermarket chain (e.g., A&P, Safeway)
> __Locally owned grocery store
> __Discount or wholesale store (e.g., Super Wal-Mart, Costco)
> __Natural food store
> __Farmers' market

Closed questions are useful in two ways. First, they give you feedback on very specific audience opinions. This allows you to tailor your speech more closely to the opinions of your audience and avoid vague generalizations. Second, the limited range of answers makes it easy to compare responses across audience members. For example, look at the scale question above. If instead you had asked an open-ended question such as "How easy is it to purchase locally grown food in your community?" some respondents might have replied with a vague answer such as "Sort of," while others might have given you a long story about their latest visit to the farmers' market. Such answers make it more difficult to identify trends and patterns in your audience.

Closed questions do have disadvantages. Because answers are limited, they can make respondents answer in ways that are not truly accurate. The multiple-choice questions above do not exhaust all the possible audience opinions. Demographic-related questions, such as race, can force an inaccurate answer if a person's complex heritage does not fit one of the categories. Yes/no questions can oversimplify one's position. For example, even if several people answer No to the question "Should organic producers get more government subsidies?" some of them might want to express that what they really oppose are subsidies but that they strongly support the production and availability of organic food.

Open Questions An **open question** permits your respondents to answer in their own words. Sometimes, the closed questions that you pose will overlook issues that are at the heart of your audience's relationship to the topic. For example, you might believe that price is a key obstacle to people purchasing organic food and generate several closed questions to confirm that belief. But if you are unaware that availability is an obstacle, you will not see that issue come up in answers to your closed questions. Open questions, then, can open you to new ideas and insights about your audience and topic.

You can think of open questions as being on a spectrum, with some questions being more broad and other being more focused. Here, "focused" does not mean that the question is completely closed. Respondents still get to answer in their own words, but the question will ask them to discuss something more specific.

- *Broad questions.* A broad question can get at an individual's overall impression or "gut reaction" to a very general idea, object, or action.

  What comes to mind when you hear the phrase "industrial agriculture"?

  What is your opinion of this year's Farm Bill?

- *Focused questions.* These questions restrict the scope of the participant's response so that he or she is less likely to give you unimportant or irrelevant information. Even though they are open, focused questions can ask for specific information but without giving the respondent a set of prescribed choices.

  What do you know about the impact of fertilizers and pesticides on water quality?

  Who or what type of person would you perceive as credible on the topic of organic food?

It can be tempting to use lots of open questions, hoping that you will learn a great deal of rich information about your respondents. But keep in mind the reasonable length guideline when adding open questions. After a few open questions, respondents might grow tired of filling out your questionnaire and give shorter and less-detailed answers.

Avoiding Poor Questions Survey results are commonly criticized because of how questions are worded. If your classmate were to ask you, "You prefer organic food, don't you?" you might feel some pressure to answer Yes. This kind of question, a **leading question**, assumes a shared perspective and encourages the answer that is desired by the questioner rather than an honest response.

Even a subtle change in wording can help you to avoid leading questions:

Leading question: Don't you think it's time to eliminate farm subsidies?

Better question: In your opinion, should farm subsidies be eliminated?

The better option allows the respondent to express his or her own attitude freely.

Similarly, a **loaded question** uses descriptive language in ways that could influence how a respondent sees the available choices.

Loaded question: Do you prefer healthy, flavorful organic food to the overprocessed dreck produced by the corporate-industrial food complex?

Better question: Overall, which do you prefer: organic food or conventional food?

Notice how the loaded question uses adjectives to make one option seem more favorable than the other.

Double-barreled questions force two ideas into the same question when they should be treated separately. Answers to these questions might reflect a response to only one part of the question or fail to reflect contrasting opinions about the different ideas. As a result, questioners are unlikely to get accurate and useful answers.

Double-barreled question: Do you favor increasing subsidies for organic food and decreasing subsidies for conventional food?

How you would interpret a No answer to this question? Perhaps it means that the respondent is opposed to both positions. Or perhaps it means that the respondent favors one position but not the other and felt compelled to answer No to the whole question since there was no way to answer No to just one part. Instead of using double-barreled questions, ask separate questions or rephrase the question in a way that explains the relationship between the two positions more clearly.

Better question: Do you favor increasing subsidies for organic food?

Better question: Would you support an increase in subsidies for organic food if it meant decreasing subsidies for conventional food?

Finally, be mindful of asking **private questions**, which might elicit information or provoke emotions that respondents would prefer to leave undisturbed. For example, people might find questions about sexual orientation or religion intrusive and unnecessary. Likewise, questions about unpleasant or traumatic personal experiences (e.g., death of a loved one, getting fired from a job) or illegal behavior (e.g., drug use) can be off-putting and might generate unreliable results. So when developing your questions, be sure to consider your respondents' possible reactions, not just the information that you would like to have.

Using Audience Analysis in Your Speeches

Once you have gathered information about your audience, what do you do with all of this material? Putting your audience analysis to work in your speeches takes some creativity. This section shows you how to move systematically through your audience research and identify opportunities for general audience adaptation.

Using Audience Demographics

Recall the tendencies of egocentrism and ethnocentrism described in the first part of the chapter. Speakers cannot assume that their audiences share their personal interests or their cultural background. Consequently, an exploration of audience demographics is necessary to see where your identity and experiences align with your audience and where they differ. Here are three practical ways to use demographics in the process of audience adaptation:

- *Use audience demographics to adjust your topic and purpose.* Where there is uniformity in a particular demographic category, define your topic and purpose in a way that highlights their relevance to that group of people. This does not mean that you should avoid topics that you think will not interest your audience. Rather, your task is to make significant topics interesting.

  For example, the topic of methamphetamine use in rural areas might not be of obvious interest to a largely urban audience, but it might have relevance for that audience if it is discussed in terms of shifting priorities for drug enforcement. In other words, use demographics to adapt, rather than abandon, your topic and purpose.

- *Use audience demographics to identify similarities and differences between you and your audience.* If you are similar to your audience in certain ways, you can emphasize those similarities early in your speech to establish common ground. Mentioning shared experiences (e.g., commuting to work) and cultural references (e.g., movies, TV shows) are an easy way to display your similarity to your audience.

  When significant differences exist between you and your audience, first consider whether those differences are likely to matter to your audience. For example, your ethnicity might not really matter to an audience that is trying to determine whether a new park should be built in their neighborhood. If differences do matter, however, explore two basic strategies: seek common ground elsewhere, or use difference to establish expertise or a unique perspective. For example, an African-American man speaking to a predominantly white audience about racial profiling might incorporate the following passage in his speech:

  No matter what our personal opinions, I think we can all agree that as a society, we need to be able to talk candidly about race. [Here, the common ground is an attitude. Next, the speaker uses demographic difference as well as personal experience to show why he is a particularly credible speaker on the topic.]

  Today, I want to share with you my personal story about being pulled over on my way home from work last month. Hopefully my experiences as a black man—along with some startling statistics and testimony from white and black folks alike—will help you understand the problem that our society calls racial profiling.

- *Use audience demographics to remind you of the need for inclusive and empowering language.* Evidence of diversity in your demographic analysis should heighten your sensitivity to language that might denigrate or disempower audience members. Overt forms, such as sexist, racist, and homophobic language and ethnic and religious slurs, have no place in public speech. More subtle forms, however, can be just as alienating and can damage a speaker's credibility.

Consider the well-meaning student who gave a persuasive speech about "the need for Americans of all different cultures" to support non-discriminatory policies in the workplace. Even though her speech was intended to bridge cultural differences, she ignored the fact that several classmates were not U.S. citizens or did not identify themselves as Americans. While these listeners might have supported her overall purpose, they might have felt that the speech was not really addressing them.

Using Audience Opinions

As with demographics, audience opinions can help you with several big-picture issues that arise at the beginning of the speech process. Consider the following ways of applying your knowledge of audience opinions:

- *Use audience opinions to adjust your topic and purpose.* For example, if an audience believes that heart disease is primarily the result of choices about diet and exercise, you might focus your speech on factors such as genetics and family history. An audience that values privacy would likely be interested in topics ranging from Internet privacy to credit card companies' use of personal information. The audience's level of prior knowledge or personal experience with Internet use or credit cards could help you to decide which topic is more appropriate.

- *Use audience. opinions to determine the depth of your speech and the supporting material you need.* Audiences with substantive knowledge of a topic might be bored by a speech that intends to give a broad overview of that topic. Conversely, audiences with little knowledge might be overwhelmed by speeches that cover too much or are filled with technical jargon. For example, you might try to use stories to inform the latter audience only about how cookies work rather than developing a detailed explanation of three types of XSS vulnerability.

- *Use audience opinions to identify areas of consensus and areas of disagreement within your audience.* Your audience might have very similar values but have wildly divergent beliefs and attitudes about the perennial public speaking topic of marijuana legalization. If the audience is split on whether marijuana's health effects are largely positive or negative, you might orient an informative speech as a mutual inquiry into the latest medical research on this topic.

PUBLIC SPOTLIGHT

Wangari Maathai

Upon receiving the Nobel Peace Prize in 2004, the Kenyan activist Wangari Maathai delivered a lecture in Oslo, Norway, that appealed to a wide range of audience members. Her situation made audience adaptation extremely complicated. Her immediate audience comprised Norwegian royalty, diplomats from around the world, and fellow Kenyans. An even broader global audience would likely hear reports about her speech. In many ways, her speech is a model of how to adapt to diverse audiences in an increasingly global society.

Maathai's own work with the Green Belt Movement in Africa provided the basis for a rhetorical strategy to appeal to multiple audiences. For Maathai, the issues of environmental sustainability, democracy, and peace are all interconnected. As a result, discussing her work on each of these issues helped her appeal to those who might be involved with one issue but not the others. In the middle of her Nobel Lecture, she summarized these connections:

> The Norwegian Nobel Committee has challenged the world to broaden the understanding of peace: there can be no peace without equitable development; and there can be no development without sustainable management of the environment in a democratic and peaceful space. This shift is an idea whose time has come.

Maathai also used inclusive and empowering language to build a sense of connection among her diverse audiences. In addition to discussing her own experiences, she encouraged others to see themselves as engaged in the same kind of work that won such a prestigious award:

> Although this prize comes to me, it acknowledges the work of countless individuals and groups across the globe. They work quietly and often without recognition to protect the environment, promote democracy, defend human rights and ensure equality between women and men. By so doing, they plant seeds of peace. I know they, too,

Global activists such as Wangari Maathai must continually adapt their messages to diverse audiences.

are proud today. To all who feel represented by this prize I say use it to advance your mission and meet the high expectations the world will place on us.

By using empowering language and showing the connections between diverse topics, Maathai's speech reached beyond the elites in her immediate audience, stretching the public sphere to include and recognize ordinary citizens enacting positive change in their communities.

 Social Media Spotlight

The Green Belt Movement has an active presence on Facebook at
http://www.facebook.com/group.php?gid=4031089747

Videos of recent Nobel Peace Prize lectures can be found at
http://nobelprize.org/nobel_prizes/peace/video_lectures.html

Additionally, the film *Taking Root: the Vision of Wangari Maathai* and an excellent set of related resources about her work can be found at
http://www.pbs.org/independentlens/takingroot/film.html

Using Demographics and Opinions Together

Audiences often will have some diversity even if they appear to be demographically homogeneous. Since it is impossible to adapt your speech to each individual listener, one of your primary tasks as a speaker is to *constitute your audience as a group.* Using both audience demographics and opinions, you can encourage your audience members to see themselves as sharing at least some characteristics.

- *Use audience demographics and opinions to constitute your primary audience.* The **primary audience**, sometimes called a target audience, is the portion of your audience that you most want to engage with your speech. Communication campaigns show the importance of identifying a primary audience. Rather than trying to persuade everyone, campaigners will orient their messages to listeners on the basis of their level of knowledge about and interest in the topic. A good example of how to think about different target audiences can be found in the "Six Americas" studies that identify different audiences for climate change communication (Maibach, Roser-Renouf, and Leiserowitz).

  For public speaking, try to identify opinions and demographic characteristics that would include a strong majority of your audience, and consider these listeners to be your primary audience. For example, consider an audience with a diverse racial composition that also places a high value on academic achievement. It might be most effective to constitute the audience as a unified group by talking about academic achievement among minorities in general rather than by trying to target a particular minority group as the primary audience. For example, your speech might focus on the role of race in your college's admissions policies or on student services geared toward minority groups. Thinking in terms of a primary audience helps you to maintain a clear sense of purpose in your speech.

  At the same time, you should not ignore your other listeners. Let's say that in the audience described above, the majority supports affirmative action policies but several listeners oppose them. A persuasive speech that targets the majority to bolster its support should not ignore the concerns of opponents. Even if you do not aspire to persuade the opponents, you might hurt your credibility with your primary audience if you appear dismissive of others in the audience, and you might make opponents even more staunch in their opposition.

  In addition, there is a fine line between appealing to your primary audience and pandering to your audience. The Ethical Dimension feature earlier in the chapter addresses this persistent challenge in public speaking.

- *Use audience demographics and opinions to constitute your audience as a "public"* One important feature of a public, as you know, is that it brings people together on the basis of both similarity and difference. In your speaking, then, use your audience analysis to display similarities and differences among your audience members with the larger goal of helping them to see how they are a public.

For example, any topic with a connection to taxes—whether it has to do with their collection or their redistribution through government programs—reflects this tension between similarity and difference. Everyone is affected by taxes, but there are differences: different rates, different types of taxes, and different exemptions and credits create an endless variety of tax situations. And taxes help to provide different types of benefits. Because we all are affected by taxes and we all are affected differently by taxes, a speech on taxes would do well to recognize those similarities and differences, perhaps showing how a particular tax proposal might affect different people in the audience.

Constituting your audience as a public, then, is a way of saying that audience analysis should be used to demonstrate the public significance of your issue. Directly identifying the aspects of an issue that unite us and separate us can help your audience to understand the broader importance of that issue.

CASE CONCLUSION

Han's Uncertainty about His Audience

The more Han thought about his audience, the more he realized that there was not one obvious way to approach his topic. He knew that an all-out criticism of U.S. policy might not fly with his audience, but he also suspected that not everyone held the "my country, right or wrong" attitude. So Han decided that he should explore his audience's beliefs and attitudes about recent policies related to terrorism as well as their broader values. Learning these things might help him to clarify his topic and speak on something that would be relevant to his audience.

Han read *Newsweek* and *Time* to get a sense of the conventional wisdom on his topics. Then he started to develop a questionnaire for his audience that included the following questions:

Do you support the Patriot Act?
**Yes   No   Undecided   Don't know
                                enough about it**

True or False: Freedom should be valued more highly than security.
What do you think is the perception of the United States in predominantly Muslim countries?

As Han worked on his questions and interviewed a few of his classmates, he thought further about how to refine his topic.

Han learned several important things from his audience analysis. First, he learned that "national security" was a key value for his audience. However, he also learned that his classmates thought that there should be something to balance the excesses of the government. This gave him a good sense of his listeners' attitudes and values. In addition, he found that his listeners knew very little about the Patriot Act.

As a result, Han made a significant decision to adjust his topic. Instead of focusing on foreign policy, he decided that his speech should focus on the value of "freedom" and raise awareness of potential threats to freedom. This focus would help him to establish an area of common ground with his audience early in the speech. His audience analysis also helped him to determine that he would need to spend a fair amount of time explaining the Patriot Act and showing his audience how it might affect them. Han hoped that by doing so, he would be able to show his audience that the domestic policies that directly affect them are connected to the foreign policies that were initially his main concern. By shifting his speech in this way, Han was not pandering to his audience; he was inventing a topic that had significance for his audience while also being consistent with his own values.

HAN'S SPEECH OUTLINE

First Draft

I. Introduction: Speaking to people who are mainly concerned with national security.

    A. "They that can give up essential liberty to obtain a little temporary safety deserve neither liberty nor safety." — Benjamin Franklin

        Constitution provides system for security but also freedom and liberty. What is this system?

    B. Checks and balances

    C. Current policies threaten this system

    D. Central idea: The Patriot Act compromises our system of checks and balances.

    E. Preview.

II. Checks and Balances

    A. Where this idea comes from

    B. How it applies in practice

III. The Patriot Act

    A. Background on the act

    B. Examples of how the act compromises checks and balances

        1. Wiretapping examples

        2. Detention examples

        3. Information-sharing examples

IV. Solutions

    A. Congressional action

    B. Judicial action

V. Conclusion

Summary

IDENTIFYING AUDIENCE DEMOGRAPHICS

- Close attention to the demographic composition of your audience can help you to craft a speech that resonates with their identity and avoids egocentrism, ethnocentrism, and stereotyping.

- Depending on the subject of your speech, you might consider these demographics: age, sex, gender, sexual orientation, race and ethnicity, religion, class and economic standing, and place.

IDENTIFYING AUDIENCE OPINIONS

- Analysis of audience opinions—their beliefs, attitudes, and values related to your topic—gives you details about your audience's engagement with the topic and the possibilities for inventing your speech.

- A speaker needs to understand an audience's beliefs regardless of whether those beliefs are actually true. Incorrect or mistaken beliefs can be a major barrier to an audience's reception of your message, or an opportunity for developing a useful informative speech.

- Values are relatively stable commitments about quality and merit. While they are not likely to be changed by one speech, they can be used to show your audience the importance of your topic to their own lives.

- Attitudes are an expression of a listener's preference based on one's beliefs and values. Investigating the beliefs and values that underlie attitudes can help you to pinpoint opportunities for informative and persuasive speaking that will resonate with your audience.

ANALYZING YOUR AUDIENCE

- In some speaking situations, your ability to analyze your audience might be limited to indirect methods—observation or interaction with persons or media that are connected to your audience in some way.

- Direct methods, such as interviews and questionnaires, can give you much more focused and detailed information. An efficient tool for audience analysis is the questionnaire, which uses a mix of closed and open questions to elicit demographic information as well as beliefs, attitudes, and values from audience members.

USING AUDIENCE ANALYSIS IN YOUR SPEECHES

- Knowledge of audience demographics can be used to adapt your speech in several ways: to adjust your topic and purpose, to identify similarities and differences, and to choose inclusive and empowering language.

- Knowledge of audience opinions can be used for those purposes, too, as well as for determining your need for supporting material and the possibilities for crafting an inclusive group identity for your audience.

Key Terms

audience adaptation
audience-centered
audience demographics
egocentrism
ethnocentrism
stereotyping
sex
gender
sexual orientation
heterosexism
heteronormative language
audience opinion
belief

value
value hierarchy
attitude
pandering
survey
questionnaire
closed question
open question
leading question
loaded question
double-barreled question
private question
primary audience

Comprehension

1. What are the three tendencies or habits that demographic analysis can help you avoid?

2. What is the difference between audience demographics and audience opinions?

3. How are attitudes different from values? From beliefs?

4. What are the advantages and disadvantages of interviews as a method of audience analysis?

5. Is a multiple-choice question open or closed?

6. What sort of information can be generated by a scale question?

7. Why should we not trust the answers to loaded questions?

8. What is a primary audience?

Application

1. What demographic factors would you want to know about if you were considering a speech in the following topic areas?

   Adoption

   Hate crimes

   Medicare

   Public transportation in your community

   The U.S. prison system

2. Choose two of the topics listed above, and determine what beliefs, values, and attitudes it would be helpful to know from your audience.

3. Identify a group in your community to whom you would like to speak. Which direct and indirect methods of analyzing that audience would you choose? Why?

4. Using the topic you have identified for your next speech, construct one example of each type of closed question described in this chapter (demographic, true/false or yes/no, multiple-choice, scaled). In class, share these with a colleague, and have him or her construct two open questions on your topic. Then discuss the quality of your questions with your classmate.

References

Butler, Judith. *Gender Trouble: Feminism and the Subversion of Identity.* London: Routledge, 1990.

Cooper, Brenda. "Boys Don't Cry and Female Masculinity: Reclaiming a Life and Dismantling the Politics of Normative Heterosexuality." *Critical Studies in Media Communication* 19.1 (2002): 44–63.

Inch, Edward S., Barbara Warnick, and Danielle Endres. *Critical Thinking and Communication: The Use of Reason in Argument.* 5th ed. Boston: Allyn & Bacon, 2006.

Kemmis, Daniel. *Community and the Politics of Place.* Norman: U of Oklahoma P, 1990.

Maathai, Wangari. "Nobel Lecture." Accessed November 10, 2007. Available at http://nobelprize .org/nobel_prizes/peace/laureates/2004/maathai-lecture-text.html

Maibach, Edward, Connie Roser-Renouf, and Anthony Leiserowitz. *Global Warming's Six Americas 2009: An Audience Segmentation Analysis.* Yale Project on Climate Change and the George Mason University Center for Climate Change Communication, May 2009. Available at environment.yale.edu/ uploads/6Americas2009.pdf

Morey, Peter, and Amina Yaqin. *Framing Muslims: Stereotyping and Representation after 9/11.* Cambridge: Harvard UP, 2011.

Rieke, Richard D., Malcolm O. Sillars, and Tarla Rai Peterson. *Argumentation and Critical Decision Making.* 6th ed. Boston: Allyn & Bacon, 2005.

Snyder, Gary. "The Place, the Region, and the Commons." In *The Practice of the Wild.* New York: North Point Press, 1990. 25–47.

Organizing the Speech: Introductions, Conclusions, and Transitions

From Chapter 10 of *Public Speaking: Strategies for Success*, Seventh Edition. David Zarefsky.

Organizing the Speech: Introductions, Conclusions, and Transitions

Listen to the
Audio Chapter at
MyCommunicationLab

After studying this chapter, you should be able to:

Objective 1	Identify the main purposes and some common types of introductions.
Objective 2	Prepare an introduction.
Objective 3	Identify the main purposes and some common types of conclusions.
Objective 4	Prepare a conclusion.
Objective 5	Use transitions to connect the elements of a speech and give its structure a dynamic quality.
Objective 6	Recognize the elements of a transition, which may be either explicit or implicit.

OUTLINE

The body of the speech is certainly its most important part; it takes up the most time, and it expresses and supports the main ideas. But if a speaker launches directly into the first main idea and ends abruptly after the last, you probably would think something was strange, perhaps even insulting, about the speech. It would be like joining a conversation that was already well along, missing the beginning completely. The ending would seem abrupt, too—like reading a book that was missing its last few pages or walking out of a movie in its last minutes. You would be surprised that the speaker had stopped, because the speech would not seem "finished."

Listeners expect a beginning, a middle, and an end. They expect to be guided into a topic, not dropped in its midst, and they expect the discussion to conclude naturally. Audiences notice when a speaker departs from this customary sense of form; if they are not disturbed by it, they at least are likely to be distracted.

In this chapter, we will explore the two elements of a speech that surround its body: the introduction and the conclusion. We will focus on the purposes of these elements, some common types, and strategies for preparing them. Finally, we will look at how speakers use transitions to connect the introduction, body, and conclusion and thus give the speech a dynamic quality.

OBJECTIVE

1

Introductions: Beginning the Speech

Both daily life and studies in the psychology of persuasion tell us that first impressions are extremely important. When you meet someone new, you quickly form impressions about that person, often based on little more than superficial characteristics such as the person's clothing and hairstyle, or car, or way of speaking. Moreover, many first impressions are likely to prove durable; they will influence how you interpret what this person says and does.[1]

The Purposes of an Introduction

The **introduction** is the beginning of the speech, which affects listeners' first impressions of the speaker and prepares them for the speech. It gives the audience clues about the speaker's personality, intentions, style, and overall perspective. And it prepares the audience for the speech by giving clues about what will follow.

The overall purpose of using your introduction to prepare the audience can be broken down into four specific goals:

1. To gain the attention and interest of your audience
2. To influence the audience to view you and your topic favorably
3. To clarify the purpose or thesis of your speech
4. To preview the development of your topic

Watch the Video "Professor Jason Warren Discusses Tips for Effective Introductions" at **MyCommunicationLab**

introduction
The beginning of the speech, which affects listeners' first impressions of the speaker and prepares them for the speech.

Gaining the Attention and Interest of Your Audience. The introduction should make the audience want to hear what will follow. Accomplishing this goal is critical because, like someone switching television channels, listeners can choose whether to pay attention. Even when the audience cannot escape a speaker physically, individuals can decide whether to be active listeners.

The primary way to make listeners pay attention is to convince them that what follows will be interesting. An effective introduction suggests to listeners that they will be stimulated by the speech. A lively narrative, startling or unexpected information, or a personal experience that listeners can identify with will suggest that the speech will be interesting and thus warrants attention.

Influencing the Audience to View You and Your Topic Favorably.

It is not enough merely to get the audience's attention. Indeed, a speaker can easily gain attention by appearing overbearing, pompous, or dogmatic.

The introduction aims to influence the audience to view you and your topic favorably so that listeners will be sympathetic and attentive. You can create a favorable first impression as follows:

- Be well prepared and confident, thereby establishing positive *ethos* (credibility).
- Identify with the predispositions of the audience, which you will discover through the audience analysis.

Like most generalizations, this one needs to be qualified a bit. Sometimes, a speaker will choose deliberately not to gain the audience's favor. For example, a dissenter who feels the need to speak out against the majority opinion may intentionally make an audience hostile by, say, accusing them of denying rights to those who are less powerful. Even though the immediate audience is unlikely to be persuaded by such a direct attack, the dissenter may, in fact, be addressing those listeners primarily to gain the attention and favor of some other audience. The real intended audience is composed of people who will hear about the speech and conclude that the dissenter is a person of courage and principle for venturing into hostile territory. This audience, of course, will then be favorably disposed toward the speaker and the topic; the dissenter will have gained both their attention and their goodwill.

Clarifying the Purpose or Thesis of Your Speech.

Listeners are more likely to follow your speech and be influenced by it if you clearly identify what you want them to believe or to do. Most introductions include an explicit statement of the speaker's thesis or purpose, as in the following examples:

Watch the Video "Introduction: Voting" at **MyCommunicationLab**

> I will argue that the United States cannot compete economically without strengthening public education.

> After you consider the facts, I hope you will call the Red Cross and volunteer to donate blood.

Speakers often state their purpose only after making introductory remarks that gain the audience's interest and make listeners favorably disposed. But, sometimes speakers can *assume* that the audience is interested and favorably disposed. For instance, a speaker addressing the student government, who discusses the benefits of student government, surely could assume interest and motivation on the part of the audience. In this case, the entire introduction might focus on an explicit statement of purpose.

Previewing the Development of Your Topic.

Besides capturing the audience's attention, influencing them to view you and your topic favorably, and clarifying your purpose, the introduction also previews how you will develop your topic in the body of the speech. Classical theorists of public speaking refer to this step as the **partition**; the speaker divides the body of the speech into selected categories for discussion.[2] For example, a speaker might say:

> First I will explain how higher education got into financial trouble, then I will describe the consequences of this for students and faculty, and finally I will tell you what we can do about it.

Basically, the speaker has revealed the pattern for the body of the speech (in this case, a problem–solution pattern) and what the major headings will be. A "road map" helps listeners to follow the speaker's thinking and to anticipate what will come next.

An Example of an Introduction

Only your own imagination and creativity limit you in devising an introduction that achieves the four primary goals. Let's look at how one student used her introduction to prepare the audience.

Michelle Ekanemesang was the third speaker in her public speaking class. To gain her listeners' attention (after all, they had already heard two speeches), she walked to the podium, paused, looked at the audience, and then suddenly dropped a large book on the floor. The resounding thud brought all eyes to Michelle as she began to speak: "Just as easily as that book fell to the floor, the innocence of a child can crash." Then, walking around to the front of the podium to retrieve the book, Michelle continued:

> However, unlike this book, a child's innocence cannot be picked up and placed back on the pedestal where it was. Children today encounter many experiences that challenge their innocence. Along with gangs, guns, and drugs, they also face another monster that is not so well publicized: sexual abuse. Approximately one child out of four is sexually abused by the age of 18. That would be four people in this classroom. Today, I want to discuss the causes and effects of childhood sexual abuse as well as to offer some tips about preventing it and what to do if you or a child you know has been a victim of sexual abuse.

Michelle's book-dropping trick could have turned into a resounding flop if she had not explained how it connected to her speech. She quickly and effectively gained her listeners' attention and then maintained it by saying that some of them might be victims themselves, thereby emphasizing the personal relevance of her topic. From the outset, it was clear that Michelle was going to talk about the horrors of child abuse. She took a serious tone of outrage and influenced the audience favorably toward her treatment of the subject. Her final statement in the introduction then clearly previewed which main topics the audience could expect her to cover: the causes, effects, prevention, and treatment of childhood sexual abuse.

 Watch the **Video** "The Process of Developing a Speech: Attention-Getting Devices" at **MyCommunicationLab**

Types of Introductions

Several types of introductions show up frequently in successful speeches, and you should be aware of them in order to decide whether they will be effective for your speech and audience.

In deciding which type of introduction to use, always try to relate the introduction directly to your speech, as Michelle did. If you quote someone famous or tell a story without showing how that connects to the speech itself, the introduction

partition
Division of the body of the speech among selected categories for discussion.

may soon seem out of place. The speech, after all, should be a unified whole. The introduction and the conclusion should work together with the body of the speech to create the response or action that you desire.

Identifying with Your Audience.

One obvious way to build goodwill and capture the audience's interest is to draw on something that you share—a common experience, common acquaintances, common values, or common goals. If listeners perceive you as being basically like themselves, they usually form a good first impression of you. And their interest should be high because, in effect, you may be telling them something about themselves or be speaking on their behalf.

Student speakers often find it easy and effective to identify with their audience because, typically, they do share many common experiences with their listeners. One student began a speech about the disillusionment felt by many of America's less fortunate youth by making a reference to a popular Hollywood movie:

> Many of you may have seen the hit movie *The Matrix*. This high-budget film paints America as one huge computerized box in which we all are trapped, with no real control of our lives and no say in our futures. We are just digits in an artificially intelligent matrix—added, subtracted, multiplied, and divided at the will of a supercomputer. When my friends and I first saw the movie, we felt strangely numb and powerless, but the feeling only lasted a few minutes. But for many of America's less fortunate youth, this is the only feeling they know.

Having gained the interest and goodwill of the audience by identifying with them, and having stated the thesis, the speaker was then well positioned to complete the introduction by previewing how the feelings of disempowerment among America's disadvantaged youth would be developed in the speech.

Referring to the Speech Situation.

Another way to establish common bonds with an audience and to strike an appropriate opening note is to refer directly to the situation. Many speeches are delivered on ceremonial occasions (for example, commencement addresses, wedding toasts, speeches of welcome or farewell), and these often are introduced effectively by an explicit reference to the occasion.

Similarly, speeches that happen to be given on a significant anniversary might make reference to the date. For example, a student speaking on September 11, 2013, might begin this way:

> Twelve years ago today, our generation and our country lost some of its innocence. Even though we were very young, none of us will ever forget the image of the planes crashing into the World Trade Center. That action started what President George W. Bush called a "war on terror." Twelve years later, do we feel safer or more secure? Can we deter or stop terrorists? In short, are we winning the war?

The speaker could go on to state the thesis and preview its development:

> I do not think we are. Our airports are safer, but our transportation system and our industrial base are vulnerable.

Similarly, Rachel Venegas used the beginning of final examination week as an opportunity to point out a disturbing trend in student study habits:

> With finals beginning, students all over campus will be frantically trying to absorb every bit of knowledge from their courses or putting the finishing touches on their papers. But during these cram sessions, students tend to put their academics before their own health,

especially by neglecting sleep. One way to bypass the urge to sleep, and an increasingly popular option, is the use of drugs meant to treat Attention Deficit Hyperactivity Disorder. Despite the serious side effects, many college students continue to take these drugs, prescribed or not, without knowing fully the risks of their misuse.

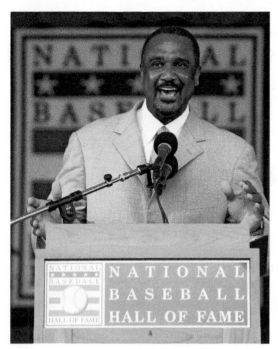

Telling an interesting story with enthusiasm is often a good way to dispose the audience favorably toward the speaker and the speech.

Other situational factors also can be the touchstone for an effective introduction. For example, the location of the speech might be important, as it was when Martin Luther King, Jr., began his famous address "I Have a Dream." Dr. King's introduction noted that he stood symbolically in the shadow of Abraham Lincoln; he was delivering his address from the Lincoln Memorial.

Referring to a previous speaker might be a natural introduction to your own speech. If your reference endorses or builds on something a previous speaker said, it creates a bridge between the two speeches and a seemingly logical flow to the discussion. And if the previous speaker was competent and credible, you even may inherit the audience's favorable disposition toward that speaker.

However, your reference does not have to support the previous speaker. In fact, that speech might provide the ammunition needed for you to disagree with something the speaker said. In this case, your introduction is both a bridge that maintains continuity and a stop sign that signals the differences between the two of you. For example, imagine that a student in a public speaking class just spoke about the ways in which Steve Jobs and Apple have revolutionized the personal computer, praising Jobs's vision and imagination. By coincidence, the next speaker had planned to condemn the overdependence by technology companies on foreign labor. Adapting the introduction to fit this situation, the second speaker could say:

> Many consider high-tech companies, such as Apple, to be ahead of their time, but in at least one respect they are dangerously behind the times: their dependence on exploited foreign labor.

Stating Your Purpose.   Sometimes, an introduction that explicitly states your purpose can be very helpful, especially if the audience is captive or is known already to be favorably disposed to your ideas. This approach is also effective when your thesis is startling or unexpected:

> In the next hour, many children in this town will suffer from abuse and neglect. We will see why this happens. Then I want you to volunteer one day a week to help stop this.

Your direct challenge will probably make the audience take notice, because you've alerted them that you expect something of them, and so they are likely to pay attention in order to decide whether or not to grant your request.

Stating the Importance of Your Topic.   Another effective opening device is to alert the audience to the significance of your topic before actually stating what the topic is. For example, a speech about preventing AIDS might begin with the statement "I have information that literally can save your lives."

Similarly, a speech about purchasing a home might begin with "Today, I want to discuss the most important financial decision most of us will ever make."

This type of introduction demands the audience's attention. Just by saying that your topic is important, you ask people to take notice. This strategy also has an element of mystery, which leads the audience to wonder just what it is that is so critical. Be aware, however, that this approach has been overused, and audiences sometimes react to such claims by being skeptical. A speaker who opens with "This speech could change the course of your life" may actually prompt listeners to think, "Oh, sure; I've heard that before."

If your speech has a formal title, be sure that its specific wording is accurate and complete. Then your introduction can "unpack" the title to forecast what will follow and to highlight your main points. In 1984, Governor Mario Cuomo of New York illustrated this introductory strategy in a speech at the University of Notre Dame:

> I would like to begin by drawing your attention to the title of this lecture: "Religious Belief and Public Morality: A Catholic Governor's Perspective." I was not invited to speak on "Church and State" generally. Certainly not "Mondale versus Reagan." The subject assigned is difficult enough. I will try not to do more than I've been asked.

Governor Cuomo then proceeded to state his perspective and to indicate how he planned to develop his ideas.

Citing Statistics, Making Claims.
Listeners sit up in interest when a speaker cites startling statistics or makes a surprising claim. Their astonishment on hearing the information causes them to pay attention. For example, to introduce the topic of poverty in the Navajo Nation, a student might begin:

> The Navajo Nation is the largest Indian reservation in the United States. It has a population of 235,000 and covers an area of 16.2 million acres. But the largest Indian reservation in America is not thriving as well as some of the country's smallest towns. According to a recent Bureau of Indian Affairs report, the unemployment rate in the Navajo Nation is almost 58 percent. Only 22.5 percent of Navajo homes have any telephone service, and many of the lines are too old to support modern Internet communication.

This type of introduction works best when the statistics are accurate but not well known—when there is a gap between what listeners think they know and what is actually the case. Statistics can show that our common assumptions are not accurate, that a problem is greater than we know, that a condition we viewed as worsening is actually improving, and so on. But the risk with this approach is that listeners may become defensive about their predispositions. Rather than considering the possibility that academic dishonesty really is more serious than they thought, for example, they may react by doubting the statistics or by denying the claim. You certainly want to encourage listeners to think critically; but if their very first response to your introduction is to doubt what you say, it will be difficult to build goodwill and regain their interest.

Telling a Story.
Speakers often begin with an anecdote—an extended illustration or example that is cast in narrative form. A speaker introduces the topic by relating a personal experience or something that happened to others. For example, when Elie Wiesel, Holocaust survivor, novelist, and Nobel Peace Prize winner, gave a speech at the White House in April 1999 on "the perils of

CHOOSE A STRATEGY: Weighing the Types of Introductions

The Situation

You are in charge of bringing a documentary about a charity to a local cinema. Before the movie starts, you will make a few comments about why you support the charity. You know that your main points will be that the charity directly benefits the community, it addresses a significant need, and it depends solely on donations. Now you want to create an attention-getting introduction.

Making Choices

1. Of the 10 types of introductions discussed in this chapter, what are some types that seem well suited to your topic and speech situation? Why?

2. You know the audience already supports the charity and you want to strengthen their commitment. Which type of introduction do you think would be more effective, (a) identifying with your audience or (b) stating your purpose? Why?

3. Suppose the charity has helped a member of your family through a tough time. What are the potential benefits and drawbacks of telling a story about your family member in your introduction?

What If...

How would your choices be affected by the following?

1. The film showing is to raise awareness for an audience that isn't familiar with the charity.

2. You are speaking at the end of a documentary festival and others have made similar introductions.

indifference," he began by relating the story of a young boy who had been rescued from a Nazi concentration camp by American soldiers:

> Fifty-four years ago to the day, a young Jewish boy from a small town in the Carpathian Mountains woke up, not far from Goethe's beloved Weimar, in a place of eternal infamy called Buchenwald. He was finally free, but there was no joy in his heart. He thought there never would be again.
>
> Liberated a day earlier by American soldiers, he remembers their rage at what they saw. And even if he lives to be a very old man, he will always be grateful to them for that rage, and also for their compassion. Though he did not understand their language, their eyes told him what he needed to know—that they, too, would remember and bear witness.

The power of an anecdotal introduction lies in its narrative form. The story is engaging, and the chronological sequence is easy to follow. A narrative is concrete—it involves specific characters in a particular situation—and therefore listeners can attend to it with less effort than is needed to follow something more abstract.

One potential drawback in using an introductory anecdote is that it may overshadow the preview of your topic or even the body of the speech. It may be so interesting that it distracts attention from your main points. To avoid this, use an anecdote that leads directly into your thesis statement and partition. Try to create unity between the anecdote and the main points so that each reminds the audience of the other.

Using an Analogy.
Closely related to the anecdote is an analogy, which is a comparison. An analogy draws attention to the similarities or the differences between two objects, events, or situations. A speaker can use an analogy to clarify an unfamiliar subject by comparing the subject with something else that the audience already understands. For example, a speech

describing the pros and cons of school vouchers might compare public and private schools with retail stores and parents and their children with consumers. In this way, the unfamiliar issue of school vouchers can be explained in the more familiar terms of shopping.

Like anecdotes, analogies help to make abstract concepts concrete. They are especially useful in introducing technical material to listeners who are not specialists in the speaker's field. For example, to inform his audience, consisting of senior citizens unfamiliar with the Internet, about search engines, student Stan Barkers began with the following analogy:

> When borrowing a book from the public library, the first thing you do is consult the card catalog, which used to be housed in a large wooden cabinet but now is online and accessible with a computer. Whether the "cards" are typed on paper or captured electronically on a computer screen, the process still works the same: you use a catalog to find where the book is located, then you proceed along the shelf and get the book. A search engine uses a process very similar to the way in which you've always searched for a book in the library. Instead of looking up an author or title, the search engine identifies key words and looks for them in billions of documents that are posted on the Internet. So it may be helpful for us to think of a search engine like Google as the Internet's card catalog.

This analogy translated what could be an unfamiliar process—using a search engine to research on the Internet—into a process that the audience easily could grasp.

During World War II, President Franklin D. Roosevelt was gifted at using analogies to explain the complexities of foreign policy to average voters. Discussing why, in 1940, the United States should lend (rather than sell) war materials to Great Britain and its allies, he offered the analogy of a man whose neighbor's house was on fire. When the neighbor ran up to ask for a garden hose, the man did not first demand payment; instead, he gave the hose to the neighbor on the promise that it would be returned when the threat was past. In just this way, Roosevelt reasoned, the United States should approach lending supplies to cash-strapped allies. This simple analogy both explained and dramatized the president's perspective, and it helped make his case with the public.

Analogies are persuasive (and thus advance the purposes of an introduction) because most listeners find it easy to focus on similarities and differences. To be effective, though, an analogy should be fairly simple and direct, like Roosevelt's. A complex comparison will force your listeners to puzzle out just what it is that you think is similar about the two things, and they will be distracted from the body of your speech. And if your analogy is too farfetched, or if it assumes key similarities without considering significant differences, listeners' first impressions of you may be negative, and they may not take your main ideas seriously. For example, several people objected to Stan Barkers's analogy, because people use card catalogs to find specific books, not to see all the places that a particular word or phrase is used.

Asking a Rhetorical Question.
What's a rhetorical question? Like the sentence you just read, a **rhetorical question** is one that you do not expect listeners to answer (even if they could). You ask the question simply to cause an audience (or a reader) to think about the answer.

A rhetorical question may prompt listeners to imagine themselves in some other time, place, or situation. For example, in urging white Americans to be sensitive to the role of race in the lives of African Americans, a student speaker might begin by asking,

Watch the Video "Introduction: Van Gogh's Incredible Life" at **MyCommunicationLab**

rhetorical question
A question for which no answer is expected but which encourages listeners to think.

> How would you feel if, at the time you were born, your earning capacity and life expectancy were automatically reduced for no reason but the color of your skin?

Then, to preview the development of the speech, the student might ask,

> Why is it that, more than 50 years after *Brown v. Board of Education*, educational opportunities still are not equal?

The first question gets the audience to empathize with African Americans, and the second question previews the development of the speech. Because the goal is to make the audience think, the speaker in this case would probably not state the thesis explicitly yet.

The pitfall in asking rhetorical questions is that speakers have overused or misused this device. Some may ask an introductory question merely to ask it, rather than to induce listeners to imagine a situation or to preview the speech. An even greater risk is that listeners will answer the question in their minds—with an answer that is different from what the speaker wants to discuss. In the worst case of all, someone in the audience may shout a response that undermines the entire introduction. One student began a speech about popular films of the 1960s by asking, "What do you think of when you hear the name 'James Bond'?" From the rear of the classroom another student called out, "A third-rate movie."

Sometimes you may ask a question that you *do* want listeners to answer orally, perhaps to get them actively involved in the development of your ideas or to start a pattern of questions and answers. In that case, you should pause after asking the question to give them time to reply. If they remain silent, you may even need to add a comment such as "This is not a rhetorical question" or "I really want to know your answer." The danger here is the reverse of the one above: your listeners may stay silent even though you want them to speak.

Quoting Someone.

Starting with a quotation is especially common and useful in sermons; the scriptural quotation then serves as the text on which the sermon is based. In secular settings, too, speakers often open with a quotation that captures the essential idea they intend to develop. For example, student speaker Clayton Hottinger introduced a speech on AIDS in South Africa by saying:

> "Cry aloud for the man who is dead, for the woman and children bereaved. Cry, the beloved country, these things are not yet at an end." So said anti-apartheid activist Alan Paton in a time of hatred and strife for South Africa, but now that trouble is over, right? Sadly, South Africa still has reason to cry, not because of apartheid, but because of a growing infection that might be mankind's greatest enemy: AIDS.

Student speaker Andrea Richards introduced a speech on cultural diversity by saying:

> In a famous speech in 1963, President Kennedy said, "If we cannot now end our differences, at least we can help make the world safe for diversity." President Kennedy was talking about ideological diversity, but today we need to apply his insight to the growing issue of racial, ethnic, and cultural diversity.

The quotation does not have to come from a famous person. It might be a simple statement such as this one:

> My father once told me that when someone says, 'It's not about the money,' then it's about the money. This is how I feel about all the politicians who keep insisting that they won't use negative campaigning.

Quoting an opposing viewpoint is a variation of this type of introduction. Abraham Lincoln did this superbly in a famous speech he made at Cooper Union in 1860. He began by quoting what his political rival, Stephen A. Douglas, had said about the intentions of the country's founders; then Lincoln used the Douglas quotation to highlight and advance his own thesis and main points.

Beginning a speech with a quotation is such a common introductory device that whole books of short quotations are published for this purpose. The warning about introductory quotations, however, is exactly the same as for anecdotes and analogies: Your introduction must relate directly to what you plan to say in your speech. If the audience cannot see the connection clearly, the introduction will seem superfluous and, therefore, will be counterproductive. A good test is to ask yourself whether the quotation will lead naturally to your thesis statement and partition and then to the body of the speech.

> ## CHECKLIST 1
>
> ## Types of Introductions
> ❑ Identifying with the audience
> ❑ Referring to the speech situation
> ❑ Stating the purpose
> ❑ Stating the importance of the topic
> ❑ Citing statistics or making claims
> ❑ Telling a story (anecdote)
> ❑ Using an analogy
> ❑ Asking a rhetorical question
> ❑ Quoting someone
> ❑ Using humor

Using Humor.   A very common introductory device is to begin the speech with a humorous reference or a joke. When it works, humor relaxes the audience, influences listeners to view the speaker favorably, and disarms skeptics. It also tells both the speaker and the audience to keep their perspective about the topic and not to take themselves too seriously.

Despite all these advantages of humor, the worst advice for preparing the introduction to a speech is that "every speech should start with a joke." Humor is not always appropriate to the subject (or the occasion or the audience), and the joke does not always relate directly to the speech. And sometimes a joke may not be as funny to your audience as it is to you. Especially with a culturally diverse audience, it is easy for a joke to backfire—to offend rather than to amuse. Despite the frequency with which accomplished speakers tell jokes, beginning speakers who have any doubt about them should avoid this type of introduction.[3]

This survey of the types of introductions is extensive, but it is not meant to be complete.[4] Anything can be used to begin a speech if it will achieve the four purposes of an introduction: gaining your audience's interest, influencing listeners to think well of you and your topic, clarifying your purpose or central theme, and previewing how you will develop the topic. The great variety and range of introductory devices, however, does not mean that you should select one hastily or without care. The introduction is clearly critical in making an effective speech, and you should prepare it as carefully as you do the body and the conclusion.

Strategies for Preparing an Introduction

OBJECTIVE
2

The multiple purposes of an introduction and the great variety of ways to achieve them may seem daunting, but the following strategies and suggestions should help you plan a successful introduction for your speech.

Prepare the Body of the Speech First.   Just as this text explains how to organize the body of the speech before focusing in this chapter on introductions and conclusions, you should follow that same sequence in preparing your speech. After all, it helps to know what you are introducing. Having already prepared the body, you now know what your main ideas are and how you will develop them. That information will help you craft an appropriate introduction that prepares the audience effectively. Another good reason to follow this strategy is that you will be less likely to delay preparing the entire speech just because you haven't yet thought of the "perfect" introduction.

Relate the Introduction to the Body.

Keep in mind that the introduction has to prepare your listeners and then lead them naturally into the body of your speech. The connection between the introduction and the body should be clear and direct. A particular anecdote, joke, or quotation might well arouse your audience's interest, but if it seems unrelated to your main points, it may not lead listeners in the direction you intend. Indeed, some introductions—no matter how engaging—may undercut your purposes, weakening the entire speech.

Keep the Introduction Brief.

Remember that the focus of the speech is on the main ideas that you will develop in the body; the introduction should lead listeners to these ideas, not obscure them. A too-long, too-strong introduction could turn into the tail that wags the dog, running away with the speech and ultimately confusing your audience. Some speechwriters advocate that an introduction should take 10 to 20 percent of the total time for the speech. Although this text resists such precise measurement, the key point remains: Limit the length of your introduction so that it does not become a speech in itself.[5]

Make the Introduction Complete.

Although exceptions exist, most introductions include the following elements: a device to gain your listeners' interest and to dispose them favorably toward you as a speaker, a statement of your thesis or purpose, and a preview of how you will develop the topic.

Keep a File of Potential Introductions.

In developing an introduction, you will doubtless run across ideas, quotations, examples, and other materials that are not immediately useful but that you can imagine shaping into an introduction for a future speech. Keep track of such materials. Do not rely on memory to recall them or find them at just the moment you need them. You might keep a folder on your computer where you will enter introductory material arranged by topic, adding new entries as you find them. Perhaps you might even download audio and video clips. You should keep track of potential introductions as well. Then, when you start preparing your next speech, you already will have resources and will not have to depend entirely on either memory or inspiration.

Be Guided by the Examples in This Text.

In this chapter, you have studied the most frequently used types of introductions; the appendix and other speeches in the text also illustrate a variety of introductions. Consider these examples not as models to be followed blindly, but as guidelines to help you think creatively about the best way to introduce your particular speech.

Plan the Introduction Word for Word.   Especially in the opening lines of the speech, you want to be sure that you say exactly what you intend. An extemporaneous opening is risky even for very confident, very experienced speakers, unless they have thought very carefully about the introduction first, because no one can entirely control the speech setting and circumstances. Nor is it wise to carry a written script to the podium, planning to read the introduction aloud. A good first impression is unlikely when your face is buried in notes. Instead, prepare and practice your opening words carefully so that you can begin speaking with confidence and good effect.

Preparing and practicing the introduction word for word will enable you to create the clearest, most compelling first impression on the audience. Moreover, knowing exactly what you are going to say at the beginning of your speech will give you greater confidence and a sense of security. So armed, you can overcome the anxiety that even experienced speakers feel when they stand to address an audience.

Conclusions: Ending the Speech

OBJECTIVE
3

Just as you want to begin your speech on the right note, so do you want to develop an appropriate, effective ending. A speech should neither end abruptly nor trail off into oblivion. As we did with introductions, we will approach conclusions by focusing on their purposes and their types and then looking at some strategies for preparing them.

The Purposes of a Conclusion

Like your introduction, your **conclusion** needs to accomplish several specific goals:

- Signal that the end is coming
- Summarize the main ideas
- Make a final appeal to the audience

Watch the Video "Professor Jason Warren Discusses Tips for Effective Conclusions" at **MyCommunicationLab**

Signaling That the End Is Coming.   Perhaps the most basic function of the conclusion is to signal to listeners that the speech is ending. No doubt you have heard a speaker who seemed to be finishing several times before the speech actually ended. Such a speech has "false conclusions"—misleading signals that the end is near. Summary statements, the use of the word *finally*, and similar cues alert the audience that the speech is wrapping up. But if you send such signals prematurely, you will confuse listeners and may even arouse their impatience when the speech does not end as expected.

You probably also have heard a speaker who ended so abruptly that you were surprised. Suddenly, although you thought the speaker was still developing a major idea, he or she came to the end of a sentence, said, "Thank you," and sat down. Somehow, that approach did not seem right either.

In both cases, the speakers failed to provide a satisfying sense of closure. If you confuse listeners with false endings or surprise them by stopping abruptly, your conclusion has not completed the sense of form. Listeners do need to be signaled that it is time to draw together their perceptions about the speech, but you should send this signal only at the appropriate time.

conclusion
The closing of the speech, which draws together what the speaker has said and indicates what the audience should believe or do in response to the speech.

An effective conclusion will reward the audience's attention by completing the form of the speech, drawing the ideas together, and making clear what listeners should believe or do.

Summarizing the Main Ideas. A second important purpose of the conclusion is to draw together the main ideas in your speech in a way that helps listeners to remember them. Even trained and experienced listeners rapidly forget what they have heard. If you want the audience to remember what you have said, you need to issue reminders at appropriate points throughout the speech. And no place is more appropriate for a **summary** than the conclusion.

To end a speech about the messages embodied in popular music, for example, you might summarize by saying, "As we have seen, popular music tells us about our own values, about our relationships with others, and about our obligations to nature, society, and the next generation." A summary does not exactly repeat the main ideas, and it certainly does not reprise their development. Rather, it reminds the audience of key points, often by highlighting particular words or phrases in a way that listeners can remember—as in the parallel structure of the three "about" phrases in this example.

An effective summary, then, is an aid to memory. By including a summary in your conclusion, you will increase the chances that listeners will recall your main ideas correctly.

Making a Final Appeal to the Audience. The conclusion is also an opportunity to say exactly what response you want from the audience. It is your last chance to remind listeners about whatever you want them to think or do as a result of your speech.

Sometimes a speaker wants listeners to take a very specific action, such as signing a petition, donating money, writing to their legislators, or purchasing a particular product. At other times, the desired response is a belief rather than an action. For example, suppose you want the audience to agree that the current president and administration have set a correct course in foreign policy matters. You are not asking listeners to take any specific action, but you do want them to be favorably disposed toward the president's international policies. Your conclusion might say, "I hope I've convinced you that the president's foreign policy is on the right track." Although you are not asking for anything directly, you do want to intensify or to change your listeners' beliefs. Either response may lead to actions later.

Sometimes the response you seek may be even more general, as in these four examples of concluding remarks:

- The next time you consider buying running shoes from one of these companies, consider the people working in the sweatshops who make it possible for you to get an affordable deal.

- You may not agree with me that Michael Phelps is the world's best athlete, but I hope you will appreciate the dedication and perseverance of professional swimmers.

- There are strong arguments on both sides of the abortion debate. I ask that you think about what I have said and come to your own conclusion about what you believe.

- You may not decide to hop a plane to the slums of Bangladesh as I did, but maybe you will consider other spring break travel alternatives that will make a difference in the lives of the less fortunate.

summary
A condensed restatement of the principal ideas just discussed.

None of these concluding statements calls for action, and yet each of them asks listeners to "do" something: to become more aware of something they had not recognized or to think critically about something they had accepted.

Virtually any speech—whether or not it is billed as a "persuasive" speech—asks for some response from the audience. In developing the conclusion of a speech, your goal is to make the audience understand exactly what response you seek.

An Example of a Conclusion

Here's how Michelle Ekanemesang ended her classroom speech about online sexual predators:

> So remember that we must commit ourselves to keeping children safe from the scourge of online sexual predators. These psychologically damaged men and women use a bag of tricks to deceive, lure, and abuse their prey—innocent children who will bear emotional and physical scars for a lifetime. We can blunt the weapons of online sexual predators by equipping children in our community with the education and knowledge they will need to detect, report, and foil the plans of sexual predators. I hope the information I've shared with you today will not fall on deaf or apathetic ears; please mention the tools I've discussed to a young person in your life. Remember that prevention is always better than a cure!

Michelle's first concluding sentence hinted to the audience that her speech was coming to an end. The next two sentences summarized the points she had made in the body of her speech. Finally, she asked the audience to take action and help stop online sexual predators by passing on the information that children need in order to prevent this form of sexual abuse.

Types of Conclusions

You already know that the types of introductions can be developed in various ways to achieve your purpose. The same is true for conclusions. Indeed, some of the following types of conclusions mirror the types of introductions you have studied; others introduce new elements into the speech.

Summarizing. We observed earlier that one purpose of the conclusion is to summarize the main points of the speech. Sometimes, summary is the *dominant* purpose. In that case, the concluding summary would be more extended than in the preceding examples. It would remind the audience not only about major topics addressed but also about the details of your argument, even repeating some memorable thematic phrases. Such an extensive concluding summary may need a "miniconclusion" of its own, to avoid ending abruptly or trailing off into insignificance.

In contrast, sometimes a succinct, bare-bones restatement of key phrases may make the most rousing finish. Consider the following conclusion from a speech by President George W. Bush outlining his strategy for responding to the terrorist attacks of September 11, 2001:

> Fellow citizens, we'll meet violence with patient justice—assured of the rightness of our cause, and confident of the victories to come.

The first part of the sentence captures the essence of Bush's policy, and the two clauses after the dash (note their parallel structure!) are a brief but powerful reminder of the attitudes the president sought to represent and to evoke.

 Watch the **Video** "The Process of Developing a Speech: Conclusions—Using Recapping/Summary" at **MyCommunicationLab**

Quoting Someone.   Just as many speeches begin with a quotation, so many end with one. In both cases, remember to tie the quotation clearly to your speech. A concluding quotation, however, may also go beyond your central ideas and give the audience something to think about; the risk of confusing listeners is much lower at the conclusion, because they have already heard your main points.

Student speaker Kim Davis found a quotation that succinctly summed up her ideas in a speech about gays in the military. Quoting a gay soldier who had been discharged for his sexual preference, she read:

> "They gave me a medal for killing two men, and a discharge for loving one."

Closing quotations should be like this one—a few neatly balanced, memorable words that sum up your central idea or advance your main purpose.

Making a Personal Reference.   Particularly if your speech is about impersonal or abstract issues, it may be appropriate in the conclusion to personalize the issues by making reference to yourself. Such a concluding device (1) illustrates your own identification with the subject—you embody the ideas and values in the speech—and (2) encourages the audience to identify with you. In this way, listeners might imagine that they have the same feelings you have about the topic.

Student Romila Mushtag used this type of conclusion effectively after arguing that hate speech should not be outlawed on campus. She ended the speech by showing the audience a handwritten racist note that had been taped to her locker door. By revealing that she had been victimized by hate speech and yet would defend someone's right to use such speech, she demonstrated a level of

Rhetorical Workout

Conclude Your Speech

You've written the body and introduction of your speech demonstrating how to ride a snowboard. Your purpose is to teach your audience a few basics about snowboarding. Think about some types of conclusions and how they could work with this speech.

1. *Summarizing:* How could an extended summary of your main "how-to" points benefit your listeners?

2. *Quoting someone:* Suppose you find three catchy quotations and you want to use one as a conclusion. How appropriate or interesting do you think each of the following might be: (a) a snowboarding instructor on how knowing the basics increases your safety; (b) a first-time snowboarder on how much fun he had learning; (c) a professional snowboarder on how much she practices.

3. *Making a personal reference:* How might concluding with a personal reference or story affect your audience?

4. *Challenging the audience:* How could you use your conclusion to challenge your listeners?

5. *Offering a utopian vision:* Suppose you chose this topic because you enjoy snowboarding and you find it to be good exercise. How could you turn these elements into a conclusion that offers a utopian, positive vision to your audience?

6. What are some potential strengths and weaknesses of each type of conclusion? Which type would you use for this speech? Why?

integrity that the audience couldn't help endorsing and trying to emulate. Her personal reference made listeners identify with her—and with the ideas in her speech.

Challenging the Audience.

Particularly when your speech asks the audience to do something, concluding with a direct challenge may be effective. This type of conclusion not only creates a common bond between speaker and audience but also transfers to the audience some of the responsibility for achieving the speaker's goals. For example, student speaker Todd McCullough, after summarizing his main ideas, ended a speech about the need for environmentally and economically responsible automobiles with this challenge:

> We need to use our power as consumers to purchase vehicles that are fuel efficient and to boycott the continued production of gas-guzzling vehicles. We are here at college to get an education so we can go out and make a living. We cannot afford to watch as our paychecks are devoured by our automobiles. It is time to rise up and demand fuel-efficient vehicles.

Offering a Utopian Vision.

Closely related to challenging the audience is this type of conclusion, which offers an idealized, positive vision of what can be achieved if only the audience will work together with the speaker. Rather than focusing on the challenge itself, however, this approach emphasizes the results of meeting the challenge successfully. The vision is called "utopian" not to dismiss it, but to emphasize that it usually transcends the immediate, practical world. One of the most famous examples of a conclusion containing a utopian vision is Martin Luther King, Jr.'s "I Have a Dream" address, delivered in 1963 at the March on Washington.

Abraham Lincoln also used this type of conclusion often. After warning of the perilous situation facing the Union in 1861, at the time of his first inaugural address, Lincoln confidently predicted in his conclusion that "the mystic chords of memory, stretching from every battlefield and patriot grave to every living heart and hearthstone all over this broad land, will yet swell the chorus of the Union, when again touched, as surely they will be, by the better angels of our nature." Yes, clouds may darken the sky at the moment, Lincoln was saying, but he promised his listeners that together they could achieve positive results in the fullness of time.

Even speeches about less momentous topics may conclude by envisioning how things will be once a problem is solved or a goal is achieved. Offering a utopian vision is particularly effective when the speaker is calling on the audience to make sacrifices or to take risks to achieve a distant goal. By predicting ultimate success, the utopian vision assures listeners that what the speaker is calling for will be worth the efforts they make.

Besides these specific types of conclusions, notice that many of the introductory approaches discussed earlier also can be used for the conclusion, including narratives, anecdotes, and rhetorical questions.[6] In the same way, some types of conclusions can be adapted effectively for use in an introduction. A quotation or a personal reference, for instance, can be as powerful at the beginning of the speech as at the end.

 Watch the Video "The Process of Developing a Speech: Conclusions" at **MyCommunicationLab**

OBJECTIVE

4

Strategies for Preparing a Conclusion

Several of the earlier suggestions for preparing an introduction apply as well to preparing a conclusion:

- Work on the conclusion after developing the body of your speech; again, it helps to know what you are concluding.
- Connect the conclusion clearly to the body of the speech so that listeners will grasp how it relates to your main ideas.
- Keep the conclusion relatively brief so that it does not detract from the speech itself.
- Aim for a complete conclusion, including both a wrap-up of your major ideas and a clear indication of how you want listeners to respond.
- Summarize your argument memorably; then tell the audience what belief or action you seek.

The following additional guidelines and suggestions will help you develop an effective conclusion.

Be Sure That it Truly Is the Conclusion.   This first principle is simple to state but no less important for that. As you begin to develop the conclusion, take care to put it at the end of the body, and lead the audience naturally into your summary and final appeal.

Recall once more that listeners get distracted or confused when a speech departs from customary structure. On the one hand, avoid any wording that might signal a false (premature) conclusion. You certainly do not want your audience to applaud when, after several false endings, you finally say, "In conclusion…," as actually happened to Arkansas Governor Bill Clinton at the 1988 Democratic convention. On the other hand, indicate clearly when you are ready to move from the body of your speech to its conclusion.

Return to Your Introductory Device When Possible.   One way to enhance the sense of form and unity in a speech is to conclude by referring again to the device you used in the introduction. If you began with a quotation, you may be able to repeat that same quotation in your conclusion, teasing a different meaning from it now that the audience has heard how you developed your topic. If your introductory device was an anecdote or a rhetorical question, your conclusion might return to that same device and embellish it based on the ideas you developed in your speech.

Of course, this suggestion cannot always be followed. The ideas in the speech may have moved far beyond where they were in the introduction, and returning to the introductory device would seem jarring ("Isn't this where we came in?"). But when you can return to the introduction, listeners will feel that the speech hangs together well, that it has a satisfying sense of structure.

Practice the Conclusion.   The inspiration of the moment is no more dependable at the end of a speech than at the beginning. Just as you developed your introduction word for word, so should you prepare a conclusion by writing out key phrases and sentences that summarize your ideas and make a strong appeal. In addition, practice the conclusion orally. Your speaking rate is likely to slow down by the end of the speech; you probably will pause briefly between the body and the conclusion; and specific words and phrases will need careful emphasis. Practicing the conclusion out loud a few times before you present the entire speech will help you craft both its content and its ultimate effect.

Transitions: Connecting the Elements of a Speech

OBJECTIVE
5

Introduction, body, and conclusion—these structural elements seem so static that, in planning one of them, you can easily forget how dynamic a speech actually is. From beginning to end, the speech represents movement. You begin with a set of ideas and a strategic objective; by moving through the ideas, you also move toward achieving the objective. Similarly, listeners begin with a certain level of understanding about the subject and a certain disposition toward you as speaker; careful listening and thinking move them through the speech as well.

This dynamic movement of both speaker and listeners is achieved by—and depends on—connections that the speaker provides to bridge any gaps between elements. **Transitions** connect the introduction to the body, connect the main ideas within the body, and connect the body to the conclusion.

The Purposes of Transitions

The most important purpose of transitions is to create this sense of movement. They also help listeners follow the speaker's movement and remember what the speaker said. Equally important, transitions keep the speaker from lapsing into nervous mannerisms that would accentuate the gaps between ideas.[7]

Even accomplished speakers sometimes neglect to think about transitions. They may organize the body of the speech carefully, labor to devise an effective introduction, and craft a compelling conclusion; yet they assume that transitions will spring up spontaneously. Facing the audience, however, their spontaneous connections may be as pedestrian as "My next point is…" or "Next, let me discuss…." The movement is halting; the sense of form is unclear.

transition
A connection, or bridge, between the main elements of the speech and between the main ideas within the body of the speech.

Strategies for Speaking to Diverse Audiences

Respecting Diversity Through Introductions and Conclusions

Introductions and conclusions are important places to recognize and adapt to the diversity of the audience. Here are some strategies that will enable you to do so:

1. Consider the variety of strategies for building goodwill with your audience. Strive to identify with them early in your speech, but recognize that you will have to make a conscious decision in your introduction about how to do so.

2. Humor is an excellent way either to build goodwill with your audience or to alienate them. Demeaning individuals or cultural groups through humor should be avoided.

3. Offer "utopian visions" that enable listeners to imagine themselves as you ideally want them to be, emphasizing common values or themes that transcend diverse cultures.

Even worse is a speaker who bridges gaps and moves forward on the basis of sheer nervous energy and repetition. You probably have heard a speaker who punctuated every pause with "Umm…" or "like…," or who completed every thought with "Okay" or "Right?" or who moved to each new point with "Now, then…." Such mannerisms can become so obvious and distracting that the audience starts counting them rather than listening to the speech.

From your experience as a listener, then, you know that an effective speaker understands the nature of transitions and includes them consciously to create movement and form. The rest of the chapter focuses on how to provide such connections in your speeches.

 **Explore** the **Exercise** "Better Transitions" at **MyCommunicationLab**

OBJECTIVE **6**

Elements of Effective Transitions

We cannot list and describe "types" of transitions, as we could with introductions and conclusions. Transitions have three basic elements: an internal summary of what has been completed, a link to what is coming next, and an internal preview of the new idea. These three elements sometimes will be found in isolation, but a complete transition will include them all.

Internal Summaries. Like a concluding summary at the end of the speech, an **internal summary** draws together the central points that were discussed within the body of the speech or even within the discussion of one main idea, serving both to aid memory and to signal closure to those points. The following are simple examples of internal summaries:

1. In a speech recommending that your college switch from a quarter to a semester system:

    So, as we've seen, abandoning the quarter system would permit students to take classes that last longer, allowing them to learn more about a particular subject and reducing the pressures they face.

2. In a speech arguing that both students and faculty would benefit if the school offered more sections of closed classes:

    I hope I've made it clear that one benefit of additional sections of closed courses is more individualized attention. The faculty will be able to answer more questions in class and students will get prompt feedback.

3. In a speech about current campaign finance laws:

    So the current campaign finance laws really do pose a serious problem, because they encourage influence peddling, because they encourage legislators to forego their legislative work to engage in time-consuming fundraising, and because they lessen public confidence in government's ability to represent the interests of ordinary working people.

4. In a speech about multiculturalism:

    As I see it, then, our commitment to cultural diversity came about through this and other key incidents that embarrassed us by showing the limitations of our perspective.

Internal summary
a summary within the body of the speech, drawing together one of the main ideas.

Each of these internal summaries wraps up one main idea of the speech. It gives the audience a brief reminder of the idea and also signals the point of completion.

A Question of Ethics

Ethical Introductions and Conclusions

Introductions and conclusions are important because they set the tone for the speech and consolidate the ideas of the speech in a memorable way. Speakers should be creative in developing their introductions and conclusions. But what if the tone or nature of the introduction or conclusion is different from that of the body of the speech? For example, does a light-hearted or engaging story in the introduction distort the audience's response to the body of the speech that is the somber explanation of the latest economic crisis? Does the speaker have an ethical responsibility not to deviate from the body of the speech when crafting the introduction and conclusion? Is it ethical to create a tone in the introduction that gets the audience interested, and then to change the tone or nature of the argument within the speech? Or is this just a matter of artistic creativity and not ethics? What are the benefits, drawbacks, and ethical concerns raised by placing ideas in the introduction and conclusion that do not appear elsewhere in the speech?

Links. Links are connections from one idea to the next. Some links are subtle and are established through careful word choice; others are explicit.

The construction *not only…but also* is an example of a subtle link. It moves from the point that was just discussed to the one that is coming up next, as in "Not only are closed classes bad for the students but also they're bad for the faculty." The speaker thus links two ideas that previously were separate in the speech.

Conjunctions such as *in addition, furthermore,* and *moreover* have the same effect. They suggest the cumulation of ideas, linking the ideas by hinting that the one to come will build on the one just considered. In contrast, conjunctions such as *however, nonetheless,* and *on the other hand* signal that the speaker is going to move from one point of view to an opposing viewpoint or in some way will qualify or limit the force of what was just said.

Sometimes links are more explicit. The speaker who finishes one idea with an internal summary and then says, "But here's the proverbial fly in the ointment," is announcing that the point just made is about to be rendered troublesome or problematic or that something calls it into question. And the speaker who says, "It's not enough to focus on the cost of higher education; we also have to be concerned with quality," is telling the audience that they need to consider one more important factor.

How subtle or explicit should a particular link be? That depends on several factors. If the connection seems obvious and listeners can be expected to see it without help, an explicit link may be insulting. But if the connection between points is complex or seems to contradict common sense, an explicit link may be appreciated. Audiences can follow narrative and chronological links more easily than they can follow analytical links. Similarly, links based on "common knowledge" and general understanding do not have to be as explicit as links that require specialized knowledge or training.

Internal Previews. A preview is a compressed version of what the speaker is about to develop; it prompts the audience to anticipate what is coming. The introduction will probably preview your main ideas. Similarly, an **internal preview** will help prepare your audience to follow along every time you introduce

internal preview
A preview within the body of the speech, leading into one of the main ideas.

a new main idea. Here are some examples of how to do that, corresponding to the examples of internal summaries that you recently read:

1. In your speech on abandoning the quarter system, an internal preview might point out,

   One of the most important reasons is that in a semester system students will have a longer time to learn what is offered in each course.

2. In your speech arguing for more sections of closed courses, an internal preview between the first and second main points might tell the audience,

   The second reason to have more sections is that the faculty will be able to give each student more attention.

3. In your speech about campaign finance laws, the body of the speech might start with an internal preview of the first major argument:

   Some argue that campaign finance laws no longer pose a serious problem. I don't agree, and let me tell you why.

4. In your speech about multiculturalism, an internal preview might signal that you are going to tell a story about how cultural diversity became a concern on campus.

Whether obviously or subtly, each of these internal previews tells the audience what to expect—each is a kind of early alert system for the audience. An internal preview signals that listeners should get ready to move on to a new aspect of the speech, and it provides clues about the nature of the movement or the new aspect itself.

 Watch the **Video** "The Process of Developing a Speech: Transitions" at **MyCommunicationLab**

Whether previewing or summarizing the entire speech or just a part, you can use repetition and restatement to alert the audience that you are beginning or ending one of your key points. For example, the first internal preview described above might be elaborated as follows:

One reason to abandon the quarter system is that students will have longer to learn what is offered in each course. More time to learn means less rush. Let me explain why this is so.

Similarly, the second internal summary above might be drawn out in this way:

I hope I've made it clear that one benefit of additional sections of closed courses is more individualized attention. The faculty will be able to answer more questions in class, and students will get prompt feedback. Opening up more sections of closed courses will truly help our teachers to interact more with us and that, in turn, will benefit us.

Complete Transitions. As we have suggested, not every element of every transition need be made apparent. But a complete transition would include an internal summary of the point being concluded, a link to connect it to the next point, and an internal preview leading into the new point. For example, a complete transition in the speech about abandoning the quarter system might go like this:

After discussing the history of the Statue of Liberty, the speaker signals a transition to considering its artistic features. Notice how the verbal transition is matched by gesture corresponding to the outstretched arm on the statue.

So there's no doubt that students will benefit from the change. Abandoning the quarter system will give them more time to write papers and study for final exams and will reduce their level of pressure and stress. [*Internal summary*] But students aren't the only ones who will gain from this change. [*Link*] The faculty will gain two benefits as well. Let me tell you about them. [*Internal preview*]

If you think that such a complete transition somehow seems stilted or unnatural, think again after imagining how a speech would be hurt by a really awkward transition such as this one:

> Uh, okay. Enough about that. Time to move on. Uh, okay. Oh yes, let me discuss…

This speaker completely sacrificed a sense of smooth progression of ideas, one of the most important contributions that transitions make to the speech.

Strategies for Preparing Transitions

Besides deciding how explicit to make each transition and whether to use repetition to emphasize the transition, consider the following brief suggestions.

Identify Main Ideas Succinctly.
In internal previews and internal summaries, quickly and clearly identify the main idea being referred to; that will make it easier to remember. Rather than restating an idea completely, use a memorable word or phrase to highlight it in the transition.

Use Parallel Structure if Possible.
When related ideas are identified in a similar or parallel fashion, that repeated pattern may make the link more memorable.

Use Signposting.
Signposting is the use of verbal cues to alert the audience to where you are in the speech. If you say that you will discuss three advantages of something, in previewing each advantage it will be helpful to identify it as "first," "second," or "third." Listeners will have no doubt that you have completed the discussion of one advantage and are about to talk about the next; and they also will clearly perceive the structure that you intended. Similarly, you can use pauses, repetition, and changes in speaking rate, pitch, or volume as signposting to guide the audience.

CHECKLIST 3

Transitions: Critical Thinking and Strategic Planning

1. Questions to ask yourself: At this point in my speech:
   - ❑ Do my listeners need a reminder or an alert about how far I've come?
   - ❑ Do my listeners need a reminder of how my last point relates to my next?
   - ❑ Do I need some verbal markers to help me and my listeners follow my outline?
   - ❑ Will my listeners follow my ideas better if I give them a brief preview?

2. If the answer is "Yes," here are some things worth doing:
   - ❑ Construct brief phrases that identify main ideas in the speech, and use them as markers and reminders at key intervals.
   - ❑ Set up your points in parallel structure whenever possible. Check your outline to help you do this.
   - ❑ Include verbal signposts that briefly show where you are and what comes next.

---

signposting
Using verbal cues to indicate to the audience where you are in the speech.

What Have You Learned?

Objective 1: Identify the main purposes and some common types of introductions.

The introduction shapes the audience's first impressions; its purposes are as follows:

- To gain attention and interest
- To influence the audience to view the speaker and topic favorably

- To state the thesis or purpose of the speech
- To preview how the speech will be developed

Some common types of introductions include the following:

- Identifying with the audience
- Referring to the speech situation
- Stating the purpose of the speech
- Stating the importance of the topic
- Citing statistics and making claims
- Telling a story (anecdote)
- Using an analogy
- Asking a rhetorical question
- Quoting someone
- Using humor

Objective 2: Prepare an introduction.

The introduction should be

- Prepared after the body of the speech is well in hand
- Related to the body
- Brief but complete
- Worded (and practiced) carefully

Objective 3: Identify the main purposes and some common types of conclusions.

The purposes of the conclusion are as follows:

- To complete the speech and signal to the audience that the end is near
- To summarize the main ideas
- To make a final appeal to listeners, asking them to adopt a particular belief or action

Among the common types of conclusions are the following:

- Summarizing
- Quoting someone

- Making a personal reference
- Challenging the audience
- Offering a utopian vision

Objective 4: Prepare a conclusion.

Guidelines for planning a conclusion are similar to those of the introduction. When possible, the conclusion should return in some way to the introductory device.

Objective 5: Use transitions to connect the elements of a speech and give its structure a dynamic quality.

Transitions serve to

- Give a sense of movement or progression to the speech by guiding listeners from one point to the next.
- Help the audience remember the main points and the structure of the speech.
- Reduce a speaker's distracting mannerisms in attempting to move from one idea to the next.

Transitions should have these characteristics:

- They should be succinct.
- They should use parallel structure if possible.
- They should provide signposting to guide the audience.

Objective 6: Recognize the elements of a transition, which may be either explicit or implicit.

A complete transition includes three elements:

- Internal summary
- Link
- Internal preview

However, not all elements are presented explicitly in every transition.

 Listen to the **Audio Chapter Summary** at **MyCommunicationLab**

Discussion Questions

1. a. Which type of introduction would be most effective in each of the following speech situations?
   - A speech introducing the recipient of a lifetime achievement award
   - An informative speech to classmates about how to improve study skills
   - A speech to warn boaters about the dangers of "mixing water and alcohol"
   - A speech to strengthen volunteers' commitment to helping the homeless
   - A speech to reverse opposition to the death penalty

   b. In those same speech situations, which type of introduction would be least appropriate? Why?

2. What does an introduction need in order to prepare the audience effectively for the speech? Meet in small groups to answer this question. Each group member will present the introduction to a speech, and the other group members then will guess the speaker's purpose, the rhetorical situation, and the content of the speech. After everyone has made a guess, the speaker will reveal the actual purpose, situation, and content so that the group can compare intent and effect and then discuss ways to improve that introduction.

3. Which factors should a speaker consider when deciding how complete to make a particular transition? Discuss how the following constraints and opportunities might or might not influence your decision:

• Your main points are organized in a dependent pattern.

• Your main points are organized in an independent pattern.

• You are moving between main ideas in the speech.

• You are moving between subpoints within a main idea.

• You are giving a speech that teaches a difficult concept to a group of students.

• You are giving a speech to a group of protesters that enumerates well-known reasons to reinforce their commitment to the movement.

Activities

1. On a copy of a speech manuscript you have retrieved from the library or the Internet, do the following:

   a. Mark the passages in the text that make up the introduction, conclusion, and transitions. What do these markings tell you about the organization of the speech?

   b. Identify the strategies used in the introduction and in the conclusion.

   c. Closely examine at least one transition in the speech. Is it complete? Can you identify the internal summary, link, and internal preview?

   d. Evaluate the effectiveness of the introduction, conclusion, and transitions. What makes them effective or ineffective? How would you improve them?

2. Create three potential introductions and conclusions for your next speech. Choose the best one of each, and explain why you think it is best.

3. Follow the instructions in Checklist 3 to plan strategic transitions for your next speech.

4. Using the three introductions that you wrote for activity two, read each to a group of other students. Together, make a list of positive aspects (to repeat) and mistakes (to avoid).

Key Terms

conclusion
internal preview
internal summary

introduction
partition
rhetorical question

signposting
summary
transition

 Study and **Review** the **Flashcards** at **MyCommunicationLab**

Notes

1 Although first impressions may be durable, even such "first-impression bias" may be overridden. See Tanya Kraljic, Arthur G. Samuel, and Susan E. Brennan, "First Impressions and Last Resorts: How Listeners Adjust to Speaker Variability," *Psychology Science* 19 (April, 2008): 332–38.

2 Classical theorists often used words such as this, from the language of architecture, to describe the organization of speeches. See Leland M. Griffin, "The Edifice Metaphor in Rhetorical Theory," *Communication Monographs* 27 (November 1960): 279–92.

3 For more on the effects of humor in speeches, see C. R. Gruner, "Advice to the Beginning Speaker on Using Humor—What the Research Tells Us," *Communication Education* 34 (April 1985): 142–47. For a contemporary view on risqué humor and the varieties of interpretation open to an audience, see Lisa Glebatis Perks, "Polysemic Scaffolding: Explicating Discursive Clashes in Chappelle's Show," *Communication, Culture & Critique* 3 (June, 2010): 270–89.

4 For another list of introduction types, see Richard Whately, *Elements of Rhetoric*, Carbondale: Southern Illinois University Press, 1963, originally published 1828, pp. 170–72.

5 One early study found that, on average, introductions made up 9 percent of the total speech and conclusions made up 4 percent. See Ed Miller, "Speech Introductions and Conclusions," *Quarterly Journal of Speech* 32 (April 1946): 181–83.

6 For a discussion on the use of metaphor in conclusions, see John Waite Bowers and Michael M. Osborn, "Attitudinal Effects of Selected Types of Concluding Metaphors in Persuasive Speeches," *Communication Monographs* 33 (June 1966): 148–55.

7 Research shows that transitions make it easier for listeners to comprehend a speech. See Ernest Thompson, "Some Effects of Message Structure on Listeners' Comprehension," *Communication Monographs* 34 (March 1967): 51–57.

Photo Credits

Credits are listed in order of appearance.

Organizing Your Speech

OVERVIEW AND LEARNING OBJECTIVES

The Elements of Sound Organization

1 Explain how the quality of your ideas influences the strength of your speech's organization.

How Patterns of Organization Connect Ideas

2 Describe basic organizational patterns you might use as you arrange your ideas strategically.

Guidelines for Organizing Your Speech

3 List and explain underlying principles of sound organization you will follow, regardless of the specific pattern you choose.

Transitions as Connectives

4 Describe different transitional devices you might use in creating a coherent presentation.

Introducing Your Speech

5 Identify the key components of a speech's introduction.

Concluding Your Speech

6 List different ways of concluding a speech effectively.

S ome speakers carefully select and focus their topics, have a clear purpose and thesis, seek out good supporting materials, and still fail to deliver a good speech. Part of their failure may be due to how they have organized their materials. This chapter is devoted to helping you understand how to organize your ideas in a way that will help you achieve your purpose.

THE ELEMENTS OF SOUND ORGANIZATION

1 Explain how the quality of your ideas influences the strength of your speech's organization.

Preview. *Nearly everyone recognizes that a speech must have strong content and be delivered effectively. Yet what impact, if any, does the organization of those ideas and supporting materials have on the listeners' response? Research and experience have shown that sound organization can have a significant effect on the audience's willingness and ability to listen and their impressions of the speaker's credibility.*

Effective speakers organize their speeches carefully. They think about what to include and what to leave out. They do not introduce irrelevant or redundant information. The best speakers understand how much background to cover, which issues to address, and how best to allocate their limited time.

Good organization is important for many reasons. Well-organized speakers appear to be competent, focused, and knowledgeable. As a result, listeners perceive them as more credible.[1] A clearly organized presentation also promotes learning and retention.[2] Delivering a well-organized presentation is one of the *best* ways for you to show respect for your listeners. When you take the time and effort to organize your comments clearly and coherently, you show that you care about making yourself understood. No listener should have to struggle to understand a presentation that is disorganized or incoherent.[3]

The quality of your organization depends on the clarity and simplicity of your ideas, as well as their appropriateness to the particular situation and audience. A well-organized speech is clear, straightforward, and easily comprehended by your listeners.

Clarity of Ideas

To be clear, an idea must first be complete. Consider, for example, Amy, who wants to speak on reforming the way appropriations for pet projects (known as *earmarks*) are inserted into legislation by members of Congress. In drafting an outline, she first clarified her specific purpose and thesis statement. These were clearly articulated and reflected the guidelines for such statements. The draft read like this:

> **Specific purpose:** *I want my audience to agree that the process through which earmarking projects are selected significantly influences the nature and outcomes of those initiatives.*
> **Thesis statement:** *Earmarking can lead to positive outcomes when sound selection procedures are used.*
> **Main Ideas**
> I. Earmark examples
> II. Criticism of earmarks

III. How earmarks waste money
IV. Benefits of earmarks
 V. Transparency and accountability

Although Amy's specific purpose and thesis statement were clear, her main points were not. None of her ideas were in the form of a complete sentence; each was undeveloped and unclear. As a result, the main points were not easily distinguished and some even overlapped. The first idea was not a main idea at all, but rather one type of supporting material—examples—that she might use throughout the speech. Amy's second point was too vague; her third point referred to one of several of the criticisms one might make of earmarks. Amy wanted to describe the potential risks and controversies of earmarking. At the same time, she sought to acknowledge that earmarks sometimes produce good results, providing funding for badly needed local projects. Ultimately, her goal was to advocate vigilance in the earmark vetting process to control the abuses sometimes associated with the practice.

Thus, Amy ultimately decided on a problem-solution pattern of organization, identifying pros and cons, and then spelling out the specifics of a sound process for examining and choosing earmarks. Her new outline reflected this pattern:

 I. The process and practice of adding earmarks to legislation in the U.S. Congress have long been controversial.
   A. Some argue that earmarks waste taxpayer dollars, with many going to support trivial projects.
   B. Others believe that legislators promote earmarks because of personal or political gain.[4]
   C. Some have called for a permanent ban on the practice of earmarking.
   D. Earmarks can lead to political corruption.
 II. In spite of these concerns, earmarking can lead to a number of positive outcomes.
   A. Projects financed through earmarking have revitalized communities, saved lives, and improved local economies.[5]
   B. Earmarks are chosen by elected representatives—who presumably are close to their communities and know their legitimate needs and concerns.
   C. The process of choosing projects to earmark can lead to bipartisan collaboration.
 III. The key is creating a rigorous vetting process for earmarks.
   A. Keep debates about earmarking open to public scrutiny and accountability.
   B. Maintain current rules that require a written statement by the sponsoring legislator(s) certifying that neither they nor their spouses have a financial interest in the proposed project.
   C. Maintain vigilance and, if necessary, require additional disclosure or documentation as earmarking projects are debated and chosen.

Amy's plan for the speech was now clear, with straightforward main ideas stated in complete sentences. Her subordinate ideas were also clear and coherent, and all that remained was for her to fill in the details with examples, testimony, and other forms of evidence.

Simplicity of Ideas

Audiences must be able to understand your ideas if they are to respond positively. In addition to clarity, the simplicity of your main ideas is important. You want to state your ideas fully and accurately, yet in terms simple enough that your listeners can understand immediately and recall your main ideas pretty much word for word.

To achieve this ideal, ask yourself whether you have stated your ideas in the most basic ways possible. Avoid combining two or three ideas in one main point. Strive for a balance among your main points, so that you allocate approximately the same amount of time to each.

Some speakers try to include too much information or even a whole series of ideas within one main point. Meleia, for example, proposed the following speech:

> **Specific purpose:** *I want my audience to become more actively involved in politics.*
> **Thesis statement:** *Political involvement leads to positive results.*

She stated her first main idea like this:

I. People who take an interest in politics can have a practical impact, help restore idealism to the process, and learn valuable personal skills.

This main point tries to do too much. It is not a single idea. Instead, it is really two and perhaps even three interrelated ideas. Meleia needs to sort out the ideas and focus separately on each. A revised version of this outline might look like this:

I. There are practical benefits to society when more citizens participate in politics.
II. The political system itself also benefits from more citizen participation.
III. Individuals who participate in the political process gain valuable personal skills.

If Meleia can convince her audience that important benefits can be gained from participating in politics, then she will have achieved her purpose. To accomplish this, of course, she will have to take the next step and develop each of her ideas with supporting materials. She will need to enumerate the benefits that come from political participation, show that they are indeed beneficial, and make them real and compelling for her audience.

Simplicity, then, goes hand in hand with clarity as a basic characteristic of a well-stated main point. What seems simple and clear to one audience, however, may not seem that way to a different audience, so it is also important that you consider the situation and audience as you prepare your speech.

Suitability to the Situation

A speech is designed for a specific audience. A speech is also influenced by the occasion that prompts it and the setting in which it occurs. Thus, your ideas must not only be clear and simple but also appropriate for the particular audience and context.

The level of complexity of any idea will be significantly influenced by the audience's relationship to the topic. If, for example, you wanted to address the threat posed by the growing federal deficit, you might choose to introduce ideas that are highly technical, sophisticated, and complex if you were addressing a group of economists at a professional conference. If, on the other hand, you were speaking to your classmates, you would probably want to offer more basic information about the deficit, including background information and definitions of key terms. How technical or complex your discussion should be, then, depends on what the audience brings to the speech in terms of their background, experience, and expectations.

HOW PATTERNS OF ORGANIZATION CONNECT IDEAS

Preview. *To make a set of ideas reasonable and coherent for your audience, you need to put the ideas together so that they relate to one another in some logical fashion. To do this, you will use such basic patterns of organization as chronological or sequential, spatial, categorical, climactic, cause-and-effect, problem-solution, and narrative.*

When you have developed a good idea or series of ideas, you then face the job of arranging them in some order. It is important to recognize that most speeches can be organized in a variety of different ways. *Your* task is to choose the most appropriate organizational pattern for the particular topic and situation in which you are speaking.

There are several organizational patterns from which to choose. Here, however, we introduce several of the most commonly used organizational patterns.

Chronological or Sequential Order

One commonly used pattern of arrangement is chronological order. You begin with a specific point in time and then move forward or backward, depending on the nature of the subject. Chronological order may be useful with a variety of topics, most notably those that deal with a process or a historical event. Thus, the development of the labor movement in the United States, the events that led up to the dissolution of the Soviet Union, or the evolution of the Tea Party as a national political force might all be appropriate subjects for chronological arrangement.

Here is how one student, providing an historical account of Nazi Germany, arranged his ideas in a chronological pattern:

> **Specific purpose:** *I want my audience to understand how the Nazis came to power in Germany.*
> **Thesis statement:** *Nazism grew out of social and political unrest.*
> I. In 1919, the Treaty of Versailles created several serious problems for Germany.
> II. Financial crises encouraged the National Socialists to attempt an unsuccessful coup in Bavaria in 1923.
> III. By 1930, the National Socialist Party had emerged as a major political party.
> IV. The violent election campaign of 1933 brought the Nazi Party to power.

Similar to the chronological pattern is the sequential pattern, which you would use if you wanted your audience to understand some step-by-step procedure or

2 Describe basic organizational patterns you might use as you arrange your ideas strategically.

Explore the Concept "Organization" at **MyCommunicationLab**

process. For instance, if you wanted listeners to understand the process involved in applying for government-subsidized housing, you could begin with the first step that the applicant takes and follow the process in order, step by step. You could similarly use a sequential pattern to help listeners understand how the Asian long-horned beetle attacks and destroys trees, how terrorists make dirty bombs, or the steps involved in adopting a child.

Spatial Order

A second common pattern is spatial arrangement. With this pattern, you use space as your ordering principle. A speech explaining the architectural plans for a new library, a presentation describing major tourist attractions of a big city (as one travels from north to south), or a speech describing the most progressive, reform-oriented prisons in the United States may all be appropriate candidates for spatial organization.

The following is an example of how one student arranged ideas in a spatial pattern determined by geography as he addressed the need for emergency preparedness in the United States.

> **Specific purpose:** *I want my audience to recognize the serious natural disasters that increasingly threaten all of our geographical regions.*
> **Thesis statement:** *Natural disasters pose a growing threat throughout the United States.*
>   I. Hurricanes threaten our coasts.
> II. Wildfires threaten our woodlands.
> III. Tornadoes threaten our Midwestern regions.
> IV. Floods threaten low-lying areas along streams and lakes.

The student then went on to offer specific examples of each of these natural disasters, as well as illustrating how each has increased in frequency.

Watch the Video "Roommates" at **MyCommunicationLab**

Categorical Order

Ideas can also be arranged in a pattern that emphasizes distinct topics—a categorical pattern. When you arrange your ideas categorically, you address types, forms, qualities, or aspects of the speech subject. For example, if you were giving a speech on the benefits of higher education, you could develop ideas related to the intellectual, social, or economic advantages of education. Similarly, you might discuss teen pregnancy in terms of those most at risk or prison reform in terms of different models that have been tried.

In the example that follows, the executive director of a small nonprofit agency arranged his ideas categorically as he described the agency's major funding sources to his board of directors:

> **Specific purpose:** *I want my audience to understand the main revenue sources that have supported our agency over the past five years.*
> **Thesis statement:** *Individual donors have provided the vast majority of the financial support that has enabled our agency to exist and thrive.*
>   I. Over the past five years, individual donations have accounted for 65 percent of our total revenue.

II. Faith communities have provided slightly less than 15 percent.
III. Grants from foundations and government agencies have averaged 18 percent.
IV. Businesses have provided only about 2–3 percent.

Under each category, the director developed his remarks by elaborating on the demographics of the individual donors category (e.g., their age, occupation, gender, etc.). He gave specific examples of faith communities most involved with supporting the agency and then commented on the funding cycles, restrictions, and stability of each granting agency with an eye toward future funding. He concluded by exploring possible reasons for underfunding by the business community. This pattern and the other patterns described so far are especially well suited for organizing informative speeches.

Climactic Order

Another way of arranging ideas is to use a climactic pattern, or a sequence that goes from simple to difficult, from least important to most important, or from emotionally neutral to emotionally intense. When the climactic order reflects audience needs and priorities, it can be an especially effective way to arrange ideas if the goal is to gain audience agreement or action. As you assess your ideas or arguments, you would then arrange them to build up to your strongest argument or most compelling idea.

Like a playwright, a speaker may wish to build on the listeners' interests and concerns until a climactic moment is reached. If, for example, you were addressing an audience with a strong concern for ethics, you might talk about a solution to a community problem in terms of its affordability and its benefits to the community, concluding with the moral imperative to act. The following is an example of ideas patterned climactically, from least to most important, with rising emotional intensity:

> **Specific purpose:** *I want my audience to agree that the United States needs a central food inspection agency.*
> **Thesis statement:** *The United States should create a central food inspection agency.*
>   I. Oversight by a central agency would yield economic advantages.
>   II. Oversight by a central agency would curb food-borne illnesses.
>   III. Oversight by a central agency would save lives.

The climactic pattern is most often used in persuasive speeches. By using this pattern, the speaker hopes that audiences will remember and be moved by the last thing they hear.

Causal Order

Ideas can be arranged in an order that leads from cause to effect or from effect to cause. This causal pattern is useful for speakers who want an audience to understand how an idea or event has unfolded or for speakers who want to suggest changes in a chain of relationships that will bring more desirable outcomes. If, for example, you wanted your audience to understand why type 2 diabetes is on the

This speaker used a causal pattern of organization as she argued that subsidized school lunch programs lead to increased achievement scores across academic subjects and improved social skills for children of all ages.

rise, you could arrange your ideas so that they would show the relationship between the disease and the contributing factors (unhealthy diet, lack of exercise). You could also use cause-and-effect order to discuss such topics as the causes of ozone depletion, the effects of gang activities on communities, or the economic factors that typically lead to a recession.

The following is an example of ideas arranged in a causal pattern. Here the president of a neighborhood association argued that the lack of traffic lights and signs produced harmful results and urged the city council to take action.

Specific purpose: *I want council members to agree that a better system of traffic lights and signs is needed in this community.*
Thesis statement: *The present system of traffic control is inconvenient and dangerous.*
  I. *Effect:* Pedestrians, young and old alike, have been struck and killed at unguarded crossings.
 II. *Effect:* At the main mall entrance, several accidents have resulted when oncoming traffic has failed to stop for the red light.
III. *Effect:* Traffic jams causing long delays occur every weekday during rush hours.
 IV. *Cause:* The real culprit contributing to this safety hazard is poor traffic control procedures.

When using causal arrangement, keep in mind that a chronological relationship does *not* necessarily equal a causal relationship. One event following another may represent chance as easily as cause. In addition, whenever you look at a given effect to seek its causes, you must guard against oversimplification. Identifying a single cause for a complex problem is usually unrealistic. Finally, sometimes cause-and-effect order is incorporated into a problem-solution pattern. Within the structure of a problem-solution speech, you will analyze the problem (effect) in terms of contributing causes, and then go on to propose solutions. The speaker who advances solutions is clearly speaking persuasively, but informative speakers may also occasionally use a causal pattern.

Problem-Solution Patterns

Watch the Video "Emergency Preparedness" at **MyCommunicationLab**

The problem-solution pattern is most common in persuasive or political speeches. In such a speech, you might identify an important problem, then propose a solution that you hope the audience will endorse. You might use this approach in proposing solutions to such problems as credit card fraud, the rise in eating disorders among college students, or the unregulated selling of drugs over the Internet.

Reflective Thinking Sequence   The traditional problem-solution pattern is based on educational philosopher John Dewey's Reflective Thinking Sequence[6] and typically addresses these questions:

1. How shall we define and limit the problem?
2. What are the causes and extent of the problem?
3. What are the effects of the problem? Who has been hurt?
4. What are the criteria by which solutions should be judged?
5. What are the possible solutions and the relative strengths and weaknesses of each?
6. What is the best solution?
7. How can we put it into effect?

Depending on the problem and the audience's prior knowledge, you might spend more or less time discussing the nature of the problem and its contributing causes. In situations where the audience is well versed on the problem, you might only briefly describe it and spend most of your speaking time exploring viable solutions.

The following is an example of ideas from a student speech that employs a problem-solution pattern:

Specific purpose: *I want my audience to join in the effort to stop deforestation.*
Thesis statement: *Deforestation must be stopped before its adverse effects make the world unfit for future generations.*

  I. *Problem (causes):* Deforestation has accelerated in recent years for a variety of reasons.
    A. One cause of deforestation is agriculture, which clears forests for farming.
    B. Another cause is cattle ranching, which needs land for grazing.
    C. In developing countries, people still cut down large numbers of trees for shelter and firewood.
    D. In general, overpopulation drives new development that threatens our remaining forests.
 II. *Problem (effects):* The effects of deforestation are often devastating.
    A. With more than 50 percent of the world's plants and animals living in 7 percent of the world's forests, most of them are headed for extinction—thus significantly decreasing biodiversity.
    B. Deforestation also leads to serious erosion and flooding.
    C. Some experts argue that perhaps the most serious effect of deforestation is global warming.
III. *Criteria for solutions:* The solutions may be weighed against such criteria as feasibility, affordability, and fairness.
 IV. *Possible solutions:* We can take a number of actions to help end deforestation.
    A. We can support *reforestation* legislation, which would prohibit clear-cutting in designated areas and allow trees to grow back naturally.

    B. We can tackle population control—by educating developing countries concerning birth control and acting responsibly in building our own families.

    C. We can inform others about the problem while setting a good example by not wasting paper and other forest products.

  V. *Best course of action:* In this case, all three solutions are interrelated, and all should be pursued. Some actions are personal and immediate; others are more long-range and deal with developing new policies and educational outreach.

The Motivated Sequence as a Special Problem-Solution Pattern One specific approach to organizing a problem-solution speech is the motivated sequence.[7] This pattern is organized around five steps:

1. *Arouse:* Capture the audience's attention and focus on the problem.
2. *Dissatisfy:* Make listeners understand that this is a serious problem that needs their attention and action.
3. *Gratify:* Reveal the solution to the problem, and assure listeners that it is within *their* power to remedy the situation.
4. *Visualize:* Show listeners *exactly* how much they can improve the situation.
5. *Move:* Appeal to the audience to take a specific action.

The motivated sequence is best suited to topics with emotional as well as logical appeal. It may work best in a speech on the need for safe housing for domestic abuse victims, or on reducing the practice of euthanizing shelter animals, or on creating after-school programs for at-risk teens. The motivated sequence allows you to engage the audience's emotions and urge them to act. It addresses the problem *and* the solution, but it concludes with an appeal designed to motivate the audience to *act*. Above all, it aims to convince the audience that they have the *power* to act, and it helps them visualize *how* they can address the problem in specific ways. Visualizing the outcomes as you conclude the speech can be especially moving. Your own passion and commitment, an awareness of the audience's needs and values, and a thorough understanding of the details of your solution are central to the effective use of this problem-solution pattern.

Narrative Patterns

Because of cultural background or personal preference, some speakers may prefer to use less direct and more organic patterns of organization.[8] For instance, a speech may be organized around telling one or more stories, using a narrative pattern. Rhetorical scholar Walter Fisher points out that the most compelling narratives are coherent, rather than scattered or fragmented.[9] The speaker may begin by introducing a theme, such as the idea that the best government leaders are highly ethical. Then, the speaker would share various stories to illustrate and reinforce the speech's thesis. Or, he or she might pay tribute to a single person by sharing an extended narrative of the person's life. The speech is a continuous narrative with various internal stories drawn out and emphasized. Each would relate to an overarching theme, perhaps by demonstrating how the person being honored lived a courageous life. Narratives should also possess what Fisher calls fidelity—that is, they must "ring

FOCUS ON CIVIC ENGAGEMENT | Amanda Shares Her Family's Journey Using a Narrative Pattern

On November 2, 2006, Amanda Cunningham spoke at a Habitat for Humanity fund-raising breakfast. In her moving speech, she shares the story of her parents' courage and determination and reveals how they qualified to become Habitat homeowners. Using a narrative pattern, this speech also functions as a tribute to Amanda's parents and offers testimonial evidence of the impact of Habitat for Humanity on the lives of real people.

My name is Amanda Cunningham. I am a student at Ivy Tech. My parents, Mark and Kim Cunningham, and I are a Habitat for Humanity partner family. Let me tell you a little bit about us. My parents were high school sweethearts and have been married for 24 years now. My dad was laid off from Otis Elevator in 1991 and decided to accept a job offer in Florida to support our family. At the age of 29, two years after moving to Florida, my dad was diagnosed with a rare type of cancer in his sinus cavity. The news from the doctors was not good; they gave my dad a small chance of survival.

After months and months of radiation treatments, the tumor had decreased in size. My brother and I were so young that we do not remember our dad being anything but sick. I remember him coming home from his radiation treatments being so tired that he would just fall asleep on the sofa. I watched him have seizures and feed himself through a tube in his nose.

My dad got very sick, but my mom stood beside him, never once giving up. Mom was not only trying to keep her and Dad's spirits up, but she was also trying to raise two small children and work her job. She ended up working long hours, seven days a week. My dad went through treatments for cancer the entire time we were in Florida. After six years there, we decided to move home to Indiana. We did not know whether the cancer was gone or not.

My dad is now 43 years old. The cancer has been in remission for 14 years, and he has completed college. The years of treatments have left him cancer-free, but his health is not perfect. The effects from the radiation treatments have been significant. Dad is now speech, hearing and visually impaired, and is fed through a tube in his stomach. His immune system is not as strong as all of ours, and we are not ever sure if or when he will end up sick and in the hospital.

My parents are the strongest people I will ever know. Their strength is not only an inspiration to my brother and me, but has also given us a solid foundation for our lives. There *are* heroes left in this world, and I count my parents among them. Giving up has never been an option for our family. Whenever a door closed on my parents, they continued to search for one that was open.

The trailer we live in is cold. It has no insulation and drafty windows and doors. The roof leaks and we have to be careful where we walk because the floor is giving way. It has been our home for the last seven years, and we have been looking for any opportunity to get into a better situation.

That opportunity was provided by Habitat for Humanity. Our family has never been looking for a handout, but rather a hand up. Habitat for Humanity offered us more than the opportunity for a place to live. It offered us an opportunity to help ourselves. *Finally*, my parents will have a home to call their own. You cannot imagine how it feels to know that my parents are going to have a home again. I speak for everyone in my family when I say that Habitat for Humanity of Monroe County is a blessing.

As blessings go, the best of blessings are those that bless others as well. We know as a family that being part of Habitat for Humanity is being part of a bigger family that offers hope for more families that need a window of opportunity like us. We can't wait to start building our home with Habitat this spring!

Now, I would like to introduce you to my parents: Mark and Kim Cunningham.

Source: Reprinted by permission from Amanda Cunningham, "Habitat: Our Window." Copyright © 2006 by Amanda Cunningham. ▸

true" with the stories that listeners know to be true in their own lives.[10] For example, a speaker might explore the meaning of *courage* by sharing a series of stories of courageous acts. While those acts might be admirable and unusual, they must also seem plausible to the audience if they are to "ring true."

If the speaker wants to build in a sense of drama or climax within a narrative pattern, he or she may choose to use a spiraling narrative. For instance, the speaker might give a speech of tribute by sharing stories that build in intensity. A person's simple acts of courage might be shared first, moving to more unusual acts, and perhaps culminating with uncommon acts of valor. Again, each would be united by the general theme. When delivered effectively, narrative patterns can contribute to a powerful, engaging presentation.

This list of organizational patterns is not exhaustive, but it does include the principal ways in which you can arrange your ideas. Some patterns of organization work best with informative speeches, whereas others work better with persuasive speeches. And some topics lend themselves to a chronological or a spatial pattern of organization better than others. In the final analysis, however, it is important to recognize that there is never just one "correct" way to organize a given speech. As you prepare your speech, you may experiment with various ways of arranging your ideas until you come upon the organizational pattern that seems to work best.

GUIDELINES FOR ORGANIZING YOUR SPEECH

3 List and explain underlying principles of sound organization you will follow, regardless of the specific pattern you choose.

Preview. *Regardless of the particular pattern of organization you choose, you will want to keep in mind some basic guidelines. It is important to view the choice of an organizational pattern as a strategic decision. At the same time, you will want to consider issues of balance, the number of main ideas to include in your speech, and where to place your strongest, most compelling ideas and information.*

Given the wide variety of organizational patterns from which you can choose, you should keep a few general principles in mind. Select your organizational pattern carefully.

Making the Pattern a Strategic Choice

The way you present your ideas and information should be *strategic*, designed to enhance the chance that you will elicit the audience response you are seeking. If you are talking to an audience about a problem that is quite complicated or one with which they have little knowledge or experience, you will want to devote a good portion of your speech to educating your listeners. A good organizational strategy in this case may be a traditional problem-solution pattern—one in which you devote substantial time to defining and exploring the problem and its causes and effects *before* moving on to propose possible solutions.

Developing Main Ideas with a Concern for Symmetry

Second, give some thought to symmetry or balance. If the idea you are addressing is one of your speech's main points, then you will want to explore it thoroughly and offer a well-developed, substantive treatment. Sometimes you may be discussing an idea that is particularly controversial or complex, so you may need to devote a bit more time to it. In general, however, you should advance the main ideas of your speech in a balanced way, giving each one the emphasis it deserves so that your listeners will understand, recall, and hopefully be moved by what you are saying.

Determining the Number of Main Ideas

Sometimes speakers have questions about how many main ideas they can convey in a single speech. In doing research on an engaging topic, the speaker may be tempted to cover a long list of key points. But including too many main ideas may result in the inadequate development of each. To some extent, the time allowed for the speech will influence how many main ideas can be fully developed. If you are delivering a six- to eight-minute speech (as is common in the classroom), you may be hard-pressed to cover more than two or three main points adequately. A twenty-minute presentation (perhaps in a community setting) may allow you to advance a larger number of main ideas (usually no more than five). But there are two constraints to keep in mind. First, many listeners cannot absorb a large number of main ideas during a single presentation. In addition, a well-formulated specific purpose statement should limit and focus the speech. You can test each idea you are considering by asking whether it advances your speech's specific purpose. If it does not, you will want to eliminate it.

Choosing the Placement of Main Ideas

Finally, be aware of primacy and recency effects. Although researchers do not agree on whether arguments are more memorable and persuasive if they are placed first (primacy) or last (recency), they *do* agree that those two positions are the most powerful—and that information or arguments embedded in the middle of a message are less likely to be as memorable or have as much impact on listeners.[11] In most instances, then, you will want to lead with and conclude with information and ideas that are especially crucial to the case you are making.

TRANSITIONS AS CONNECTIVES

Preview. *Transitions add clarity and smoothness to a speech. Without strong transitions, even a well-organized speech may strike listeners as confusing or disorganized. When crafted well, transitions can contribute significantly to the impact of the speaker's overall message.*

As a responsible speaker, you need to help the audience see the relationships among your ideas. Once you have drafted your speech, you must consider how you will progress from one idea to another so that listeners can see the connections.

A transition is a bridge that connects one idea to another. Listeners cannot be expected to pay complete attention to the speaker, nor can they be expected to understand the sequence of ideas and information as clearly as the speaker does. You must alert your listeners to a new idea about to be introduced and help them see how it relates to your overall message.

As structural elements, transitions are small but mighty. They are, perhaps, the most unappreciated and underused components of effective speech making.

4 Describe different transitional devices you might use in creating a coherent presentation.

Explore the Concept "Better Transitions" at **MyCommunicationLab**

A transition links one major idea with another in a speech, showing their relationship to each other. However, a transition does more than show how an idea fits into a speech. It also reinforces an idea that a speaker wishes to share. Transitions often provide a quick glance back at the idea just discussed and then a quick look forward to the next main idea. A transition, then, may function as a miniature review and preview of ideas, reinforcing key ideas in the speech.[12] For example, a speaker identifying factors that have contributed to the rise in rates of type 2 diabetes may make the following two points:

I. Poor dietary choices have contributed to the rise of type 2 diabetes.
II. Sedentary lifestyles have contributed to the rise of type 2 diabetes.

A transition that bridges the two, simultaneously reinforcing the ideas, could be as follows:
Not only does a poor diet make developing type 2 diabetes more likely, so does a lack of exercise.

Sometimes, in longer, more intricately developed speeches, this reviewing and previewing should be done more extensively. When this is the case, the speaker can rely on an internal preview or an internal summary, both of which are extended transitions.

Internal Previews

Explore the Concept "Connecting to Key Ideas" at **MyCommunicationLab**

When moving from one idea to the next, you can give your audience a brief internal preview of the point you are about to make to help focus listeners' attention on what's to come. For example, suppose a speaker has just discussed this point: "Pollution of air and water in this community has direct consequences for your health." The next main idea he plans to take up is the following: "Pollution effects can drastically alter the standard of living in this country." To transition into this second point, he might combine a simple restatement of the first idea with an internal preview in this way:

> Pollution, then, can cost you (and those you love) your health. But its effects are even more far-reaching. If pollution isn't controlled now, drastic steps will have to be taken that will impact the way we live every day. Let us consider now the ways in which our standard of living is at risk because of pollution.

You may benefit from using an internal preview when you want to set the stage for a particular portion of your speech, perhaps by explaining *why* you will focus on the programs you have chosen. Suppose, for example, you have been addressing the problems with public education in the United States, with a particular focus on young children from low-income families. Now, you want to explore programs in your community that represent "best practices" in after-school programming for these children. To transition into this portion of your speech, you might say the following:

> Our community is filled with many interesting after-school programs for children. But three in particular have recently won awards for their excellence and creativity: the Boys and Girls Club After-Hours Program, the Girls, Inc. Leadership Program, and the Mother Hubbard's Cupboard Growing Food for Healthy Bodies Program. In the time that remains, I would like to focus on each of these programs and explore how they have truly enriched the lives of our children.

Internal Summaries

Sometimes, getting from one idea to another has to be more elaborate because the material is complex. In these cases, you may use an internal summary, briefly going over the information covered so far before moving on to the next point. A speaker who is advocating for green burials as an alternative to traditional funerals, for example, used an internal summary in her transition:

> As you can see, green burials are a growing trend in many parts of the United States, with certified green cemeteries in over forty states. We've seen how green burials help protect the environment and ecology by reducing the use of toxic chemicals, nonbiodegradable materials, and fossil fuels. We've seen pictures of peaceful green burial sites that are typically planted with natural grasses and wildflowers that require little or no maintenance. Now let's look at two other advantages of green burials: affordability and family members' feelings of involvement as they participate in laying their loved ones to rest.[13]

This kind of transition—a short summary of what has been said—helps keep the audience mentally on track. It also reinforces key ideas.

Sometimes internal summaries can be brief phrases embedded in new ideas. This is how one speaker used transitions to develop her first main idea in a speech on poverty and dental health:

I. Poor people with impaired dental health confront a variety of problems.
   A. Their general health can be at risk (including heart disease).
   B. *Not only can poor dental health lead to other serious health consequences,* it also adversely influences the individual's ability to get a job.
   C. *In addition to basic health and employment problems,* those with poor dental health often find it challenging to establish meaningful relationships with others in their daily lives.

These sample transitions illustrate how words and phrases can help listeners process information and ideas as they are advanced by the speaker.

Signposts

Watch the Video "The Process of Developing a Speech: Transitions" at **MyCommunicationLab**

In some instances, you may merely want to provide verbal markers to alert your audience to the fact that you are moving from one idea to another by enumerating each point or by signaling the next point to be made. If so, you can rely on what are known as signposts. You may, for example, tell your listeners that you have three good reasons for asking them to sign up for the Big Brothers/Big Sisters program. You may simply say: "*The second reason* for you to sign up now is that the need is so urgent in our community." As you move into the third reason, you may go on to say: "*A final reason* for volunteering is that you will derive great satisfaction from knowing you have really made a difference in a child's life."

Other signposts include words such as *next, another,* and *finally.* Here are some examples:

"*The next* good reason is…"
"*Another* reason you should sign up is…"
"*Finally,* you should join now because…"

213

Rhetorical Questions

A speaker can also use rhetorical questions to highlight movement and assist flow, with the added benefit of encouraging listeners' involvement. Rhetorical questions stimulate thought and interest without seeking an oral response. Suppose a speaker has been discussing the need for a Volunteers in Medicine clinic in her community. She has described the medical services currently available in the area. As she moves on to address the issue of those who fall through the cracks of the present system, she asks, *But what happens if you have no health insurance? Who will take care of you when you are sick?*

These rhetorical questions should engage listeners' emotions and make them eager to hear what the speaker has to say. They should also encourage movement in the minds of the audience, allowing the speaker to focus their attention on the community's real need for a VIM clinic.

Taken together, these transitional devices help listeners make the right connections and follow the progression of ideas in your speech. In addition, transitions reinforce ideas and encourage listener involvement.

So far in the chapter, we have discussed organizational principles and approaches that largely apply to the way you will arrange the main ideas in the body of your speech. Now we turn our attention to how you will begin your speech. The effectiveness of your speech's introduction will likely influence the audience's frame of mind as you move into the presentation of your main ideas.

INTRODUCING YOUR SPEECH

5 Identify the key components of a speech's introduction.

Watch the Video "Jason Warren Discusses Tips for an Effective Introduction" at **MyCommunicationLab**

Preview. *Although speech introductions may be structured in different ways, the most effective introductions establish common ground with the audience, capture and hold the listeners' attention, stress the relevance of your topic, establish your credibility as a speaker, clarify your purpose, and provide a preview of your ideas.*

No matter which organizational pattern you follow, you will need to introduce your speech in an effective way. It is not enough to say, "Today I am going to talk with you about why the community needs a free health clinic." Hardly any listener will be riveted by that. Instead, the introduction needs to be structured so that audience members *want* to listen to your speech, view you as a credible source, and have some idea of your speech's purpose and main ideas.

Establish Common Ground

Many speakers seek to establish common ground with listeners as they begin to speak. Audiences tend to listen to speakers with whom they share common experiences, problems, or goals. For example, when giving a speech on student loans in a class with several other working students, Yuko began her speech this way:

> When I get to this class at 8:00 A.M., I have had four hours' sleep. I work full-time as a waitress at Nick's and do not get home until about 2:00 A.M. Like many of you, I need to work to support myself while going to school. Some of you have full-time jobs and some are part-timers. Some of you also have families to care for as well as working and going to school. And I know that at least one of you is also a single parent. For us, getting an education and making ends meet is not easy.

In speaking contexts outside the classroom, the speaker may also want to emphasize similarities between himself or herself and the audience. Perhaps the speaker is perceived as someone whose life experiences have differed significantly from those of the audience. In this case, establishing common ground with listeners creates a sense of "we-ness" that invites the audience to listen. In 1993, President Bill Clinton addressed the convention of the Church of God in Christ in Memphis, Tennessee, speaking from the pulpit where Martin Luther King had given his last sermon. This white president used the occasion to connect with the African-American community by stressing their common goals.

> By the grace of God and your help, last year I was elected President of this great country. I never dreamed that I would ever have a chance to come to this hallowed place where Martin Luther King gave his last sermon. I ask you to think today about the purpose for which I ran and the purpose for which so many of you worked to put me in this great office. I have worked hard to keep faith with our common efforts: to restore the economy, to reverse the politics of helping only those at the top of our totem pole and not the hardworking middle class or the poor; to bring our people together across racial and regional and political lines, to make a strength out of our diversity instead of letting it tear us apart; to reward work and family and community and try to move us forward into the 21st century. I have tried to keep faith.[14]

Establishing common ground (together with other devices described in upcoming sections) may also engage the audience's attention and make them want to hear more.

Capture and Maintain the Listeners' Attention

When you first get up to speak, listeners usually give you their full attention. But that attention may be fleeting. Let us consider several approaches to maintaining the audience's attention and how some speakers have used them.

Watch the Video "Investing in Our Future" at **MyCommunicationLab**

Tell a Story   An interesting story—whether it is emotional, humorous, puzzling, or intriguing—commands attention. The story can be real or hypothetical. It can be a personal story that reveals something of your own experience, or it can be something you have read. Speaking to a group of teachers, Carmen Mariano, an assistant superintendent in the Massachusetts public school system, began with this narrative:

> Ernest Hemingway tells the story of a Spanish man who has a bitter argument one morning with his young son, Paco. When he arrived home later that day, the man discovered that Paco's room was empty—he had run away from home.
>
> Overcome with remorse, the man realized that his son was more important to him than anything else. He went to a well-known grocery store in the center of town and posted a large sign that read, "Paco, come home. I love you. Meet me here tomorrow morning. Signed, your father."
>
> The next morning, the man went to the store. There, he found his son and seven other young boys who had also run away from home. They were all answering the call for love, hoping it was their dad inviting them home.[15]

Mariano used this opening to lead into the point that teaching children who come from tension-filled homes where they do not feel loved or wanted is a great challenge for teachers in the public school system.

Use Rhetorical Questions   Earlier in the chapter, we discussed how rhetorical questions may assist movement in a speech and encourage involvement. Similarly, in an introduction, rhetorical questions can prompt listeners to think about an issue or idea without seeking an immediate response.

Lin began his speech by raising questions that challenged listeners to consider how they might deal with ethical dilemmas:

> This is an honors public speaking class, and, as honors students, we're all used to getting good grades. Grades are very important to us and we can be very competitive. Well, you might not kill for an A—but, what *would* you do for an A? Would you consider peeking at the answers to someone's exam if you had the chance to do so and were sure you wouldn't get caught? Would you tell a professor that he or she made a mistake in grading an exam if it meant that your grade was lowered? Would you let a friend write a short paper for you and turn it in as your own? Can you think of any time when you've done something that you wouldn't like anyone else to know about to get a good grade? If we're perfectly honest with ourselves, we know that these questions are not so easy to answer in a "socially acceptable" way. Maybe you've never cheated or plagiarized or lied to a friend—but, have you ever been tempted?

Lin's audience will likely find their thinking stimulated by these rhetorical questions that relate directly to their lives as students.

Begin with a Memorable Quotation   No doubt someone has said or written something that captures the thesis of your speech. The idea has been expressed so well, perhaps by a person whom the audience respects and admires, that you know it will get the listeners' interest and attention right away. An esteemed scholar, scientist, or political figure can be quoted. Or you can use the words of a popular entertainer, author, athlete, singer, or other well-known and highly respected figure.

As a concerned citizen, David wanted to persuade his audience to volunteer with a new community initiative called New Leaf, New Life. The program sought to make the local jail a more humane and educational environment and to provide mentors for prisoners who were about to be released. David began his speech by quoting the famous nineteenth-century union organizer and Socialist Party presidential candidate Eugene V. Debs:

> Eugene V. Debs devoted most of his life to seeking justice for the most vulnerable members of society. Debs once said, "While there is a lower class, I am in it; while there is a criminal element, I am of it; and while there is a soul in prison, I am not free."[16]

By quoting Debs, the speaker hoped to move his listeners to seek social justice by participating in what he described as a life-altering program.

Use Humor   Some speakers like to begin a speech with a humorous story, but you need to approach humor with caution. No matter how funny a story may be, it must also be relevant to the point you want to make. Just telling a few jokes is not a good way to begin a speech, and a joke that falls flat is embarrassing. Humor should never be disrespectful or aimed at ridiculing someone or something, so you need to be careful. In the following introduction, Richard Lamm, representing the University of Denver's Center for Public Policy and Contemporary Issues, began his speech to the World Future Society by telling the story of a priest who ended up sitting next to a drunk while riding the subway. The man was disheveled and smelled strongly of liquor. At the same time, he was deeply engrossed in reading a newspaper. Lamm continues:

> After a few minutes, the man turned to the priest and asked. "Excuse me, Father, what causes arthritis?"
>
> [Without hesitation] the priest said roughly, "Loose living, drink, dissipation, contempt for your fellow man and being with cheap and wicked women!"
>
> "That's amazing," said the drunk [as he] returned to his newspaper.
>
> A while later, the priest, feeling a bit guilty, turned to the man and asked nicely, "How long have you had arthritis?"
>
> "Oh," said the man, "I don't have arthritis. I was just reading that the pope did."
>
> The parable, of course, is a lesson on assumptions.[17]

Of course, these techniques are not mutually exclusive; you can use several at once. You may, for example, tell an interesting story that also establishes common ground and arouses curiosity. And you will want to deliver the introduction effectively. For example, pausing after telling a compelling story, posing an engaging rhetorical question, or sharing a memorable quotation may help listeners ponder what you are about to say. The key factor is capturing and holding the audience's attention and interest.

Stress Relevance

Either consciously or unconsciously, your listeners will ask themselves why they should care about your topic. Even when we find something interesting, we soon begin to wonder whether it has any relevance to us or any real impact on the lives of those we care about. In the introduction, you should take the time to establish the significance of your topic, answering for your audience such questions as, "What does this have to do with me?" or "How will this course of action make for a better world?"

Sarah, a student speaker, wanted to get her audience to take an active role in the university's new fund-raiser, the Dance Marathon. In her introduction, she emphasized how her classmates could make a real difference in the lives of children while participating in a wonderful, truly engaging event. She pointed out that dance marathons had been held on campuses around the country, such as Penn State and Indiana University, for quite a few years. This year, however, was to be Southeast Missouri State's first year to host such an event. Here is how she emphasized the importance of her topic:

> Why would anyone force themselves to dance for 48 hours? The student who chaired the Dance Marathon steering committee at Indiana University put it this way: "Dance Marathon is about learning what is a priority in life....A true priority in someone's life should be giving back to others who need your help." As a dancer, you too can discover the incredible experience of knowing you helped save children's lives. One dancer summed up his experience like this: "I love this. My feet hurt, but the feeling in my heart won't go

away." When you participate in the Dance Marathon, you are raising money for the Children's Miracle Network. Money from our marathon will be split between St. Louis Children's Research Hospital and Cardinal Glennon Children's Miracle Center in St. Louis. I have known several children who have been patients at these hospitals, and I know you have too.[18]

No one listening to these introductory remarks could fail to see the importance of this cause and how it could positively impact their lives as well as the lives of countless children.

Well known for his courageous actions during the civil rights movement, Congressman John Lewis possesses strong credibility on issues of social justice and human rights.

Establish Your Credibility

The audience should know of any special relationship you have with the topic that would enhance your ethos. Of course, credibility is an ongoing issue throughout any speech, but the introduction represents an especially critical time for establishing your credentials. For seasoned professionals, this process may be less daunting. We expect doctors to know about medicine, attorneys to know about law, and accountants to be able to answer questions about our taxes. For student speakers, however, establishing ethos can be more challenging.

Yet student speakers can establish their ethos in compelling ways. Let us look at how one student did it. In her speech urging students to volunteer for a summer work project, Kristin began by relating her own experience:

Last year I took a different kind of summer vacation. I did not go to the beach to try to get a fabulous tan. I did not go to a lake and learn to water-ski. I did not go to a big city to visit museums and see shows. I went to a hot, dry desert. There was no air conditioning anywhere. After a night spent sleeping in a sleeping bag on a bare floor, I got up, had breakfast, got into an old truck with about a dozen other kids and took off over a dusty road to a house that badly needed repair. In the hot sun I helped plug cracks in the wall, learned how to mix and apply plaster, and stripped and painted peeling boards.

I did this for nothing. Well, that isn't right. I did not get paid money, but I did get something a lot more valuable. Working as a volunteer in a remote town in an Indian reservation, I learned so many things about a different culture. I made close friends among the people I worked with. I helped to make a real difference in real people's lives. I came back from this experience a different—and richer—person than I was when I went. I am going to tell you today how you can enrich your life, too.

Having established her credibility, this speaker is well positioned to use her personal experience to convince her listeners that they should get involved as well.

If you lack the kind of direct topic-related experience illustrated in the preceding example, you can still establish your credibility as a student speaker by telling your audience that you have had a long-standing interest in your topic and have become motivated to do further research to learn even more about it. You may briefly explain what sparked your interest and then go on to show listeners that you really *are* knowledgeable, widely read, and able to respond to challenging questions.

Clarify Your Purpose/Advance Your Thesis

A key function of the introduction is to advance your speech's thesis—stating, in a single declarative statement, the central idea of your speech. By articulating your thesis as part of the introduction, you help the audience discern your central theme, overarching point, or principal argument. No speaker wants to move into the body of the speech with the audience still wondering, "What's the point? Where is this going?"

One speaker, Joel, decided to give a persuasive speech about the U.S. prison system.[19] In his introduction, he pointed out that the U.S. prison population has increased dramatically over the past 35 years. He noted that one out of every 200 U.S. residents is incarcerated, resulting in steeply rising prison costs.[20] He then advanced his thesis: *The government needs to reform the U.S. prison system.* He went on to argue for lighter sentences, a reduction in mandatory sentencing, and an increased emphasis on rehabilitation.

Often, the thesis statement is soon followed by a preview of the speaker's main ideas.

Preview Your Main Points

Before moving into the body of your speech, you should provide a preview. The preview introduces your main ideas, offering a road map so that listeners can more easily follow your speech. In previewing, you are also signaling what you feel is most important—those things you want the audience to remember and reflect on long after you have finished speaking. By providing a preview, you increase the likelihood they will.[21] If, after giving your preview, you follow through with your plan, you will have further enhanced your credibility by demonstrating your careful organization and preparation.

Consider, for example, the speech given by a student speaker, Erin, whose thesis was as follows: *Students should explore exciting alternatives to traditional college majors before making a final choice.* The speaker began by reminding her audience that more than two-thirds of college students change majors before settling on a final plan of study—some switching three or more times. She pointed out "Many of us think we have to choose a major in a traditional area, such as accounting, English, computer science, or education. But that's not necessarily the case." She then went on to preview the ideas she would develop:

> There are three exciting programs at our university that offer creative alternatives to the traditional college major, and these may be of interest to you if you have not yet found your niche here at I.U. First is LAMP, the Liberal Arts and Management Program, which combines a strong liberal arts education with specialized business skills and knowledge. Second is PACE, the Political and Civic Engagement program which helps you develop skills for participating

in political and civic life. Finally, there is the Individualized Major program, where you literally design your own major from scratch—choosing from courses all over the university.[22]

Having forecast what she planned to do in the speech, the speaker's challenge was to deliver on the promise by developing each point she mentioned in the preview.

Final Tips about Introductions

Remember the power of *first impressions*. Part of your first impression as a speaker will be based on the way you introduce your speech. Following are some tips to keep in mind:

- Craft your introduction with care. Most speakers wait until after they have outlined the body of the speech to develop the introduction. For instance, they may experiment with several different attention-getting devices before they settle on the one they feel is most compelling.
- The length of the introduction will vary with the needs of the speaking situation. Some formal events require the speaker to offer an introduction that refers to the events at hand and acknowledges or thanks several significant persons related to the event. Usually, however, introductions should be *brief*. We have all heard speakers who ramble on for some time, and then say, after ten minutes or so, "What I'd like to talk about today is…" This can prompt the frustrated listener to tune out.
- Each introduction should be tailored to the situation. If the person introducing you fully establishes your credibility, for example, you may have little need of augmenting what has already been said. If the audience is already keenly aware of the significance of the problem you are addressing, you will not need to offer an elaborate justification. Instead, you may simply say, "We are all aware of the urgency of the problem that has brought us here tonight." In short, each introduction should be crafted not according to a formula but based on the demands of the topic, the listeners, and the situation.
- If you develop your introduction carefully and deliver it effectively, you will set the stage for the audience to attend to the main ideas that you will develop throughout the rest of your speech. A strong introduction makes the audience want to hear more.

Bringing your speech to an effective conclusion is also important. Sometimes speakers primarily think about how to arrange and present their main ideas, without paying attention to what they will say at the end of their speech. Yet the conclusion is the last thing the audience hears. If it is memorable and compelling, the conclusion can truly enhance the overall impact of the speech.

CONCLUDING YOUR SPEECH

Preview. *Carefully planning your speech's conclusion is an essential part of preparing to speak. By summarizing your main ideas, challenging your audience, appealing to your audience, visualizing the future, using good quotations, or referring to the introduction—or by using a combination of these techniques—you can craft an effective ending for your speech.*

Watch the Video "Jason Warren Discusses Tips for an Effective Conclusion" at **MyCommunicationLab**

6 List different ways of concluding a speech effectively.

Many speakers do not really conclude their speeches—they simply stop talking. Others may stumble through their concluding remarks, reducing the effectiveness of the presentation. Sometimes speakers say something like, "Well, I guess that's about it. Any questions?" The conclusion is very important. If you construct it properly, you will bring your speech to a strategic close and create a final positive impact.

As you approach the speech's conclusion, you will want to signal to the audience that you are, in fact, concluding. One of the major vehicles for signaling the conclusion is a summary of your main points.

Summarize Your Ideas

Summaries are especially important when the speech is complex or long. The summary reinforces your ideas and reminds the audience of your most important points. When combined with the preview in your introduction and the development of each main idea in the body of your speech (including the transitions that connect them), the summary provides a final chance to reiterate key ideas and help the audience remember them.

Summaries are often used in conjunction with another concluding device. In the summary that follows, Patti, a long-time volunteer with a local nonprofit agency, the Shalom Community Center, offers a summary and extended quotation as she concludes her speech:

Watch the Video
"The Process of
Developing a Speech:
Conclusions: Using a Summary"
at **MyCommunicationLab**

> I hope I have been able to help you better understand what critical services the Shalom Community Center provides for people experiencing extreme poverty and homelessness in our community. Shalom offers the basics: food for the hungry—serving breakfast and lunch every weekday, shelter during the day where guests can take a shower, do their laundry, store their belongings, and receive their mail, *and* opportunities for day-by-day problem-solving and empowerment.
>
> As part of their mission statement, Shalom lists their basic values on their Web site. I think they really capture the essence of Shalom:
>
> 1. *Hospitality*—We extend community beyond the margins to include those unserved by society. We invite all people into our safe and welcoming space.
> 2. *Dignity*—We value the worth and dignity of every person, treating all with compassion and respect. We honor the lives, concerns, and stories of people who have been marginalized by society and expect our staff, volunteers and guests to do the same.
> 3. *Empowerment*—We strive to increase the economic and social strength of people in need. We help people develop confidence in their own capacities. We support people in making choices that improve the quality of their lives.
> 4. *Hope*—We believe in the possibility each person possesses to create a sustainable, healthy, and happy life. We work to nurture that hope in all people.[23]
>
> Shalom is a special place. I hope you will join me at the next Shalom open house and Community Conversation on May 10. You will be able to take a tour, meet Shalom's new executive director, chat with volunteers and guests, and learn how you can become involved in serving the most vulnerable citizens of our community.

The speaker then distributed a flyer that offered details about the Community Conversation (including time and place) and provided agency contact information.

Challenge Your Audience

Most of the time, summaries do not stand alone. Often they are—or should be—accompanied by some other interesting concluding device. One device that can be effective is a challenge to the audience to act on what you have said. This was the strategy used by then-senator Barack Obama in his keynote speech to the 2004 Democratic Convention:

> Hope—Hope in the face of difficulty. Hope in the face of uncertainty. The audacity of hope!

Speakers who feel strongly about their topic will make every effort to challenge their listeners to act.

> In the end, that is God's greatest gift to us, the bedrock of this nation. A belief in things not seen. A belief that there are better days ahead.
>
> I believe that we can give our middle class relief and provide working families with a road to opportunity.
>
> I believe we can provide jobs to the jobless, homes to the homeless, and reclaim young people in cities across America from violence and despair.
>
> I believe that we have a righteous wind at our backs and that as we stand on the crossroads of history, we can make the right choices, and meet the challenges that face us.
>
> America! Tonight, if you feel the same energy that I do, if you feel the same urgency that I do, if you feel the same passion that I do, if you feel the same hopefulness that I do—if we do what we must do, then I have no doubt that all across the country, from Florida to Oregon, from Washington to Maine, the people will rise up in November...and this country will reclaim its promise, and out of this long political darkness a brighter day will come.[24]

Appeal to Your Audience

In your conclusion, you can make a final attempt to move your audience to act or believe more strongly about your proposition. Speaking to an audience of representatives of companies honored as *Parents* magazine's "Best Companies for Working Families," Richard Lamm concluded his speech with this appeal:

> I close with a metaphor on the need for cooperation and community....The metaphor is an Amazon legend which tells of a priest who was speaking with God about heaven and hell.
>
> "I will show you hell," said God.
>
> They went into a room that had a delicious beef stew on the table, around which sat people chained to their benches and who looked desperately famished. They held spoons with long handles that reached into the pot, but were too long to put the stew back into their mouths. Their suffering was terrible.

"Now, I will show you heaven," said God.

They then went into an identical room with the savory stew on the table, around which sat people with identical spoons and handles, but they were well nourished and joyous.

The priest was baffled until God said, "Quite simply, you see, these people have learned to feed each other."[25]

Lamm's appeal is for the audience to recognize their responsibility for taking care of *everyone* who is part of the organizational family.

Visualize the Future

In a speech in which you advocate important changes, visualizing the results of those changes is an especially appropriate and powerful way to conclude. This device (which is built into the motivated sequence) allows you to picture or imagine the projected results of your ideas in an appealing way. In a speech delivered to a large group of students at Liberty Baptist University, the late Senator Edward M. Kennedy concluded his speech by offering this compelling vision of America:

I hope for an America where neither "fundamentalist" nor "humanist" will be a dirty word, but a fair description of the different ways in which people of goodwill look at life and into their own souls.

I hope for an America where no president, no public official, no individual will ever be deemed a greater or lesser American because of religious doubts—or religious beliefs.

I hope for an America where the power of faith will always burn brightly, but where no modern Inquisition of any kind will ever light the fires of fear, coercion, or angry division.

I hope for an America where we can all contend freely and vigorously, but where we will treasure and guard those standards of civility which alone make this nation safe for both democracy and diversity.[26]

Kennedy then goes on to invite his listeners, many whose views differed sharply from the speaker's in terms of politics and religion, "to live peaceably with men and women everywhere."

End with a Quotation

Ending your speech with a good quotation can help reinforce your thesis and restate the major points you made. Poetry, plays, songs, speeches, and literary works can all supply effective quotations. Quotations should be pertinent, compelling, and brief. In his speech to the nation on October 1, 1979, President Jimmy Carter concluded with a striking quotation:

The struggle for peace—the long, hard struggle to bring weapons of mass destruction under the control of human reason and human law—is the central drama of our age.

At another time of challenge in our nation's history, President Abraham Lincoln told the American people: "We shall nobly save, or meanly lose, the last best hope of earth."

We acted wisely then, and preserved the nation. Let us act wisely now, and preserve the world.[27]

Refer to the Introduction

You can achieve a sense of symmetry and reinforce your major theme by coming back to the introduction in the conclusion of your speech. This commonly happens when a speaker uses both a preview and a summary, but you can find more interesting ways to do this, often by using one of the techniques we have already discussed in the chapter. For example, you may return to a story, quotation, or rhetorical question that you used in the opening.

Consider the following example from a speech given by Robert C. Purcell, executive director of General Motors Advanced Technology Vehicles, at the 1998 MBA Recognition Ceremony at the Kelly School of Business, Indiana University. He had introduced his speech with a riveting story from May 1961, in which a group of black and white students, riding on a bus together, were attacked by an angry white mob. One young black seminary student, John Lewis, was nearly killed. His life was saved only because a white Alabama public safety officer, Floyd Mann, chased off the crowd by firing shots into the air. Purcell concluded his speech like this:

> There's a postscript to the story I shared with you when I began today. Not long ago, John Lewis, the young seminary student, returned to Alabama, to the site of that historic attack 37 years ago, for the dedication of a civil rights memorial....By that time, Lewis had a long and distinguished career.
>
> As we waited for the ceremony to begin, an older gentleman, who seemed vaguely familiar, came over to him.
>
> "You're John Lewis, aren't you?" the man said. "I remember you from the Freedom Rides."
>
> It was Floyd Mann—the same Floyd Mann who had waded into that mob with his revolver, more than 35 years before.
>
> Lewis was overcome with emotion. "You saved my life," he said. And then he embraced Floyd Mann. Not sure as he did so, if even then, black men and white men hugged each other in contemporary Alabama.
>
> But Mann hugged him back, and John Lewis began to cry.
>
> And as the two men released each other, Floyd Mann looked at Lewis and said, "You know...I'm right proud of your career."
>
> And if there is one hope that I hold for each of you today—it is that 10 or 20 or 30 years from now, when you look back on your careers, you'll be just as proud.[28]

Many speakers use a combination of techniques. Patti combined a summary with an extended quotation. Barack Obama offered a challenge while also visualizing the future. Robert Purcell brought closure to his speech through an extended story that referred to his introduction. These combined approaches are fairly typical and often work more effectively than any one technique used alone.

Final Tips about Conclusions

Just as the introduction of your speech contributes to the audience's first impression of you, the conclusion represents your last chance to reach out to listeners and reinforce your speech's purpose. Guidelines to help you include the following:

- The conclusion should be *brief*; this is no place to introduce new information or to tack on something you forgot to say earlier.
- Speakers sometimes have trouble ending their speeches. A speaker may say, "Let me leave you with this thought," and then ramble on for several more minutes. Or the speaker may pepper his or her remarks with signposts such as *finally* or *in conclusion*—but not stop talking. Soon, listeners will become frustrated or bored. Even a good speech (and a good speaker) can lose ground if the conclusion is poorly crafted and delivered.
- You can signal to the audience that you are concluding by your content and your delivery. Offering a summary clearly communicates that you are approaching the end of your speech, as do signposts such as *finally* or *in closing*. You may also move physically closer to the audience and connect with them directly through eye contact and vocal expressiveness as you offer a concluding quotation, help them visualize the future, or call them to action. Your conclusion is your last opportunity to connect with your audience, and it should never be lost.

 Study and Review materials for this chapter are at **MyCommunicationLab**

SUMMARY

 Listen to the Audio Chapter Summary at **MyCommunicationLab**

The Elements of Sound Organization

1 Explain how the quality of your ideas influences the strength of your speech's organization.

- Effective speakers strive to organize their ideas carefully and strategically.
  - Well-organized speakers are usually viewed as competent and knowledgeable.
  - They are also viewed as being invested in their topic and respectful of the audience.
  - The better organized the speaker, the more likely the audience will learn from the speech and be influenced by it.
- The foundation of a well-organized speech is a set of main ideas that are clearly formulated.
  - Design ideas with a specific purpose in mind, making sure that they are clear, simple, and appropriate to the situation.

How Patterns Connect Ideas

2 Describe basic organizational patterns you might use as you arrange your ideas strategically.

- Ideas should be organized in a coherent and reasonable fashion. The principal patterns of organization follow:
  - Chronological or sequential (arranged in a time or step-by-step order)
  - Categorical (a pattern that emphasizes distinct topics)
  - Climactic (arranged according to importance, size, or degree of simplicity)
  - Causal (moving from causes to effects or from effects to causes)
  - Problem-solution (a logical progression that moves from perceived difficulties to an examination of alternatives to a best solution)
  - Narrative (based on a story-telling model)

Guidelines for Organizing Your Speech

3 List and explain underlying principles of organization you will follow, regardless of the specific pattern you choose.

- Every speech should be organized with underlying principles in mind.
  - Ideas and information should be presented strategically, always guided by the specific purpose of the speech.
  - Each idea should be well developed, with a concern for balance and symmetry.
  - Main ideas should relate directly to your specific purpose and should be limited in number.
  - The most important information and ideas should be presented first or last.

Transitions as Connectives

4 Describe different transitional devices you might use in creating a coherent presentation.

- A transition is a connective that provides a bridge as you move from one idea to another. Transitions include the following:
  - Internal previews
  - Internal summaries
  - Signposts
  - Rhetorical questions

Introducing Your Speech

5 Identify key components of a speech's introduction.

- Once you have chosen the basic organizational pattern and worked on good transitions, you are ready to think about how to introduce your speech. In most situations, your introduction should do the following:
- Establish common ground with the audience.
  - Capture and hold the audience's attention.
  - Show them why your topic is relevant to them.
  - Establish your credibility.
  - Advance the speech's purpose.
  - Preview your main ideas.

Concluding Your Speech

6 Describe different ways of concluding a speech effectively.

- Crafting an effective conclusion is also important. The conclusion is your last opportunity to connect with your audience and realize your specific purpose. Conclusions allow you to do the following:
  - Summarize your main ideas.
  - Challenge your audience.
  - Appeal to listeners.
  - Visualize the future.
  - Offer a memorable quotation.
  - Create balance and closure by referring to the introduction.

QUESTIONS FOR REVIEW AND REFLECTION

The Elements of Sound Organization

1 Explain how the quality of your ideas influences the strength of your speech's organization.

1. Why is good organization important?
2. In what ways does the purpose of your speech influence the main ideas?
3. What makes an idea a good one? Examine the main ideas you advanced in your last speech. How do they measure up in light of these criteria?

How Patterns of Organization Connect Ideas

2 Describe basic organizational patterns you might use as you arrange your ideas strategically.

4. What are the principal patterns of organization?
5. Why would you choose one pattern over another?

Guidelines for Organizing Your Speech

3 List and explain underlying principles of sound organization you will follow, regardless of the specific pattern you choose.

6. How might each of the following concepts be important to you as you go about organizing your next speech?
   a. Strategic organization
   b. Balance/symmetry
   c. The number of main ideas to include
   d. Primacy and recency effects

Transitions as Connectives

4 Describe different transitional devices you might use in creating a coherent presentation.

7. What is the function of transitions?
8. What are the different kinds of transitions that you might use as you move through your speech? Briefly define each, and describe whatever advantages each may offer.

Study and Review the Flashcards at **MyCommunicationLab**

Introducing Your Speech

5 Identify the key components of a speech's introduction.

9. What are the major components of the speech introduction? Why is each important?
10. Give some examples of how you might capture the listeners' attention in your introduction.
11. As you look toward your next speech, what preliminary ideas do you have for good ways to introduce your topic?

Concluding Your Speech

6 List different ways of concluding a speech effectively.

12. What should you accomplish in the conclusion to your speech?
13. What are some devices you might use to conclude your speech in an effective and compelling way?
14. Thinking of your next speech topic, begin to focus on what kind of device might work effectively in your conclusion. Offer an example of one quotation or other device that you might use.

PHOTO CREDITS

TEXT CREDITS

GLOSSARY

categorical pattern An organizational pattern in which several independent, yet interrelated, categories are used to advance a larger idea.

causal pattern An organizational pattern in which ideas focus on causes or effects, or are arranged to reveal cause-to-effect or effect-to-cause relationships.

chronological pattern An organizational pattern in which ideas are arranged in a logical, time-based or sequential order.

climactic pattern An organizational pattern in which the ideas being advanced in a speech are arranged so that they build in intensity.

Dewey's Reflective Thinking Sequence A problem-solution pattern that takes listeners through a thorough problem exploration before considering possible solutions and arguing for the preferred course of action.

fidelity Narratives that seem authentic to listeners because they ring true with their own life experiences.

internal preview A quick look ahead at what will be covered under one of the main points or within a particular section of a speech.

internal summary A brief review of what one has presented under a main point or within a particular section of a speech.

motivated sequence An organizational pattern for a persuasive speech that is based on psychological studies of what engages people's emotions and motivates them to act.

narrative pattern An indirect, organic organizational pattern that often uses a coherent series of stories to convey the main ideas of the speech.

preview A glimpse of the major points one will be treating in a speech or in a section of a speech.

primacy effects The presumed impact of placing the most compelling information or arguments first in a speech.

problem-solution pattern An organizational pattern in which a problem is identified and one or more specific solutions are proposed.

recency effects The presumed impact of saving the strongest argument or the most important information for near the end of a speech.

rhetorical questions Questions posed by a speaker to stimulate audience interest and thought, not to solicit information or answers.

sequential pattern An organizational pattern in which the various steps of a process or phenomenon are identified and discussed, one by one.

signposts Words that alert listeners to where you are in your speech, particularly in relation to the speech's overall organization.

spatial pattern An organizational pattern in which ideas are arranged according to their natural spatial and/or geographical relationships.

spiraling narrative A narrative pattern that builds in intensity from the beginning to the end of the speech.

symmetry Using a balanced approach to developing and presenting ideas in a speech, so that each idea is developed with a similar level of elaboration.

transition A word, phrase, or sentence that helps the audience perceive the relationship of ideas and the movement from one main idea to another.

NOTES

1. James C. McCroskey and R. Samuel Mehrley, "The Effects of Disorganization and Nonfluency on Attitude Change and Source Credibility," *Communication Monographs* 36 (1969): 13–21.

2. Studies generally show that organized speeches are better understood than those that are less well-organized. See, for example, Ernest C. Thompson, "An Experimental Investigation of the Relative Effectiveness of Organizational Structure in Oral Communication," *Southern Speech Communication Journal* 26 (1960): 59–69.

3. When listeners are forced to listen to a disorganized presentation, they are unlikely to respond in a way that is consistent with the speaker's specific purpose. See Raymond G. Smith, "An Experimental Study of the Effects of Speech Organization upon Attitudes of College Students," *Communication Monographs* 18 (1951): 292–301.

4. For example, a Michigan legislator sponsored a $486,000 earmark to add a bike lane to a bridge within walking distance of her home. See David S. Fallis, Scott Higham, and Kimberly Kindy, "Congressional Earmarks Sometimes Used to Fund Projects near Lawmakers' Properties," www.washingtonpost.com/investigations/congressional-earmarks-sometimes-used-to-fund-projects-near-lawmakers-properties/2012/01/12/gIQA97HGvQ_story.html (accessed February 10, 2012).

5. See Peg McGlinch, "Don't Ban Earmarks—Fix Them," www.usnews.com/opinion/blogs/peg-mcglinch/2012/02/09/dont-ban-earmarks-fix-them (accessed February 12, 2012).

6. John Dewey, *How We Think* (Boston: Heath, 1910).

7. This pattern was originally introduced by Alan H. Monroe in *Principles and Types of Speech* (New York: Scott, Foresman, 1935) and has been refined in later editions. See, for example, Kathleen M. German, Bruce E. Gronbeck, Douglas Ehninger, and Alan H. Monroe, *Principles of Speech Communication*, 17th edition (Upper Saddle River, NJ: Pearson, 2010).

8. See Karen Zediker, "Rediscovering the Tradition: Women's History with a Relational Approach to the Basic Public Speaking Course," paper, Western States Communication Association, Albuquerque, New Mexico, 1993.

9. Walter R. Fisher, "Narration as a Human Communication Paradigm: The Case of Public Moral Argument," *Communication Monographs* 51 (1984): 1–22.

10. Ibid.

11. See James C. McCroskey, *An Introduction to Rhetorical Communication*, 7th ed. (Boston: Allyn & Bacon, 1997), 205–22; and Howard Gilkinson, Stanley F. Paulson, and Donald E. Sikkink, "Effects of Order and Authority in an Argumentative Speech," *Quarterly Journal of Speech* 40 (1954): 183–92.

12. Assuming that recipients find the message relevant, moderate repetition (such as that provided by transitions, a preview, and a review within a speech) prompts listeners to better understand and better recall what is said as well as process it more deeply. See, for example, Heather M. Claypool, Diane M. Mackie, Teresa Garcia-Marques, Ashley McIntosh, and Ashton Udall, "The Effects of Personal Relevance and Repetition on Persuasive Processing," *Social Cognition* 22 (2004): 310–35. Also see Robert F. Lorch Jr., Elizabeth Pugzles Lorch, and W. Elliot Inman, "Effects of Signaling Topic Structure on Text Recall," *Journal of Educational Psychology* 85 (1993): 281–90.

13. Bob Scott, "Green Burials Gaining Popularity," *The Herald-Times,* Sunday, January 29, 2012, A2.

14. From Bill Clinton, "Memphis Church of God in Christ Convention Address," November 13, 1993. Published 1993 by Bill Clinton.

15. Carmen Mariano, "You as Teachers Are Saving the World," *Vital Speeches of the Day* 71 (October 1, 2005): 642.

16. From Eugene Debs, "Statement to the Court," Federal Court of Cleveland, September 18, 1918.

17. Richard Lamm, "Unexamined Assumptions: Destiny, Political Institutions, Democracy and Population," *Vital Speeches of the Day* 64 (September 15, 1998): 712.

18. Reprinted by permission from Sarah Snyder. Published 2007 by SC 105 Speakers Showcase.

19. Joel Grass, "When Prisons Suffer We All Suffer," Persuasive Speech Two on the Website for SC 105: Fundamentals of Oral Communication, http://cstl-cla.semo.edu/williams/sc105/samples.htm (accessed February 24, 2012).

20. See, for example, Michael Jacobson, *Downsizing Prisons* (New York: New York University Press, 2005).

21. See Claypool et al., "The Effects of Personal Relevance and Repetition on Persuasive Processing"; and Lorch et al., "Effects of Signaling Topic Structure on Text Recall."

22. Office of Admissions, Indiana University, "Academic Opportunities," http://admit.indiana.edu/academics/opportunities.shtml (accessed February 1, 2012).

23. To read more about Shalom Community Center, go to http://shalomcommunitycenter.org/about/our-mission (accessed February 7, 2012).

24. From Barack Obama, "Keynote Address to the 2004 Democratic National Convention," July 26, 2004. Published 2004 by BarackObama.com.

25. Richard Lamm, "Family Friendly Institutions," *Vital Speeches of the Day* 72 (October 15, 2005): 30.

26. Edward M. Kennedy, "Faith, Truth and Tolerance in America," http://www.americanrhetoric.com/speeches/tedkennedytruth&tolerance.htm (accessed: February 7, 2012).

27. Jimmy Carter, "U.S. Response to Soviet Military Force in Cuba," *Vital Speeches of the Day* 42 (1970): 4.

28. Robert C. Purcell, "Values for Value: Integrity and Stewardship," *Vital Speeches of the Day* 64 (October 1, 1998): 766.

Ethos

This chapter discusses how a rhetorical public speaker develops a relationship with an audience. A "relationship" means more than simply letting an audience know a speaker's identity and his or her qualifications. A relationship is something personal that involves an emotional attitude toward another person or group and negotiates their reciprocal identities. This chapter explores the strategies that can be used to develop a relationship between speaker and audience that is most conducive to persuasion. Starting with the classical definition of ethos as a combination of goodwill, practical wisdom, and virtue that make us think a speaker is credible and trustworthy, this chapter moves into more specific concepts that help define ethos, including persona, evoked audience, identification, distinction, and polarization.

Perhaps what most distinguishes public speaking from any other form of persuasion is the fact that its effectiveness relies heavily on the character of the speaker. As an oral performer, a public speaker steps before an audience and effectively asks them a favor—to listen attentively as the speaker rewards their time and energy with a speech that is tailored specifically to their interests. An advertisement or a YouTube clip or an e-mail has no analogous constraint. Because of their reproducibility, these media can be watched or read at any time that is convenient to an audience and can be turned off or ignored just as easily without offending anyone. Yet when members of an audience ignore the speaker entirely or walk out of the room, we think of it as highly rude or antagonistic. That is why the choice to actually attend a public speech is usually a more personal and important decision than simply clicking on a video link. When we decide to be a member of an audience, we do so because we want to listen to the *speaker*, and we have done so because we have put trust in that speaker to reward our time commitment. Any successful public speech must therefore begin with the existence of mutual trust that forms a temporary relationship between speaker and audience. Without a sense of this "bond," a speaker's words fall on deaf ears.

For the purposes of rhetorical public speech, **ethos** represents this sense of public character that is recognized by an audience and influences their reception of the speaker's arguments. Ethos is thus the capacity to influence an audience based on the audience's perceptions of the credibility and character of the speaker in relationship to the audience's own interests and values. Importantly, even though the Greek word for ethos is "character," this does not have the modern connotation of being something private and inside of us that others cannot see.

That is why it is perhaps more appropriate to call it *public* character. Ethos in the rhetorical sense is not something absolute and stable that one carries around wherever one goes; it is determined by the relationship one has with an audience. The president of a country may possess great ethos with respect to his or her own constituency and yet be despised by a foreign population. This is because any act can be interpreted differently by different groups. A presidential declaration of war may be seen as a courageous defense of freedom by one side and a brutal act of imperialism by the other. To understand the possible effects of one's rhetoric, then, a person must understand how an audience perceives his or her character.[1] For the Greeks, people with ethos were those people who earned respect, admiration, and allegiance rather than those who simply possessed a good "soul" that went unseen by others.[2]

The concept of ethos has distinctly rhetorical implications because it deals with aspects of credibility and authority that influence our choice of whom to trust when faced with important decisions.[3] In other words, because we often do not have the time or resources to be able to make crucial judgments on our own, we look to those who possess strength of character, or ethos, to help guide our actions. For this reason, Aristotle believed that among the three forms of rhetorical proof (ethos, pathos, and logos), ethos was often the most powerful. He writes:

> There is persuasion through character whenever the speech is spoken in such a way as to make the speaker worthy of credence; for we believe fair-minded people to a greater extent and more quickly than we do others, on all subjects in general and completely so in cases where there is not exact knowledge but room for doubt. And this should result from the speech, not from a previous opinion that the speaker is a certain kind of person; for it is not the case as some of the handbook writers propose in their treatment of the art at fair-mindedness on the part of the speaker makes no contribution to persuasive this; rather, character is almost, so to speak, the most authoritative form of persuasion.[4]

The reason that ethos is the most authoritative form of persuasion is simply because we tend to accept the opinions of those people who we feel are more like us and who have our best interests at heart. Particularly when hundreds of different messages surround us every day, demanding our attention for this thing and that, ethos provides us an efficient and usually reliable way of selecting those few that we think are tailored specifically to our lives and our concerns. This is why public speaking, as an oral performance, still remains a powerful medium of persuasion in a digital age. It is the only medium that establishes a meaningful bond between speaker and audience and distills from the cacophony of popular and political culture a single message that creates a sense of shared experience between both speaker and audience and between audience members themselves.

---

[1]For more on speaker credibility, see chapter 5 of Gary C. Woodward and Robert E. Denton, Jr., *Persuasion and Influence in American Life*, 5th ed. (Long Grove, IL: Waveland, 2004).

[2]For more on the Greek notion of public life, see chapter 2 of Hannah Arendt, *The Human Condition*, 2nd ed. (Chicago: The University of Chicago Press, 1958).

[3]For excellent essays exploring the concept of *ethos*, see Michael J. Hyde, ed., *The Ethos of Rhetoric* (Columbia: University of South Carolina Press, 2004).

[4]Aristotle, *Rhetoric*, 1356a.

Because it is so central to the act of public speaking, establishing ethos is a complex process that involves more than simply offering an audience a list of accomplishments and admirable characteristics. Developing ethos in a public speech is not the same as presenting a written resume for a job application. The goal of developing ethos is to establish a relationship, not to document facts. Aristotle explains the difficulty of establishing ethos and its three components:

> There are three reasons why speakers themselves are persuasive; for there are three things we trust other than logical demonstration. These are practical wisdom (*phronesis*), and virtue (*arête*), and goodwill (*eunoia*): for speakers make mistakes in what they say through failure to exhibit either, all, or one of these; for either through lack of practical sense they do not form opinions rightly; or through forming opinions they do not say what they think because of the bad character; or they are prudent and fair-minded but let goodwill, so that it is possible for people not to give the best advice although they know what it is. These are the only possibilities.[5]

Understanding the subtleties of Aristotle's argument requires a clear distinction between these three components of ethos. By **practical wisdom**, he means a proven ability to size up problematic situations and make judgments that show prudence and forethought, as a military commander might possess due to actions during past battles. By **virtue**, he means excellence in performing particular activities that are held in high regard and embody the best cultural values, as one might think of the virtues of motherhood. By **goodwill**, he means the presence of conscious and thoughtful consideration of the audience's well-being, as we would expect from a good friend rather than from a stranger on the street.

In summary, we prove practical wisdom by boasting of our track record of past decisions, we prove virtue by showing how we have committed ourselves to certain noble habits of action, and we prove goodwill by addressing the concerns and interests of our audience and by revealing our willingness to sacrifice our own self-interest in service of their prosperity. As Aristotle remarks, however, it is difficult to show all three in a speech. For instance, a criminal may have demonstrated practical wisdom in his ability to rob banks, but lack virtue and goodwill. A reclusive monk might be well esteemed in virtue, but have little practical wisdom for everyday situations and perhaps might not care. And an old high school friend might have all the goodwill in the world toward you, but lack good sense and most components of virtue. In each case, we might have interesting conversations with each of these individuals, but rhetorically we would not necessarily look to them for counsel in times of crisis or uncertainty. It is during these times that ethos becomes a powerful persuasive tool because it focuses an audience's attention on the message that comes from one respected individual. Developing this rhetorical ethos will be the subject of the rest of this chapter.

Discussion: Many times celebrities whose ethos comes from their acting ability try to also establish ethos in the political sphere. Which celebrity activist do you think has successfully established goodwill, practical wisdom, and virtue with respect to some political issue? And who do you think has done the opposite?

---

[5]Aristotle, *Rhetoric*, 1358a.

PERSONA

Most people step into any familiar social situation with an **inherited ethos**, which is the actual reputation that rhetors "carry with them" because of an audience's acquaintance with past behavior. When an inherited ethos is strong, such as the ethos of a mother for her child or that which close friends have with each other, the rhetor rarely has to spend any time establishing his or her reputation or credibility. It certainly would be strange for a mother to say to her child, "Because I have worked hard these many years learning how to cook healthy meals (good sense), because I care deeply for your future (goodwill), and because I am a just and honorable soul (virtue), please listen to my recommendation to eat your spinach." Having already established her ethos, she simply says "Eat your spinach." Inherited ethos is this kind of unspoken credibility that needs no mention to function. In Aristotle's language, it is "inartistic."

Ethos becomes a uniquely rhetorical concern of *art* only when rhetors, in some form, create or modify the perception of an audience about them. **Persona** is this rhetorical creation; it represents the constructed ethos that a rhetor creates within the confines of a particular rhetorical text. Persona, in other words, is more a creation of language rather than an inheritance of history. Like the costume that transforms an actor into a new personality on stage, rhetoric can create a "public face" that best suits the immediate needs of a rhetor. Unlike inherited ethos, which is the product of cumulative interactions or exposure over time with an audience, one's persona is always tied to a specific discourse and is completely contained within that discourse. For example, a convict before a parole board enters the hearing with an inherited ethos as a liar and a thief, and he attempts to counter that reputation by describing himself as a "changed man" who has seen the error of his ways. The decision of the board rests on whether the convict's persona of a "changed man" is more convincing than the inherited ethos of a liar and a thief.

Deciding when to construct a persona and when to rely on the strength of one's inherited ethos depends upon the presence and quality of one's reputation within an audience. On the one hand, when a speaker is unknown to an audience, creating a persona is necessary in order to present a favorable "first impression."[6] We are all familiar with those first job interviews when we must define ourselves as an ideal employee. On the other hand, when a speaker enters a situation as a respected leader, there is no need for such self-promotion; indeed, it would be seen as being in bad taste. Rarely do we enjoy listening to famous and powerful people talking about their fame and power. But most speaking situations usually fall somewhere in between these two extremes. In these cases, one must construct a persona that somehow addresses, modifies, and transcends the limits of one's inherited ethos.[7]

Because the construction of personae deals not just with possession of knowledge or skills, but with notions of character, it relies heavily on personal stories and the form of delivery. **Personal stories** are narrations of one's life experience that

---

[6]An interesting account of an actual scholarly persona is found in James Darsey, "Edwin Black and the First Persona," *Rhetoric & Public Affairs* 10, no. 3 (2007), 501–507.
[7]The relationship between rhetor and audience can be described in terms of the ratio between the level of credibility and the level of agreement. These considerations are explained in detail in chapter 7 of Woodward and Denton, *Persuasion and Influence in American Life*.

provide insight into the speaker's practical wisdom, virtue, or goodwill. Phrases like "The time I was behind enemy lines . . ." or "When I saved my sister's life . . ." or "Growing up in a tough neighborhood . . ." signify to an audience that a person is relating a story that offers a window into his or her deeper self. The **form of delivery** reveals character by using phrases, words, accents, or gestures commonly associated with certain "types" of people. Hence, a president often vacillates between acting "presidential" by speaking in firm, calm, and authoritative terms in formal settings and behaving as an "ordinary American" by doing volunteer work with rolled-up sleeves and telling jokes around a barbeque. Form of delivery is important because we trust those who speak like us, not just because it is familiar, but because it shows a mastery of the type of language that can only be acquired through life experience. It is thus an expression of goodwill.

The personae available for a rhetor are literally infinite. However, there are general types of personae that are always familiar and that conform to our social conventions. Take, for instance, just a few popular personae: the country lawyer, the wise sage, the teenage rebel, the religious prophet, the CEO, the father/mother figure, the loyal friend, the iconoclast, the president, the confidant, the drill sergeant, or the door-to-door salesperson. Any person attempting to create his or her own persona, of course, will always individualize his or her character such that no two personae will ever be alike. But these models provide general guides for action.

In their review of the research on the roles typically played by rhetors in rhetorical situations, Roderick Hart and Susanne Daughton identify four recurring personae: the apologist, the agent, the partisan, and the hero.[8] These roles represent fitting responses to situations that also take into account the personality and intentions of the speaker.

1. **Apologist:** The role of **apologist** is employed when speakers wish to rebuff attack, including both attacks on one's personal character and more often on one's position. The essential characteristic of the apologist is *righteous indignation*. The apologist does not actually "apologize." Like Socrates in front of the jury, the apologist instead corrects the mistaken impression of the audience and seeks to clarify the essential rightness of his or her position. The most powerful way to do this is by employing one of three strategies: *bolstering*, which supports one's case by "correcting" the erroneous facts and narratives held by the audience ("My accusers have been deceived by liars and are in turn distorting the truth about my position"); *differentiation*, which clarifies misunderstanding by more clearly separating, or differentiating, two issues that have been carelessly conflated ("My critics do not understand the difference between making policy statements and telling jokes."); and *transcendence*, which resolves tensions by invoking a higher principle that clarifies apparent contradictions ("I am accused of inciting violence, and yet the only thing I want is peace. But sometimes peace must be achieved through war."). Successful apologists appear noble because they're willing to suffer for their cause while seeking to clarify the truth.

---

[8]Roderick Hart and Susanne Daughton. *Modern Rhetorical Criticism*, 3rd ed. (Boston: Pearson, 2005), 220–221.

2. The **agent** speaks on behalf of some institution as a spokesperson of legitimate authority, thereby standing as a "representative" of a recognized institution, such as church body, a government, or a corporation. The essential characteristic of the agent is *enthusiastic loyalty*. Typical people who fit the role of agent in society are public relations specialists, priests, presidents, CEOs, chancellors, community leaders, and ambassadors of all kinds. What makes a successful agent is the fact that he or she charismatically can "stand in" for a larger institution, thereby putting a personal face on a sometimes abstract entity. It is difficult to have affection for the Catholic Church or the United States or Microsoft simply as institutions; but we can generate great enthusiasm at the prospect of meeting the pope or the president or Bill Gates. At the same time, our enthusiasm at meeting these individuals is only because they "stand for" a form of organized authority that is greater than them as individuals. In other words, a successful agent conveys personal charisma while at the same time being an effective representative of a larger and more powerful group that asks our allegiance.

3. The **partisan** is one who represents not a group or institution but an idea or ideal. This individual tends to thrive in heated debates during times of turmoil and upheaval, when people are looking for new directions based on new ideas. The essential characteristic of the partisan is *critical idealism*. Partisan are idealists because they are advocating a vision of society or politics or religion that is not yet real but that might be possible with faith and effort; and they are critical because in order to make this possibility a reality, they must remove many obstacles in the path, obstacles that are usually tied to tradition, law, or institutional inertia. Partisans are most influential, therefore, on the margins of politics, often as social movement leaders or public intellectuals or iconoclastic artists, musicians, and poets. The biggest difference, therefore, between the partisan and the agent is that the partisan can hypothetically stand alone, whereas the agent is always a representative of an established institution; ironically, then, when partisans actually succeed in promoting their ideas, they become agents.

4. Finally, the **hero** is defined as an individual who is willing to actively confront power in the name of helping others even if it means that great suffering might come upon him or her. The essential characteristic of the hero is therefore *romantic courage*. Heroes are "romantic" because, unlike the partisan, they do not have a coherent political vision they are promoting, but instead boldly stride into the unknown against all obstacles with the optimistic faith that things will work out for them in the end. And they are courageous because they do not simply "talk the talk" but also "walk the walk." Without a commitment to action, particularly the type of action that directly and physically confronts a more powerful foe, the hero is merely a big talker. It is for this reason that heroes are often spontaneously found or discovered in moments of crisis, because the hero reacts spontaneously to defend the weak and challenge the strong in the name of an abstract value that is shared by the community the hero fights for. Finally, what makes heroes capable of making such self-sacrifices is their confidence that even if they die in the struggle, their legacy will live on as martyrs.

It is important to also keep in mind that these roles are not mutually exclusive. Some of the greatest orations combined many or even all of these roles, with the speaker taking on new personae during different phases of the speech. For instance, an American president might assume the role of the apologist in defense of the wisdom of some military policy ("Those who question the wisdom of toppling this dictator do not properly understand the nature of evil"), then might take on the role of agent ("As the commander-in-chief of this nation, I will not allow its foreign policy to be determined by petty tyrants"), only to then transition to being a partisan ("Furthermore, this campaign is not simply about our national self-interest. I advocate this policy not simply because I am president, but because I believe that the true task of humanity is to spread freedom and democracy around the globe") and then end on a heroic note ("Finally, I can no longer stand to see children suffer and mothers weep; when evil shows its face it must be confronted at all costs if we are to live with ourselves"). A role is not something that locks us permanently into any type of performance; it is a type of script we perform to accomplish a specific rhetorical task.

Sojourner Truth: "Ain't I a woman?"

One of the most fascinating orators in American history is civil rights champion and former slave Sojourner Truth. Born Isabella Van Wagenen (a Dutch name given by her Dutch slave owners) in about 1797, Truth endured many years of abuse until finally achieving her freedom in 1827 and changing her name in 1843. Despite growing up illiterate, she was a woman of remarkable intelligence and presence. She was tall for her era—almost six feet—with a low and powerful voice that had a song-like quality to it. Her straight-talking and unsentimental style, combined with her imposing figure, made her a national symbol for strong women, both black and white. Her most famous extemporaneous address, "Ain't I a Woman?" was delivered at the Women's Convention in Akron, Ohio, on May 29, 1851. This type of convention was a major component of the early women's rights movement, which involved the organization of women's conferences to bring together feminists to discuss goals and strategies. However, many of these conferences attracted men (including several ministers) who came largely to heckle the speakers and to argue that women's proper place was one of being both subservient to and cared for by men.

It was the heckling of one of these ministers that inspired Truth to speak. Reacting to a black-robed minister who argued for male superiority based on "superior intellect" and "manhood in Christ," Truth argued that women were in fact more powerful than men and also that black women had been denied even the limited rights given to white women. Her argument constructs a persona that establishes her superior strength, capability, and authority. A firsthand account described how "Sojourner walked to the podium and slowly took off her sunbonnet. Her six-foot frame towered over the audience. She began to speak in her deep, resonant voice."

> Well, children, where there is so much racket there must be something out of kilter. I think that 'twixt the negroes of the South and the women at the North, all talking about rights, the white men will be in a fix pretty soon. But what's all this here talking about?

That man over there says that women need to be helped into carriages, and lifted over ditches, and to have the best place everywhere. Nobody ever helps me into carriages, or over mud-puddles, or gives me any best place! And ain't I a woman? Look at me! Look at my arm! I have ploughed and planted, and gathered into barns, and no man could head me! And ain't I a woman? I could work as much and eat as much as a man - when I could get it - and bear the lash as well! And ain't I a woman? I have borne thirteen children, and seen most all sold off to slavery, and when I cried out with my mother's grief, none but Jesus heard me! And ain't I a woman?

Then they talk about this thing in the head; what's this they call it? [member of audience whispers, "intellect"] That's it, honey. What's that got to do with women's rights or negroes' rights? If my cup won't hold but a pint, and yours holds a quart, wouldn't you be mean not to let me have my little half measure full?

Then that little man in black there, he says women can't have as much rights as men, 'cause Christ wasn't a woman! Where did your Christ come from? Where did your Christ come from? From God and a woman! Man had nothing to do with Him.

If the first woman God ever made was strong enough to turn the world upside down all alone, these women together ought to be able to turn it back, and get it right side up again! And now they is asking to do it, the men better let them.[9]

Truth masterfully combines elements of all four roles within her unique personae. First, her sheer act of standing up to speak at the convention implies she is an agent who speaks on behalf of the women gathered together. Indeed, her speech made many of the other women in the audience anxious because they were not sure that an imposing former slave with a thick accent was the best choice of representative for their group. Second, she acts the apologist by refuting the false accusations (made by the "man in black") that women are fragile and cannot take care of themselves without men. She accomplishes this by bolstering her assertion that women are equally competent to men by citing specific facts of her life that show her physical and emotional strength. Third, she plays the hero when she directly challenges the men in the audience, thus taking a real personal risk on behalf of other women who might not have had the courage to do so. Finally, she takes on the role of partisan by advocating the radical notion that it is women, not men, who are the true seat of power and authority because of the heritage of Eve (who turned the world upside down on her own) and Mary (who gave birth to Christ on her own). Anyone who doubts the power of *ethos* to leave a lasting rhetorical legacy need only recognize how this short and impromptu speech became one of the most famous orations in history almost entirely due to Truth's mastery of the power of personae.[10]

---

[9]Ibid.

[10]The changing narrative surrounding Truth's rhetoric is explored in Roseann M. Mandziuk and Suzzane Pullon Fitch, "The Rhetorical Construction of Sojourner Truth," *Southern Communication Journal* 66, no. 2 (2001), 120–137.

Discussion: Moving to a new place (either long term, such as for college or a new career, or short term, such as an exchange program or summer camp) often creates a new opportunity to create a novel persona that is no longer constrained by one's inherited ethos. Have you ever consciously tried to create a new persona after making such a move? Did you change your role as apologist, partisan, hero, or agent?

EVOKED AUDIENCE

If the persona is the image that the rhetor constructs of him- or herself as a speaker, the **evoked audience** is the attractive image that the rhetor constructs of and for the audience. If the speaker's constructed self-image can be considered as the "first" persona (in which the speaker tells the audience who "I" am), then the evoked audience can be considered as the "second" persona (in which the speaker tells the audience who "you" are). The concept of the second persona was advanced by Edwin Black. For him, an astute rhetorical critic can thus see "in the auditor implied by a discourse a model of what the rhetor would have his real auditor become."[11] The function of the evoked audience, or this "second persona," is to create an attractive image of unity that makes members of an audience desire to be a part of a common group rather than an aggregate of separate individuals.

In its most general form, we find politicians using evoked audiences whenever they speak of the *American people* as a collective body of people who love liberty, freedom, and democracy. By creating a category of identity that can unify a group of separate individuals, an evoked audience creates the possibility of cooperative action because it contributes to the creation of a sense of unity that may not have existed before the speech. For example, we often take for granted that everyone who is born within the geographic boundaries of the United States is an "American," but prior to the revolution, people identified themselves more with their local city or region. For revolutionaries to start using the term *American* thus helped make possible a national identity that stood apart from the British Empire.[12]

Like the concept of persona, the evoked audience is a partly fictional identity that usually overstates the unified character of the people listening to a speech (who in reality are far more diverse). Like persona, the evoked audience often is what a rhetor *wants* an audience to be rather than what it literally *is*. Yet this ideal often brings a new reality into existence. For instance, a collection of teenagers may all be talented at a certain sport, but they do not think of themselves as a "team" until the coach starts telling them to act like one ("Go Tigers!"). The coach's rhetoric creates a sense of commonality by evoking the team spirit within the individual players that may not have been fully present before. The most typical sign that such a team spirit is being attempted by a speaker is the repetitive use of "we" or "you," such that an audience feels it is being grouped together under a single category. One can imagine a parent telling his or her children, "If we are a family, then we will eat

---

[11]Edwin Black, "The Second Persona," *Readings in Rhetorical Criticism*, ed. Carl R. Burgchardt (State College, PA: Strata Publishing Co., 1995), 90.

[12]For more on the "public" as an evoked audience, see Michael McGee, "In Search of the People," *Quarterly Journal of Speech* 71 (1975), 235–249.

together at the dinner table." The implicit choice now placed upon the audience is whether or not to accept that group membership.

Therefore, although there is a fictional quality about an evoked audience, this does not mean that it is an illusion. Clearly, a speaker who speaks to an audience of school children as if they were all members of Congress is not literally accurate. However, motivational teachers *can* speak to them as "future leaders of America" and anticipate an energetic response. In other words, the evoked audience should always select and amplify shared qualities that are already present (or at least potentially present) within an audience. The average audience of college students, for instance, can be referred to as "university students," or "citizens," or "eager young people," or "future leaders," or "party-goers." Each of these designations may be partly true, but each of them only speaks to one portion of that group's identity. Consequently, deciding what identity to evoke in an audience has different consequences for rhetorical persuasion.

Despite what has been said, however, one should not think that the evoked audience is something that the speaker always *does* to the audience. Many times, an audience goes to a speech, as with a "rally," precisely to feel a part of a common identity. In this case, the evoked audience is merely the vehicle through which this desire is actualized. In other words, the audience must be *active*, not *passive*, in generating its sense of common identity. It is this constitution of a common emotional bond between members of an audience that makes public speaking, as an oral performance, so powerful.

Tecumseh: "Brothers, we all belong to one family."

One of the greatest Native American leaders and warriors was Tecumseh, a Shawnee leader who resisted colonization of native lands by uniting the various tribes into a Native Confederacy spreading from the Great Lakes to Mexico. As part of this campaign, Tecumseh supported the British during the War of 1812, hoping that alliance with the enemies of the United States might stem the tide of settlers. This speech to the Osages in winter of 1811–1812 attempted to create a common identification between tribes as a necessary means of self-defense by evoking an audience who saw themselves as "brothers" of one "family":

> Brothers we all belong to one family; we are all children of the Great Spirit; we walk in the same path; slake our thirst at the same spring; and now affairs of the greatest concern lead us to smoke the pipe around the same council fire!
>
> Brothers, -We are friends; we must assist each other to bear our burdens. The blood of many of our fathers and brothers has run like water on the ground, to satisfy the avarice of the white men. We, ourselves, are threatened with a great evil; nothing will pacify them but the destruction of all the red men...
>
> Brothers, -We must be united; we must smoke the same pipe; we must fight each other's battles; and more than all, we must love the Great Spirit; he is for us; he will destroy our enemies, and make all his red children happy.[13]

---

[13]Tecumseh, available at <http://www.historyisaweapon.com/defcon1/tecumosages.html> (accessed 6 September 2012).

Although Tecumseh's speech also had explicit deliberative intent insofar as it advocated an explicit policy, the primary function of the speech was to construct a common identity as "brothers" who all share a kinship with the Great Spirit. Consistent with speeches of identification, Tecumseh speech spends a great deal of time talking about the common characteristics of his audience that make them all "one," including a shared environment, a shared history, shared rituals, shared appearance, and a shared spirituality. From his perspective, only by evoking an audience capable of sharing a common identity and purpose can any of them stop their inevitable annihilation.

Discussion: The creation of "team" spirit has become as common a goal in business as in athletics. When have you participated in some activity as an employee that was intended to evoke a group identification with fellow employees? Did the activity have any unintended consequences in actual practice?

IDENTIFICATION

When we "identify" with someone, we see ourselves as sharing some quality or experience with another person or group. Usually this feeling comes after the revelation of a life experience that we see as similar to our own. The process of making friends with people often begins with this step of identification in which two strangers find themselves sharing in some common interest, habit, belief, or feeling. In this sense, the process of identification is how two or more people come to form a bond that generates commonality out of what might seem, at first, to be different perspectives. What we "identify," then, is some quality in another person that he or she shares with us. Identification is not merely labeling something; it is identifying the qualities in others that we find in ourselves as well.

In rhetoric, **identification** is the strategy of creating a common bond with an audience by drawing parallels between the characteristics of speaker and audience. For Kenneth Burke, *identification* is a broad term that ranges from the simple schoolyard attempt to make friends by asserting a common quality or interest (e.g., "we are all baseball lovers") to religious or nationalistic attempts to create a unified group with common goals and characteristics.[14] What each of these examples has in common is a sense that two or more distinct and unique individuals share in some "essence" or "quality" that transcends their individuality (love of farming, class identity, and divine origin, respectively). This sense of commonality thus leads to people uniting in a common purpose. For instance, when Sojourner Truth argues that she also possesses "masculine" qualities, she creates a commonality between men and women that had not previously been present. In short, identification represents the persuasive attempt on the part of the rhetorical agent to say "I am one of you" in order to create a sense of "we." The justification for such a strategy is that we tend to prefer listening to people who feel and think like we do.[15]

[14]For more on identification, see Kenneth Burke, *A Rhetoric of Motives* (Berkeley: The University of California Press, 1969), xiv.
[15]For more on identification, see Gary C. Woodward, *The Idea of Identification* (Albany: State University of New York Press, 2003).

Benjamin Banneker: "We are all of the same family"

As the Tecumseh example demonstrates, identification can be used to solidify a preexisting similarity. However, identification can also be one way in which previously marginalized groups attempt to include themselves as active parts of the general public. For instance, after the American victory in the Revolutionary War, many opponents of slavery—particularly the slaves themselves—hoped it would lead to an end of that oppressive institution. One such person was Benjamin Banneker, a child of a freed slave who taught himself mathematics and astronomy and eventually published several successful almanacs. On August 19, 1791, he sent one of his almanacs to Thomas Jefferson along with a letter that rebuked Jefferson for his proslavery views. He went on to compare black slavery to the British rule over the colonies. One strategy Banneker used to convince Jefferson of the evils of slavery was identification. However, the power of his identification comes only after beginning with the appearance of difference and division:

> I suppose it is a truth too well attested to you, to need a proof here, that we are a race of beings, who have long labored under the abuse and censure of the world; that we have long been looked upon with an eye of contempt; and that we have long been considered rather as brutish than human, and scarcely capable of mental endowments.
>
> Sir I hope I may Safely admit, in consequence of that report with hath reached me, that you are a man far less inflexible in Sentiments of this nature, then many others, that you are measurably friendly, and well disposed towards us, and that you are willing and ready to Lend your aid and assistance to our relief from these many distresses and numerous calamities to which we are reduced.
>
> Now Sir, if this is founded in truth, I apprehend you will embrace every opportunity, to eradicate that train of absurd and false ideas and opinions, which so generally prevails with respect to us; and that your sentiments are concurrent with mine, which are, that one universal Father hath given being to us all; and that he hath not only made us all of one flesh, but that he hath also, without partiality, afforded us all the same sensations and endowed us all with the same faculties; and that however variable we may be in society or religion, however diversified in situation or color, we are all of the same family, and stand in the same relation to him.[16]

Banneker's persuasive strategy clearly is meant to draw from the very principles of equality that Jefferson had enshrined in the Declaration of Independence. In short, he argues that Jefferson's statement of "all men are created equal" clearly includes all human beings, including African-American slaves. Notably, Banneker makes his case by "identifying" the qualities that are shared by human beings despite their skin color, including possessing the same flesh, the same sensations, the same faculties, and ultimately the same relation to God. This shows that a strategy of identification requires more than simply saying "we are all in this together." It requires identifying the specific characteristics that a speaker shares with an audience and that members of an audience share with each other.

---

[16]Benjamin Banneker, available at <http://mith.umd.edu/eada/html/display.php?docs=banneker_letter.xml&action=show> (accessed 6 September 2012).

However, this particular example also shows the limits of this strategy when it does not occur in a face-to-face oral environment. Banneker writes a *letter* to Jefferson, thereby allowing Jefferson to read the letter at his convenience or even skim over the parts that make him uncomfortable. Consider how different this message would have been received had Banneker stood before Jefferson and shook his hand while looking him in the eye. The fact that Jefferson never acknowledged Banneker's letter or directly confronted the institution of slavery shows how even the most brilliant minds find it easy to rationalize their own behavior when they are left to their own resources in the comfort of their private homes.

Discussion: Politicians notoriously strive to be all things to all people, trying to find parts in their lives that somehow connect to a particular constituency. What are the most common identifications made between politicians and American audiences? And what does the ubiquity of the strategies say about the actual character of the American public?

DISTINCTION

Identification is a mainstay of rhetorical persuasion, but it is not always sufficient. Especially in times of uncertainty in which we seek good advice rather than loyal friendship, we often look to those people who are very *unlike* us because they possess uncharacteristic excellence in character or special expertise in a very specific subject. In other words, we often want speakers not to "fit in" but to "stand out." In this case, we look not for identification but for **distinction**, which is the attempt to establish credibility by the possession of special knowledge and/or unique experience that are superior to those of the audience. **Special knowledge** refers to the kind of knowledge one receives by learning technical discourses and procedures, such as the knowledge one receives from attending a university. Whether experts are scientists, theologians, ethicists, economists, or movie critics, they all base their arguments on knowledge not accessible to the general public. **Unique experience** refers to the kind of expertise one acquires by having "been there" or "gone through that." For example, it is a common dramatic technique used in all war movies that the highly educated new officer always defers to the practical experience of the veteran soldier once combat begins. The officer might be more capable to discuss broader military strategy (thus having special knowledge), but the enlisted soldier usually knows better what to do in the heat of battle (thus possessing unique experience). The ideal, of course, is a fusion of both qualities within a single person.

In cases of *distinction*, the persona of the rhetor stands apart from the evoked audience; in cases of *identification*, it is aligned with it. Both represent forms of credibility, but distinction is credibility from *difference* (even if it is just difference in degree), whereas identification is credibility from *likeness*. Frequently, some combination of the two is most useful.[17] To continue the military metaphor, a four-star general cites the possession of superior knowledge and broader experience in

---

[17]The desirability of a mixture of both qualities is exemplified by the notion of "source credibility" as explained by Jack Whitehead in "Factors of Source Credibility," *Quarterly Journal of Speech* 54 (1968), 59–63.

order to justify leading a campaign, but he or she usually makes an effort to also establish how he or she is still a common soldier "at heart" in order to command loyalty. Presidential candidates, too, often spend a great deal of time touting their expertise while simultaneously spending most of their days eating hot dogs, going bowling, or kissing babies. They want to appear as ordinary citizens and extraordinary leaders simultaneously.

Gorgias: "What is there greater than the word?"

Perhaps the original masters of speeches of solicitation were the Greek Sophists themselves. As the practitioners of a new art of rhetoric, they had discovered a new commodity that was in much demand in the new democracies of the fifth century B.C.E. It was therefore natural that they also would use their own persuasive skills to market themselves much in the way that contemporary universities compete for students. However, their aggressive salesmanship and at times arrogant tone did not sit well with aristocrats like Plato, who thought that paying fees to acquire wisdom and virtue corrupted the very nature of wisdom and virtue. However, before criticizing the Sophists in his dialogue, Plato has the fictionalized portrayal of Socrates question Gorgias about what he teaches and why he considers himself an expert in his field. Gorgias's answer employs the strategy of distinction to set himself (and his art) above others:

SOCRATES   What is that which . . . is the greatest good of man, and of which you are the creator? Answer us.

GORGIAS   That good, Socrates, which is truly the greatest, being that which gives to men freedom in their own persons, and to individuals the power of ruling over others in their several states.

SOCRATES   And what would you consider this to be?

GORGIAS   What is there greater than the word which persuades the judges in the courts, or the senators in the council, or the citizens in the assembly, or at any other political meeting? If you have the power of uttering this word, you will have the physician your slave, and the trainer your slave, and the money-maker of whom you talk will be found to gather treasures, not for himself, but for you who are able to speak and to persuade the multitude....

SOCRATES   I had that in my admiring mind, Gorgias, when I asked what is the nature of rhetoric, which always appears to me, when I look at the matter in this way, to be a marvel of greatness.

GORGIAS   A marvel, indeed, Socrates, if you only knew how rhetoric comprehends and holds under her sway all the inferior arts. Let me offer you a striking example of this. On several occasions I have been with my brother Herodicus or some other physician to see one of his patients, who would not allow the physician to give him medicine, or apply a knife or hot iron to him; and I have persuaded him to do for me what he would not do for the physician just by the use of rhetoric. And I say that if a rhetorician and a physician were to go to any city, and had there to argue in the Ecclesia or any other assembly as to which of them should be elected state-physician, the physician would have no chance; but he who could speak would be chosen if he wished; and in a contest with a man of any other profession the rhetorician more than any one would have the power of getting himself chosen, for he can speak more persuasively to the multitude than any of them, and on any subject. Such is the nature and power of the art of rhetoric.[18]

In the voice of Gorgias we hear the voice of distinction insofar as he offers proof—through both knowledge and experience—of his possession of a skill that gives its possessor power and money and freedom. Like any good salesman in a speech of solicitation, Gorgias does not deny that he is selling something for his own personal gain; he simply wishes to make very clear, through exaggerated examples that mark his distinction, that what he is selling will bring even more benefit to the one spending money.

Discussion: One way to think about the strategy of distinction is the effort to be the "best of the best" (rather than the good amidst the bad). Distinction is to have a special quality of excellence that is admired by those with comparable virtues. In what context are speeches of distinction the most common? What kind of audience is most receptive to the speeches in a way that does not produce resentment?

POLARIZATION

Understanding of the complex ethics behind strategies of ethos would not be complete without a consideration of polarization (or "division"). Just as any action has a reaction, any attempt to establish unity inevitably also creates a division between "in" groups and "out" groups that results in inevitable polarization. For something to be "polarized" is to have two objects that repel each other from a distance. For instance, the North Pole and the South Pole represent two sides of the earth, but they are not antagonistic toward one another. They are simply far apart. Two magnets of the same polarity, however, will literally repulse each other when brought together. Similarly, two friends separated by thousands of miles are not polarized, but simply distant; two enemies in the same room, however, will create a palpable tension. Polarization thus represents a division based on antagonism. For example, we are often forced to choose between aligning ourselves with one group or another with little room for compromise. Either we are "with them or against them." And those who seek compromise in this situation are thus usually attacked from both sides for being wishy-washy. In a polarized environment, the decision not to choose is also a choice that puts us at risk of being abandoned, rejected, or ignored.

By its nature as an art that thrives in conflict and uncertainty, rhetorical discourse often magnifies these choices and uses the contrast to force a decision. In rhetoric, **polarization** is the strategy of dividing an audience into a positive "us" and a negative "them" in order to create unity through difference. The "them" in this case is usually a **criticized audience** that represents a group antagonistic to the rhetor's interests, such as another political party, or simply a demonized audience

---

[18]<http://classics.mit.edu/Plato/gorgias.html>.

that is used as a convenient foil, such as a group of "traitors" or "evil-doers." The strategy is then to argue that if one does not follow the path preferred by the rhetor (a path that ends in belonging to an evoked audience), then this person will align him- or herself with a group of people who lack ethical or practical judgment. Most children become acquainted with this strategy early on in their lives when they are encouraged to behave during the year so that Santa Claus includes them on his "nice" list rather than his "naughty" list. This same model can be applied effectively in the analysis of contemporary partisan politics.[19] In summary, if the first persona presents the "I" who is speaking and the second persona defines the "you" who is being spoken to, polarization defines a "third" persona representing the undesirable "they" who are not present but who are used to define who the "I" and "you" are not.[20]

Including "polarization" within a public speaking discussion may appear to border on the unethical. After all, are we not usually advised to invite as many people as possible to hear our speech? Is it not completely inappropriate in a tolerant age to pick out a group of people (or a type of person) to criticize or condemn? The work of Kenneth Burke is instructive here. Throughout his writings, Burke lamented the tendency for **scapegoating** in public rhetoric, in which all of a public's "sins" are placed upon a largely defenseless group that is then run out of town. At the same time, however, Burke also recognized that division is a natural state of human nature, and that rhetoric arises whenever individuals and groups are in conflict with one another. Moreover, rhetorical action cannot avoid the effects of polarization. For instance, even the statement "we should all love one another" can be used to divide those who love from those who hate. Burke's point is that we must be aware of the implicit acts of polarization that occur in all our identifications, make them explicit, and do our best to make our criticisms of others intelligent, precise, just, and sympathetic.

One common strategy to make polarization less ethically problematic is to base it more on hypothetical values or attitudes than on actual characteristics of specific social groups. Certainly, parents who ask their children whether they want to be a "doctor" or a "couch potato" are using polarization primarily to inspire them to do their best. In this case, the negative audience is not real but hypothetical—it represents a "type" of behavior we find distasteful. This still involves ethical responsibility, but it often can be used for purposes of genuine encouragement. The responsibility of speakers is thus to identify all possible divisions and to avoid unnecessary or unintentional castigation of other groups, even in the name of the most noble and respectable goal or virtue. As history has shown, many of the greatest

---

[19]Some examples discussing the rhetoric of polarization include Andrew King and Floyd Douglas Anderson, "Nixon, Agnew, and the 'Silent Majority': A Case Study in the Rhetoric of Polarization," *Western Speech* 35, no. 4 (1971), 243–255; William D. Harpine, "Bryan's 'A Cross of Gold': The Rhetoric of Polarization at the 1896 Democratic Convention," *Quarterly Journal of Speech* 87, no. 3 (2001), 291–304; and David E. Foster, "Bush's Use of the Terrorism and 'Moral Values' Issues in His 2004 Presidential Campaign Rhetoric: An Instance of the Rhetorical Strategy of Polarization," *Ohio Communication Journal* 44 (2006), 33–60.

[20]See Philip Wander, "The Third Persona: An Ideological Turn in Rhetorical Theory," *Central States Speech Journal* 35 (1984), 197–216.

atrocities were committed by those who truly believed they were fighting in the name of truth and freedom and goodness. As important as it is to be motivated by noble values and inspiring identifications, it is also important to analyze who is being excluded or condemned.

Clarence Darrow: "The cruel and the thoughtless will approve"

Polarization becomes a particularly potent strategy when an audience is faced with an absolute decision to say "yes" or "no" to something without the possibility of middle ground. When we are faced with an either/or decision, our alternatives are immediately polarized into two competing paths from which we must choose. Not surprisingly, then, courtroom arguments are often the most polarized of all arguments. The prosecution warns us that a judgment of innocence will render us dupes; the defense ominously predicts that a judgment of guilt will convict the jury of cruelty and thoughtlessness. A prime example of the strategy was given by Clarence Darrow on May 29, 1924, in defense of two wealthy and highly educated university students from Chicago named Nathan Leopold, Jr., and Richard Loeb. These two young men had kidnapped 14-year-old Bobby Franks by luring him into a car and had then subsequently killed him, taking care to cover their tracks by burning the body and pretending the boy had been taken for ransom. In reality, the two students had murdered Franks to test a theory that they were "Nietzschean supermen" who could commit a perfect crime without being caught. Predictably, when the method and motives of their crimes were revealed after their capture, there was widespread public demand for their execution.

In the midst of this turmoil, lawyer Clarence Darrow took the case for their defense. His intention was not to prove their innocence but rather to put capital punishment itself on trial. After convincing his clients to plead guilty, he embarked on a defense that the two young men weren't completely responsible for their actions, but were the products of the environment in which they grew up, an environment that condoned intolerance and cruelty. At the conclusion of his summation, Darrow polarized two competing value systems in an effort to make his audience choose the path of "love" over that of "hatred." The first path he described as the path of execution:

> The easy thing and the popular thing to do is to hang my clients. I know it. Men and women who do not think will applaud. The cruel and the thoughtless will approve. It will be easy today; but in Chicago, and reaching out over the length and breadth of the land, more and more fathers and mothers, the humane, the kind, and the hopeful, who are gaining an understanding and asking questions not only about these poor boys but about their own, these will join in no acclaim at the death of my clients. These would ask that the shedding of blood be stopped, and that the normal feelings of man resume their sway . . .
>
> I know the easy way. I know Your Honor stands between the future and the past. I know the future is with me, and what I stand for here; not merely for the lives of these two unfortunate lads, but for all boys and all girls; for all of the young, and as far as possible, for all of the old. I am pleading for life, understanding, charity, kindness, and the infinite mercy that considers all.

I am pleading that we overcome cruelty with kindness and hatred with love I . . . am pleading for the future; I am pleading for a time when hatred and cruelty will not control the hearts of men. When we can learn by reason and judgment and understanding and faith that all life is worth saving, and that mercy is the highest attribute of man.[21]

According to Darrow, pursuing the easy path of cruelty has long-term negative consequences for "the humane, the kind, and the hopeful" who are struggling to raise their children in a peaceful country. For this virtuous group of people, crime needs to be punished without falling victim to the very forces of cruelty that motivated the criminals. Hence, he effectively polarizes two groups of people—those who would hate and those who would love—and implies that a judge or jury who would condemn murderers to death belong to the same group as the murderers themselves. This is certainly not a fair fight by the end. On the one side stands the "easy way" of cruelty and hatred; on the other side stands the "future" of life: understanding, charity, kindness, infinite mercy, love, reason, judgment, and faith. Who would chose to be a party to the first group? Certainly not the judge, who decided to sentence the two boys to life in prison—where they were subsequently murdered by other inmates who chose the other path.[22]

Discussion: When do you think polarization is ethically warranted? We often do not think that it is ever right to speak in terms of "us" versus "them," and yet nothing is more common in political and moral discourse. How can you tell between an ethical and unethical use of polarization?

---

[21]Clarence Darrow, available at "PBS: American Experience," <http://www.pbs.org/wgbh/amex/monkeytrial/filmmore/ps_darrow.html> (accessed 3 September 2012).

[22]For more on Darrow's courtroom rhetoric, see Martin Maloney, "The Forensic Speaking of Clarence Darrow," *Speech Monographs* 14, no. 1 (1947), 111–126. For more on the trial of Leopold and Loeb, see Charles E. Morris III, "Passing by Proxy: Collusive and Convulsive Silence in the Trial of Leopold and Loeb," *Quarterly Journal of Speech* 91, no. 3 (2005), 264–290.

KEY WORDS

Agent

Apologist

Criticized audience

Distinction

Ethos

Evoked audience

Form of delivery

Goodwill

Hero

Identification

Inherited ethos

Partisan

Persona

Personal stories

Polarization

Practical wisdom

Scapegoating

Special knowledge

Unique experience

Virtue

SUMMARY

Ethos is something given to a speaker by an audience based on how a speaker displays himself or herself within a particular rhetorical situation. We should therefore not confuse ethos, as a rhetorical concept, with personal concepts such as affection or trust or reputation. Each of these things is certainly relevant to considerations of ethos, but they are not determining conditions. Indeed, sometimes we grant ethos to people we hate, distrust, and think of low repute. These situations occur, for example, when these individuals testify against their own best interests about something that they have specialized knowledge about, as when an executive convicted of insider trading testifies at a congressional committee about the need to regulate insider trading. As Anthony Pratkanis and Elliot Aronson observe, "a communicator can be an immoral person and still be effective, as long as it seems clear that the communicator is not acting in her or his self-interest by attempting to persuade us."[23] Although this particular strategy is only relevant to a small class of people in extraordinary circumstances, it nonetheless shows that we should consider *ethos* not as a quality of a person's character but as a criterion for judgment in a specific speech situation.

In most of our everyday interactions, the Aristotelian categories of goodwill, practical wisdom, and virtue are usually sufficient for acquiring ethos. Goodwill represents an emotional attitude of the speaker toward the audience such that he or she appears to wish the very best for the person or people to whom the rhetor is speaking. We tend to think people have goodwill toward us when they make

sacrifices on our behalf, sometimes in the moment but usually over a longer course of a relationship. Practical wisdom represents an intellectual capacity to make decisions in complicated situations that make those situations turn out for the better far more often than they turn out for the worse. Those with practical wisdom are people with much experience and knowledge to whom we look for specific advice. Whereas our close friends might give us the emotional support of goodwill, oftentimes we look to professionals or even strangers for counsel about complicated judgments. Finally, virtue represents a condition of character that embodies multiple values, such as courage, temperance, generosity, humility, and the like. We look to people with character because they seem to be "well rounded" and thoughtful, thus assuring that their counsel will not be based on narrow criteria but broader considerations. It is no accident that we often associate virtue with age, as it takes a great deal of time and diverse life experience to accumulate multiple virtues in a coherent and stable character.

Developing a message that also supports one's ethos requires further conceptual strategies, however. Persona provides a way of developing a specific presentation style that can balance the needs of a specific situation with the imperative to maintain consistency in character. *Persona* should not be considered a way of simply "acting," and thereby putting on a mask, for narrow purposes of persuasion; rather, it should be considered a method of amplifying or diminishing certain characteristics in one's own personality in order to best respond to

---

[23]Anthony Pratkanis and Elliot Aronson, *Age of Propaganda: The Everyday Use and Abuse of Persuasion* (New York: Henry Holt, 2001), 134.

a situation and an audience. Similarly, the evoked audience is not a purely fictional creation that is offered to an audience as in a fantasy role-play exercise. An *evoked audience*, like persona, is rather a selective amplification of certain qualities that are already shared by members of an audience and then given a concrete name and identity that serves as an appropriate response to a rhetorical situation. Turning a group of teenagers interested in basketball into the "Fighting Tigers" does not invent their interest in being a part of an athletic team out of the blue; it simply solidifies this interest and gives it a concrete manifestation. Identification is thus a natural bridge between persona and the evoked audience, as it represents a way of creating a common "we" out of an "I" and "you," even while retaining certain differences. A general may still be a general and a platoon a platoon, but they are all soldiers fighting for their nation and for "freedom."

The categories of distinction and polarization, being categories of difference, are usually only effective once such a common identification has been made. Distinction takes for granted the assumption of identification but seeks to add extra qualities to make the speaker stand out from the group. For instance, once the "Fighting Tigers" have been identified and their emotional bond solidified through various practices and rituals, it comes time to select a team captain. This is the time for speeches of distinction, in which each member of the team justifies why he or she stands apart from others (while still retaining the members' common unity). Distinction is thus a delicate balancing act of sameness and difference.

Last, polarization occurs when a speaker attempts to further solidify the identification of a group by comparing its members with an outsider group that represents the opposite in values and goals. Polarization presents an unsavory "other" (real or fictional) that usually serves to increase competitive motives. Of all the strategies, therefore, polarization has the most potential for ethical abuse, as speakers all too easily descend into vicious caricature of competing groups. As with all strategies of ethos, one must be careful of exaggerating one's own virtue while condemning the vice of others for narrowly selfish ends. Some degree of polarization is virtually inevitable in any speech, but one must at all times be careful to reduce its possible negative impacts to a minimum. We can have goodwill, after all, even toward those who disagree with us or are unlike us.

EXERCISES

1. Select a speech on americanrhetoric.com that you will explore. This will be called your "rhetorical artifact." No two students should have the same speech. Analyze your rhetorical artifact. Which was the primary strategy used to constitute ethos with the audience? Choose one and explain, using quotations from the speech for support.

2. Break into groups of two and briefly interview your partner about the accomplishments in his or her life, drawing on specific examples. Then give impromptu speeches of introduction for each other, creating for the partner an exaggerated persona (by using the strategy of distinction) that presents him or her in a heroic light. Did the speech about yourself sound anything like you?

3. Divide yourselves into groups either by year (freshman, sophomore, etc.) or by major. Have each group come up with a speech that argues why its year or major has distinction and then use polarization to show why it is better than the others. Were any elements of these speeches persuasive to the other groups?

4. Randomly break into groups of four. For a few minutes, try to find what you have in common. Then create a name for a "club" to which you all belong and give a list of characteristics (which you all possess) that are necessary to be part of that club. (The name of the club should also reflect something about these shared qualities.) Present your club and its characteristics to the class. How many other people belong to that club? Which club is the most exclusive and which is the most inclusive?

5. Come up with some absurd ethical argument (e.g., clothing should be optional when coming to class). Now create an impromptu speech that relies on creating an evoked audience that would naturally favor this argument (e.g., we are all "free spirits" who reject any kind of constraint on our freedom). Which speech was the most persuasive? Why?

Reasoning

From Chapter 8 of *Public Speaking: Strategies for Success,* Seventh Edition. David Zarefsky.
Copyright © 2014 by Pearson Education, Inc. All rights reserved.

Reasoning

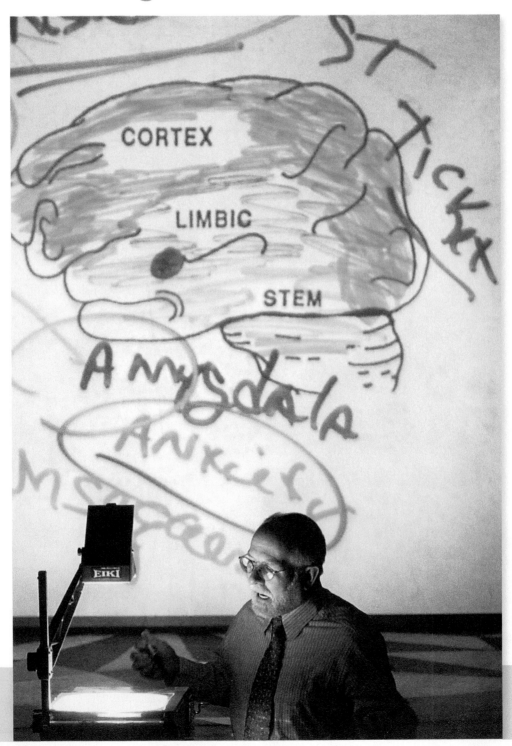

LEARNING OBJECTIVES

After studying this chapter, you should be able to:

Objective 1	Explain the nature of rhetorical proof in public speaking and identify its three components.
Objective 2	Describe six basic patterns of reasoning, focusing on their types, appropriate tests of their soundness, and how to use them in a speech.
Objective 3	Define what a fallacy is and identify both general fallacies and fallacies that correspond to particular patterns of reasoning.
Objective 4	Explain how an understanding of reasoning processes helps in preparing and delivering a speech and in being an active, critical listener.

OUTLINE

Proof, Support, and Reasoning
Rhetorical Proof as Support | Proof and the Audience | Components of Proof
An Example of Rhetorical Proof | Using Rhetorical Proof in Your Speech

Example
Types of Inference from Example | Tests for Inference from Example
Guidelines for Reasoning Through Example

Analogy
Types of Inference from Analogy | Tests for Inference from Analogy
Guidelines for Reasoning Through Analogy

Signs
Types of Inference from Signs | Tests for Inference from Signs
Guidelines for Reasoning Through Signs

Cause
Types of Inference from Cause | Tests for Inference from Cause
Guidelines for Reasoning Through Cause

Testimony
Types of Inference from Testimony | Tests for Inference from Testimony
Guidelines for Reasoning Through Testimony

Narrative
Tests for Inference from Narrative

Avoiding Errors in Reasoning
Six General Tests of Inference

Reasoning in Public Speaking

B y now, you have analyzed your situation, picked a good topic, and assembled some useful supporting materials. But how do you know whether these materials actually prove the point you want to make? In this chapter, you will learn about proof in public speaking and how to strengthen the reasoning in your speech.

Suppose that you are planning a speech on the ways that technological and economic forces are changing the newspaper industry. You have found examples of newspapers that have stopped publication altogether, statistics showing a drop in advertising revenue for large-city papers, and testimony from an expert who says that it may be that more people get news from the Internet than from the paper. You want to use this evidence to support the following claim:

> The daily newspaper as we have known it for generations is now a thing of the past.

Notice that this claim goes beyond what the evidence actually says. What enables you to make the claim on the basis of the evidence is *reasoning*—thinking through a connection between the evidence and the claim. This chapter examines various types of connections you can make and the factors that determine whether they are strong or weak.

OBJECTIVE 1

Proof, Support, and Reasoning

Consider the following claims:

- $2 + 2 = 4$
- The sum of the angles of a triangle equals 180 degrees.
- Light travels at about 186,000 miles per second.
- The *Mona Lisa* is Leonardo da Vinci's most beautiful painting.
- The semester academic calendar is best for our university.
- The government's economic policy is bad for the country.

The first three statements are mathematical or scientific claims; they are based on a system of rules by which they can be proved with absolute certainty—as long as you operate within that system. The last three claims are different; they involve beliefs, values, and judgments. Although for any of these three you could find evidence that convinces *you* of their truth, someone else might be unimpressed by your evidence or might find counterevidence to argue an opposing point. Therefore, the "proof" of these claims is not offered with the same level of certainty that supports the first three claims.

The ideas in a speech almost never take the form of a fixed mathematical principle as in the first three claims above. Instead, the basic material of public speaking is like the last three claims, involving matters of belief or value, judgments about what ought to be, norms of conduct, or predictions about the future. Such statements require agreement between the speaker and listeners, not only about the truth of the claim, but also about what should count as proof in the first place.[1]

rhetorical proof
Proof established through interaction between the speaker and the listeners; provides support for a conclusion but not assurance that it is true.

Rhetorical Proof as Support

Rhetorical proof is established through interaction in which the speaker and listeners reason together. This type of proof does not *ensure* that a conclusion is correct, but it offers *support* for a conclusion. It gives listeners confidence that the conclusion is probably correct and that they can share it, make it part of their working knowledge, and act on it if they are able to do so. Rhetorical proof *justifies* claims. Although it does not establish that they are unquestionably true, it gives a critical listener good reason to accept them.

Suppose you are speaking to first-time employees about how they should save and invest their money. Research and analysis have convinced you that buying stocks is the best long-term investment, but you can't be absolutely certain of that conclusion because it involves value judgments, predictions, and speculations. Moreover, the substantial drop in stock values during the recession of 2008 and 2009—in some cases as much as half the value of a stock was lost—certainly would give pause to anyone investing in stocks. Therefore, to help listeners reach the conclusion that an investor thinking of long-term strategies should purchase stocks, your speech might draw on statistics, historical accounts of the growth of the stock market, examples of successful investors, and testimony from economists showing that by early 2012 the stock market had recovered from the losses it suffered during the 2008–2009 recession. These are called "supporting materials," precisely because their function is to *support* your conclusion. They do not guarantee that your conclusion is correct, but they give listeners good reasons to accept what you say and to act on it.

Unlike mathematical proofs, then, rhetorical proofs have degrees of support ranging from strong to weak. As a result, both speakers and listeners must evaluate rhetorical proofs critically, testing them rather than taking them for granted. Your goal as a speaker is to provide the strongest support possible for your conclusion. What factors make rhetorical proof strong?

Watch the Video "Persuasive Speech: Mass Transit" at **MyCommunicationLab**

Proof and the Audience

The overriding factor in supporting a claim is, of course, the audience. Listeners who pay attention to the reasoning in a speech are critical and active; they are willing to be convinced but are skeptical enough to ask whether the speaker's reasoning withstands scrutiny. Critical listeners will ask whether your causal links are valid, whether your comparisons are apt, and whether the people you quote are authorities in the subject—all tests that you will study in this chapter. Knowing that you will face a critical audience helps you as a speaker, because you will work hard to make your reasoning strong. In this way, you and your listeners work together to achieve the highest possible standard of rhetorical proof.

Audiences differ, of course, and so you might need different proofs to convince, say, an audience of Democrats that the current president's economic policy is flawed than you would need for an audience of Republicans. But if you focus too narrowly on the immediate audience, you could run into a serious ethical: Yes, you may be *able* to convince the specific audience, but *should* you? Not all audiences are made up of critical listeners (as advertisers know only too well). Indeed, some listeners probably would accept just about any conclusion.

When many Americans accepted the U.S. government's call for the internment of Japanese and Japanese-Americans during World War II, did that prove the government's argument true? The answer to this difficult question turns out to be "yes and no." In a purely functional sense, yes: For those people in that situation, calls for Japanese internment could be considered proved; believers incorporated the government's claims into their working knowledge and acted on them. But in a

Diagramming the structure of proof can help you identify the warrants justifying your inference from evidence to claim.

larger sense, no: Regardless of what the supporters of the government's policies did or did not believe, they *should not have* accepted his claims, because the government's reasoning and evidence were flawed.

Speakers need to focus not only on proofs that listeners *actually do* regard as solid but also on proofs that they *ought* to regard as solid. Generally, a proof is **reasonable** if it would be taken seriously by a broad and diverse group of listeners exercising their best critical judgment.[2] Such an audience includes people who actually hear your speech as well as a larger, more culturally diverse audience who might "overhear" it through word of mouth or the media. When you offer rhetorical proofs, you are making strategic choices about the reasoning patterns that your immediate audience and this larger audience would accept. Think of a well-selected jury of peers in a well-run courtroom as your audience; if such a group of critical listeners would accept your proof, the inference is reasonable.

Even if your actual audience does not resemble such a group, do not abandon your standards. In offering a rhetorical proof, you must satisfy the immediate audience and also must meet a broader standard of reasonableness that would satisfy a larger imagined audience of critical thinkers.

Components of Proof

Any idea in the speech—whether a main point or a subordinate point—can be regarded as a *unit of proof* that has three principal components: the claim, the supporting material, and the reasoning.

Claim. The **claim** is the statement that you want the audience to accept; it is what you are trying to prove. The claim could be your broad thesis:

> The shift to digital music formats has changed the nature of the recording industry.

Or the claim could be a specific subpoint:

> Because record labels can now distribute their music over the Internet without producing compact discs, they can affordably and efficiently offer consumers a wider variety of artists and genres.

Supporting Material. This second component of a proof provides *evidence* for your claim. To prove your claim, you must show that evidence supports it.

Reasoning. It is reasoning that links the supporting material to your claim so that you and your listeners together can decide whether the evidence really does support the claim.

Usually, the claim and the supporting material are stated explicitly in the speech and are easy to identify. But the essential link, reasoning, is usually implied; it involves a mental leap from the supporting material to the claim. This leap is called an **inference**. The inference enables us to say that, even though we are going beyond

reasonable
Would be inferred by most people when exercising their critical judgment.

claim
A statement that a speaker asks listeners to accept and that the speaker tries to prove.

inference
A mental leap from the supporting material to the claim.

what the supporting material literally says, we feel justified in doing so because similar inferences in the past have usually led to acceptable results.[3] Exploring different kinds of inference and how they work is the primary purpose of this chapter.

An Example of Rhetorical Proof

After introducing a speech about the effect of tax increases on a family's budget, student Catherine Archer claimed

> Taxes have taken a bigger bite out of the average paycheck each year. Just look at the record. Our state sales taxes have gone up faster than our income. Local property taxes have gone through the roof. And now the federal government is proposing to raise gasoline taxes again. Where does it all stop?

After the speech, she invited questions from the floor. "What about Social Security?" one woman asked. Catherine replied

> Thank you. That's still one more example of a tax that has gone up faster than income. In fact, many people today pay more in Social Security tax than in their income tax.

Then a man in the audience said, "Since you mentioned income taxes, I want to remind you about the significant cuts in income tax rates that were passed by Congress and signed by President Bush in 2001 and 2003. Congress also has cut taxes on capital gains and on dividends. Many of these tax cuts were extended in 2004 and 2006, and President Obama's budget left many of these tax cuts in place, so it's not true that the government always raises taxes."

This man seemed to imply that Catherine had not considered all the possible taxes and had jumped to a conclusion. She didn't disagree with the man but restated her claim: "You're right about some of these specific cuts, but other taxes have gone up so much that my main point is still true. Besides, not all of these proposed tax cuts actually were enacted."

This example illustrates five important aspects of rhetorical proof:

1. Reasoning plays the crucial role in linking supporting material to the claim. Catherine's reasoning connected specific examples to her claim that taxes take a larger share of the paycheck each year.

2. Reasoning depends on an inference but cannot guarantee that the inference is "right." Nonetheless, we still can apply tests of soundness. In this case, for instance, do the examples really represent the overall tax picture, or has Catherine left out some important categories?

3. An inference often takes the form of an implicit statement that a general rule is being followed. Catherine's reasoning implied, "These examples of tax increases are significant and representative."

4. The speaker and listeners together decide whether the inference is sound. This audience participated by asking questions that helped to identify possible problems with Catherine's inference, and she had a chance to address their concerns. Together, speaker and audience probably became more confident about the inference. Even if audience members do not explicitly voice concerns, the speaker needs to think about what a critical audience might be asking and then build answers to those potential questions into the speech.

5. Nothing can guarantee that the inference of a rhetorical proof is correct, but tests have evolved over time to distinguish between good and bad inferences. Asking whether Catherine's examples represent all categories of taxes is one such test.

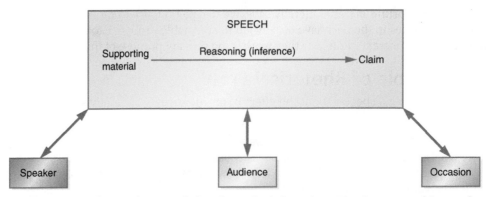

Figure 1 An enhanced view of the rhetorical situation: The inner workings of a speech.

Using Rhetorical Proof in Your Speech

Figure 1 shows the relationships among claims, supporting material, and reasoning. It shows the "inner workings" of the speech.[4] The other elements of the rhetorical situation are also shown, to remind you that the speech interacts with the speaker, the audience, and the occasion. Choices of reasoning patterns are influenced by each of these other elements.

The best time to construct effective reasoning relationships is after you research the speech. Your outline will help you to see what is used as supporting material for each claim. As Figure 2 shows, each Roman numeral in the outline identifies a main idea that supports your thesis statement, and each capital letter represents supporting material for that main idea. At a smaller level, each capital letter marks a claim that is supported by all the Arabic numerals under it, which, in turn, are supported by the lowercase letters, and so on.

Beginning with the smallest claims in your outline, identify the supporting material; then determine what kind of link (inference) will best connect the supporting material to each claim. This chapter presents practical methods to help you discover appropriate links and to test whether they will make the connection that you want to make with your audience.

To help you develop convincing rhetorical proofs, we will discuss six broad categories of reasoning: example, analogy, sign, cause, testimony, and narrative. For each category, the discussion first will focus on the variety of types, then on some tests to discover errors in reasoning, and finally on suggestions for using each reasoning pattern in a speech.

II. Lack of variety is not a valid complaint against Campus Food Service.
    A. You get more choices than you would at home.
        1. Each day, there are three main entrees and a vegetarian meal.
        2. There also are other options.
            a. A salad bar
            b. Cereals
            c. Breads
            d. Soups
    B. A special dinner is offered once each month.

Figure 2 An outline reveals links in reasoning.

It may seem confusing that some of the reasoning patterns have the same names as types of supporting material (reasoning through example, for instance). However, the reasoning pattern is not the same thing as the supporting material. Rather, it explains why the supporting material should count as support for the claim. Suppose you were to say, "Politicians are corrupt; just look at Smith, Baker, and Jones." The presumably corrupt politicians Smith, Baker, and Jones would be your examples (supporting material), and the inference that the three of them are representative or typical of politicians would be your reasoning (reasoning through example).

These categories were chosen because, at least in Western culture, they have been found over time generally to yield reliable results. Not all cultures will share all these norms of reasoning or give them the same emphasis. For example, some Eastern cultures are easily able to embrace contradictory positions. Western culture, however, usually adheres to the "law of noncontradiction": that something cannot have one feature (call it x) and its opposite (not-x) at the same time. Likewise, some cultures prize storytelling and therefore would give more weight to narrative inferences, whereas others are more concerned with prediction and control and hence give more weight to inferences from cause. When speaking to a culturally diverse audience, you will want to use multiple reasoning patterns in order to take these differences into account. Still, most of these reasoning patterns will be applicable across cultures, even if the emphasis differs.[5]

Example

OBJECTIVE
2

Probably the most common reasoning pattern in public speaking is inference from example. **Examples** are specific instances that are used to illustrate a more general claim; the inference is that the specific is typical of the general. For *example*:

- A tourist notices that three downtown streets are deserted at midday and infers that businesses in that town are generally not doing well.

- On four occasions, a student succeeds in visiting faculty members during their office hours and infers that most instructors are conscientious and accessible.

- A researcher discovers that 15 percent of the people in one community lack health insurance and infers that about 15 percent of the country's population has no health insurance.

- Believing that most politicians cannot be trusted, a citizen infers that neither of the candidates for mayor can be trusted.

In each example, someone has brought together a statement about a particular situation and a statement making a general claim and has attempted to relate the two. Whether proceeding from specific to general (the first three examples) or from general to specific (the last example), the inference is that particular cases are **representative** of the general category. To say that they are representative is to say that they are typical cases and that there is nothing unusual about them.[6]

A moment's thought shows why representativeness is important. Suppose that, although three downtown streets were deserted, traffic jams occurred near all of the city's shopping malls; then, the tourist would not be justified in drawing a general conclusion from the specific case observed. Or imagine that the student's four successful visits were all on days when faculty members were careful to hold office

examples
Specific instances used to illustrate a more general claim.

representative
Typical of the larger category from which a case is selected.

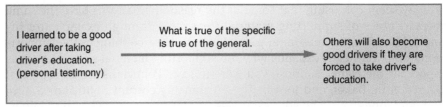

Figure 3 Inference from example.

hours because they were advising majors for next semester's registration; then, it would not be valid to infer that instructors are accessible at other times.

In short, if the particular cases are *not* typical (not representative), we cannot confidently infer that what is true of them is true in general. Again, inferences cannot be guaranteed as can mathematical proofs. But even if we can't be absolutely certain that examples are representative, we can still try to select them in a way that removes all known causes of distortion or bias.

The strategic advantage of inference from example is that it makes a general or abstract statement more concrete and tangible. The politician who says, "My economic program will benefit middle-class families," may help her audience to accept her claim by talking about specific families—preferably people with whom listeners can identify—who will gain from the program. Of course, the power of the appeal depends on whether the specific cases will be accepted as representative.

Figure 3 maps an inference from example, applying the general pattern shown in Figure 1. A student speaker says:

> I learned to be a good driver after taking driver's education. Others will also become good drivers if they are forced to take driver's education.

Notice something else about Figure 3. This student is offering herself as an example, but her supporting material is personal testimony. *Example,* as we have said, refers to *both* a reasoning pattern *and* a type of supporting material, but these are not exactly the same thing. *Any* type of supporting material could provide the specific cases you use when you reason from example.

Types of Inference from Example

Speakers use many different types of examples, depending on their purposes. The following three considerations are especially pertinent in selecting examples.

Individual Versus Aggregate Examples.
Sometimes a speaker describes individual occurrences of an example. For instance, a speaker is friends with John, Martha, and Claude, all of whom had to interrupt their education for financial reasons; by talking about each of them, the speaker supports the inference that the cost of a college education is a serious concern.

At other times, individual cases will be less convincing than an aggregate statistical example. Because 50 percent of students in a national survey report that they have seen someone cheat on an examination, a speaker infers that probably half the students on campus have witnessed such behavior.

Factual Versus Hypothetical Examples.
Factual examples are actual occurrences; whether individual or aggregate, they are "real." In contrast, a speaker may construct hypothetical examples, creating a vivid (but imaginary) illustration of something abstract. To describe the problems of homelessness, for example, a

Watch the Video "Business Presentation: Large Group" at **MyCommunicationLab**

CHOOSE A STRATEGY: Using Examples Strategically

The Situation

You are preparing a five-minute presentation to give to your city's planning commission, opposing a plan to build a big-box retail store close to a residential neighborhood. You are concerned about increased traffic and pollution, and you have also learned that the proposed building site includes a wetlands area that hosts 10 different rare and endangered bird species.

Making Choices

Which would be more effective to include?

1. An individual example of an endangered bird *or* an aggregate example of how many rare species live in the wetlands area?

2. A factual example of how much pollution increased in a different neighborhood after a similar store was built there *or* a hypothetical example of how much pollution could increase after the proposed store is built?

3. A brief list of neighborhoods that experienced increased traffic accidents and congestion after similar stores were built *or* an extended example of a fatal traffic accident in one neighborhood?

What If...

How would your choices be affected by the following?

1. A report by state engineers predicts that, due to water drainage issues, pollution increases at the proposed building site could be much greater than they have seen at past building sites.

2. Store officials have offered to install, at their own expense, a new traffic light and a bike trail to manage and reduce car traffic.

speaker might invent a hypothetical character whose daily experiences are typical of homeless people generally.

A speaker may have good reasons to offer a hypothetical example rather than a factual one, but the invention should be acknowledged and should never be treated as fact. One journalist received a Pulitzer Prize for a series of stories describing the plight of a child who was addicted to drugs; when it came to light that this child was hypothetical rather than a real person (as the stories had intimated), the prize was withdrawn.

Brief Versus Extended Examples. Sometimes a quick list of examples is effective because the speaker's emphasis is on the existence and number of cases rather than on their details. Thus, to establish that many students are worried about the cost of education, a brief mention of John, Martha, and Claude should support the claim.

But suppose the speaker wants listeners to understand what students go through when financial problems make them leave school. It would then be more effective to offer a more complete description of just one case. Better than to simply report that John had to leave school for financial reasons would be to describe the events that led to his decision—the conversations between him and his parents, how he broke the news to his friends, and what his life has been like since leaving.

Tests for Inference from Example

Inference from example will be accepted as reasonable if listeners have no good reason to doubt it. Ask yourself these questions when using inference from example to support your claim:

1. *Are there enough examples?* If the number of examples is very small, particularly in making a statistical generalization, the sample may not include

significant features of the population as a whole. If you claim that more students are graduating from high school than ever before because your high school graduated a record number of students, the audience may doubt your inference; your high school is only one of thousands.

2. *Do the examples represent the whole category?* If all the cases you cite are alike in some way that distorts your inference—say you use only fraternity members as examples to support some point about all college students—your claim will be weakened.

3. *Are the examples ambiguous?* Sometimes a single example can support different inferences, making it a poor example. If 70 percent of employees are dissatisfied with the company's new computer system, one speaker may claim that the new system is flawed; but another speaker may claim that employees need more training to understand the new system. Which claim is the audience to believe?

4. *Are the examples fallacious?* A **fallacy** is an inference that appears to be sound but that, on inspection, contains a significant flaw. In the case of inferences from example, which relate parts to wholes, the flaw is that the whole is not always the same as the sum of the parts. The **fallacy of composition** results from assuming that what is true of the part is automatically true of the whole. For instance:

Each individual student will gain a better chance of getting into a popular course by registering for it at the very start of the enrollment period, so if all students register for it right away, everyone will have a better chance of getting in.

You should be able to spot the fallacy: If everyone tries to register for the same class at the same time, no one will have gained an advantage; instead, there will be a bottleneck in the registration system. What is true of the part individually is not true of the whole collectively. Conversely, the **fallacy of division** results from assuming that what is true of the whole is automatically true of the part. For example:

The campus is excited about the homecoming game, and so each instructor must be excited, too.

fallacy
An inference that appears to be sound but that, on inspection, contains a significant flaw.

fallacy of composition
Assuming that what is true of the part is automatically true of the whole.

fallacy of division
Assuming that what is true of the whole is automatically true of the part.

CHECKLIST 1

Tests for Inference from Example

1. Are there enough examples?

2. Do all the examples represent the whole category?

3. Are the examples ambiguous?

4. Are the examples fallacious? Do any examples assume that:

   ❏ What is true of the part must be true of the whole (fallacy of composition)?

   ❏ What is true of the whole must be true of the part (fallacy of division)?

Guidelines for Reasoning Through Example

Here are suggestions for effective reasoning through example:

1. *Limit the number of examples.* You want enough examples to indicate a pattern that supports your inference, but you don't want to risk boring the audience with unnecessary examples. Consider your purpose and audience carefully; a single example may be enough.

2. *Make sure each example is believable.* Even one unbelievable example can undermine your inference—and your entire point.

3. *Avoid obvious, overused examples.* If you tell listeners what they already know, your inferences may seem trivial or trite. Seek novel examples that might surprise the audience. Arguing against censorship, for example, student Sarah McAdams skipped the standard example of book burning in Nazi Germany; instead, she surprised listeners by citing examples of U.S. censorship:

In 1925, anyone caught teaching Darwin's *Origin of Species* in a Tennessee public school was fined. In 1933, a young actor was arrested for smuggling an illegal item into the United States. That item was James Joyce's *Ulysses*—a book that is now considered a literary masterpiece. In 1980, some high school students were forced to read an edited version of Shakespeare's *Romeo and Juliet* because parents and teachers thought the original play was too racy.

And in the aftermath of September 11, there have been quite a few attempts to stop critics of the war on terror from speaking out.

4. *Match the details of examples to your purpose.* If your main point is the very existence of the example, few details are needed. But if you want to show the audience exactly how the example illustrates your inference, supply more detail about the example.

5. *Make the examples memorable.* After selecting enough believable, fresh examples, bring your inference to life for the audience by carefully selecting details and describing the examples vividly.

Analogy

An **analogy** is a comparison of people, places, things, events, or more abstract relationships. Whereas the key feature of inference from example is the link between the parts and the whole, the key feature of inference from analogy is a comparison between the known and the unknown.

An inference from analogy asks the audience to accept the idea that items that are basically alike in most respects will also be alike in the particular respect being discussed. For example, in a speech on gun deaths, a student speaker said:

The United States would have fewer gun deaths if it made guns illegal. Japan has few gun deaths and guns are illegal there.

Figure 4 offers a map of this analogy.

Analogical inferences are prominent in public speaking because they are psychologically appealing to an audience. They enable us to accept something that is unknown because it is similar to something that we do know.[7]

Types of Inference from Analogy

Depending on whether the comparison between things is direct or concerns their relationships, an analogy is either literal or figurative.[8]

analogy
A comparison of people, places, things, events, or more abstract relationships.

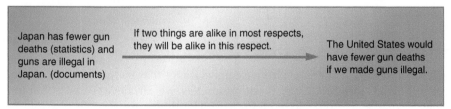

Figure 4 Inference from analogy.

Literal Analogies. A **literal analogy** is a *direct* comparison of objects, people, or events. Suppose a speaker says:

> Illinois will not be able to escape the massive job cuts that have already hit Michigan—another midwestern industrial state.

This speaker is directly comparing Illinois to Michigan. The inference is that, because Illinois is basically like Michigan, it, too, will probably face a major loss of jobs.

Speakers often use literal analogies to suggest that one action or event is a precedent for another—that actual experience with one enables us to predict what will happen with the other. Former Senator Charles Robb of Virginia took this approach in arguing that a law to prohibit the federal government from recognizing same-sex marriages was discriminatory:

> Until 1967, 16 states, including my own state of Virginia, had laws banning couples from different races to marry. When the law was challenged, Virginia argued that interracial marriages were simply immoral.... The Supreme Court struck down these archaic laws, holding that "the freedom of choice to marry" had "long been recognized as one of the vital personal rights essential to the orderly pursuit of happiness by free men."
>
> Today, we know that moral discomfort—even revulsion—that citizens then felt about legalizing interracial marriages did not give them the right to discriminate 30 years ago. Similarly, discomfort over sexual orientation does not give us the right to discriminate against a class of Americans today.

Figurative Analogies. A **figurative analogy** compares the *relationships* between objects, people, or events in order to make complex or abstract statements more vivid and more concrete. Again, the comparison begins with something the audience already knows.

Suppose you wanted to claim that the Social Security System will face financial problems around the year 2020 as many "baby boomers" reach retirement age. You could support your claim with only statistics, of course, but that could be tedious and would work far better in print than in a speech. Instead, you might say:

> Depending on Social Security for your retirement income is like betting all of your money on one horse in a race.

Then your comparison would make the statistics—and your point—clear: Social Security is a gamble. Similarly, the speaker predicting major losses of jobs in Illinois might add:

> Trusting the politicians to find a way to avoid it is like putting the fox in charge of the chicken coop.

This speaker is not directly comparing politicians to foxes or job losses to a chicken coop. Rather, the comparison is figurative; it points to *relationships*. The politicians stand in the same relationship to the job losses that the fox does to the chicken coop. In both cases, those who supposedly are protecting something are really a grave threat to it.

literal analogy
A direct comparison of objects, people, or events.

figurative analogy
A comparison of the relationships between objects, people, or events.

Tests for Inference from Analogy

As we saw concerning inferences from example, things may be *similar*, but they are never completely *identical*. Thus, as with examples, we can never be sure that an analogy is completely valid. No matter how similar things are, they are also different in some respects.

For an analogy to be strong and compelling, listeners have to believe that the basic similarities between two items outweigh their basic differences. An analogy raises two closely related questions:

1. *Are there basic differences as well as similarities?* Suppose a speaker claims that Detroit and Chicago have similar economic concerns because they are alike in so many ways: Both are northern metropolitan areas, both have large populations, both are surrounded by suburbs that erode the city's tax base, and so on. Besides these similarities, however, there is an obvious and important difference between the two cities: Detroit's economy historically has depended on one industry, automobiles, whereas the economy of Chicago is more diversified.

2. *Do the differences outweigh the similarities?* The discovery of differences between items being compared is not, in itself, reason to question the analogy. One has to demonstrate that the differences really do matter. For instance, if a diversified economy protects a city better against recession because workers who lose jobs in one industry can find new jobs in another, then this difference outweighs the similarities between Detroit and Chicago, and the analogy is questionable. But if a weak national economy hurts cities in general—whether or not they have a diversified economy—then this difference between Detroit and Chicago would not matter much, and the analogy would stand.

Guidelines for Reasoning Through Analogy

Here are suggestions for effective reasoning through analogy:

1. *Avoid analogies that are trite or farfetched.* An overused analogy will lose the audience's attention and make the entire speech seem stale, whereas an analogy with no basis in common sense may call so much attention to itself that it distracts from the point it is supposed to prove. A well-known televised public service announcement (PSA) compared the brain to an egg and heroin to a cast-iron frying pan that "smashes" the brain. The PSA also compared the heroin user's family, friends, job, and future to various kitchen utensils and appliances and implied that heroin also "smashes" the user's relationships and life. Though its shock effect gained it attention, the PSA was viewed by many as farfetched and trite. Its target audience of young people knew that their friends who use heroin did not immediately and irreversibly "smash" their brains and everyone and everything around them. The comparison was exaggerated and, consequently, the target audience dismissed it.

2. *Analyze what you are comparing.* Make sure that you understand the essential similarities and differences of the items in your analogy so that you can argue convincingly that their similarities outweigh their differences and will not be surprised if a listener suggests otherwise. The speaker who compared Detroit's and Chicago's economic outlooks must be ready to respond to a listener's observation that the cities differ in the important factor of economic diversification. If that difference wasn't important to the speaker's main point, the analogy could be defended.

A Question of Ethics

Ethical Issues in Reasoning

We employ reasoning to make our arguments and positions clear. One powerful mode of reasoning is analogy, because it compares something new to something that the audience already knows and understands. Analogy heightens similarities, but in doing so does it distort the items being compared? For instance, if a manager compares her company's precarious position in the marketplace to the United States' involvement in Vietnam during the 1960s and 1970s, is that a fair comparison? Does the manager trivialize the Vietnam conflict or, alternatively, make the company's position seem disproportionately dire? Do such comparisons properly respect the memory of the different events? Do they raise ethical issues?

3. *Use analogies sparingly.* Although analogies are a form of inference, they also are like ornaments (to use an analogy of our own). Too many ornaments may hide what they are intended to decorate, and too many analogies in a speech may obscure the main point. Governor Rick Perry of Texas, while seeking the 2012 Republican presidential nomination, used so many attention-grabbing figurative analogies that they probably overwhelmed his audience at times.[9]

4. *Use analogies sensitively.* The benefits of using analogy may be undone if the comparison strikes listeners as insensitive. This can happen if they focus on an embarrassing aspect of the comparison, one that the speaker did not intend. During the 2008 presidential campaign, for example, "change" was a key theme, so some messages presented Republican candidate Senator John McCain as the candidate of change. Democrats responded with a figurative analogy: "You can put lipstick on a pig, but it is still a pig." What they intended to suggest was that calling McCain a candidate for change did not make it so, just as another superficial change (lipstick) did not change the basic nature of a pig. But the analogy struck many as insensitive because Republican vice presidential candidate Governor Sarah Palin of Alaska, after referring to herself as a hockey mom, had joked that the only difference between a hockey mom and a pit bull was lipstick; thus, the "lipstick on a pig" analogy could be interpreted to suggest that Democrats were calling Palin a pig. Similarly, in early 2009 President Obama compared his skill at bowling to that of a contestant in the Special Olympics. His goal was to poke fun at his own low score, but the analogy easily could be misunderstood as belittling the Special Olympics, where some contestants in fact bowl very well.

Signs

sign
Something that stands for something else.

A **sign** is something that stands for something else—which is usually an abstraction or something that we cannot observe directly. The presence of the sign causes us to infer the existence of what it stands for.

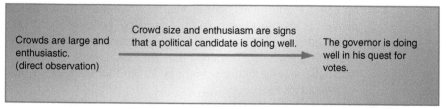

Figure 5 Inference from signs.

If the number of students absent from class increases suddenly, that may be a sign of a flu epidemic. If today's average grades are higher than 10 years ago, that may be a sign that grading standards have changed. If homeless people are living on the streets, that may be a sign that public policies are not meeting the needs of the disadvantaged. If wages differ for male and female workers doing similar jobs, that may be a sign of gender discrimination. In each case, we infer that something exists based on something else that presumably is a sign of it. The strategic benefit of inferences from sign is that they enable listeners to reach a conclusion about something that they can't know directly, by linking it in this way to something that they do know. As another example, a newspaper reporter covering a political campaign writes:

The governor is doing well in his quest for votes since his crowds are large and enthusiastic.

Figure 5 offers a map of this inference from signs.

Types of Inference from Signs

In theory, anything can stand for anything else. In practice, however, inferences from signs fall into several types:

- Physical observation
- Statistical indexes
- Institutional regularity

Physical Observation. If the alarm goes off and you don't check the time but you look out the window and see a bright sun, you probably infer that the sun means it's morning. Similarly, through **physical observation** of a bulldozer on an empty campus lot, a student inferred that the university was about to construct a new building. The sun and the bulldozer were observable signs of other things that could not be observed.

Statistical Index. Many statistical measures are taken as signs. High scores on exams, for instance, are widely accepted as a sign of intelligence. Similarly, the ups and downs of the Dow-Jones Industrial Average are seen to indicate the health of the economy, and a rising Consumer Price Index is regarded as a sign of inflation. Intelligence, economic health, inflation—these are all abstract concepts that cannot be observed directly. But in each case, a **statistical index** that we *can* see is regarded as a sign of something that we cannot observe.

Institutional Regularity. **Institutional regularity** is an observable pattern that results from some norm or social convention. For example, because athletic competitions usually begin with the singing of the national anthem, if you turned

physical observation (as a sign)
Regarding something that can be observed as a sign of something that cannot.

statistical index (as a sign)
A statistical measure that is taken as a sign of an abstraction.

institutional regularity (as a sign)
A sign relationship that results from norm or social convention.

on your TV and heard people singing it, you might infer that a game was about to begin. In the same way, because diplomatic disagreements often are described by such polite phrases as "They had a frank exchange of views," that phrase in a news story about international negotiations might be a sign that discussions had reached an impasse.

CHECKLIST 3

Tests for Inference from Signs

- ☐ Is an alternative explanation more credible?
- ☐ Can the alleged sign be found *without* the thing for which it stands?
- ☐ Is the sign part of a pattern, or a single unusual case?

Tests for Inference from Signs

If a sign *always* stood for the same thing, then whenever we observed the sign, we could infer that the abstract concept was present as well. Thus, *whenever* someone scored high on a test, we could infer that the person was intelligent; and *whenever* we heard the national anthem, we could expect a sports event to follow. So certain a sign would be said to be *infallible*, meaning that it predicts with certainty the existence of the thing it signifies.

Reality offers few (if any) infallible signs. To say that something is a sign, then, means that it *usually* signifies something else, although in a given circumstance it might not. The high rate of absenteeism from class may well signify an epidemic, but are students suffering from the flu or spring fever? Because most signs are *fallible* and can be interpreted variously, critical listeners and speakers will subject them to the following tests of reasonableness:

1. *Is an alternative explanation more credible?* Is it more reasonable to suppose that today's higher grades signify harder-working students, or changes in grading standards, or changes in admissions policies? The question can be resolved by gathering other information. If the credentials of entering students have been similar for the past 10 years, then it is more reasonable to infer that the higher grades signify changes in grading standards. Examine alternative explanations for a sign before accepting inferences based on it.

2. *Can the alleged sign be found without the thing for which it stands?* Although the national anthem is often sung before an athletic contest, it also is sung on many other occasions—at the opening of a patriotic rally, for example, or at the beginning of a school day. A sign that can be found in a variety of circumstances is not a solid basis for an inference.

3. *Is the sign part of a pattern, or a single unusual case?* If only one instance of gender-based wage differences can be found, that is not a strong sign of pervasive, widespread discrimination. But if a pattern of wage differences can be identified, it is more reasonable to see that as a sign of gender discrimination.

Guidelines for Reasoning Through Signs

Here are suggestions for effective reasoning through signs.

1. *Use sign inferences to link the abstract with the concrete.* Keep in mind that the primary purpose of a sign inference is to predict the existence of something that cannot be observed on the basis of something that can be. Use sign inferences to convince listeners that something they cannot see does, in fact, exist.

2. *Explain the sign relationship clearly.* Make sure your listeners understand exactly what you are alleging to be a sign of something else and why you think

it predicts what you claim. A student speaker left her audience wondering when she said:

All we have to do is turn on the television set to see signs of the glory of modern civilization.

Was she referring to the technological achievements of broadcasting? Did she believe that the content of television programs showed the triumph of the human spirit? Or was she actually being sarcastic and preparing to criticize typical television fare?

3. *Point to multiple signs of what you want to infer.* Student Roger Berkson used several signs in a speech. Alone, each sign could be fallible, but together they all pointed in the same direction and gave his inference more credibility:

Personal commitment combined with effective reasoning from evidence to claims makes this speaker's presentation convincing.

When I saw that many more students were absent from class lately, I wasn't sure that it meant that they were sick. After all, it was close to midterm exams, and everyone could use more time to study. But then I found out that visits to the infirmary went up, sales at the pharmacy were on the rise, and more beds were in use at the city hospital. Those signs suggest to me that we have a flu epidemic on campus.

4. *Do not claim more for a sign inference than it can establish.* A sign inference claims a predictable relationship between the sign and the thing for which it stands, but it does not establish that either one affects the other. Although a rise in the Consumer Price Index may predict inflation, it certainly does not influence, cause, or lead to inflation. This last point highlights an important distinction between sign inferences and our next form of reasoning: inference from cause.

Cause

Unlike a sign inference, a **causal inference** explains the relationship between things by pointing to the influence of one thing on the other.

Suppose the state legislature significantly raises the gasoline tax, which service stations pass along to consumers by raising the price of gasoline, and sales then decline. Is this chain of events a coincidence? We can never know for sure. But it may be reasonable to infer that the price increase affected consumption patterns—that as the cost of gasoline rose, more consumers decided to limit their driving and to conserve gasoline as well as their money.

A causal inference relates things by identifying one as the cause (higher price) and the other as the effect (lower sales). The cause must both precede and lead to the effect. Moreover, the speaker should provide reasons that the cause–effect relationship makes sense and that no alternative explanation is more plausible.

causal inference
A pattern of inference that suggests that one factor brings about another.

| California has eliminated affirmative action in college admissions. (documents or common knowledge) | Affirmative action policies have been the cause of minority enrollment until now. ⟶ | The number of minority students in California colleges and universities will decrease. |

Figure 6 Inference from cause.

The strategic advantage of inferences from cause is that they enable listeners to see a pattern among what otherwise might be unconnected events. Recognizing the pattern, they can predict what will happen next or they can determine what must be done to avoid that outcome. Listeners are made to feel that they know "what is going on"and that they can do something about it.

Figure 6 maps an inference from cause. When California eliminated affirmative action in college admissions, some higher-education officials alleged that the end of affirmative action would drastically reduce the number of minority students.

Types of Inference from Cause

There are several types of causal inference. Among the most common are prediction, assignment of responsibility, explanation, and steps to a goal. Each of these types is a different use you can make of the inference from cause.

Watch the Video "Persuasive Speech: Mandatory Minimums (Problem–Cause–Solution)" at **MyCommunicationLab**

Prediction.   Some causal inferences explain changes by predicting what leads to what. In a speech about energy efficiency, a speaker might say:

> When you replace a standard light bulb with a compact fluorescent one, you are not merely changing a light bulb. You are changing the world.

The inference is that the act of using energy-efficient compact fluorescent light-bulbs, if adopted on a wide scale, has the potential to make a major positive impact on the environment.

Assignment of Responsibility.   Another common use of causal inferences is to assign responsibility for something, to tell why it occurred. Suppose you were asked to speak about the question"Why would someone run for president if there were no chance of being elected?" In thinking about the question, you may see other reasons to run for office: to get publicity, to establish political relationships, to add certain issues to the agenda for public discussion, to position oneself to run for vice president, to have a good time, and to be ready in case leading candidates falter. Through a causal inference, you could present these as reasons or motivations—as causes—for the decision to run.

Explanation.   A causal inference also can be used to explain something that otherwise doesn't make sense. Consider this paradox: Why, in the richest nation on earth, are there shortages of funds for virtually every social program? Answering such a question involves finding an element—often unexpected or obscure—that explains the situation. If your inference explains that Americans strongly prefer private over public investment, you would have identified a possible cause of the paradox.

Rhetorical Workout

Reason Through Cause

You are researching a speech about the effectiveness of red-light cameras at intersections. You want to carefully assess the information you have to be sure you are making correct inferences.

Supporting material: You read an article about five major cities that installed red-light cameras. The cities reported fewer driver fatalities after installing the cameras.

Claim: You draft the following claim: Red-light cameras improve public safety.

Reasoning: Use the tests for inference from cause to evaluate your claim:

1. Has a *sign* relationship been confused with a *causal* relationship? Could either factor—(a) use of red-light cameras or (b) fewer driver fatalities—be a sign of the other, rather than a cause or effect?

2. Does some common cause of both factors make it seem that they have a cause–effect relationship? Suppose all the cities in the article also reduced speed limits in and around the intersections where they installed red-light cameras. How could this factor be a common cause of the two factors in your claim?

3. Does your claim contain a *post hoc* fallacy, assuming that one factor caused another only because the second factor occurred after the first? Why or why not?

4. Have important multiple causes or multiple effects been overlooked? What questions could you research to learn if your cause (use of red-light cameras) has more than one effect or if your effect (fewer driver fatalities) has more than one cause?

5. Is there likely an alternative cause? What questions could you research to learn if fewer driver fatalities were directly linked to the use of the cameras?

Steps to a Goal.   A causal inference also can relate the means to the ends, as when we know our goals and want to determine the best way to attain them. This form of reasoning is used often in problem–solution speeches. If you advocated the development of solar power in order to avoid risking an energy shortage, you would be employing this type of causal inference.[10]

Tests for Inference from Cause

As with the other patterns of reasoning, the rhetorical proof in a causal inference is not ironclad. We may think we understand how one aspect of a situation influences another and yet we may be mistaken—as examples throughout this chapter have shown. In the case of Figure 6, for instance, some people have maintained that, except for an initial drop, the number of minority students did *not* decline after affirmative action was abolished. (There was considerable disagreement about whether this was true and what these results meant, but that is another story.) Any of the following analytical errors will make a causal inference less reasonable:

1. *Has a sign relationship been confused with a causal relationship?* Because we know that two things are somehow related, we mistakenly assume that one causes the other. Student Michael Leu, for example, let enthusiasm for his subject overpower his ability to test inferences when he made the following argument:

   Only the best professors on this campus teach their classes at noon. If Professor Walker really wanted to be a better teacher, he would change the time of his class so that it met at noon instead of 10.

Had Michael tested his inference carefully, he might have recognized a serious flaw in his reasoning. Teaching at noon might be a *sign* that one was a good teacher, because only the best professors teach at that hour right now. But there is no reason to believe that teaching at noon *causes* anyone to be a good teacher. Professor Walker's changing his class time won't make him a better teacher; instead, it will make Michael's first sentence no longer true.

2. *Does a common cause of both factors make it seem that they have a cause–effect relationship?* This reasoning error alleges that one factor is the cause of another, although in fact both manifest a third cause. If you fall prey to the **common cause fallacy**, you may mistakenly remove what you think is the cause of a problem, only to discover that nothing changes.

   For example, the fact that students in wealthy school districts generally score higher on standardized tests than do students in poorer districts may seem at first glance to prove that higher spending for education results in higher test scores. But some have argued that the real reason wealthy districts score better is that the families who live in them can afford to give their children reading and travel experiences and personal computers—and that this enrichment at home leads *both* to higher test scores *and* to pressure on school districts to spend more for education.

3. *Is there a* post hoc *fallacy?* In Latin, *post hoc* means "after this"; thus, a **post hoc fallacy** occurs if you assume that, because one event occurred after another, it was caused by the earlier event. This reasoning error comes up often in political speeches. Republicans observe that the Cold War ended after President Reagan took office and assume that he should get credit for it; Democrats point to a strong economy while President Clinton was in office and credit him for it. Can we reasonably infer that the end of the Cold War and the sustained economic growth at the end of the twentieth century were caused by these two presidents just because they were in office at the time?

4. *Have important multiple causes or multiple effects been overlooked?* If a problem has multiple causes, acting to remove a single cause is unlikely to solve the problem. Consider the disparities in educational achievement between urban and suburban schools. One important cause is the difference in budgets—suburban districts often are able to spend more on education. But simply equalizing budgets will not solve the problem, because other factors also contribute to the disparity: the preference of many talented teachers for suburban settings, the greater presence of books and other educational stimuli in suburban homes, and the greater involvement of suburban parents in their children's education.

   Likewise, a particular action may have multiple effects, some of which may be undesirable. Student speaker Demetris Papademetriou overlooked this when he used a causal inference to argue in support of economic globalization:

The globalization of business has produced tremendous benefits for the world as a whole. Stockholders receive better returns on their investment because of lower production and labor costs. Workers around the world are given new opportunities to earn a respectable living. The telecommunications and shipping industries have seen major growth as they work to connect producers and consumers in every place on the globe.

Talking with classmates after his speech, Demetris found that he had not convinced them because he had neglected several *other* possible effects of

common cause fallacy
Assuming that one thing causes another when in fact a third factor really is the cause of both.

post hoc **fallacy**
Assuming that, because one event occurred before another, the first is necessarily the cause of the second.

economic globalization that were not so pleasant. Besides the benefits he listed, globalization has led to the loss of millions of domestic jobs, the exploitation of some workers overseas, and other negative developments. These were multiple effects that should at least have been considered in the speech.

5. *Is there a likely alternative cause?* Sometimes what appears to be the cause really isn't. Things may be related, but for a reason different from the one the speaker suggests. Student Muhammad Gill pointed out this mistake in arguments that endorse racial profiling (the practice of making traffic or other investigative stops on the basis of a person's race or ethnicity):

Some people argue that racial profiling is justified. And in rare cases, such as those involving suspected terrorists, it may be. But it is wrong when people look at the high arrest and conviction rates for illegal drug possession among African Americans and they infer that the reason that there are more blacks in court and more blacks in jail is that blacks are more likely to commit crime. The real reason our courts and jails are disproportionately black is that there has been long-standing racial discrimination in both arrests and sentencing.

> **CHECKLIST 4**
>
> ## Tests for Inference from Cause
>
> ❑ Has a sign relationship been confused with a causal relationship?
>
> ❑ Does a common cause of both factors make it seem that they have a cause–effect relationship?
>
> ❑ Does the fact that one event occurred after another falsely signify a cause–effect relationship?
>
> ❑ Have important multiple causes or multiple effects been overlooked?
>
> ❑ Is there a likely alternative cause?

Guidelines for Reasoning Through Cause

Here are suggestions for effective reasoning through cause:

1. *Analyze what the alleged cause is and how it exerts its influence on the effect.* A student speaker who ignored this advice argued that the position of the stars on a person's birthday causes that person to show certain personality traits. When listeners asked questions, though, the speaker was unable to explain the astrological cause or how it worked its influence.

2. *Realize that causal relationships are often complex and subtle.* A cause can have multiple effects, and an effect can have multiple causes. Be sure that your analysis of the cause–effect relationship is plausible and that your inference will be accepted as reasonable. For example, few people will accept that spending more money on a social problem, by itself, will solve the problem.

Testimony

When you rely on other people for the accuracy of supporting materials, their *testimony* stands in for your own direct encounter with the materials. You have confidence in their judgment and are willing to argue that the claim is true because they say so.

When a claim involves, for example, various economic indicators, or the long-term significance of a Supreme Court decision, or adequate safeguards for removing toxic waste, few speakers know enough to support the claim based on their own knowledge. In such cases, both speaker and listeners are usually willing to

Reasoning

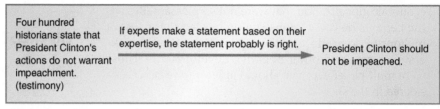

Figure 7 Inference from testimony.

defer to the judgment of someone whose training, experience, or esteem might all be reasons to trust that person's judgment.

Using testimony, like any other form of reasoning, is a strategic choice. The benefit of inferences from testimony is that they make use of the source's authority in two ways: her expertise makes the audience more disposed to accept the claim and her *ethos* becomes associated with that of the speaker.

Figure 7 offers a map of an inference from testimony. It is based on an event that occurred in late 1998 when the House of Representatives was considering the impeachment of President Clinton. A large group of professional historians published a newspaper ad contending that the president's actions were not "high crimes and misdemeanors" as that term was understood in historical context and, therefore, that he should not be impeached. Citing this ad, Clinton's supporters urged that we take the historians' judgment seriously because of their professional expertise.

Types of Inference from Testimony

Testimony can be either fact or opinion. Each of these forms of testimony can be classified further according to (1) the type of person who offers it and (2) whether it is quoted or paraphrased.

Expert Versus Lay Testimony. In most cases, we seek **expert testimony**—the support of someone who is recognized as an authority on a particular subject, who has studied the subject in detail, and whose knowledge and interest in the subject far exceed the average person's. It is not unusual, however, for an expert in one field to make judgments about another field, as when a sports figure endorses a breakfast cereal or an economist comments on fashion trends. When experts testify about matters outside their field of expertise, we should examine their claims closely.

Although expert testimony usually provides stronger support for a claim, speakers sometimes deliberately use **lay testimony**, citing the opinions of "ordinary people" to show what nonexperts think about the subject. Speeches urging teenagers to avoid drugs may cite reformed addicts, not because they are experts but because the audience can imagine these former drug abusers as not all that different from themselves. The speaker hopes that, for just this reason, listeners will learn from the mistakes of those who abused drugs.

Quoted Versus Paraphrased Testimony. Quoted testimony repeats the exact words of the source, whereas paraphrased testimony gives only a general idea of what the source said. For example:

expert testimony
Testimony from a person who is generally recognized as an authority on a particular subject.

lay testimony
Testimony from a person who is not an expert.

QUOTED: Police Chief Walters said, "The rate of burglaries in our town is an
           embarrassment to civilized society."
PARAPHRASED: Police Chief Walters said that the burglary rate was unacceptably high.

Although quoted testimony usually provides stronger support, at times a quotation is too long, too confusing, or too technical for listeners to follow. In that case,
a paraphrase may allow you to cite what the source said without losing the audience's attention. The paraphrase, of course, must render the quotation accurately,
or else you will *misquote* the source.

Tests for Inference from Testimony

Enticed by fame or fortune, some people will say just about anything. Therefore,
even the quoted testimony of an expert is not always strong support for a claim.
Like other forms of reasoning, inferences from testimony must meet certain tests.

 Watch the **Video** "Bill
Gates Criticizes America's
High Schools" at
MyCommunicationLab

1. *Does the statement accurately reflect the source's views?* Imagine that a student,
   in arguing that the theory of intelligent design should be taught in public
   schools, paraphrased a well-known paleontologist as saying that Darwin's
   theory of evolution is wrong. Listeners could find this hard to believe, and
   their doubts would turn out to be well founded if the paleontologist actually said:

   Darwin was wrong. Natural selection is not the most important way in which evolution
   occurs. Other mechanisms that Darwin did not consider play a role just as crucial to
   the evolution of species.

   This exact quotation shows that the scientist would not have questioned
   Darwin's theory but only the importance of one proposed means of evolution-
   ary change. The speaker's paraphrase of the statement as an attack on the theory
   of evolution would not be accurate, and the audience should reject the claim.

2. *Is the source an expert on the topic?* As noted earlier, an expert in one field sometimes offers opinions about other fields. A physicist is not necessarily an expert
   on international relations, nor is an actor the most credible source for a claim
   about nuclear energy. It is not enough that a source be regarded as *generally*
   well qualified; the source needs to be an expert in the *particular* subject about
   which you are making a claim. (Although it always applies to expert testimony,
   adapt it to assess lay testimony by asking, "Does this person have experience
   relating to the claim?")
      Student speaker Trisha Butcher gave a speech about the benefits of build-
   ing more prisons as a way to reduce crime. She based many of her arguments
   on what she had heard from her father, the owner of a company that spe-
   cializes in large-scale industrial construction projects and that had received
   several contracts to build new prisons:

   During a personal interview with my dad, I learned that building more prisons is an
   effective way to reduce the crime rates in our cities. My father also assured me that,
   compared to other methods of rehabilitation and punishment, prisons will prove the
   most economically feasible for the country in the long run.

   Listeners were unconvinced—as they should have been, because this testimony failed several tests. As the owner of a construction company, Trisha's
   father was hardly in a position to compare approaches to reducing crime;

nor was he qualified to make national economic forecasts. And because he earned money from industrial construction, and specifically from building prisons, his opinions were likely to be biased. But Trisha recovered when she revised this speech for her final class project. She found a criminologist to comment about how prisons might deter crime and an economist to assess the economic effects of prisons. Then she used her father's testimony to illustrate the personal experience of someone involved in building prisons—a point on which he *was* well qualified to speak.

3. *Is there a basis for the source's statements?* A speaker who offers judgments without providing any basis for them is said to **pontificate**. Unfortunately, experts as well as lay people can do this. But if the source is offering judgments, listeners need to be confident that he or she is familiar with all aspects of the topic and has reasons for making the claim.

4. *Is the source reasonably unbiased?* No one is completely free of bias, of course, but if a source has a vested interest in a claim, the pressure will be strong to offer testimony consistent with that interest. An environmental engineer who owns land at a particular site, for example, may be more likely to downplay hazards on the site than would an engineer who has no economic interest in the matter. Similarly, claims by industry experts—whether automakers, cigarette manufacturers, or health-care providers—should be scrutinized. Now, just because an expert stands to gain from the consequences of his or her testimony does not mean that the testimony itself is wrong. But when expertise and self-interest are mixed, you need to be a skeptical, critical listener.

5. *Is the testimony up to date?* Some issues are timeless, and so it will not matter when a person's testimony was offered. Moral and philosophical principles may be timeless matters, although even here advances in knowledge and technology may affect what once seemed settled matters. On most matters, though—and particularly when data and statistics are involved—recent testimony may be more valuable than older support.

Even when testimony meets all these tests, you still may have to choose among the conflicting claims of qualified experts who disagree. Do not simply pick what supports your thesis and ignore other testimony. Instead:

- Ask what each expert's record of previous statements may imply about the quality of judgment in this case.
- Ask which expert's testimony is closest to consensus in the field.
- Ask which expert's statement is most consistent with other things you already know or believe.

Guidelines for Reasoning Through Testimony

Here are suggestions for effective reasoning through testimony.

1. *Be sure you quote or paraphrase accurately.* Obviously, a direct quotation must be exactly what the source said. But it is equally important that a paraphrase be faithful to the context and meaning of the original statement and that it fairly reproduce its subtleties. For example, if the context suggests that the source favors an action but has reservations about it, you would not paraphrase accurately if you suggested that the source wholeheartedly supports the action.

pontificate
To offer judgments without providing any basis for them.

2. *Usually, draw on multiple sources of testimony.* If all your testimonial evidence comes from a single source, listeners may infer that no one else agrees or that your research is shallow; this could undermine even an authoritative source's credibility.

3. *State the credentials of your source.* Because an inference from testimony depends on listeners accepting the source as an authority, you should specify whom you are quoting or paraphrasing. Don't include every credential of the source, but list qualifications that support the claim in the quotation. Similarly, in selecting sources to quote, focus on people whose credentials are pertinent to your subject, and make sure that the audience understands why you are using the source. The endorsements of celebrities who lack subject-matter expertise carry little weight.

4. *Your own ethos affects the credibility of testimony you cite.* If listeners regard you as highly credible, they will be more likely to accept what you say; they will make inferences about the truth of your claims based on your own credibility. When basketball star Magic Johnson, after being diagnosed HIV-positive, urged others to avoid contracting the virus, he was a highly credible source because he was directly affected. Beyond that, if listeners love basketball and admire Magic Johnson, your use of his testimony will be more credible than it would be if they had no interest in him or the sport.

CHECKLIST 5

Tests for Inference from Testimony

❒ Does the statement accurately reflect the source's views?
❒ Is the source an expert on the topic?
❒ Is there a basis for the source's statements?
❒ Is the source reasonably unbiased?
❒ Is the testimony up to date?

When qualified experts disagree, ask:

❒ What does each expert's record of previous statements imply about the quality of judgment in this case?
❒ Which expert's testimony is closest to consensus in the field?
❒ Which expert's statement is most consistent with other things you already know or believe?

Narrative

This final category of inference, called *narrative*, comes into play when a speaker tells a story. A story is often more powerful than other ways of developing an idea. It is *personalized*, presenting a broad, general, or abstract idea as a specific situation involving particular people. Listeners become involved in the action and wonder what will happen; the story thus adds an element of suspense. A narrative works just like an extended example, and so *representativeness* serves to test the inference, just as it does for inference from example.

The dramatic structure of a narrative inference makes it powerful, which is apparent to anyone who reads novels or watches television and movies. The narrative structure consists of *characters*, a sequence of episodes or moves (often called a *plot*), the resolution of some sort of *conflict* (broadly defined), and an *ending* to which the resolution points. But the ending—the "moral of the story"—often is not stated explicitly. Audience members infer it for themselves.[11]

Narratives take many forms in speeches and have many uses. They may be personal—a story in which

A speaker may use narrative reasoning to talk about hypothetical, real, or fictional events. To be effective, the story should be coherent, plausible, and consistent, and should resonate with the listeners.

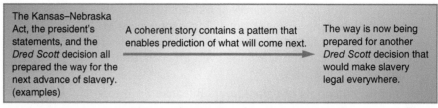

Figure 8 Inference from narrative.

the speaker is the main character—or they may be about other people. They may describe real events or a hypothetical situation; fictional narratives are also common in speeches, as in the retelling of children's stories, fables, biographical accounts, and historical scenarios.[12]

Figure 8 maps a famous historical case of inference from narrative. During the 1850s, some Northern politicians, including Abraham Lincoln, believed that a group of Southern sympathizers were plotting to extend slavery over the entire country. In the "House Divided" speech, Lincoln arranged a series of recent events into narrative form so that they told a story of the work of this "slave power." Each of these events, such as the Kansas–Nebraska Act opening formerly free territories to slavery and the *Dred Scott* Supreme Court decision preventing Congress from outlawing slavery in the territories, prepared the way for more drastic action to extend slavery. Lincoln used the coherence of the story to predict what these plotters would do next: Bring about a second *Dred Scott* decision that would prevent *states* from outlawing slavery anywhere. Figure 8 paraphrases his argument.

We have referred to narrative as a kind of verbal storytelling, but narrative inferences can also be made from visual evidence. In interpreting a picture, for instance, one might reveal the "story" that the picture tells.

Tests for Inference from Narrative

To test whether a narrative inference is sound, examine various elements of its structure. Some important questions follow:

1. *Is the narrative coherent?* Does the story hang together and make sense? Is everything tied together at the end? Or do unexplained factors and loose ends make the story seem "unfinished" and its point unclear?

2. *Is the narrative plausible?* Is the story realistic, or is it farfetched? Because the narrative is offered to explain or support some claim, an implausible narrative will call that claim into question as well.

3. *Are characterizations consistent?* Do individuals in the story act as the audience has been led to expect? Just as you must be credible as a speaker and just as the experts you quote must be credible as authorities, so the characters in a narrative must be credible. If they are not, the audience will question the story—and the claim.

4. *Does the narrative have resonance?* **Resonance** is a feature that makes a narrative strike a responsive chord with listeners, allowing them to identify with the story and to relate it to their own experience. If your narrative has resonance, listeners will realize that you are telling the story not primarily for its entertainment value, but to speak directly to them and to make them understand your point.

resonance
The quality of striking a responsive chord with listeners, causing them to identify with what one is saying.

CHECKLIST 6

Tests for Inference from Narrative

- ❏ Is the narrative coherent?
- ❏ Is the narrative plausible?
- ❏ Are characterizations consistent?
- ❏ Does the narrative have resonance?

Avoiding Errors in Reasoning

We have examined a variety of inferences and some tests for each of them. The best way to ensure that your reasoning is sound is to apply those tests to specific inference patterns. But there are also some general errors in reasoning. As we have seen, these also are called *fallacies*. The inference appears at first to be sound but, on inspection, it contains a major flaw. Although fallacies often seem persuasive, critical listeners quickly realize that the reasoning goes astray.

Sometimes the term *fallacy* refers very broadly to any claim that people disagree with or any statement that they do not like. At other times, the term refers very narrowly to defects in formal logic only. In public speaking, however, fallacies are inferences that would generally be regarded as unreasonable by a broad and diverse audience of listeners exercising their best critical judgment.[13]

Six General Tests of Inference

For any argument, regardless of the type of inference, these are important questions to ask:

1. *Does the claim follow from the supporting material?* This is the most basic question. Suppose a speaker stated:

   Because our school is 100 years old, it needs higher academic standards.

   We would be hard pressed to find any relationship between the supporting material (the age of the school) and the claim (that higher academic standards are needed). The claim might be correct, but it probably could not be inferred from this supporting evidence. The technical term for an inference in which the claim does not follow from the supporting material is **non sequitur** (Latin for "It does not follow").

2. *Does the claim advance our understanding beyond the supporting material?* Because we reason from what we already know (the supporting material) to what we wish to establish (the claim), an inference moves beyond the supporting material. Sometimes an inference has no real movement; the claim simply restates the supporting material in slightly different words. Such an inference is said to be a **circular argument**, as in this statement:

   Freedom of speech is for the common good [*claim*] because the expression of opinions is ultimately in the best interest of all [*supporting material*].

3. *Is the claim relevant to the issue?* Sometimes, a speaker makes a claim that is not pertinent to the topic at hand. Consider the following argument from a student who was claiming that the Scholastic Assessment Test (SAT) does not predict academic success:

   The test numbers do nothing to measure a student's potential for success in college. I am so tired of the way the modern world reduces us all to numbers. The college admissions process has become a clear example of this. When students want most of all to be seen as unique persons, they are instead reduced to an SAT score.

   By noting the dehumanizing effect of using test scores to assess college applicants, the speaker was making a claim about modern life, and supported it with reference to the SAT, but the claim had nothing to do with the issue

non sequitur
A claim that, on its face, is unrelated to the supporting material.

circular argument
Only restating the claim in slightly different words, rather than supporting the claim.

of whether the exam is a poor measure of students' potential. Whereas test number one (above) refers to the relationship between the supporting material and the claim, this test concerns the relationship between the claim and the issue. An inference that diverts attention from the issue is said to be **ignoring the question**. (More commonly it is called a *red herring*, from the practice in earlier centuries of dragging a smoked fish along a trail to confuse hunting dogs that were tracking the scent of a fox.)

4. *Is the language clear and unequivocal?* The important point here is that the clarity of language may affect the quality of an inference. When the language of a speech can have multiple meanings, it is said to be **equivocal**; and any inferences based on that language will also be open to interpretation.

    Suppose that a politician promises "no tax increases." This sounds straightforward but can be interpreted in many ways. Is the politician promising that there will be no new taxes, or that the current tax rate will not increase? Or that the percentage of a family's income paid in taxes will not change? Or that the family will spend no more on taxes this year than last year? Furthermore, what is a "tax"? Is it limited to such obvious categories as income, sales, and property taxes, or does it also include fees for driving on toll roads or camping in national parks?

5. *Has probability been clearly distinguished from certainty?* Speakers sometimes forget that inferences cannot be guaranteed, and they regard as certain what is really only probable. A speaker might argue, for example, that viewing violent television programs unquestionably inspires people to act violently. But this claim is hardly a sure thing; some researchers suggest that television violence may have little or no effect on behavior, and some even argue that television violence reduces aggression by providing a relatively harmless outlet for it. When a speaker suggests that all the evidence is clear-cut in one direction, listeners will do well to be wary that he or she is overstating the case.

6. *Is the speaker's emotional response appropriate to the situation?* Although over 20 years old, there is a still-famous example of what happens when the speaker's emotional response is not appropriate to the situation. During the 1988 presidential debates, Democratic candidate Michael Dukakis, who opposed capital punishment, was asked whether he would favor it were his wife raped and murdered. Dukakis virtually ignored the hypothetical situation posed by the questioner and proceeded in analytical fashion to restate his position on capital punishment:

    > I think you know I've opposed the death penalty during all my life. I don't see any evidence that it's a deterrent, and I think there are better and more effective ways to deal with violent crime. We've done so in my own state. And that's one of the reasons we have had the biggest drop in crime of any industrial state in America.

Many viewers reacted negatively to this response because Dukakis seemed to show no emotion; nothing in his answer suggested the rage people might expect from a husband in this situation. As a result, many listeners both discounted Dukakis's views on capital punishment and decided that he was not credible. Both conclusions were reached by inference from the mismatch between Dukakis's emotional reaction and what would be expected.

Watch the Video "Mark Knapp on the Accuracy in Detecting Deception" at **MyCommunicationLab**

ignoring the question
Making an inference that diverts attention from the issue at hand.

equivocal
Having multiple meanings.

As this example illustrates, appropriate emotional response sometimes is more important than the details of the inference. This point was made vividly in August 1998 when President Clinton spoke to the nation about his improper relationship with Monica Lewinsky. Although many people believed that an overzealous special prosecutor was the real cause of his problems, Clinton's use of that claim in his speech did not go over well. At that moment, the audience was expecting to see the emotions of contrition and remorse, not causal arguments.

The first key issue is the *appropriateness* of the speaker's emotional response. Some situations, such as the presentation of scientific research, call for straightforwardness and calm; others, such as the ones Dukakis and Clinton faced, call for a passionate response. But because the meaning of situations is not given and because inferences from emotions—like other inferences—cannot be guaranteed, the speaker should analyze the norms of appropriate emotional response as part of the audience analysis.

Second, should speakers always respond in the "appropriate" way? At times, a speaker may deliberately violate listeners' expectations by making an "inappropriate" response, perhaps becoming emotionally aroused about a subject that the audience regards as "no big deal" or finding humor in a subject that the audience takes seriously. Usually, when a speaker violates norms of appropriateness, the purpose is to shock listeners, to make them pay attention, and to convince them to reexamine their ideas. But such a strategy is risky, because the discomfort produced by an inappropriate response may turn the audience against the speaker instead.

Finally, be aware that emotional responses are sometimes misused, as when a speaker labels ideas he or she does not like as "anti-American" or "sexist" or "racist." Unsupported appeals to fear, to prejudice, or to pride are actually devices to prevent inference, an attempt to substitute emotional reactions for substantial proof.

CHECKLIST 7

General Tests for Inferences

- ☐ Does the claim follow from the supporting material?
- ☐ Does the claim advance our understanding beyond the supporting material?
- ☐ Is the claim relevant to the issue?
- ☐ Is the language clear and unequivocal?
- ☐ Has probability been clearly distinguished from certainty?
- ☐ Is the speaker's emotional response appropriate to the situation?

Reasoning in Public Speaking

OBJECTIVE
4

How can you apply the reasoning process to preparing, delivering, and listening to speeches? When preparing a speech, ask yourself why listeners should regard the supporting material as grounds for your claim. Then apply the tests for the particular kinds of inferences (Checklists 1 to 6) and the general tests for inferences (Checklist 7) to determine whether your reasoning seems sound. Then imagine a relatively skeptical listener—not someone hostile to the topic, but someone who really does need to be convinced. Would that person regard your reasoning as sound?[14]

Proceed to higher levels of claims and repeat this process. Finally, ask whether all the statements marked by Roman numerals in your outline taken together provide a basis for inferring your central claim. If so, then you have done a good job

Strategies for Speaking to Diverse Audiences

Respecting Diversity Through Reasoning

Not all individuals or cultures reason in the same way. The following strategies will help ensure that you do not unconsciously assume that all audience members reason in the same way that you do.

1. Think about how your audience may expect certain types of reasoning more than others. This is certainly true across cultures, where narrative (for example) may be expected in one case and scientific facts in another. But this is also true within U.S. audiences; a group of engineers would expect different evidence from that for literary scholars.

2. Be sure that your inferences (from example, analogy, sign, cause, testimony, and narrative) avoid stereotypes of individuals or cultural groups. Resorting to such stereotypes weakens your *ethos*. Not only does it potentially alienate your audience, but it also generally does not employ sound reasoning.

3. Pay attention to differences in the assumptions that your audience may have. Some things that you may consider so obvious that they require no explanation, may not be so obvious for others. Rhetorical proof relies on both audience and speaker, so keep in mind how reason and audience are linked.

in working with your speech materials. But if you find any questionable inferences, your listeners are likely to find them, too.

When presenting a speech, remember that the audience is a critical factor in establishing rhetorical proof; the speaker and listeners reason together. As we have seen throughout the chapter, your selection of one reasoning pattern rather than another is a strategic choice, because each pattern reflects a different aspect of how listeners think along with you. Moreover, you will not always make every step in your reasoning explicit; sometimes the supporting material or, more likely, the inference will seem to be assumed. This means that you are drawing on the audience's knowledge and expectations to establish the inference.

For example, audience analysis might suggest that your listeners believe that mergers of media companies threaten the ability of the press to be both a government watchdog and a guardian of democracy. You might never mention that inference explicitly in your speech, instead say:

> This week we heard news reports of yet another media corporation merger. We know what that means for the strength of American democracy.

Occasionally, of course, the audience analysis will be mistaken. Suppose that the last statement was met by blank stares—or, worse, by frowns. Such feedback signals that the audience is not ready to participate in this inference. Even while giving the speech, you may modify your strategic plan, deciding in this case to make the inference explicit—not only stating that media mergers threaten democracy, but also giving evidence to support your claim.

You can help listeners follow your reasoning process by signposting its steps and inferences. For instance:

> Let me provide three examples…
> An analogy is in order here…

Phrases like these will prompt listeners to anticipate the inference and its appropriate tests. Or you may ask (and later answer) such a question as:

How do we know that the statistical sample was representative?

This will suggest that you know the relevant tests of reasoning and are confident that your speech satisfies them. Even the use of reasoning terms (*consequently, therefore, the premise is, the implied conclusion is,* and so on) will help listeners understand where you are in reasoning through the speech. Your care in reasoning appropriately from supporting material will also help to promote your audience's critical thinking and listening skills—just as their critical listening will provide you with an incentive to reason carefully.[15]

What Have You Learned?

Objective 1: Explain the nature of rhetorical proof in public speaking and identify its three components.

Rhetorical proof in public speaking is different from proof in mathematics or science:

- Rhetorical proof depends on an interaction between the speaker and the audience.
- Although their joint conclusions cannot be guaranteed absolutely, they can be supported and shown to be probable.

A rhetorical proof includes three main components:

- The claim is the statement that listeners are asked to accept.
- Supporting material provides the foundation for the claim.
- Reasoning links the supporting material to the claim.

Reasoning involves making an inference:

- An inference is a mental leap.
- The leap is the judgment that the supporting material really does support the claim.
- Inferences cannot be guaranteed, but certain patterns of inference can be shown as generally reliable.
- An inference is reasonable if it would be made by most people when exercising their critical judgment.

Objective 2: Describe six basic patterns of reasoning, focusing on their types, appropriate tests of their soundness, and how to use them in a speech.

The major forms or patterns of inference include the following:

- Example
- Analogy

- Signs
- Cause
- Testimony
- Narrative

Each of these reasoning patterns has

- Several different types
- Specific tests to determine whether it is a strong inference
- Guidelines for use

Objective 3: Define what a fallacy is and identify both general fallacies and fallacies that correspond to particular patterns of reasoning.

In addition to the specific tests for each reasoning pattern, there are general tests of reasoning in order to avoid such fallacies as the following:

- *Non sequitur*
- Circular argument
- Ignoring the question
- Equivocal language
- Confusing probability with certainty
- Inappropriate emotional response

These are fallacies because the inferences appear to be sound but actually are seriously flawed.

Objective 4: Indicate how an understanding of reasoning processes helps in preparing and delivering a speech and in being an active, critical listener.

The chapter concluded with suggestions for using your understanding of the reasoning process in preparing, delivering, and listening to speeches.

 Listen to the Audio Chapter Summary at MyCommunicationLab

Discussion Questions

1. In class, watch a recording of a recent political speech and discuss its reasoning process. What patterns of inference were used? Why do you think the speaker chose to use those patterns? Did they work? Did you recognize any fallacies?

2. If you knew that your audience would be uncritical, why would you still take time to test your inferences before speaking? With a group of peers, discuss the ethics of proper reasoning.

3. In what ways might emotion help someone or prevent someone from making a proper inference? Discuss situations in which particular emotions (love, fear, hate, anger, boredom) might advance or detract from the reasoning process.

4. As we have seen in this chapter, telling a story (narrative inference) is an effective way for speakers to make a point in very concrete terms. Share examples of speeches or other presentations where you have seen this technique used well. How in-depth were these examples?

Activities

1. Now expand your evaluation of each link on a map. Identify each type of inference, and conduct appropriate tests to understand why each link is positive or negative.

2. Identify examples of each type of inference that you plan to use in your next speech. Which reasoning patterns are most appropriate for your topic? Which do you think will be most effective with your audience? How would your reasoning patterns need to be modified for a different audience, such as elderly veterans or mostly international students?

3. Using Checklist 7 as a guide, for the next few days, think critically about the everyday communication events around you. Identify claims in the wide variety of messages that surround you (TV commercials, newspaper editorials, or arguments with friends, for

example). Demonstrate how at least three of these messages fail one of the general tests, and explain the fallacy of each.

4. Find a letter to the editor in the campus or local newspaper. Identify and analyze the inferences the writer makes. What patterns are employed? Are the tests for each pattern satisfied? Are there any general errors in reasoning?

5. Watch on television or listen on the radio to a highly partisan "news" and opinion show. List the fallacies and other lapses in reasoning you perceive the host or guests to be making, and supply examples.

Key Terms

analogy	fallacy of composition	physical observation (as a sign)
causal inference	fallacy of division	pontificate
circular argument	figurative analogy	*post hoc* fallacy
claim	ignoring the question	reasonable
common cause fallacy	inference	representative
equivocal	institutional regularity (as a sign)	resonance
examples	lay testimony	rhetorical proof
expert testimony	literal analogy	sign
fallacy	non sequitur	statistical index (as a sign)

 Study and **Review** the **Flashcards** at **MyCommunicationLab**

Notes

1 Although scientists and mathematicians may argue about what counts as proof, their institutional standards for agreement are usually clearly defined. See Philip J. Davis and Reuben Hersh, "Rhetoric and Mathematics," *The Rhetoric of the Human Sciences: Language and Argument in Scholarship and Public Affairs*, ed. John S. Nelson, Allan Megill, and Donald N. McCloskey, Madison: University of Wisconsin Press, 1987, pp. 53–68. For a discussion of the similarities that may ground different standards of proof, see Stephen Pender, "Between Medicine and Rhetoric," *Early Science and Medicine* 10 (2005): 36–64.

2 See also Chaim Perelman and Lucie Olbrechts-Tyteca, *The New Rhetoric: A Treatise on Argumentation*, translated by John Wilkinson and Purcell Weaver, Notre Dame, IN: University of Notre Dame Press, 1969, pp. 31–35.

3 For a more detailed map of the reasoning process, see Stephen Toulmin, Richard Rieke, and Allan Janik, *An Introduction to Reasoning*, 2nd ed., New York: Macmillan, 1984. See also J. Ramage and J. Bean, *Writing Arguments*, 3rd ed., Boston: Allyn & Bacon, 1995; and Douglas N. Walton, *Argumentation Schemes for Presumptive Reasoning*, Mahwah, NJ: Lawrence Erlbaum, 1996.

4 This is an adaptation of a model developed by a contemporary British philosopher, Stephen Toulmin, in *The Uses of Argument*, Cambridge: Cambridge University Press, 1958. Toulmin's model includes some additional elements that need not concern us here.

5 For recent research on the influence of culture on reasoning patterns, see Erica Goode, "How Culture Molds Habits of Thought," *New York Times* (Aug. 8, 2000): D1, D4.

6 Also consult a theoretical discussion of inferences from example in speeches, such as John Arthos, "Where There Are No Rules or Systems to Guide Us: Argument from Example in a Hermeneutic Rhetoric," *Quarterly Journal of Speech* 89 (November 2003): 320–44.

7 For research detailing the persuasive effects of literal and figurative analogies, see Pradeep Sopory and James Price Dillard, "The Persuasive Effects of Metaphor: A Meta-Analysis," *Human Communication Research* 28 (July 2002): 382–419.

8 Our modern understanding of literal and figurative analogies developed from the classical tradition. For more on the genesis of analogical reasoning, see James S. Measell, "Classical Bases of the Concept of Analogy," *Argumentation and Advocacy* 10 (Summer 1973): 1–10. For an example of the prevalence of analogy in speeches, see David Hoogland Noon, "Operation Enduring Analogy: World War II, the War on Terror, and the Uses of Historical Memory," *Rhetoric & Public Affairs* 7 (Fall 2004): 339–65.

9 For more on the use of analogies in speeches, see James R. Wilcox and Henry L. Ewbank, "Analogy for Rhetors," *Philosophy and Rhetoric* 12 (Winter 1979): 1–20.

10 For a more detailed theoretical discussion of inferences from cause, see David Zarefsky, "The Role of Causal Argument in Policy Controversies," *Argumentation and Advocacy* 13 (Spring 1977): 179–91. Marketing and consumer research also depends heavily upon causal claims. See Elise Chandon and Chris Janiszewski, "The Influence of Causal Conditional Reasoning on the Acceptance of Product Claims," *Journal of Consumer Research* 35 (April 2009): 1003–1011.

11 According to some, storytelling is the most important aspect of speechmaking. See Walter R. Fisher, "Narration as a Human Communication Paradigm: The Case of Public Moral Argument," *Communication Monographs* 51 (March 1984): 1–22.

12 For a good practical discussion of the power of narrative in speeches, see Theodore F. Sheckels, "The Rhetorical Success of Thabo Mbeki's 1966 'I Am an African' Address," *Communication Quarterly* 57 (July 2009): 319–33.

13 Several books explore fallacies in detail. See Alex C. Michalos, *Improving Your Reasoning*, 2nd ed., Englewood Cliffs, NJ: Prentice-Hall, 1986; T. Edward Damer, *Attacking Faulty Reasoning*, 2nd ed., Belmont, CA: Wadsworth, 1987; Howard Kahane, *Logic and Contemporary Rhetoric*, Belmont, CA: Wadsworth, 1980; and Christopher W. Tindale, *Fallacies and Argument Appraisal*, Cambridge: Cambridge University Press, 2007.

14 It has been said that "arguments are found in people," meaning that listeners are responsible for making the inferential leaps between supporting material and claim. See Wayne Brockriede, "Where Is Argument?" *Argumentation and Advocacy* 11 (Spring 1975): 179–82.

15 For a more detailed discussion of how speakers (and audiences) develop skill in reasoning, see Dale Hample, "Arguing Skill," *Handbook of Communication and Social Interaction Skills*, ed. John O. Greene and Brant R. Burleson, Mahwah, NJ: Erlbaum, 2003.

Photo Credits

Credits are listed in order of appearance.

Argument

The cover of the July 2008 issue of *National Geographic* shows a close-up of the face of a gorilla, with the question superimposed: "Who murdered the mountain gorillas?"[1] Mark Jenkins's feature story opens by describing the conditions in central Africa's Virunga Park, the forests of which are stripped by charcoal producers and the borders of which are crowded by refugees from the conflict in the Democratic Republic of Congo. During the summer of 2007, seven mountain gorillas were killed in the park. The story describes the killing this way:

> On July 22 of last year unknown assailants crouched in the forest, preparing to execute a family of gorillas.... [A]rmed with automatic weapons, the killers had hunted down the twelve-member Rugendo family, well known among tourists and well loved by the rangers of Virunga National Park ... On foot patrol the next morning [park rangers] found three female gorillas—Mburanumwe, Neza, and Safari—shot to death, with Safari's infant cowering nearby. The following day Senkwekwe was found dead: blasted through the chest that same night. Three weeks later the body of another Rugendo female, Macibiri, would be discovered, her infant presumed dead.
>
> Just a month earlier, two females and an infant from another gorilla group had been attacked. The rangers had found one of the females, shot execution style in the back of the head; her infant, still alive, was clinging to her dead mother's breast. The other female was never found.
>
> All told, seven Virunga mountain gorillas had been killed in less than two months. Brent Stirton's photographs of the dead creatures being carried like royalty by weeping villagers ran in newspapers and magazines around the world. The murders of these intelligent, unassuming animals the park rangers refer to as "our brothers" ignited international outrage....
>
> One thing seemed certain from the moment the bodies of the gorillas were found last July: Poachers had not killed them. Poachers who prey on gorillas leave an unmistakable calling card: They kidnap the infants and cut off the heads and hands of the

---

[1] Mark Jenkins, "Who Murdered the Virunga Gorillas," *National Geographic* 214, no. 1 (July 2008): 34–65. The full story is available online at http://ngm.nationalgeographic.com/2008/07/virunga/jenkins-text (accessed October 12, 2011). A video that accompanies the story is available at: http://ngm.nationalgeographic.com/2008/07/virunga/gorillas-video-interactive (accessed October 12, 2011).

adults—to be sold on the black market. But these bodies were left to rot where they fell, and the motherless infants left to starve to death.[2]

Notice how the essay speaks of the gorillas in human terms, describing them as members of a family, calling them by name, explaining how an infant was found clinging to her dead mother, and referring to execution-style shootings. Additionally, the magazine cover is a commanding piece of visual rhetoric: it shows a close-up image of a gorilla, eyes staring directly back at the readers with a face much like their own. The essay proceeds to lay out a forensic argument about who was most likely guilty of the "murders."

In the magazine's November 2008 issue, debate emerged about this story. One letter disagreed with the use of term "murder," arguing "the word 'murder' (the unlawful premeditated killing of one human being by another) is and should be reserved for people."[3] The writer worried that not only would the term be redefined, its meaning would be minimized "by equating people to animals," which would further desensitize people to the murder of millions of people in Darfur. Another letter referred to the images of women begging for charcoal that accompanied the original story, and argued: "The plight of these human beings should be our very first concern."[4]

Which author is right? Either what was done to the gorillas constitutes murder and people should feel about and react to it the same way they would to the murder of a human family of seven, or the killing of animals is not murder even though it may be a cause for sadness and a reaction. Which position is most persuasive? Is it murder? Can a nonhuman be murdered? When a gorilla is murdered/killed, what should be the government response? What penalty is appropriate for the murderer/killer?

Many people might rightly say Jenkins and the letter writers all have a right to their own opinions, but that misses the point. You have been exposed to different opinions. Which makes the most sense to you? You cannot accept them both, even if you can see both sides. Either you agree it is murder, or you do not. Arguments require people not only to understand another person's point of view, and that person's reasons for that position, they also require them to choose between competing arguments.

THE PLACE OF ARGUMENT IN A CIVIL SOCIETY

Argument is not something to be avoided. The letter writers did not start a fight by disagreeing or attacking the *National Geographic* article's author. Instead, a reasoned exchange of arguments occurred. Such an exchange is something to encourage. Citizen participation in decision making distinguishes a democracy from all other forms of government. If that distinction is to be more than superficial, and if democracy is to remain vibrant, citizens must be trained in the skills

---

[2]Jenkins, "Who Murdered," 39, 45.
[3]Chris Falzon, letter to the editor, *National Geographic* 214, no. 5 (November 2008), 8.
[4]Bryan Berry, letter to the editor, *National Geographic* 214, no. 5 (November 2008), 8.

that enable reasoned and reasonable decision making. Influential US political philosopher John Dewey explains:

> [T]he faith of democracy in the role of consultation, of conference, of persuasion, of discussion, in formation of public opinion . . . [is] faith in the capacity of the intelligence of the common man [and woman] to respond with common-sense to the free play of facts and ideas which are secured by effective guarantees of free inquiry, free assembly and free communication . . . [T]he heart and final guarantee of democracy is in free gatherings of neighbors on the street corner to discuss back and forth what is read in the uncensored news of the day, and in gatherings of friends in the living rooms of houses and apartments to converse freely with one another."[5]

Argumentation is a skill central to democracy. Thus, this section offers a definition of argument and an explanation of its role in decision making, then outlines argument as interactive, contingent and, at its best, cooperative.

Argument is a complex concept. It can be defined as *reasoned discourse that seeks to persuade by presenting support for a position.* Aristotle outlined three types of proof for an argument: ethos (proof from the character of the speaker), pathos ("disposing the listener in some way"), and "argument [logos] itself, by showing or seeming to show something."[6] Some have simplistically defined "logos" as "logic." However, the Greek term "logos," like "argument," is complex. Classical rhetoric scholar George Kennedy points out that "logos" can mean "anything that is 'said,' but that can be a word, a sentence, part of speech or of a written work, or a whole speech."[7] "Logos" refers to the content of persuasion, usually the reasoning, but it is a broad concept.

"Argument" refers both to a thing one makes and an exchange in which one engages. Communication scholar Daniel O'Keefe divides argument into two types, describing argument$_1$ as a "kind of utterance" and argument$_2$ "as a particular kind of interaction."[8]

Argument$_1$ is *argument as a thing, the particular speech act in which one presents a claim and provides sufficient reasons to warrant assent to that claim.* Jenkins's story about the gorillas advances a number of arguments$_1$, including the arguments that gorillas were murdered, that there were many suspects, and that the battle over charcoal provoked the attacks. The letters responding to the story also contain examples of argument$_1$, including the arguments that gorillas by definition cannot be murdered because they are not human and that people should be more worried about the refugees than the gorillas.

---

[5]John Dewey, "Creative Democracy," *1939–1941/Essays, Reviews, and Miscellany,* vol. 14, *John Dewey: The Later Works, 1925–1953* (Carbondale: Southern Illinois University Press, 1988), 227.

[6]Aristotle, *On Rhetoric,* trans. George A. Kennedy (New York: Oxford University Press, 1991), 1.2 [1356a].

[7]George A. Kennedy, *A New History of Classical Rhetoric* (Princeton, NJ: Princeton University Press, 1994), 11.

[8]Daniel J. O'Keefe, "The Concepts of Argument and Arguing," *Advances in Argumentation Theory and Research,* ed. J. Robert Cox and Charles Arthur Willard (Carbondale: Southern Illinois University Press, 1982), 3–23, esp. 3–4, and "Two Concepts of Argument," *Journal of the American Forensic Association* 13 (1977): 121–128.

Argument$_2$ is *argument as a form of interaction, the way in which arguments-as-things and the people using them interact with each other*. The exchange between the feature story and letters constitutes an argument$_2$, in which differing points of view are represented and contrasted to one another. At its best, argument$_2$ highlights areas of agreement just as much as it might represent a disagreement. It can create the conditions where agreement can be reached, not just where disagreement is solidified. For example, these authors could decide that regardless of whether the killing of gorillas rises to the level of the murder of a human, it is still an egregious act that deserves prosecution. As this example demonstrates, argument$_1$ forms the *basis* on which decisions are made; argument$_2$ is the *process* through which they are made.

In democratic systems in which members participate in decision making (systems as small as a shared household and as large as a nation-state), argument is indispensable. It provides the means through which the relative benefits and costs of a proposal can be assessed. Roommates may consult each other about whether their pooled resources should be used to buy a stereo or a new outdoor grill. Residents of a city may discuss whether a 1 percent local option sales tax should be assessed to raise funds to improve local schools, as Waterloo, Iowa, did in 1992. Residents of a state may debate about whether to vote for a ballot initiative banning same-sex marriage, as California did in 2008 with Proposition 8. Residents of a nation may argue about whether to ban flag burning. In a representative democracy, such arguments may find their focus in debates conducted by legislators. Extensive debate occurred in Congress in 1989 as part of the decision to pass the "Flag Protection Act."[9] The location of the debate then moved to the Supreme Court, which heard arguments about whether a ban on flag burning was constitutional. The Court ultimately decided such a ban violated the First Amendment and voided the law.[10]

These examples highlight two important themes: (1) arguments are necessarily interactive and (2) all decisions based on argument are necessarily contingent.

First, let us consider how argument is interactive. An exchange of arguments$_1$ creates argument$_2$. In the debates over California's Proposition 8, people offered a number of arguments$_1$. After California's Supreme Court declared unconstitutional Proposition 22 (a 2000 initiative that altered the state Family Code to ban same-sex marriage), people opposed to same-sex marriage proposed an initiative to amend the state constitution to declare: "Only marriage between a man and a woman is valid or recognized in California."[11] Amending the state constitution, proponents of the initiative believed, would block the state Supreme Court from declaring a same-sex marriage ban unconstitutional.

The former Speaker of the US House of Representatives, Newt Gingrich, released a video in support of the initiative. In it, he argued,

> Throughout American history, the people have defeated the threat of judicial tyranny ... Our courts have an important role to play in our government, but it is not their role to define American values. That right belongs with the

---

[9]For examples of the congressional debate, see *The Congressional Record*, September 12, 1989.
[10]*United States v. Eichman*, 496 U.S. 310 (1990).
[11]California Secretary of State, Elections and Voter Information, http://www.sos.ca.gov/elections/bp_11042008_pres_general/prop_8_text_law.pdf (accessed March 18, 2009).

people . . . On November 4, the people can overrule the judges and undo what they did. They can vote yes on Proposition 8 to restore California's long-standing history of protecting marriage. . . . I can't overstate the danger of tyranny from elitist judges who believe they have the right and the power to dictate their values to the American people. . . . keeping the courts in check is one of the most important issues of the 2008 election. It is central to the future of America. On November 4, overrule the judges. Vote yes on Proposition 8 to defend and protect marriage.[12]

Gingrich advanced two arguments in support of Proposition 8. First, he said, it would protect marriage. Second, he argued, a vote for Proposition 8 would check activist judges; and it is the people's duty to resist judicial tyranny. He heightened the importance of this issue by asserting that checking the threat of judicial tyranny was among "the most important issues" in this particular election.

The *Los Angeles Times,* as well as California's nine other largest newspapers, editorialized against the initiative, arguing:

[T]he California Supreme Court overturned Proposition 22. . . . and ruled that marriage was a fundamental right under the state Constitution. As such, it could not be denied to a protected group—in this case, gay and lesbian couples. . . . Proposition 8 seeks to embed wording in the Constitution that would eliminate the fundamental right to same-sex marriage.

It's a rare and drastic step, invoking the constitutional-amendment process to strip people of rights. Yet in California, it can be done with a simple majority vote. All the more reason for voters to weigh carefully what would be wrought by this measure. . . . [T]he very act of denying gay and lesbian couples the right to marry—traditionally the highest legal and societal recognition of a loving commitment—by definition relegates them and their relationships to second-class status, separate and not all that equal.

To be sure, the court overturned Proposition 22, a vote of the people. That is the court's duty when a law is unconstitutional, even if it is exceedingly popular. Civil rights are commonly hard-won, and not the result of widespread consensus. . . . Californians have accused the state Supreme Court of obstructing the people's will on marriage before—in 1948, when it struck down a ban on interracial marriages.

Fundamental rights are exactly that. They should neither wait for popular acceptance, nor be revoked because it is lacking.[13]

The newspaper advanced two arguments in opposition to Proposition 8: First, marriage is a fundamental right for Californians and, hence, cannot be denied to any group. Second, it is the courts' job to protect fundamental rights from the tyranny of the majority.

As citizens of California listened to this interplay of arguments, they were pushed to form their own conclusions about the law. Even though some voters may

---

[12]Newt Gingrich, "Stop Imperial Judges . . . Support Proposition 8," YouTube, http://www.youtube.com/watch?v=73Q4V8WNF6k (accessed March 19, 2009).

[13]"Reneging on a Right" [editorial], *Los Angeles Times,* August 8, 2008, http://www.latimes.com/news/opinion/la-ed-marriage8-2008aug08%2C0%2C1229155.story (accessed March 19, 2009).

not have come to a firm conclusion, they still had to cast their vote on November 4, 2008. Decisions often are made before people have attained certainty, but a decision can be reconsidered. Proposition 8 passed, but the debates over it have not ceased. Opponents filed court cases to have the law overturned. The California Supreme Court heard oral arguments on those cases on March 5, 2009.[14] An additional ballot initiative was also placed in circulation to replace the word "marriage" with the phrase "domestic partnership" throughout California law.[15]

This continuing argument$_2$ illustrates our second point: argument is contingent. Human beings must make decisions and act even when complete information is lacking. People had to vote on the proposition even though debate had not finished. Thus, people make decisions that are contingent, meaning the conclusions depend on the circumstances and information available at a particular point in time, information which necessarily deals in probabilities and not certainties. These decisions are useful for the time being, but if new information arises, or times change, the conclusions people reach through argument may change.

Even when humans believe they possess all possible information, they still lack certainty. Human beings are not perfect and always possess incomplete knowledge. They often only know what is probable, not certain. That is why the goal of argument is not to achieve absolute certainty about what is true, but to resolve what is probably right and, hence, what should be done. New facts can always emerge, general beliefs change; thus, conclusions can shift. Although arguments may be presented in absolute language, the decisions based on them are not necessarily absolute, final, or the only option. The domain of argument is the probable. Still, a decision reached through argument is better than a decision made randomly.

For example, when you considered which college to attend, you used arguments to make that decision. You gathered information from various schools, came up with reasons why each school was better or worse, and came to a decision based on those information-backed reasons. When people asked you why you chose a particular school, you offered reasons, such as: "the university has a good reputation," "the university is the most affordable," "the school has a good program in the area I want to study," or "the location of the college and the programs it offers suit my interests." All these are reasons why you chose the school, and evidence for your claim that a particular school is best for you. Even if you could never be 100 percent certain that you chose the best college, these reasons enabled you to make a decision that is better than one made randomly.

An example of how the conclusions of *all* arguments are contingent, even arguments about facts, can be found in the recent debates over Pluto. First discovered in 1930, Pluto was demoted from planet status in 2006 when the General Assembly of the International Astronomical Union (IAU) voted to accept a definition of "planet" that would exclude Pluto. Neil deGrasse Tyson, an astrophysicist at the American Museum of Natural History and director of the Hayden Planetarium,

---

[14]All the legal briefs and filings concerning this case can be found at the California Supreme Court website: http://www.courtinfo.ca.gov/courts/supreme/highprofile/ prop8.htm (accessed March 19, 2009).

[15]Initiative 1356 (09-0003), Substitutes Domestic Partnership for Marriage in California Law, Summary Date: 03/09/09, Circulation Deadline: 08/06/09, Signatures Required: 694,354, http://www.sos.ca.gov/elections/elections_j.htm#circ (accessed March 18, 2009).

chronicles Pluto's rise to and fall from planet status.[16] When it was initially discovered, scientists declared the mass of rock and ice to be a planet. It was located where the scientists thought a planet should be, given the orbital path of other planets. However, Pluto was idiosyncratic: it was very small compared to the other planets; its orbit is eccentric (it crosses the orbit of Neptune) and tips more than seventeen degrees from the plane of orbit of other planets in the solar system; and other icy objects share its orbital space. Thus, the claim "Pluto is a planet" was contingent and open to revision as more information became available.

Knowing that even scientific knowledge is contingent, when they planned the new $230-million Rose Center for Earth and Space at the museum, Tyson and other exhibit planners made determinations of the "shelf life of various astrophysical subjects,"[17] in other words, of the degree of reservations attached to various scientific conclusions. Since the Copernican revolution, scientists have possessed a high degree of certainty that the earth revolves around the sun. The exhibit planners were willing to cut such claims into permanent metal displays at the museum,[18] knowing they would have a long shelf life. In the "moderate shelf-life category" resided claims about water on Mars, which were displayed with "replaceable rear-lit transparencies." For knowledge claims with a brief shelf life, the exhibit would show videos that could easily be swapped out.[19]

Given that the subject of argument is the contingent and probable, people need an attitude toward argument that induces a willingness to argue. Just because a conclusion has been reached does not mean it cannot be reconsidered. Thus, the process of argument$_2$ works best when it is a cooperative, rather than combative, process. People need to want to engage in argument, to test ideas, and to work through disagreements.

Unfortunately, argument seems to have been given a bad rap. If you ask someone "Do you want to have an argument?" the other person would probably look at you as if you were crazy. People tend to view arguments as harmful rather than productive. This view is based on misconceptions about argument. People often understand argument through a structural metaphor, which organizes the concept of argument in terms of war. Linguists George Lakoff and Mark Johnson believe this understanding has implications not only for how people talk about argument, but also how they engage in it, for people "conceive of arguments, and execute them, according to the ARGUMENT IS WAR metaphor because the metaphor is built into the conceptual system of the culture in which you live."[20] People involved in argument perceive themselves "as having something to win and something to lose, territory to establish and territory to defend. In a no-holds barred argument, you attack, defend, counterattack, etc."[21] Even in the most systematic, rational arguments, these parallels between war and argument prevail: "There is still a position

[16]Neil deGrasse Tyson, *The Pluto Files: The Rise and Fall of America's Favorite Planet*, (New York: Norton, 2009).

[17]Tyson, *Pluto*, 63.

[18]Tyson, *Pluto*, 64.

[19]Tyson, *Pluto*, 64.

[20]George Lakoff and Mark Johnson, *Metaphors We Live By* (Chicago: University of Chicago Press, 1980), 63–4.

[21]Lakoff and Johnson, *Metaphors*, 62.

to be established and defended, you can win or lose, you have an opponent whose position you attack and try to destroy and whose argument you try to shoot down. If you are completely successful, you can wipe him [or her] out."[22]

Unfortunately, the argument-is-war metaphor works against seeing argument as cooperative. If you think of those with whom you disagree as enemies, your goal is not to communicate with them, but to vanquish them. Concomitantly, they are unlikely to want to talk to you if they are beaten down by the end of every exchange. Argument-is-war induces a worldview in which people who disagree are vicious enemies, opponents are to be vanquished, and the outcome of a dispute is final, without any possibility (or desire) for reliving the fight. For example, is there a person in your life with whom you do not want to argue under any circumstances? That person may not view argument as a way to work through a disagreement, but as a way to emotionally and intellectually beat you down.

Fortunately, argument-is-war is not the only way to view argument. Consider how the way you think about argument would change if you instead used another metaphor: argument-is-play. Viewing argument as play allows you to see how it can be productive and enjoyable. Play is a way in which people learn, cooperate, and experiment. It can be quiet or raucous; a solitary enterprise or a team sport. The outcome is uncertain and the goal is indeterminate, but you'll probably have fun while playing. Just as in play, argument can be a contest with only one winner (as in organized sports) or a form of engagement in which the goal is not to win (as in role-playing or playing house). In play, the goal is not to chase others from the field (or to deter them from even entering the game), but to induce them to join the argument. In play, you do not want to completely defeat your opponent, because you want to play again. The play metaphor represents an attitude adjustment about argument, and can influence the way you engage in the process.

Using the play metaphor, people can frame the argumentative interaction differently. In contrast to a metaphor that uses combat terms, the play metaphor talks about argument in a way that encourages other people to participate. For example, when a difference of ideas occurs during a class, class members can play out an idea to see all its nuances. When a student group is debating what to do, its members can see themselves as all members of the same team, working together to reach a goal.

In a democratic society, participation in argument is essential. Without it, decision making is left in the hands of the few people who are in positions of power. Arguments occur about many topics, with greater or lesser degrees of importance. If the only disagreement that people had with others was about which movie to attend, the world would be a much simpler (and more boring) place, but arguments arise over much graver issues: war and peace, life and death, justice and equality. Aristotle recognized the importance of such topics when he wrote about the subjects of political oratory in his *Rhetoric*. To be equipped to make decisions about these issues, an understanding of argument is essential. The next sections review the parts of an argument$_1$ and introduce the concept of presumption. The final section explores the various ways in which argument$_2$, as an interactional process, occurs in various spheres of argument.

---

[22]Lakoff and Johnson, *Metaphors,* 63.

CLASSICAL CONCEPTIONS

Aristotle's approach to logic has long influenced argument studies. At the heart was the concept of the **syllogism,** *a statement in which a conclusion is inferred from the truth of two premises.* You may have heard of this process as deductive reasoning, which is composed of a major premise, a minor premise, and a conclusion. In a perfect syllogism, the major premise speaks to a universal truth.

The minor premise speaks to a specific example of the universal. The conclusion is the result of combining the two premises.

> Major premise: All human beings are mortal.
> Minor premise: John is a human being.
> Conclusion: John is mortal.

The conclusion of a formal syllogism is certain only if the premises are certain. Of course, because humans are fallible, virtually no premise can be absolutely certain.

An example of deductive reasoning can be found in congressional arguments that genocide was committed in Darfur, Sudan. In July 2004, the US House of Representatives considered Concurrent Resolution 467 "Declaring Genocide in Darfur, Sudan."[23] The Resolution opened by citing the first three Articles of the 1948 United Nations Convention on the Prevention and Punishment of the Crime of Genocide. In particular, it quoted the definition of genocide in Article 2:

> genocide means any of the following acts committed with the intent to destroy, in whole or in part, a national, ethnical, racial or religious group, as such: (a) killing members of the group; (b) causing serious bodily or mental harm to members of the group; (c) deliberately inflicting on the group conditions of life calculated to bring about its physical destruction in whole or in part; (d) imposing measures intended to prevent births within the group; and (e) forcibly transferring children of the group to another group.

The Resolution then cites evidence that "an estimated 30,000 innocent civilians have been brutally murdered, more than 130,000 people have been forced from their homes and have fled to neighboring Chad, and more than 1,000,000 people have been internally displaced," killing, causing harm, and inflicting destructive life conditions being elements of genocide. The conclusion of the Resolution "declares that the atrocities unfolding in Darfur, Sudan, are genocide." The Resolution passed in the House with a vote of 422-0 and in the Senate by a voice vote. Within a year, President George W. Bush would call the events in Darfur genocide, breaking with the United Nations, which considered the killings to be crimes against humanity but did not think they rose to the level of genocide.[24]

Notice how the Resolution uses deductive reasoning. It begins by establishing a major premise regarding actions that constitute genocide. Next it develops the minor premise by citing specific instances fitting within the definition

---

[23]US Congress. House., 108th Cong., 2d sess. H. Con. Res. 467.

[24]Jim VandeHei, "In Break With U.N., Bush Calls Sudan Killings Genocide," *Washington Post,* June 2, 2005, http://www.washingtonpost.com/wp-dyn/content/article/2005/06/01/AR2005060101725.html (accessed February 22, 2011).

of genocide. Finally, it concludes that these actions are genocidal. The argument moves from the general major premise, through the instances of the minor premise, to a conclusion.

Aristotle recognized that people typically do not speak in formal syllogisms, especially because human beings rarely can be certain of their premises. Thus, he developed the enthymeme, which he defined as a "rhetorical syllogism."[25] Although much scholarly debate exists over exactly what Aristotle meant by the term, the definition we find most helpful is offered by communication scholar Lloyd Bitzer, who says that an **enthymeme** is *"a syllogism based on probabilities, signs, and examples, whose function is rhetorical persuasion. Its successful construction is accomplished through the joint efforts of the speaker and audience, and this is its essential character."*[26] What most distinguishes the enthymeme is not its form or content, but the process through which it is constructed—jointly by the speaker and the audience. Often the speaker will leave some of the premises unspoken so that the audience fills them in. Bitzer argues the process of co-construction makes the enthymeme extremely persuasive because *"the audience itself helps construct the proofs by which it is persuaded."*[27] The concept of enthymeme also suggests that the distinction between argument$_1$ and argument$_2$ may be too rigid. The making of an argument$_1$ can also be interactive.

Enthymemes are widely used. Advertising slogans, political campaigns, and conversations with friends often rely on enthymemes. People do not systematically lay out every premise, but rely on shared beliefs and values to fill them in. An illustration of how the audience fills in reasoning can help to clarify how enthymemes function. In 1991, Gatorade developed a marketing campaign featuring Michael Jordan, arguably the greatest basketball player of all time. The slogan of the campaign is "Be Like Mike." The commercial features highlights of Jordan playing basketball and drinking Gatorade, interspersed with images of regular people playing basketball, while the "Be Like Mike" jingle plays in the background." The commercial ends with the slogan "Be Like Mike. Drink Gatorade."[28]

Given that the Gatorade marketing campaign was one of the most successful in history, it is reasonable to conclude that many members of the audience complete the reasoning by filling in the principle that, if you mimic the behavior of another person, you become more like that person.[29] The power of the campaign occurs largely because the reasoning is left for the audience to provide. If made explicit, the reasoning becomes suspect. If members of the audience were told that by drinking Gatorade, they would become better basketball players, they would obviously be skeptical. When allowed to fill in the reasoning on their own, they are more likely to accept it.

---

[25]Aristotle, *On Rhetoric*, 1.2 [1356].

[26]Lloyd F. Bitzer, "Aristotle's Enthymeme Revisited," *Quarterly Journal of Speech* 45, no. 4 (December 1959): 399–408, 408, italics added. See also Thomas M. Conley, "The Enthymeme in Perspective," *Quarterly Journal of Speech* 70 (1984): 168–187.

[27]Bitzer, "Aristotle's Enthymeme," 408.

[28]The full video is on YouTube at http://www.youtube.com/watch?v=b0AGiq9j_Ak (accessed October 12, 2011).

[29]Darren Rovell, *First in Thirst: How Gatorade Turned the Science of Sweat into a Cultural Phenomenon* (New York: AMACOM, 2005).

Enthymemes consistently appear in presidential campaign rhetoric, as candidates tap into beliefs shared by the people they see as their base.[30] During the 2007 primary for the Republican presidential nomination, Mitt Romney's campaign aired a sixty-second spot known as the "Ocean" advertisement.[31] Within the advertisement, Romney voices over the image of waves crashing on a beach as children play on the shoreline. He begins by referring to a *Wall Street Journal* editorial, penned by Reagan speechwriter Peggy Noonan in the wake of the 1999 Columbine shootings, in which she described contemporary culture as "the ocean in which our children swim" and a "culture of death," full of television, radio, magazines, and newspapers that bombard children with images of violence and sex, and said, "The boys who did the killing, the famous Trench Coat Mafia, inhaled too deep the ocean in which they swam."[32] Extending Noonan's metaphor of ocean, Romney explains he wants to: "clean up the water" where people swim. He also wants to limit Internet pornography, drugs, and violence on TV and in video games. The advertisement concludes with the simple statement: "Mitt Romney. President."[33]

The unspoken part of the enthymeme—the part the audience is asked to fill in—is that any person who wants to clean up the culture should be supported in a bid for the presidency and that Romney is more committed to doing these things than any of the other Republican candidates. The advertisement also relies on the audience to fill in the premise that controlling pornography, drugs, sex, and violence on TV should be one of the primary goals of the president. The spoken part of the argument is that Mitt Romney would like to control pornography, drugs, and violence on TV. The main conclusion (contained in the slogan that ends the advertisement) is: you should vote for Mitt Romney for president of the United States.

The process of arguing can involve a variety of strategies. The central question is: how can you know when you have presented (or heard) a good argument? In order to present a coherent argument$_1$, you must be able to: (1) provide any parts of the argument for which other people ask or about which they are uncertain, and (2) understand what type of claim you are advancing and what type of data are needed to support that claim.

THE TOULMIN MODEL

Philosopher Stephen Toulmin was troubled by the inadequacy of the syllogism as a model for actual argument in which premises are never certain.[34] For instance, a person may understand the data offered and the conclusion advocated, but not *why* that particular data supports the conclusion. Toulmin believed an explanation

---

[30]Kathleen Hall Jamieson, Erika Falk, and Susan Sherr, "The Enthymeme Gap in the 1996 Presidential Campaign," *PS: Political Science and Politics* 32, no. 1 (March 1999): 12–16.

[31]The spot can be viewed on YouTube, at http://www.youtube.com/watch?v=vFyDWjATbok (accessed November 7, 2007).

[32]Peggy Noonan, "The Culture of Death," *Wall Street Journal* (April 22, 1999), http://peggynoonan.com/article.php?article=40 (accessed February 20, 2011).

[33]Script for "Ocean," http://www.mittromney.com/News/Press-Releases/Ocean_Ad (accessed November 7, 2007).

[34]Stephen Toulmin, *The Uses of Argument* (Cambridge, UK: Cambridge University Press, 1969), 130.

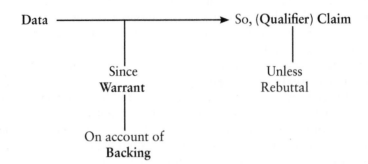

Data ──────────────────► So, (Qualifier) Claim

Since
Warrant

Unless
Rebuttal

On account of
Backing

of the relationship between the data and the conclusion was needed. He developed a description of argument patterns composed of the following parts: claim, data, warrant, qualifications, backing, and conditions for rebuttal. Based on Toulmin's work, argument scholars Wayne Brockriede and Douglas Ehninger developed a model that we adapt here:[35]

PARTS OF ARGUMENT₁

Toulmin defines the claim as "*the conclusion whose merits we are seeking to establish,*"[36] or what the rhetor is trying to persuade the audience to believe. For example, Mark Jenkins, the author of the article about the gorillas, claims "Poachers had not killed them."[37] Because neither he nor the readers were present when the gorillas were killed, he had to provide data for that claim.

Argumentation scholars distinguish between four types of claim: fact, definition, value, and policy. A **claim of fact** is what it sounds like, *a claim that advances an empirically verifiable statement*. Say, for example, Jo shot and killed Sam. In a courtroom, the claim of fact might be: "Jo ended Sam's life." Evidence to support such a claim likely would include Sam's body, the murder weapon, and testimony that Jo was the one to use the weapon against Sam. (Although the claim is called a claim of fact, it is possible that it will be disputed or controversial.)

A **claim of definition** is *a claim that identifies how a concept or term should be defined*. Definitions enable people to make distinctions among things that at first glance might appear quite similar. In the legal realm, various labels and definitions are applied to the act of one person taking the life of another. If Jo shot and killed Sam, the act could be defined as self-defense, manslaughter, first-degree murder, or second-degree murder. Courts establish criteria to determine when an act meets a particular definition, then apply them to the particular act to determine which crime, if any, was committed. For example, when a woman kills a boyfriend or husband who has battered her, it was once considered murder, and often first-degree murder, because her action was premeditated and with intent to cause death.

---

[35]Wayne Brockriede and Douglas Ehninger, "Toulmin on Argument: An Interpretation and Application," *Quarterly Journal of Speech 46*, no. 1 (February 1960): 44–53.

[36]Toulmin, *The Uses*, 97, italics added.

[37]Jenkins, "Who Murdered," 45.

As people better understood domestic abuse and accepted the concept of "battered-wife syndrome," they have come to see women who kill their abusers as acting in self-defense.[38] By definition, what these women did changed from murder to self-defense, although the act was factually the same.

A **claim of value** is *a claim that advances a statement about what is worthy.* A claim of value may be based on arguments about what is good or bad, just or unjust, right or wrong, or beautiful or ugly. Such claims are not empirically verifiable; instead, they are based on the judgments of the audience. People often assume that killing another person is wrong, but in some instances killing another person is generally considered acceptable. If Jo killed Sam in self-defense, it would not be considered wrong. Of course, what constitutes self-defense is not self-evident. The arguments about when taking another life should not be punished are arguments about claims of value.

Finally, a **claim of policy** is *a claim that addresses what should be done.* A claim of policy usually contains the words "should" or "ought to." It is up to legislators to determine what the appropriate punishment should be for each type of crime, although juries and judges have some discretion. For example, "The death penalty should be the punishment for first-degree murder" is a claim of policy. Embedded within a claim of policy is a complex series of related arguments, wherein the arguer establishes that a significant problem exists, the proposed policy can solve the problem, the benefits of the policy outweigh any potential costs, and the policy is necessary given the limits of alternative solutions.

Most extended arguments include all of these types of claims. Distinguishing between types of claims can help you figure out what is really at issue. For example, if you wanted to organize a debate about global warming on your campus, the first thing you would need to figure out is whether you want the debate to be about a question of fact (is human activity the primary cause of global warming?), a question of policy (should the federal government enact higher fuel efficiency standards for autos in order to reduce global warming?), or a claim of value (is stopping global warming more important than preserving our fossil fuel—based economy?).

The example that began this chapter is an illustration of claims of definition, which play a central role in debate. Before you could answer the question of fact, "who murdered the Virunga gorillas?" you would first need to answer the definitional question of whether killing a gorilla is murder. The way claims of definition complicate public debate is also illustrated by the controversy over regulating pornography and obscenity. Before you can debate a question of fact (does viewing pornography encourage men to accept rape myths?), a question of value (is pornography morally wrong?), or a question of policy (should pornography be regulated through civil or criminal law?), you need to first figure out what "pornography" is. Is "pornography" best defined by activist Andrea Dworkin and legal scholar Catharine MacKinnon as "the graphic sexually explicit subordination of women through pictures and/or words,"[39] or by the US Supreme Court as that

---

[38]Lauren K. Fernandez, "Battered Woman Syndrome," *Georgetown Journal of Gender and the Law* 8 (2007): 235–250.

[39]Andrea Dworkin and Catharine A. MacKinnon, *Pornography & Civil Rights: A New Day for Women's Equality* (Minneapolis: Organizing Against Pornography, 1988), 138–139.

which "the average person, applying contemporary community standards would find … taken as a whole, appeals to prurient interest";[40] or is it just speech like other speech? Depending on how you define the term, you would answer the questions of fact, value, and policy differently.

Toulmin describes **data** as the "*information on which the claim is based.*"[41] Data are sometimes referred to as evidence or supporting materials. Jenkins's description of the gorillas provides data to support the claim that poachers were not at fault: infants were left clinging to their dead mothers; and the gorillas' bodies had not been cut up after death.

Supplying incorrect or insufficient data to support a claim is an example of bad argument. Improperly collected statistics, poorly chosen examples, or quotations that are taken out of context are some of the ways in which evidence can be incorrect. For instance, an argument may rely on a public opinion poll, but the statistics summarizing the poll may not be useful if the poll was not properly conducted. Many television news programs conduct call-in polls in which viewers are encouraged to call and vote. The results cannot be generalized to the entire public, because only those people watching that particular news show and sufficiently interested in the topic will participate.[42] The data generated is not necessarily representative of the entire population's opinions.

Someone might also present a bad argument by providing insufficient evidence to justify the claim. When you reason from example, you must provide a sufficient number of examples before you can warrant a generalization. Almost everyone knows someone who has lived a long life in spite of a less-than-healthy lifestyle. If you were to justify smoking cigarettes and eating a poor diet on the basis of one person, you would be engaging in a hasty generalization. If Jenkins based his claim that poachers had not killed the gorillas on the data that only one of the seven gorillas was left unscathed, he would have provided insufficient data.

The need to guard against accepting a claim supported by insufficient data is demonstrated by social satirist Stephen Colbert's concept of *truthiness*. Selected by *Merriam-Webster's Dictionary* as the Word of the Year 2006, *truthiness* is defined as "1: 'truth that comes from the gut, not books' (Stephen Colbert, Comedy Central's *The Colbert Report*, October 2005) 2: 'the quality of preferring concepts or facts one wishes to be true, rather than concepts or facts known to be true' (American Dialect Society; January 2006)."[43] Colbert explains further: "It used to be, everyone was entitled to their own opinion, but not their own facts. But that's not the case anymore. Facts matter not at all. Perception is everything. It's certainty."[44] Colbert is being humorous; but he is also making a serious point. Too frequently, people jump to conclusions based on an impulsive reaction without researching the facts and sometimes, even despite facts.

---

[40]U.S. Supreme Court, *Paris Adult Theatre I et al.* (413 U.S. 24) 1973.

[41]Toulmin, *The Uses*, 97, italics added.

[42]Muzzio, Doug, "The Savvy Voter: Analyze a Poll," PBS's By *The People: Election* 2004, http://www.pbs.org/elections/savvyanalyze.html (accessed January 22, 2009).

[43]"Truthiness," Merriam-Webster's Words of the Year 2006, http://www.merriam-webster.com/info/06words.htm (accessed January 22, 2009).

[44]Stephen Colbert, interview by Nathan Rabin, January 25, 2006, http://www.avclub.com/articles/stephen-colbert,13970 (accessed January 22, 2009).

To avoid this reliance on unjustified opinion, when presented with a claim, you need to ask: What data support this claim? Simply saying that you "feel" something is true is not sufficient. Why does Jenkin's description of the condition of the dead gorillas serve as data proving poachers were not involved?

Toulmin describes **warrants** as *bridges, or the generalizable "rules" and "principles" that link the data to the claim*.[45] Warrants show that the jump from the data to the conclusion is reasonable, that the conclusion is warranted. Jenkins uses empiricial knowledge about poaching to connect his data to his claim: "Poachers who prey on gorillas leave an unmistakable calling card: They kidnap the infants and cut off the heads and hands of the adults—to be sold on the black market."[46] Thus, if the "calling card" was not present, the killers were not poachers.

Toulmin explains warrants are needed because a listener may not understand why the data provides proof of a claim. For example, last summer, John told his spouse, "I need new golf clubs (claim). The grooves on my irons are smooth (data)." To him, that was sufficient. However, his spouse did not understand the connection and asked, "What does that mean?" John then explained the warrant: grooves are what put spin on the golf ball, and the spin is what makes the ball stop on the green. Thus, when the grooves are smooth, it is time to get new clubs. Happily, John got his new golf clubs.

The rhetor provides the warrant by explaining why the data warrants the conclusion. Some warrants, however, are faulty. For example, people often assume that because one thing happened after another, the first thing caused the second. (This assumption is called the *post hoc ergo propter hoc* fallacy.) If you have a superstition, chances are it is based on this error in reasoning. If you claim you always do better on a test if you go to a movie the night before, you probably have based your claim on faculty reasoning. Just because the movie came before the successful test does not mean it caused the successful test. Thus, the warrant "when a thing happens after another, the thing is caused by the event preceding it" is flawed. This mistake is common because it is difficult to distinguish causation from correlation. Correlation is found when two events happen at about the same time, but one does not necessarily cause the other.

For Toulmin, **conditions of rebuttal** indicate "*circumstances in which the general authority of the warrant should be set aside.*[47] Conditions of rebuttal provide reasons why the argument may not be correct and offer challenges to the data or the strength of the warrant. In the gorilla story, one condition of rebuttal might be that the poachers were interrupted before they could "kidnap" the infant or take the hands and feet. That condition seems unlikely, however, given that the killings happened over many days.

Toulmin defines **qualifiers** as *those statements indicating the "strength conferred by the warrant.*"[48] Not all claims have the same level of certainty. The level is often determined by the strength of the conditions of rebuttal. Claims can be qualified with terms such as "usually," "possibly," "likely," "in all probability,"

---

[45]Toulmin, *The Uses*, 98, italics added.

[46]Jenkins, "Who Murdered," 45.

[47]Toulmin, *The Uses*, 101, italics added.

[48]Toulmin, *The Uses*, 101, italics added.

"presumably," and "always." Notice that each qualifier represents different levels of certainty.

One of the best examples of using qualifiers in argument is a weather report. Meteorologists make an argument when forecasting tomorrow's weather. They claim the weather will be of a particular type, based on the data from weather stations, models, and radar. Usually, meteorologists will qualify a forecast with a probability; for example, "there is a 50 percent chance of rain tomorrow." We might say: "it will *probably* rain tomorrow." That is a different claim from "it will *certainly* rain tomorrow" (a claim few, if any, meteorologists would ever make).

Jenkins provides no qualifiers in his essay. He does not say: "Poachers probably had not killed the gorillas." Instead, his is an unequivocal statement: "Poachers had not killed them."

Finally, Toulmin describes **backing** as *assurances that the warrants are authoritative and/or current*. The backing says the warrant is supported. Usually, backing will provide an answer to the conditions of rebuttal. Although Jenkins provides no explicit backing for his description of poaching, if pressed he could likely point to studies and past experiences with poaching. In other words, his warrant is based on inductive reasoning, which is based on his accumulated experience of poaching.

In discursive form, an example of an argument$_1$ that contains all the parts of the Toulmin model would read as follows:

> The Smithsonian American Art Museum displays quilts as art (data), so a quilt is a form of art (claim) almost always (qualifier), unless the quilt is machine-made (conditions of rebuttal), given the Smithsonian Institute is a qualified arbiter of what constitutes art (warrant) because it is the nationally endowed museum of the United States (backing).

Just as most arguments are not formal syllogisms, arguments are not usually laid out following Toulmin's pattern. You will have to figure out the components. (As this example demonstrates, rigidly following the Toulmin model results in overly complex sentences.)

What would an argument containing the elements of the Toulmin model look like in prose form? What follows is an argument that Elizabeth Cady Stanton advanced in 1892 in a speech to the Committee of the Judiciary of the United States Congress. Her "Solitude of Self" speech is fascinating because it provides a philosophical foundation for granting women the right to vote.[49] As you read the following passage, which outlines her argument, notice how it fulfills each part of argument Toulmin identifies.

> The strongest reason for giving woman all the opportunities for higher education, for the full development of her faculties, forces of mind and body; for giving her the most enlarged freedom of thought and action; a complete emancipation from all forms of bondage, of custom, dependence, superstition; from all the crippling influences of fear, is the solitude and personal responsibility of her own individual life. The strongest reason why we ask for woman a voice in the government under which she lives; in the religion she is asked to believe;

---

[49]For an analysis of the speech, see Karlyn Kohrs Campbell, "The Humanistic Underpinnings of Feminism: 'The Solitude of Self,'" *Man Cannot Speak for Her* vol. 1 (New York: Praeger, 1989).

equality in social life, where she is the chief factor; a place in the trades and professions, where she may earn her bread, is because of her birthright to self-sovereignty; because, as an individual, she must rely on herself. No matter how much women prefer to lean, to be protected and supported, nor how much men desire to have them do so, they must make the voyage of life alone, and for safety in an emergency they must know something of the laws of navigation. To guide our own craft, we must be captain, pilot, engineer; with chart and compass to stand at the wheel; to match the wind and waves and know when to take in the sail, and to read the signs in the firmament over all. It matters not whether the solitary voyager is man or woman.[50]

Stanton's argument could be broken down as follows:

Qualifier, Claim: "woman [should be given] all the opportunities for higher education . . . a complete emancipation from . . . all the crippling influences of fear." In this passage, "all . . . most enlarged . . . complete" make clear the claim is unqualified; Stanton does not recognize a less than exhaustive application.

Data: "the solitude and personal responsibility of her own individual life"

Warrant: each person has a "birthright to self-sovereignty"

Backing: "as an individual, she must rely on herself"

Rebuttal: Stanton anticipates that someone might argue "women prefer to lean" on men, so she says "No matter how much women prefer to lean" they ought to experience full freedom.

Because Stanton delivered this speech toward the end of her career, after decades of debate on the issue of woman suffrage, it makes sense that she would deliver the argument₁ in its most complete form. As people engage in argument₂ and are challenged to explain themselves, the various parts of an argument₁ are filled in. In other words, argument₂ usually is necessary to call forth a complete argument₁.

Knowing the parts of an argument₁ will help you understand what a person is arguing, become better at constructing an argument, and understand where you disagree with someone. For example, is the disagreement on the level of the data or the warrant? The answer allows you to locate the point of disagreement. Knowing the parts of an argument also helps you critique and analyze an argument. You can understand whether someone is making a warranted argument; that is, you can determine whether a rhetor's claim is supported by data and reasons, or parts of the argument are missing.

This knowledge also will help you understand when people introduce an argument that is irrelevant–that does not speak to the claim, data, or warrant, but introduces an irrelevant issue. For example, *ad hominem* attacks are arguments against the person making the claim that are irrelevant to the claim. The title of Al Franken's 1999 book, *Rush Limbaugh is a Big Fat Idiot,*[51] contains an ad hominem attack. Even if some of Limbaugh's arguments are wrong, Franken cannot demonstrate

---

[50]Elizabeth Cady Stanton, "The Solitude of Self," *Man Cannot Speak for Her,* vol. 2, ed. Karlyn Kohrs Campbell (New York: Praeger, 1989), 373.

[51]Al Franken, *Rush Limbaugh Is a Big Fat Idiot* (New York: Dell, 1996).

this by highlighting Limbaugh's girth or by calling him an idiot. If someone attacks you, rather than a part of your argument, you could point out that the attack is irrelevant: your claim is still warranted.

Ad hominem arguments are not always irrelevant. During the 2007 presidential primary campaign, they can be seen not only in verbal comments, but also in multimodal forms, such as YouTube videos. In what is considered the first video to go viral during that campaign, ParkRidge47 (Phillip de Vellis) posted an attack advertisement against Hillary Clinton and supporting Barack Obama, titled "Vote Different."[52] A mashup of the famous "Apple/1984" advertisement,[53] the "Vote Different" video replaces the original advertisement's image of a movie screen, showing a male face speaking to undifferentiated and gray-clad masses, with a screen showing Hillary Clinton's face.[54] In both advertisements, amid the wash of gray, sprints a woman in red and white running shorts and top. At the end of the ad, she flings a sledgehammer at the screen, smashing it and freeing the masses. The original commercial ended with the January launch date of the Macintosh computer and a hint that this is a reason why 1984 will differ from George Orwell's *1984.* The mashup remake ends with a reference to *1984,* then jumps to a simple graphic "BarackObama.com" accompanied by a mashup of the Apple and Obama logos.

The advertisement represents an ad hominem attack insofar as it does not offer an assessment of Hillary Clinton's policies, but instead creates a visual analogy between Clinton and the controlling face and voice of the Orwellian dystopia. The mashup wants you to see Clinton as controlling and dangerous.

When a question of character is at issue, or when arguers claim they should be believed because of their characters (in other words, their characters are what warrants their arguments), ad hominem arguments become relevant. Particularly in contemporary politics, when candidates run on their personalities and images as much as on their political positions, arguments concerning their characters become highly relevant.[55] To the extent that Hillary Clinton's campaign argued she was the better candidate because her experience formed her character as presidential, the advertisement had a point. It argued one could engage in politics as usual, voting for a person perceived to be part of the Washington establishment, or one could "vote different."

A statement that sounds as if it has all of the parts of a complete argument does not necessarily justify assent. It may provide bad data. A warrant may be nonsensical. A qualification may not be strong enough. The connections between the data, claim, and warrant may be weak. Not only must people be able to identify the parts of an argument, they also need to be able to assess the strength of those parts.

---

[52]Chris Cillizza, "Creator of Hillary Attack Ad Speaks," washingtonpost.com Politics Blog, March 30, 2007, http://blog.washingtonpost.com/thefix/2007/03/author_of_hillary_attack_ad_sp.html (accessed November 21, 2007).

[53]"1984 Apple's Macintosh Commercial," YouTube video, http://www.youtube.com/watch?v=OYecfV3 ubP8 (accessed November 21, 2007).

[54]"Vote Different," You Tube video, http://www.youtube.com/watch?v=6h3G-1MZxjo (accessed November 21, 2007).

[55]John F. Cragan and Craig W. Cutbirth, "A Revisionist Perspective on Political *Ad Hominem* Argument: A Case Study," *Central States Speech Journal* 35, no. 4 (Winter 1984): 228–237.

Argument Fields

Although a complete argument ought to contain all the component parts outlined by Toulmin, not all arguments sound alike. An argument between friends about what movie to see proceeds differently from an argument in a legislative hearing about what regulations ought to be placed on movies. In a debate between friends, the argument "It's my turn to pick," may be perfectly reasonable, but a legislator who said "It's my turn to have a law passed" would likely be laughed out of the assembly. The idea that the norms and rules of argument change from field to field was introduced most completely by Toulmin. He explains that an **argument field** is *an argument type in which the types of data used and conclusions reached are of the same logical type.* Arguments "come from different fields when the backing or the conclusions in . . . arguments are not of the same logical type."[56] The elements involved in argument (claim, data, warrant, and so on) do not change, regardless of the field in which the argument occurs, but the criteria for examining an argument do vary. As examples of field dependent argument, Toulmin points to argument in the fields of law, marine biology, and mathematics, which are field dependent because they each use different types of data and warrants to support claims. In law, citing previous court decisions as precedent is a central way to provide data, but court decisions would be unpersuasive at a presentation on marine biology. All fields require data and the other parts of the Toulmin model, but what counts as legitimate data, warrants, and so on, varies from field to field.

PRESUMPTION AND BURDEN OF PROOF

Regardless of the type of claim, your argument will not take place in a vacuum. All arguments have claims and data that precede them; thus, audience members are predisposed to believe one side more than the other. Presumption as a concept was developed in 1830 by Richard Whately, Anglican Archbishop of Dublin, in his book *Elements of Rhetoric.* Whately defines **presumption** as *a predisposition to believe that a claim is correct until overwhelming evidence proves otherwise.*[57] This definition makes clear that arguments do not occur in a political or social vacuum; instead, as rhetorical scholar Karen Whedbee explains, they are "'grounded' within a context of commonly accepted opinions, practices, and institutions."[58] Whately's view is that the most commonly and widely held ideas deserve presumption and should only be set aside if there is good reason to do so.

The Pluto controversy described earlier contains appeals to presumption, with defenders of Pluto arguing that until exploratory missions had flown to Pluto and "additional factual details" were uncovered, Pluto should remain a planet.[59]

---

[56]Toulmin, *The Uses,* 14, italics added.

[57]Richard Whately, "From *Elements of Rhetoric, The Rhetorical Tradition,*" in *The Rhetorical Tradition: Readings from Classical Times to the Present,* ed. Patricia Bizzell and Bruce Herzberg (Boston: Bedford, 1990), 846–847.

[58]Karen Whedbee, "Authority, Freedom and Liberal Judgment: The Presumptions and Presumptuousness of Whately, Mill and Tocqueville," *Quarterly Journal of Speech* 84 (1998): 176.

[59]Julian Kane, quoted in Tyson, *Pluto,* 66.

One Pluto defender articulated a particularly strong presumption for maintaining Pluto's planet status: "I believe that until we land on Pluto and find incontrovertible evidence that that world does not wish to be called a planet, that we should leave things as they are."[60] Despite substantial evidence that Pluto is not like other planets, Plutophiles argued that overwhelming evidence was necessary to overcome the presumption that Pluto was, indeed, a planet.

Whately also explained the relationship between presumption and the **burden of proof,** or *the obligation to offer reasons sufficient to overcome presumption.* Whately claimed that the burden of proof "lies on the side of him [or her] who would dispute" the claim presumed correct.[61] Burden of proof is an important concept for determining when you should assent to a claim that another person advances. The burden of proof lies on people who support ideas that lack presumption.

People most commonly hear of presumption and burden of proof in relation to courts of law. The accused are "presumed innocent." This does not mean they *are* innocent, or that they are more likely innocent than not. Instead, it means that before anyone concludes the accused is guilty, the prosecution must meet its burden to prove the accused is guilty. Presumption is almost always fixed and unchanging in a criminal court of law. Presumption can be overcome and the burden of proof fulfilled if the prosecution provides evidence proving guilt beyond a reasonable doubt, but it cannot shift (unless there is a defense such as insanity, in which case the defense bears the burden of proving insanity).

In other debates, presumption may not be predetermined. In fact, debate can begin with where presumption rests and who, then, carries the burden of proof. Often, arguers spend time establishing that presumption is on their side, and that if any doubt exists in the audience's mind, the audience should side with them. For example, people who oppose abortion often appeal to presumption about when life begins. In a 1988 speech, then-President Ronald W. Reagan advanced a presumption appeal when he said: "Isn't there enough evidence for even skeptics to admit that those who assert the personhood of the fetus may be right? And if we are to err, shouldn't it be on the side of life?"[62] In other words, President Reagan was arguing that unless overwhelming evidence is presented that proves otherwise, people must assume a fetus is a full person. This appeal does not prove abortion is wrong because the fetus is a person, but instead seeks to sway those who may be uncertain about the fetus's personhood.

Another example of a presumption appeal comes from the debates over the 2003 invasion of Iraq, which was justified by the claim that Saddam Hussein possessed weapons of mass destruction (WMDs). As time passed and no WMDs were found, administration officials were pressured to justify the invasion. On August 5, 2003, Secretary of Defense Donald Rumsfeld held a Pentagon press briefing. When asked why the United States had not yet found the weapons that were the reason for the war, he answered: "as we all know, the absence of evidence is not evidence

---

[60]David Levy, quoted in Tyson, *Pluto,* 100.

[61]Whately, *"Elements,"* 847, italics added.

[62]Ronald W. Reagan, *Weekly Compilation of Presidential Documents* (Washington, DC: GAO, 1988), 74.

of absence."[63] This statement clearly located presumption with those who believed Saddam Hussein possessed WMDs. According to Rumsfeld, the burden of proof was not on those who believed weapons existed, but on those who argued that they did not.

SPHERES OF ARGUMENT

Although many arguments in which you engage on a daily basis may be technical (such as the communication in a classroom as you discuss specialized scholarly articles) or personal (such as the interpersonal interactions you have with friends), one purpose of this book is to orient your thinking about communication toward a public sensibility. How can people resolve disagreements about public issues such as global warming, immigration, the war in Iraq, abortion, or desegregation? To understand the dynamics of public argument, it helps to understand the distinctions between the processes of public, personal, and technical argument.

Philosopher Chaïm Perelman emphasizes that arguments are always addressed to an audience.[64] Although people often think of the strength of an argument in terms of how well it will convince a **universal audience,** that is, *an audience composed of all reasonable and competent members of humanity,* the reality is that people address arguments to **particular audiences,** or *actual audiences.*[65] The debate between creationism/intelligent design and evolution provides an example. For scientists, only peer-reviewed scientific data count when determining which theories should be taught; thus, citing evidence from the Bible to explain creation would be unpersuasive to an audience of scientists. In contrast, evidence from the Bible might be sufficient to persuade a religious audience that data from nonscientists pointing to intelligent design should be taught as a theory. In each case, the arguers are addressing particular audiences. Arguments are different according to their audiences and purposes (resolving a technical dispute, working through a personal issue, or developing public policy.)

Communication scholar G. Thomas Goodnight recognizes that the persuasiveness of an argument and the form it takes depend on the sphere of argument in which it occurs.[66] According to Goodnight, **spheres of argument** are *"branches of activity—the grounds upon which arguments are built and the authorities to which arguers appeal."*[67] Goodnight recognizes that what is persuasive depends on the purpose of the argument. To explain how different grounds for argument emerge, Goodnight posits three spheres of argument: personal, technical, and public. He

---

[63]Donald Rumsfeld, "DoD News Briefing—Secretary Rumsfeld and Gen. Myers," August 5, 2003, United States Department of Defense, http://www.defenselink.mil/transcripts/2003/tr20030805-secdef0525.html (accessed January 13, 2005).

[64]Chaïm Perelman, *The Realm of Rhetoric,* trans. William Kluback (Note Dame, IN: University of Note Dame Press, 1982), 9–20.

[65]Perelman, *The Realm,* 14.

[66]G. Thomas Goodnight, "The Personal, Technical, and Public Spheres of Argument: A Speculative Inquiry into the Art of Public Deliberation," *Argumentation and Advocacy* 18 (Spring 1982): 214–227.

[67]Goodnight, "The Personal," 216, italics added.

argues that particular warrants and data count differently depending on the sphere in which they are argued.

Think about the last time you and friends were talking. What did you talk about? Music? Your favorite TV show? The newest movie? What a friend should do about a family conflict? You and your friends may have covered a range of topics, from arts to interpersonal relations. It is doubtful that any of you declared another friend incapable of speaking about a topic because s/he was unqualified. The next day, probably no one in your group remembered the specific arguments. Your experience in this instance is an example of the **personal sphere,** *the place where the most informal arguments occur, among a small number of people, involving limited demands for proof, and often about private topics.*

Argument in the personal sphere tends to be ephemeral, meaning it is not preserved. No preparation is required. Many things count as evidence, which is pulled from memory. All topics are open to discussion even if the participants have no special knowledge about them. Expertise is not necessary; anyone can talk on any subject. The test of what constitutes a valid argument in the personal sphere is truthfulness: are the people with whom you disagree honestly representing their beliefs? The time limits imposed probably have nothing to do with the nature of the disagreement, and more to do with when people must leave. Ultimately, the relationships involved do not require agreement among everyone.

Contrast this to the **technical sphere,** *the argument sphere that has explicit rules for argument and is judged by those with specific expertise in the subject.* An example of a technical sphere argument occurs any time medical professionals try to publish their scholarship in a specialized journal such as *Journal of the American Medical Association* or *The Lancet.* Technical arguments are judged by referees, or peer reviewers, who have special expertise in the area being discussed. When the arguments are deemed valuable, they are preserved and published. Other members of the specialized medical community may then join the discussion.

The function of this type of argument is, as Goodnight states, to "advance a special kind of knowledge."[68] It takes special expertise to contribute to a technical dispute. It also takes special expertise to read or understand it. Terms, phrasings, and the complexity of the argument make it relatively inaccessible to anyone not trained in medicine. The argument in a medical essay may be difficult for you to follow because the data being used is unknown to you, or because the warrants were left unstated and you did not know how to provide them.

Another example of technical argument can be found in courts of law. Judges oversee disputes between trained lawyers and must themselves possess special expertise in order to apply the rules of argument fairly. Lawyers must not only have received training, they must also have passed a test (the bar exam) that deemed them competent to practice law. Very specific rules govern who may speak, when they may speak, and what they may say. The proceedings are recorded. Not all evidence counts. (For example, hearsay evidence is usually excluded in criminal cases.) The ultimate authority for determining punishment is the law; a jury may decide a case, but its decision is bound by the rules of law and the judge's instructions. Many

---

[68]Goodnight, "The Personal," 219.

times, the test of argument in the technical sphere is truth, either in terms of objective facts or in terms of which claim best approximates people's understanding of the world.

In many ways, the technical and personal spheres of argument represent two extremes. The **public sphere** is *the argument sphere that exists "to handle disagreements transcending personal and technical disputes."*[69] Ultimately, the issue at hand is broader than the needs of a group of friends or of a specialized technical community. For example, arguments about whether the university should raise tuition, a parking ramp is the best way to solve the parking problem downtown, or the local school bond referendum should be passed are all public sphere arguments. Generally, the issues affect a broad range of people and, hence, a broad range of people may speak to them. The demands of proof are not as rigid as in technical argument or as fluid as in personal argument. The test of validity for such an argument tends to be whether it is right, as in "just" (not as in "correct"). People, as members of a community, try to serve the community's interests with public argument and, thus, need to assess whether they can come to agreement about what is the right thing to do.

The Pluto controversy offers an example of the distinction among public, personal, and technical claims. In the February 1999 issue of *Natural History*, Tyson wrote an essay titled "Pluto's Honor." In it, he argued:

> As Citizen Tyson, I feel compelled to defend Pluto's honor. It lives deeply in our twentieth-century culture and consciousness and somehow rounds out the diversity of our family of planets, like the troubled sibling of a large family. Nearly every schoolchild thinks of Pluto as an old friend. And there was always something poetic about being number nine. As Professor Tyson, however, I must vote—with a heavy heart—for demotion. Pluto was always an enigma to teach.[70]

In other words, Tyson recognizes that arguments that might matter in a personal or public sphere (such as public perception, schoolchildren's beliefs, and the poetry of nine) are not relevant in the technical realm, where technical questions of how planets are grouped are the only criteria. Children's sadness at not finding Pluto along with the terrestrial and gas giant planets in the Scales of the Universe exhibit (which portrays the relative size of things in the solar system) simply does not count as relevant data in the debate.

Other scientists also recognized this distinction among argument spheres. In a debate Tyson organized at the American Museum of Natural History on the status of Pluto, Jane Luu, codiscoverer of the first actual Kuiper belt object (the belt in which Pluto resides), argued Pluto was not a planet and made clear that continuing to refer to it as a planet "would only be due to tradition and sentimental reasons. . . . So, in the end, the question goes back to this: Should science be a democratic process, or should logic have something to do with it?"[71] Luu was basically asking: Is this a technical or public sphere debate? Substantial public outcry arose over the IAU's vote to demote Pluto from planet status, but the data used by the scientific community was what mattered. As Tyson explains, "Science is not a democracy. As

[69]Goodnight, "The Personal," 219, italics added.

[70]Neil de Grasse Tyson, "Pluto's Honor," *Natural History* 108, no. 1 (February 1999): 82.

[71]Quoted in Tyson, *Pluto*, 71.

is often cited (and attributed to Galileo), the stated authority of a thousand is not worth the humble reasoning of a single individual."[72]

Just because an argument belongs in the public sphere does not mean technical arguments are irrelevant. In debates over what individuals and governments should do to combat global warming, technical debates about the causes and rate of warming, as well as about the effectiveness of solutions, play an important role. Other arguments might start in the technical sphere, but become public sphere arguments. Communication scholars Valeria Fabj and Matthew J. Sobnosky explore how HIV/AIDS activists challenged the medical establishment's drug-testing protocol (a technical issue) because it failed to serve public interests. The traditional requirements of double-blind studies to administer placebos to terminal patients seemed to magnify, rather than lessen, the public health crisis of HIV/AIDS.[73] Fabj and Sobnosky argue that public sphere deliberation was enhanced by activists' introduction of a personal and technical issue (individuals get diseases doctors treat) into the public sphere of deliberation. Activists trained themselves in the technical language of medicine so they could persuasively argue that public, and not just technical, concerns should govern drug-testing protocol.

Spheres of argument do not denote locations. The most technical arguments might occur in the most private locations: imagine two doctors debating the best treatment for a patient while in the restroom, or two lawyers having a heated personal discussion, while preparing for court, about where they should eat lunch. Spheres of argument do influence argumentative practices—the norms and rules that govern how the argument ought to proceed and that may influence who is allowed to speak, from what location, and on what topics.

The person, topic, or location does not determine the sphere; instead, the sphere influences who may speak on what topic and in what location.

CONCLUSION

"Argument" refers both to the complex relation of claim, data, warrant, backing, qualifications, and conditions for rebuttal and to the process by which people engage each other in the exchange of reasons. Most important, however, arguments are a central part of communication in a democratic society. The attitude people take into argument influences how they engage in argument. Believing argument is war induces you to treat people with whom you disagree as enemies to be vanquished. This perspective is not conducive to creating an environment that encourages open communication. In contrast, if you conceive of argument as play, you are likely to see debate as a cooperative enterprise. Argument only works in deliberation and judgment if people are willing to change their minds when they hear a sound argument. Interlocutors are not enemies, but fellow humans, vulnerable to the same dangers, injuries, and harms as other humans, and thus deserving of the full measure of respect due to people considered to be friends.

---

[72]Tyson, *Pluto*, 127.

[73]Valeria Fabj and Matthew J. Sobnosky, "AIDS Activism and the Rejuvenation of the Public Sphere," *Argumentation and Advocacy* 31 (Spring 1995): 163–184.

We do not mean to imply that argumentative processes are just play without real consequence. The outcomes of argument have real consequences to which campus project is funded, which job candidate is hired, which political candidate wins, whether or not a country is invaded, and so on. Our objective with this argurment-is-play metaphor is not to suggest the stakes involved in argument are less important, but to heighten our sense of responsibility to the people with whom we argue.

Deliberation, judgment, and decision making—all crucial elements of democracy—require that members of a community be able to explain and justify their positions. Deliberation also requires that people compare and contrast competing arguments so they can make decisions even when faced with incomplete information. Every person makes decisions every day; and it is always better to make a decision based on sound evidence, strong reasoning, and warranted conclusions. When argument is conceived of as a cooperative enterprise in decision making, its utility as a way to resolve differences, rather than magnify them, becomes clear.

You may have found that an argument that works for one audience is not persuasive to another. As you listen to public discussion of a policy, you realize the way that argument progresses is different from the way that you and a friend may resolve a disagreement. Argument is a process: the best argumentative engagements are those in which people engage with each other and are open to persuasion.

We think a good principle for arguing is as follows: you should be as open to persuasion and change as you hope the person with whom you are arguing is. When you walk into an argument$_2$, you should be willing to alter your position in the face of other arguments. The willingness to alter your own position is the basis of democratic government, the First Amendment, and the marketplace of ideas, all of which rely on the assumption that people will make reasoned decisions when presented with information and arguments. As an argument progresses, data is accepted and discarded, warrants are challenged and reinforced, qualifications and reservations are added to claims, and claims are rejected or accepted. Rejection of a claim influences the other arguments$_1$ offered, because that claim may actually function as backing or warrant for other arguments. As particular arguments are abandoned, the argument$_2$, itself, evolves.

KEY CONCEPTS

argument	data
argument field	enthymeme
argument$_1$	particular audiences
argument$_2$	personal sphere
backing	public sphere
burden of proof	presumption
claim	qualifiers
claim of definition	spheres of argument
claim of fact	syllogism
claim of policy	technical sphere
claim of value	universal audience
conditions of rebuttal	warrants

DISCUSSION QUESTIONS

1. Read an article advocating a policy, a letter to the editor, or an editorial. Diagram one of the arguments in that essay, identifying as many components of the Toulmin model as you can.
2. Read a newspaper or magazine in which a public policy issue is discussed. Identify places where appeals to presumption are used.
3. Identify a topic about which much debate proceeds. Create examples of the four types of claims (fact, definition, value, policy) that could be made in relation to that topic. In other words, craft four topics that people could debate, each topic focusing on a different type of claim.
4. Read an article advocating a policy, a letter to the editor, or an editorial. Identify examples of faulty or incomplete arguments. Are the data adequate? Is a warrant unclear? Are the examples too few from which to generalize? Can you construct an argument that advances the same claim, but without faulty reasoning?

RECOMMENDED READINGS

Fabj, Valeria, and Matthew J. Sobnosky. "AIDS Activism and the Rejuvenation of the Public Sphere." *Argumentation and Advocacy* 31 (Spring 1995): 163–184.

Goodnight, G. Thomas. "The Personal, Technical, and Public Spheres of Argument: A Speculative Inquiry into the Art of Public Deliberation." *Argumentation and Advocacy* 18 (Spring 1982): 214–227.

O'Keefe, Daniel J. "Two Concepts of Argument." *Journal of the American Forensic Association* 13 (1977): 121–128.

Inventing and Organizing Your Persuasive Speech

Joel Page/AP Images

This chapter is intended to help you:

- Identify the purposes of persuasive speaking
- Explore and generate ideas for your persuasive speech
- Use organizational patterns that are adapted to your audience and purpose

Persuasion has always been at the heart of public speaking. One traditional definition of rhetoric describes the primary skill of public speaking as the speaker's ability to identify the "available means of persuasion" in a situation (Aristotle). But persuasive speaking can be especially challenging today. One of the main challenges is your competition in the public sphere. Considering only commercial messages, the average American has approximately 3,000 exposures each day (Jacobson and Masur). The numbers might be even higher among younger people; one study of youth in the United States showed an average of eight hours of daily media exposure (Roberts).

As a result, listeners have developed some defense mechanisms against this onslaught of persuasion. Some communication scholars have referred

CASE SCENARIO

Anne's Speech on Disability Access

Earlier in the semester, Anne had given an informative speech about access to campus buildings for disabled people. In that speech, she shared a memorable story about a class project that required her to move around campus for a few hours in a wheelchair. Her vivid story captured her audience's attention, but she was not sure how motivated they might be to act on this issue. She decided to revisit this issue for her persuasive speech. Would her audience be willing to do something outside of class about disability access? It would be a challenge to identify the right purpose and set of persuasive strategies that fit her classmates' level of concern.

to a general state of **distraction**, or fleeting attention to a single message, among contemporary audiences (DeLuca and Peeples). Because traditional and social media are saturated with messages, we give little attention to any one message. The next time you walk past a bulletin board of flyers and announcements on your campus, note how many you notice and how few you bother to read. Audiences also may develop **cynicism**, a distrustful and largely negative attitude, when it comes to persuasive messages. When everyone is trying to persuade—and when many people appear to be untrustworthy—it can be difficult to treat every persuasive message seriously (Hart and Hartelius; Hariman).

The challenges of distraction and cynicism are just two of the prominent obstacles in contemporary public speaking. This chapter will help you to confront these obstacles by guiding you through the invention process for persuasive speaking. This chapter will begin by looking at the primary purposes of persuasive speaking and the resources for invention that are available. The last section of the chapter will focus on the organizational strategies that are standard ways of engaging the typical challenges of persuasive speaking. ■

Purposes of Persuasive Speaking

Speaking to persuade means that your primary aim is to influence the attitudes and actions of your audience. In some situations, this may mean reinforcing the beliefs and feelings that your audience members already hold. In others, it may mean challenging their beliefs or weakening their commitments to open the way for other views. Or it may mean encouraging the audience to act on the attitudes they already hold. As a result, the general purpose of persuading your audience can take many specific forms depending on the situation and your audience.

Civic and Political Purposes of Persuasive Speech

Persuading audiences is a vital part of civic and political engagement. If you are working on a community project such as a new park or playground, you might need to persuade local residents of the importance of public space or convince them to donate time or money to the project. If you are trying to improve relationships between your campus and the surrounding community, you might need to persuade your fellow students that their weekend parties are having a negative impact on the community

Often, these civic activities can set the groundwork for political persuasion. If audiences see the importance of public space, it might be easier to persuade them to support a local bond initiative. Students with greater sensitivity to campus–community relationships might be more willing to participate in discussions of your campus's building plans or engage in advocacy about transportation and development near campus. In all of these scenarios, persuasion is necessary for promoting certain courses of action, as well as for electing and supporting leaders who will make the ultimate decisions.

In these contexts, persuasive speaking typically focuses on one of three purposes: strengthening commitments, moderating opposition, and advocating action. The first two purposes are concerned primarily with influencing the audience's attitudes; the third is concerned with translating audience attitudes into action.

Strengthening Commitments An *attitude* can be thought of as a preference—a favorable or unfavorable disposition toward some idea or practice or some judgment of that idea or practice as either desirable or undesirable. Much persuasive speaking has the purpose of strengthening a favorable or neutral audience's commitments, making those attitudes or preferences more pronounced. You are trying to strengthen an audience's commitment to an attitude when you speak to a sympathetic audience about an important civic or political issue, when you encourage a neutral audience to see certain ideas as desirable, or when you encourage any audience to see one option as better than another.

Civic and political speech often attempts to strengthen an audience's commitment by heightening their concern about some issue. This type of persuasive speech often flows naturally from an informative speech that intends to raise awareness of an issue. The persuasive speech differs because you are going beyond raising awareness in an attempt to influence the audience's feelings and responses to that new awareness. For example, if you are speaking about cancer treatments, your speaking goal might be to persuade your audience to favor reducing restrictions on experimental drugs. In this way, you are trying to clarify the audience's preference.

Attitudes are based on both beliefs and values. Therefore, strengthening an audience's commitments often requires that you engage audiences

THE ETHICAL DIMENSION

Preaching to the Choir

Speaking to people who already agree with you is sometimes called "preaching to the choir." As was mentioned earlier in the chapter, this might seem like the easiest type of public speaking, but it raises challenges all its own. Some of these challenges are explicitly ethical and worth considering before you engage in persuasive speaking.

Your choices of supporting material and language have significant ethical implications when you are speaking to a sympathetic audience. Using only the most outrageous examples or appealing primarily to emotion certainly can excite an audience—you have probably heard this kind of "red meat" rhetoric in political campaigns—but also can distort the audience's judgment.

However, there is a larger ethical issue about preaching to the choir: Should you do it in the first place? In some situations, you might not have a choice. If you are asked to give a presentation to your organization and most of its members see things the same way, then you need to be careful with the tactics and appeals mentioned above. But in other situations, you might have more flexibility in how you constitute your audience. Imagine that you are a student leader who is speaking to students about a proposed tuition increase. Even if a majority of the student body opposes the increase, is it ethically sound to give a speech that speaks only to the majority with the purpose of strengthening their commitment?

In such situations, think about the range of possible short-term effects as well as potential long-term consequences of your rhetoric. In the short term, you might get the majority on board and riled up, but ignoring other viewpoints could create a backlash where none existed before. In the long term, this kind of rhetoric can lead to **polarization**, in which one group in a society perceives itself as absolutely opposed to another group. Many observ-

Political campaign speeches can often involve "preaching to the choir." How can speakers invigorate their supporters without demonizing their opponents?

ers believe that polarization is detrimental to effective democratic decision making. Finally, it might not serve you well to constitute audiences that are unwilling or unable to engage in critical thinking about important public issues. Even if preaching to the choir seems easy, its ethical dimensions should make you think carefully about how you constitute your audience and about the most appropriate ways to persuade them.

WHAT DO YOU THINK?

1. If you are speaking to a sympathetic or like-minded audience, what sort of language should you use to refer to your opponents? What types of language would be inappropriate?

2. Think of a public issue about which you are undecided or uncertain of your position. How would you respond to a speaker who seems to be preaching to the choir? What lessons does this suggest about your own choices as a speaker?

on both of those levels. For example, if you want to persuade your classmates that the amount of money that is allotted to student groups is undesirable, then you might need to address factual issues about the size of the budget and which groups get funding, as well as the value of extracurricular groups and ideals such as fairness and financial responsibility. All of these points could affect whether your audience sees the current budget as desirable or not or whether they might prefer an alternative budget.

Moderating Opposition When an audience does not favor your position, an appropriate persuasive purpose is to moderate their opposition to your position. For instance, imagine that you are trying to extend the library hours on campus but the library staff is opposed to that change. If you are going to speak to the staff, your initial task should be to determine the basis for their opposition. If you can address some of their reasons and therefore weaken some of their commitments, you might be able to moderate that opposition to make them more open to your viewpoint.

Moderating opposition is a staple of civic and political engagement. Because democratic principles require us to respectfully engage people with opposing points of view, the skill of being able to moderate that opposition is necessary if one want to be an effective agent in the civic and political arena. For example, an advocate of abstinence-only sex education is likely to face opposition from people who prefer sex education that directly discusses sexual activity. Opponents might not ever support abstinence-only education, but they might be persuaded to moderate their opposition if abstinence is taught as one of many options for promoting sexual safety. Moderating opposition, then, is not about getting opponents to completely switch their position but instead about encouraging them to see your position in a somewhat more favorable light.

Advocating Action The other major purpose of persuasive speech is *advocating action*. Persuading people to vote in a certain way, encouraging elected officials to make certain decisions, and simply motivating other citizens to get up and do something are all examples of how persuasive speech can advocate action. All of these examples may involve influencing people's attitudes in some way, but in some situations, simply generating a favorable attitude is not enough from the viewpoint of the persuasive speaker. For that speaker, the real goal is getting a favorably disposed audience to move from attitude to action.

Advocating action takes a variety of forms. In terms of civic engagement, the challenge might be getting co-workers to volunteer for a Saturday charity event or soliciting contributions from individual or institutional donors. In terms of political engagement, advocacy might involve encouraging other students to vote for a student government candidate. Once a candidate is in office, you might attempt to persuade

Ted Powers/AP Images

MODERATING OPPOSITION
A classic example of a speech designed to moderate opposition is John F. Kennedy's speech to the Houston Ministerial Association during his campaign for President. His speech was intended not to shift votes, but to moderate opposition that was based on prejudice against his religion.

him or her to address certain issues or to vote a certain way on legislation. In all of these situations, persuasive speech is designed to direct the action of others in consequential ways.

Aligning Your Purpose and Your Subject

The persuasive purposes described above are ultimately shaped by your consideration of audience. But the *subject* of your speech also shapes your persuasive purpose. Persuasive speaking in the public sphere tends to address one of four subject areas: facts, attitudes, policies, and direct action. Once you have clarified both the subject area of your speech and the desired movement that you seek from your audience, your invention process will be much more focused.

Addressing Questions of Fact It might seem odd that persuasive speeches would focus on facts. Aren't facts just true statements? Why would we need to waste our time speaking about facts?

Certainly, some facts are beyond dispute and do not require much discussion. For example, there are many facts about the September 11, 2001, attacks that can be stated conclusively. We know the precise times when the World Trade Center buildings were hit. We know which people hijacked which planes. And we know that a network called al-Qaeda orchestrated the attacks.

But many questions remain about the facts surrounding those attacks. A key question is why the attacks were not stopped ahead of time. Did government officials downplay or ignore the signs of a threat? Was there a failure of communication among intelligence agencies? Was there inadequate monitoring of sites where the attackers trained? The 9/11 Commission Report stands as one attempt to assemble the available evidence and offer a persuasive answer to these and other questions about the facts surrounding 9/11.

Whenever there is a dispute about the facts, a difference in interpretation, or a lack of conclusive evidence, there is an opportunity for persuasive speech to play an important role in the public sphere. Some disputes involve *questions about the past:*

> Did our university ever have discriminatory admission policies?
>
> What caused the recession that started in 2008?

Others are *questions about the present:*

> How does participation in extracurricular activities affect academic performance?
>
> Is organic food healthier than conventional food?

Still other factual disputes involve predictions, or *questions about the future:*

> What are the prospects for the nuclear energy industry in the next decade?
>
> Will the Social Security system be available when my audience retires?

Each of these questions could have a conclusive answer. But because there is likely to be disagreement about the answer, persuasive speaking can help us to figure out the answer. A persuasive speech that tries to answer questions of facts does not simply inform an audience about what is already known. It attempts to persuade the audience that this explanation of the available evidence is the correct or most plausible one. Consequently, speeches about facts involve strengthening commitment or moderating opposition to a particular explanation.

Addressing Attitudes Speeches that focus on attitudes also attempt to strengthen an audience's commitment or moderate its opposition to an idea or practice. This focus can be a smart choice depending on your rhetorical situation. For example, if you are involved in a campaign to increase your college's support for the arts, you might need to heighten concern among the student body—in other words, strengthen students' commitments—before trying to get them to support a policy or take action. If you are speaking in support of gay marriage to an audience that has diverse viewpoints, you might decide that it is more important to moderate opposition and seek common ground than to promote a policy that is supported by only a portion of your audience.

Inventing and organizing a speech that focuses on attitudes will depend on the specifics of your topic and whether you want to strengthen or moderate your audience's existing commitments. In some instances, speakers will start by offering a coherent account of the evidence and then connecting that evidence to shared values. In other situations, speakers will start by amplifying shared values, offering criteria for evaluating an idea or practice, and then applying the criteria to the specific idea or practice under consideration.

Addressing Policies Policy speeches attempt to persuade audiences about the decisions that some group should make. It might be a decision that is made jointly by you and your audience, as when you are trying to persuade other people on your residence hall floor to agree on a policy about quiet hours. Or it might be a decision that you want other people to make, such as encouraging the city council to pass an ordinance that restricts panhandling.

Speeches focusing on policies might pursue any of the three audience-oriented purposes discussed above. However, the typical policy speech advocates action; the entire speech is designed to explain why some group should take a particular action or resist taking action. Depending on your audience, though, your speech may involve the other purposes. For example, advocating less regulation of industry in front of a liberal audience would mean moderating opposition, while discussing it with a group of students who are interested in joining Young Republicans might lead to a speech that is primarily about strengthening commitments.

PUBLIC SPOTLIGHT

Eboo Patel

Eboo Patel has emerged as one of today's leading voices for religious pluralism and interfaith dialogue. After nearly dropping out of college, he founded and now directs the Chicago-based Interfaith Youth Core (IFYC), which brings together high school students from diverse religious backgrounds to engage in service projects in their communities. A key part of Patel's vision for IFYC is that it encourages young people to "identify values they share with one another and then articulate how their religious traditions speak to those shared values" ("Eboo Patel"). Patel was named one of "thirty social visionaries under thirty changing the world" by *Utne Reader* in 2002 and was selected to be on the President's Faith Advisory Council in 2009.

Patel is a compelling speaker, both for his organization and for the broader importance of interfaith dialogue and bridging cultural divides based on shared values. His speech to the Nobel Peace Forum in 2004, for example, suggests that the religious mix of the contemporary United States is reflective of America's historical cultural diversity:

> America is a grand gathering of souls, the vast majority from elsewhere. A century ago it was Jews and Catholics from Southern and Eastern Europe who came, adding new texture to the American tradition. A century ago, it was Jane Addams who imagined and created a new America. Her conviction was that America needed to invite its new Catholic and Jewish immigrants to sit at its table. Her creation, Hull House, succeeded in deepening American democracy. More recently it has been Buddhists, Hindus, Muslims and a range of new Christians from Asia, Africa, the Middle East and the Latin world that have come. America is now the most religiously diverse nation on the planet (Patel).

Throughout his work, Eboo Patel persistently challenges his audiences to observe the overlap between different religions—not only to enrich their understanding of their own religious tradition, but also to create more favorable attitudes toward different religious perspectives.

 Social Media Spotlight

The Interfaith Youth Core has an active social media presence. In addition to Facebook and Twitter sites, its website includes a blog and podcasts that feature the voices of IYC alumni as well as staff members describing ongoing projects and issues. Their YouTube channel catalogs videos of participants and highlights media coverage of the organization.

Facebook: http://www.facebook.com/pages/Interfaith-Youth-Core/29924369552

Twitter: http://twitter.com/IFYC

Blog: http://www.ifyc.org/category/topics/blog

YouTube: http://www.youtube.com/user/InterfaithYouthCore

Excerpt from Eboo Patel's Nobel Peace Forum in 2004 by Eboo Patel. Reprinted with permission by the author and Interfaith Youth Core.

Discussions of policy have always been a part of public discourse. Over time, theorists of rhetoric and public speaking have identified the recurring issues in policy speeches and have developed organizational strategies that address these issues. The most fundamental strategy, as you will learn, is the problem–solution strategy, which provides evidence of a problem, outlines a solution, and justifies the solution in relation to its effects.

Addressing Direct Action When you want your audience to act directly rather than merely to support the actions of others, you are developing a speech that truly addresses action. The action may be individual-level behavior change, as in a speech encouraging students to be a designated driver. Or it may be collective action, as in a speech that asks students to join in a rally at the state capitol.

Speeches that attempt to motivate direct action often look similar to policy speeches, since both offer good reasons in support of some position on a significant issue. But direct action speeches ask for something more from an audience. It is one thing to solicit an audience's support for building a new gym on campus. It is quite another to persuade audience members to write a letter to the college president or donate some of their hard-earned money. Therefore, speakers who are focusing on action need to consider what would move the audience beyond passive agreement to direct action.

One tried-and-true format for speeches that promote action is known as Monroe's motivated sequence. It follows a pattern that is similar to a problem-solution strategy, with each step leading audiences toward a call to action that comes at the end of the speech.

Clarifying Your Persuasive Purpose

The above material suggests a variety of ways in which you can tailor your persuasive purpose for a more effective speech. Let's look at further examples to see how you might clarify your purpose.

Narrow Your Purpose At first, the most important way of narrowing your topic is to decide whether you are trying to influence your audience's attitude, either by strengthening a commitment or by weakening opposition, or whether your primary purpose is to promote action.

> *Topic:* Puppy mills
>
> *General purpose:* To persuade
>
> *Specific purpose:* To influence my audience to have a less favorable attitude toward puppy mills.

> *Topic:* Music with explicit lyrics
>
> *General purpose:* To persuade
>
> *Specific purpose:* To persuade my audience to boycott stores that refuse to sell music with explicit lyrics.

If your speech is attempting to influence attitudes, narrowing also can help you to identify whether your speech will focus on questions of fact or on values.

> *Specific purpose:* To influence my audience that puppy mills are unhealthy for both puppies and humans.
>
> *Specific purpose:* To influence my audience that limiting the sale of music is a threat to our freedoms.

In the first example, the specific purpose clearly intends to shape *attitudes* by casting puppy mills as a problem. But the focus on health suggests that the speech will answer factual questions about the impacts of puppy mills. The second example intends to influence attitudes about limitations on music sales by linking those limits to the value of freedom.

Identify Specific Audience Attitudes Reflecting on the specific attitudes of your audience is another means for clarifying your persuasive purpose. For example, a persuasive speech on nuclear energy might have a slightly different specific purpose depending on the audience.

> *Topic:* Nuclear energy
>
> *General purpose:* To persuade
>
> *Specific purpose* (sympathetic audience): To intensify my audience's attitude that nuclear energy is superior to coal as a fuel for electricity.
>
> *Specific purpose* (neutral audience): To influence my audience that nuclear energy is a desirable energy source for the twenty-first century.
>
> *Specific purpose* (hostile audience): To influence my audience to have a more favorable attitude toward nuclear energy.

Notice how the wording of the specific purpose does not change the general purpose of the speech: to persuade the audience by influencing their attitudes. But the wording does show how the speaker's purpose changes depending on the existing attitude of the audience. Unlike the first two audiences, a hostile audience is not likely to believe that nuclear energy is "a desirable energy source" after a single speech. But trying to moderate that audience's opposition by influencing them to have a slightly more favorable attitude might be a realistic goal.

Purpose statements for speeches that advocate action also can benefit from careful tailoring in light of audience attitudes. For example, if you are advocating that your college should build a new activities center, an effective specific purpose statement for a speech to administrators might look like this:

> *Topic:* Building a new student activities center
>
> *General purpose:* To persuade
>
> *Specific purpose:* To advocate that our college should build a new student activities center.

Different audiences and different obstacles could lead to more focused statements:

> *Specific purpose:* To persuade my audience that they should contribute to the fund for a new student activities center.
>
> *Specific purpose:* To persuade my audience that building a new activities center is a better use of resources than building a new residence hall.

Check with your instructor about how specific your purpose statement needs to be. The point is not to achieve a "perfect" statement, but to allow the process of writing your specific purpose statement to help you invent your persuasive speech as a whole.

Inventing Your Persuasive Speech

Invention cues are useful for identifying potential main points and supporting material in your persuasive speech. However, the rhetorical situations of persuasive speaking raise additional constraints and opportunities for you to consider.

Using Audience Feedback

In the classroom, you can use feedback that you received on previous speeches to help you prepare later speeches. What were your audience's questions? What ideas generated a lot of interest? Did your audience give you new information or share how your speech was relevant to them? Especially if you are continuing with the same topic in your persuasive speech, audience feedback can suggest a starting point for inventing a persuasive speech.

Audience questions provide an easy entry point into a subsequent speech. For example, after Kim's informative speech on credit cards, her audience was left wondering what rules their college had for allowing credit card companies to promote products on campus. Even though this was not the initial focus of Kim's interests, she learned that her audience wanted to know how this issue affected their campus and what they might do. As a result, Kim decided to explore her university's policies and determine how students might influence those policies.

Flashpoints of *audience interest* also can stimulate thinking about later speeches. Calvin's informative speech on genetically modified foods, for example, touched off a discussion about the high price of organic and natural food. His audience had a generally favorable attitude toward organic food, but they were convinced that it was too expensive for the average college student. Calvin knew that if he wanted to persuade people to eat more organic food, he would have to address the price issue in a compelling way.

Information provided by the audience also can help a speaker to find new possibilities for speeches. Aziz gave a speech about the tenets of Islam for his informative assignment, and during the feedback period, one of his classmates mentioned that she had seen a report about unfair and inaccurate media representations of Muslims. Aziz looked up the report and found several examples from U.S. media and popular culture that would provide a familiar point of reference for his audience in his persuasive speech.

Incorporating this kind of feedback into your next speech can help you to boost your ethos. By referring back to earlier speeches or mentioning specific statements from your audience, you will show that you have listened to their comments and taken them seriously enough to address. For example, Calvin decided to begin his persuasive speeches by acknowledging the strong opinions of his audience about food prices:

> "Organic food is so expensive!"
>
> "On my budget, I can hardly afford to pay for regular groceries, much less organics."
>
> "I don't call it Whole Foods—it's Whole Paycheck!"
>
> Have you ever found yourself thinking or saying any of these things? Some of you mentioned them after my last speech, and I have thought these same things when I make my weekly food run. But after doing a little investigating, I'm having a change of heart about organic food.

Here, Calvin is attempting to moderate his audience's opposition with regard to the price of organic food. He directly acknowledges his audience's beliefs and attitudes based on prior feedback and states that he shares some of those opinions. This helps him to establish common ground with his audience before posing challenges to their opinions.

Using Audience Research

Researching audience opinions is absolutely necessary for inventing an effective persuasive speech. This process can be broken down into two phases: identifying the crucial audience obstacles to persuasion and potential adaptation strategies and developing questions that help you to see which obstacles and strategies have relevance for your topic.

Identify Obstacles Each of the three persuasive purposes raises specific obstacles to persuasion that invite different adaptation strategies. At first, it might seem that there would be few obstacles for a speaker who is trying to strengthen a commitment. This purpose is typically appropriate for a sympathetic or neutral audience—in other words, people who are already open to the speaker's ideas if not outright supportive. But even these audiences might not be especially concerned about the issue. Therefore, a primary adaptation strategy is to *heighten the public significance of the issue* so that audience members perceive it as worthy of exploration. This is a necessary first step if you want the audience to make an informed judgment about whether something is favorable or desirable. In addition, speakers can adapt by *emphasizing the personal connection of the issue to the audience* so that the audience members' abstract concern for the issue becomes concrete. Finally, if an audience's support is based on limited awareness of alternatives, then you might decide to *inoculate the audience members against counterarguments* so that they can resist opposing messages.

For oppositional audiences, the primary obstacle is a difference of opinion with the speaker in terms of *values*. Audience members might simply have a different set of value priorities that lead them to see very different things as desirable. With such an audience, a speaker should focus on *establishing common ground* and *identifying shared values*, a topic that will be discussed in more detail later in this chapter. In other instances, opposition may come from incomplete or incorrect knowledge; in this case, a speaker should focus on *connecting new facts to strongly held audience values* or possibly *shifting to an informative speech*.

As with other types of persuasive speaking, advocates of policy and action may confront audiences that perceive a lack of urgency and importance. But these purposes raise additional obstacles. Taking then, action has costs as well as benefits, so the perceived costs—both to the individual and to the society as a whole—are always a primary obstacle for this type of persuasive speaking. In turn, speakers need to *minimize the costs of action, highlight the benefits, and show the audience members how they can act effectively*. When speaking to a hostile audience, an additional obstacle is the audience's attraction to alternatives, whether that is the current state of affairs or a different course of action. For these situations, speakers need to *highlight the flaws or limitations of possible alternatives*. Because oppositional audience members are not likely to completely change their mind, this strategy focuses instead on weakening their commitment to alternatives. You might even decide that influencing the attitudes of a hostile audience is a more appropriate purpose than trying to get the audience to act.

Table 1 shows how each of the persuasive purposes faces particular obstacles and suggests possible adaptation strategies.

TABLE 1 Persuasive Purposes, Obstacles, and Adaptation Strategies

Persuasive Purpose	Potential Obstacles	Adaptation Strategies
To strengthen commitments	Lack of commitment	Intensify commitment Heighten significance
	Awareness of other points of view	Inoculate, address objections
	Lack of coherent viewpoint	Provide a perspective
To moderate opposition	Incomplete/incorrect knowledge	(*Try informative speech*)
	Value conflicts	Establish common ground, shared values
To advocate action	Costs and barriers	Minimize costs, show efficacy
	Lack of urgency	Emphasize timeliness, costs of inaction
	Lack of importance	Heighten significance, emphasize outcomes
	Commitment to status quo/ other options	Show limits/flaws of other options

Develop Questions Once you have considered the typical obstacles to persuasion and the potential adaptation strategies, develop questions that you can ask your audience directly or determine indirectly. Your goal is to find opportunities for overcoming key obstacles or pursuing adaptation strategies that might resonate with their existing attitudes. Consider the following categories for developing questions:

- *Beliefs*. Incorrect, incomplete, or inadequate knowledge of your topic is often a critical obstacle in speaking to a general audience. Without adequate information, an audience may lack strong commitments on an issue, may not perceive the issue as urgent, and may not understand the practicality or desirability of certain courses of action. Therefore, it is important to identify whether your audience shares beliefs that are supportive of your point of view.

  True/false questions and carefully crafted multiple-choice questions can reveal areas of belief that may deserve elaboration in your speech. For example, Cameron found out that his audience had a wide range of strong opinions about delisting wolves as an endangered species, but hardly anyone knew how many wolves were needed to maintain a viable population. Consequently, he spent more of his speech talking about the latest ecological research on wolf populations.

- *Values*. Taking stock of your audience's values can give you a sense of why audience members perceive the topic the way they do. Values can affect their perception of the problem and its importance, the coherence of their viewpoint, and the desirability of certain actions. For example, an audience that values material well-being over intellectual stimulation is likely to have different attitudes about what your college's academic requirements should look like.

  In addition, values point to opportunities for motivating your audience. Classmates who value material well-being may be persuaded to take more communication classes when they find out that employers rank strong communication skills as one of the highest criteria for making hiring decisions. As this example suggests, effective persuasion is often a matter of sharing important information to shape beliefs and then attaching those beliefs to key values.

- *Relevance and perceived significance*. Does your audience see the topic as personally relevant or important on a public level? In the context of persuasive speaking, relevance and significance are directly related to whether your audience will have strong commitments on your topic, whether audience members have become aware of alternative viewpoints, and whether they see the issue as urgent.

- *Resistance to action.* Listeners have all sorts of reasons for not taking action on some issue: It's too difficult; it costs too much; they don't know where to start; it's inconvenient; they don't have time; it won't make a difference; it might not work. By finding out what is really stopping your audience from acting, you can give special attention to minimizing or eliminating those barriers to action. For example, Amber's audience was sensitive to the plight of restaurant servers and supported the idea of tipping. But they also thought that tipping restaurant servers really had no effect on the quality of service. So Amber spent a fair amount of time in her speech describing how servers talk about and react to getting a poor tip and a great tip.

Ultimately, using audience research as well as audience feedback is a matter of honest, patient, and respectful listening. If you really listen to what your audience knows about your topic and what really concerns and motivates the audience members, then you are in a much better position to engage their viewpoints directly with effective, ethical persuasion.

Using Topic Research

As with audience research, your first step with topic research should be to revisit your invention cues. The common topics—existence, definition, comparison, causality, correlation, and time and space—are just as pertinent to persuasive speeches, and several are absolutely necessary to examine, depending on the organizational pattern you use.

On civic and political matters, topical analysis also takes the form of identifying the stock issues that are related to a proposed policy. **Stock issues** are similar to common topics because they apply regardless of the subject matter. However, stock issues are specific to questions of policy or action; when a change is being proposed, stock issues are the typical issues on which people are likely to disagree or resist change. If you are considering a speech that proposes some policy, consider the following stock issues:

- *Need for change.* Does the current state of affairs need to be changed? If the audience does not see a need for change, then a persuasive speech should focus on shifting audience attitudes or advocating a very limited course of action. For example, Thomas believed that there was a need to repeal the Patriot Act, but his audience did not see the Act as a relevant issue in their lives. As a result, he stepped back from advocating a repeal of the Act; instead, he attempted to persuade his audience to have unfavorable attitude toward it.

- *Barriers to change.* What is standing in the way of change? If the current situation is framed as a problem, then the barrier is often an underlying cause of that problem. If the situation is framed as "OK but needs improvement," then the barrier is some obstacle that is preventing things from being ideal. For Amy, the barrier that related to her speech on healthy food options on campus was the college's contracts with outside vendors. If those contracts could be changed, then more nutritious foods would be available. Her speech would need to spend a fair amount of time explaining those contracts before advocating a change.

- *Proposal for change.* What should be done? Thinking about alternative proposals for change is absolutely necessary for speeches that advocate action. If there are several proposals for change circulating in public discourse, then a persuasive speech might need to spend time comparing those proposals. Kira's speech on repurposing a nearby mall, for example, compared three different proposals before advocating her preferred choice. If the only alternative is doing nothing, then speakers might need to explore why doing nothing is still appealing. Eric's speech proposing a city ordinance mandating helmets for bicyclists focused on people's strong resistance to wearing helmets.

- *Practicality of change.* Is the change feasible? It is one thing to have a great idea for change but quite another to plan how that change will actually happen. Therefore, a key issue for any proposed change is whether it can be implemented practically. Tanner's speech on "greening the campus" had a lot of great ideas about sustainability, but without a clear idea of the steps that would make that change real and the funding and staffing that would be needed to implement the changes, his audience thought his speech seemed too idealistic. Additional research on how other campuses have put similar ideas into practice would have been a great addition to his speech.

- *Advantages of change.* Will the change create benefits? If your audience is trying to decide between different courses of action or is uncertain about the benefits of adopting your proposed action, then you might spend time discussing the many ways in which your proposed action will be better than the current state of affairs or other actions. In Eric's speech on bicycle helmets, he vividly compared the effects of bike accidents on helmet wearers and nonwearers.

Using stock issues for analysis also can help you to reflect further on the purpose of your speech. A speech that advocates policy or action may spend a fair amount of time trying to shift attitudes about the feasibility of that proposal. For example, a speech that advocates boycotting of a product or company might need to overcome resistance to the idea of boycotts in general by showing audiences how a boycott can be a practical and effective strategy for pursuing change.

Organizing Your Persuasive Speech

As with invention, the organizational strategies that you learned for informative speaking also can be applied to persuasive speaking situations. Sequential and analytical strategies can be useful for developing specific sections of a persuasive speech. For example, a speech might track the progression of a public issue such as AIDS or illustrate a shift over time in social attitudes about interracial relationships. The compare-and-contrast strategy and the key issues strategy both can be useful for showing how one position—whether on facts, attitudes, policy, or action—is superior to another.

In most situations, though, you will be best served by employing organizational patterns that serve particular persuasive purposes. This section identifies some of these patterns and provides concrete suggestions for when and how to use those patterns.

Criteria–Application Pattern

The **criteria–application pattern** offers audiences a set of standards or criteria and then applies those standards to a specific situation. This pattern is especially useful when you want to make a clear-cut judgment about factual issues or when you want to use shared values or goals to evaluate a specific practice or policy. In relation to your audience, the criteria help you to establish common ground by stating broad, general ideas before getting into the details of a particular situation.

The criteria-application pattern works well to focus attention on the most relevant criteria for establishing facts. Often, a speech like this will define key terms in the process of developing the criteria in the first part of the speech (Inch and Warnick). Consider this basic outline for a speech about standardized tests:

> *Specific purpose:* To persuade my audience that standardized tests do not accurately measure a student's capabilities.
>
> *Central idea:* Standardized tests fail to measure important student capabilities.
>
> Main points:
>
>   I. Definitions
>
>   A. Standardized tests are examinations of general intellectual skills that are scored in a consistent way for all students.
>
>   B. In this context, capabilities are the behaviors, attitudes, and skills needed to succeed in school and in the workplace.
>
>   II. Criteria
>
>   A. Tests need to measure writing skills.
>
>   B. Tests need to measure speaking skills.
>
>   C. Tests need to measure one's ability to adapt to new situations.
>
>   D. Tests need to measure skills fairly, without cultural bias.

III. Application
    A. Most standardized tests explicitly measure writing skills.
    B. However, no standardized tests measure speaking skills.
    C. Standardized tests are not designed to measure or evaluate intangible capabilities.
    D. There is some evidence that standardized tests are culturally biased.

After defining the key terms, this speech provides criteria for considering the supporting material. Think of these criteria as providing ground rules for the rest of the speech: What should count as evidence? What conditions need to be met to support the central idea? The application section of the speech then presents supporting material that addresses each of those points. In this speech, for example, the subpoints under "Application" might include examples of specific standardized tests or testimony from educational experts.

The criteria–application pattern also can be used in speeches that attempt to influence attitudes or advocate policies. For example, the criteria may be broad goals or values that are intended to shape the audience's attitudes about a specific practice or policy:

Specific purpose: To moderate my audience's opposition to new graduation requirements.

Central idea: Our new graduation requirements are better than the current requirements.

Main points:

    I. Definitions
    II. Criteria
        A. In general, requirements should ensure that students understand and appreciate different cultures.
        B. Requirements also should ensure that students have basic competency in writing, speaking, and mathematics.
        C. Requirements should also be focused and straightforward so that students can complete them efficiently.
    III. Application.
        A. The new Global Cultures requirement will better prepare graduates for our multicultural world.
        B. The new Public Speaking requirement will give students practical skills that employers desire most.
        C. The new distribution requirements have fewer categories, and each category requires exactly one course.

Here, the speaker uses criteria to put specific requirements in a positive light. If the audience is resistant to the idea of having new requirements, the criteria encourage them to see that these requirements may in fact have some benefit for them.

Problem–Solution Pattern

The **problem–solution pattern** offers audiences a policy that will contribute to fixing some damaging conditions. This pattern is a standard option for most policy speeches. Beyond an explanation of the problem that motivates the policy, this pattern invites speakers to spend roughly half of the speech discussing how the policy will be implemented and what the likely consequences will be. The stock issues that you learned about earlier in the chapter should be used to flesh out this basic organizational pattern.

For problem–solution speeches, the stock issues are generally addressed in the following order:

I. Problem
    A. Need for change
    B. Barriers to change

II. Solution
    A. Proposal for change
    B. Practicality of change
    C. Advantages of change

In this pattern, the first half of the speech is devoted to demonstrating the existence of the problem and identifying causes or factors that perpetuate it. The second half of the speech proposes a solution and provides support for it in two main ways: by showing that the proposal can be implemented practically and by showing that it will have advantages over the current state of affairs or rival plans. Examine this working outline:

Specific purpose: To persuade my audience to support "take-back" laws for consumer electronics.

Central idea: Congress should pass a law requiring producers of consumer electronics to sponsor collection and recycling programs for computers and televisions.

Main points:
    I. Electronic waste is a growing problem in the United States.
        A. Millions of tons of e-waste are dumped in U.S. landfills annually. This waste presents clear risks to human health and the environment.
        B. There is little incentive for producers to take responsibility for this unique type of garbage.
    II. This problem can be solved with a national "take-back" law.
        A. Congress should pass a take-back law requiring electronics companies to collect and recycle computers and televisions.
        B. This law would direct environmental agencies to work with companies to coordinate the collection of used consumer electronics.

   C. Funds for the program would be generated by a surtax on new computers and televisions.

   D. Take-back laws would have several advantages over our current situation.

    1. They would increase the rate of recycling.

    2. They would direct e-waste into safe recycling programs, thereby protecting workers' health.

    3. They would keep toxic metals from leaching into ground water, thereby keeping our drinking water safe.

    4. By forcing companies to deal with their own waste, these laws would encourage companies to produce more environmentally friendly products.

Notice how the solutions section is organized to address each of the stock issues. First, it states the specific proposal for change; then it explains how that change would be put into practice. Finally, the advantages section starts by describing how the proposal solves the problem and then adds an additional benefit of the proposal. In a more developed outline, these portions of the speech should be carefully tailored to the knowledge level of the audience.

Comparative Patterns

Two types of comparative patterns work well for persuasive speaking. The **comparative advantages pattern** pits two competing solutions against one another to highlight the advantages of one solution. This pattern is essentially a version of the compare/contrast pattern for informative speeches, and it can be used in conjunction with the key issues pattern.

For example, suppose that your campus is considering where to build a new residence hall and has narrowed down the available areas to two choices. A persuasive speech could advocate for one location over the other:

> *Specific purpose:* To persuade my audience that North Campus is the best location for the new residence hall.
>
> *Central idea:* North Campus is a better location for the new residence hall than South Campus.
>
> Main points:
>
> I. North Campus has better automobile access than South Campus.
>
> II. North Campus is closer to most academic buildings.
>
> III. North Campus would have less impact on wildlife.

Because the need for change is usually well established, a comparative advantages approach like this one begins by presenting the proposal for change. Then the bulk of the speech focuses on the key issues for decision makers, showing how, on each issue, the proposal is superior to alternatives.

The **elimination of alternatives pattern** offers audience a series of proposals and shows the flaws of each one before settling on the speaker's preferred alternative. This pattern can be useful when you are trying to help your audience work through competing factual explanations or several potential policies or actions. Thus, it works well when the audience is already aware that alternatives exist but is uninformed about their strengths and weaknesses or perhaps committed to a different alternative than the one you are proposing. The following example identifies alternative policies, eliminating two ideas before advocating the third.

> *Specific purpose:* To persuade my audience that the best way to improve the state's financial situation is to lower taxes on businesses.
>
> *Central idea:* Our state should reduce business taxes by 2%.
>
> *Main points:*
>
> I. There is widespread agreement that the state's financial situation is shaky. In recent months, legislators, the governor, and advocacy groups have been debating how to improve the state's financial situation.
>
> II. Increasing government spending may stimulate the economy in the short term, but it will significantly increase the state's budget deficit.
>
> III. Implementing a statewide lottery could yield a significant amount of money, but it is essentially a regressive tax.
>
> IV. Reducing business taxes is the option most likely to spur long-term economic growth in our state.

In this example, the speaker begins by establishing common ground by discussing the public controversy. The speech then proceeds to explain the various alternatives that have emerged in that controversy. It saves the preferred alternative for the final point, showing how it has the greatest strengths compared to the others.

Motivated Sequence Pattern

The **motivated sequence pattern** is the primary strategy for speeches that ask audiences to take action. As the title suggests, this organizational pattern takes an audience through a sequence of steps that are designed to increase listeners' motivation to act. The specific action is the central idea of the speech.

The motivated sequence shares some characteristics of the problem–solution and elimination patterns. Like the elimination pattern, the motivated sequence delays statement of the central idea. But instead of examining alternatives, the motivated sequence focuses on the speaker's preferred alternative—an action that the speaker wants the audience to take. The speaker sets up the desirability of this action by evoking a need in the audience that can be satisfied by the action.

The sequence of steps moves as follows:

I. *Attention:* Arouse the audience's interest in your topic.

II. *Need:* Evoke a need or unmet goal.

III. *Satisfaction:* Offer a course of action that satisfies the need.

IV. *Visualization:* Depict how life will be better if the audience acts.

V. *Action:* Direct the audience to take specific action.

Notice that these steps are similar to the problem–solution pattern. Both patterns attempt to show some need in the first half of a speech. The satisfaction and visualization steps show the fulfillment of that need, in much the way that the solution section shows how a public problem can be solved. Both patterns have the same underlying logic; they simply apply that logic differently depending on whether the purpose is passive agreement with a policy proposal or a direct action by listeners.

For example, consider how you could make minor adjustments to shift between a motivated sequence speech and a problem–solution speech:

Motivated Sequence Pattern	**Problem–Solution Pattern**
I. Attention	I. Introduction
Think about the majesty of our national parks.	Think about the majesty of our national parks.
II. Need	II. Problem
National parks have big staffing shortages.	National parks have big staffing shortages.
	This problem results from dwindling public funding and limited training opportunities.
III. Satisfaction	III. Solution
This summer, volunteer at a national park.	Congress should increase funding for staff and volunteers in the National Park Service.
	This increase could be achieved with a small increase in user fees.
IV. Visualization	
Imagine the people you will meet and the positive experiences you will create.	Better staffing would enhance visitor experiences and strengthen public support for the National Park Service.
V. Call to Action	IV. Conclusion
In early spring, contact a park to get involved with their Volunteers-In-Parks program.	Congress can sustain the majesty of our national parks by increasing funding for staff and volunteers.

As you can see, the main points of the motivated sequence correspond with the problem–solution pattern. If you are still wrestling with the specific purpose of your speech, experiment with the different patterns to see how they can help you to generate different possibilities for your purpose as well as your central idea.

MOTIVATING AUDIENCES

Individuals may resist taking action if they believe that their input will not make a difference. Persuasive speakers can remind them that their individual voices are amplified when they are part of a larger collective effort.

Jim West/Alamy

CASE CONCLUSION

Anne's Speech on Disability Access

Anne considered advocating for institutional changes to improve handicapped accessibility, but the solution would have been long and difficult to explain, and her classmates were not much interested in campus politics. Instead, she decided to ask for direct action on a personal level. She crafted her specific purpose as follows:

Specific purpose: To persuade my audience that they have the power to alleviate handicap inaccessibility on our campus.

Another round of audience questionnaires showed that Anne had convinced listeners of the problem. The main resistance to action was that they simply did not know what to do and whether any action would be feasible. This made the motivated sequence an appropriate pattern for her speech. She gained attention with a clever quotation and statistic about wheelchair

use and picked up on this appeal in the need step by describing all the challenges she experienced when she was put in the position of a disabled student for an afternoon. Anne also made an explicit connection to how this problem had personal relevance for her listeners.

Her satisfaction step then offered an acronym that identified simple, personal actions that her audience could take on a daily basis. She took advantage of her audience's feeling of disempowerment about influencing bigger changes to explain that these personal actions were something they could do right away that would help other students immediately. Then her visualization step envisioned a ripple effect: a campus where the spirit of helpfulness was pervasive. Finally, her call to action reinforced the acronym and reminded the audience of what they could do as soon as they left the classroom that day.

WORKING OUTLINE

Anne's Speech on Disability Access

Specific purpose: To persuade my audience that they have the power to alleviate handicap inaccessibility on our campus.

Central idea: Overcoming architectural and attitudinal barriers to accessibility starts with every individual becoming "A.W.A.R.E."

I. Introduction

Anne starts with a quotation that has a twist at the end to gain the audience's attention.

    A. "From sea to shining sea, like Lady Liberty. She reigns over all she sees. She's beauty and she is grace, she is queen of 50 states. She is elegance and taste, she's Miss <u>wheelchair</u> United States."

    B. According to researchers at the University of California in San Francisco, 1.6 million people use wheelchairs in the United States to get around. With a number like this, this also means that more people in wheelchairs are becoming active in wheelchair beauty pageants, but more important, we are going to be increasingly more likely to encounter these individuals on our campus.

Her brief reference to personal experience enhances her ethos and gets developed in the body of the speech.

The central idea introduces the acronym that she returns to in the satisfaction step.

    C. I may not be in a wheelchair today, but I have been, and every day I am one of many people on this campus who see handicap inaccessibility and feel that they can do nothing about it.

    D. Overcoming the architectural and attitudinal barriers to accessibility on our campus starts with every individual becoming "aware." A-W-A-R-E: Attitude for Willingness to Act, and Reinforcement Everywhere.

    E. Today in my speech, I will illustrate everyday problems with accessibility and how becoming AWARE will empower these individuals and make our campus fit for a "Miss wheelchair United States."

    (Transition: First let's take a look at some common problems on our campus that cause wheelchair inaccessibility.)

II. Problem/Need

    A. One fall day in my freshman year of college, my classmates and I decided to sit down for what we believed in and spend a day in the life of someone who spends all the days of their life in a wheelchair. Having never been handicapped before, much like many of you, I must say that this experience opened my eyes to the way the world sees, or doesn't see, people in wheelchairs on this campus.

    B. I experienced several architectural barriers when I was in a wheelchair.
        1. Doors
            a. Even though many buildings on campus have automatic doors, several do not.
            b. Classroom doors also present accessibility barriers.

    2. Bathrooms

        a. A handicap bathroom is not just a bathroom with more room for people who do not live in a wheelchair.

        b. Story about my experience in waiting for bathroom.

C. Now if I were Miss Wheelchair Montana and the announcer asked me what I'd like to change about the world, I'd have to say, "I'd like to be able to open a door."

D. This accessibility problem is relevant to students who are not handicapped.

    1. Blocking ramps with bikes.

    2. Using handicap bathrooms.

    3. Blocking doorways.

(Transition: Now that we understand some common accessibility issues, I want to show you how you can help.)

III. Plan/Satisfaction

Many of you may think that handicap accessibility is an important issue but feel that there is nothing that you personally can do about it. Overcoming architectural and attitudinal barriers to accessibility starts with a simple step: Every individual needs to become "A.W.A.R.E." A-W-A-R-E.

A. <u>A</u> is for attitude. Attitudes can promote or preempt action. What are your attitudes about your ability to foster change? What are your attitudes toward people in wheelchairs? Having the right attitude is the first stage in becoming AWARE.

B. <u>W</u> is for willingness. You must be willing to take a moment out of your day to open the door for someone who is struggling. You must be willing to wait for an open stall in the bathroom that is not the handicap one. You must be willing to see these people for who they are, not how they get from point A to B.

C. <u>A</u> is for action. Join or simply support ADSUM or measures on campus that make accessibility more achievable. Advocate for a change in the way those around you see people in wheelchairs.

D. <u>R</u> is for reinforcement. Reinforcement among your group of friends or your classmates, reinforcement of the attitudes and willingness to change. Talk to your peers, and look for opportunities to raise awareness.

E. <u>E</u> is for everywhere. Here in this building, here on campus, here around town. Everywhere all the time, for everyone.

(Transition: Now that you know what to do, I'd like you to imagine yourself doing it and the cascading consequences of your actions.)

Side notes:

Tangible, concrete examples give listeners a clear sense of the existence of this problem.

This portion of the speech heightens personal relevance and identifies a cause of the problem without directly blaming listeners.

This section states the central idea and gives students a concrete guide for action.

These five elements incorporate both individual-level change and larger policy-level change, but the emphasis is on individual action in this speech. The motivated sequence is thus an appropriate organizational pattern.

IV. Practicality/Visualization

 A. Awareness is knowledge, and knowledge is power. You have the power to change this campus for the better and change the lives of your fellow classmates in the process.

 B. Think about how you appreciate it when someone opens a door for you. It may be a small thing for you, but it makes a real difference for students with disabilities.

 C. When you reinforce these ideas among your friends, it is like a ripple in a lake. People all across campus can benefit just from a few words you say.

V. Conclusion/Call to Action

 A. Sometimes people need a ramp to create a level playing field. You have the power to make yourself and our campus more AWARE of accessibility issues on campus.

 B. Albert Einstein once said, "A mind that has been stretched will never return to its original dimension." I dare you to stretch your mind and attitudes through this plan of awareness, and I promise you it is an attitude you will never regret.

Summary

PURPOSES OF PERSUASIVE SPEAKING

- The purpose of a persuasive speech is determined by aligning the audience response you desire with the general subject of the speech.

- Persuasive speeches usually seek to strengthen an audience's commitment, moderate their opposition, or advocate some form of action. Their subject may be a question of fact, an attitude, a policy, or direct action.

INVENTING YOUR PERSUASIVE SPEECH

- Audience research for persuasive speeches should focus on beliefs, values, perceptions of significance and relevance, and sources of resistance.

- Topical analysis can highlight the stock issues that speakers are expected to address, especially for speeches about policy or action.

- Linguistic analysis can direct attention to key values as resources for persuasion.

ORGANIZING YOUR PERSUASIVE SPEECH

- The criteria–application pattern establishes clear standards or guidelines for answering questions of fact, shaping attitudes, or evaluating policies.

- The problem–solution and motivated sequence patterns share the logic of identifying a need or problem and then proposing an action or solution to address it.

- Comparative patterns can be used to evaluate the strengths and weaknesses of competing solutions systematically. Finally, the motivated sequence relies on a psychological pattern of need arousal and fulfillment to encourage listeners to take action.

Key Terms

distraction

cynicism

polarization

stock issues

criteria–application pattern

problem–solution pattern

comparative advantages pattern

elimination of alternatives pattern

motivated sequence pattern

Comprehension

1. What are two obstacles that speakers face in a public sphere that is overloaded with persuasive messages?

2. What are two primary adaptation strategies for trying to strengthen an audience's commitment to their current point of view?

3. When speaking to an audience that is opposed to your point of view, should your goal be to get audience members to switch their position? Why or why not?

4. How can speeches on questions of fact be persuasive, not just informative?

5. What is the difference between a speech that addresses policy and a speech that addresses direct action?

6. What are three ways in which audience feedback on prior speeches can help you invent a persuasive speech?

7. What are the stock issues in persuasive speeches?

8. Which organizational patterns would be appropriate for a speech addressing a question of fact?

9. What are the five steps of the motivated sequence?

Application

1. Take an informal survey of your classmates' attitudes about a current campus issue. Then come up with central ideas for three speeches: one that strengthens their commitments, one that moderates opposition, and one that advocates action.

2. Look at a national newspaper or magazine that discusses current events, and identify two articles: one that appears to be *informative* and another that seeks persuasion on a question of fact. How can you tell the difference between the two?

3. Find the website of your Congressional representative or Senator, and locate a page that describes this person's position on a particular issue. Which of the stock issues does he or she address, and what sort of language does he or she use to describe the issue?

4. Using the same issue that you chose for question 1, develop a simple outline for a problem–solution speech. Then, with a small group of classmates, play the roles of different people or groups on campus that might disagree with that speech. Have these people raise disagreements on the stock issues.

5. Develop a motivated sequence speech that encourages students to take this course next semester. Feel free to tailor different speeches to different groups of students who provide ready-made audiences for you.

I'm looking out here at this mountain and it's got—it looks like somebody has been out there plowing across the side of it. It's like one sort of terrace after another, right up the side.[6]

There can, however, be a negative side to this power of picturing. When listeners don't have previous experience to compare with the picture formed by the speaker's words, they can easily be deceived. For example, the so-called "moonlight and magnolias" school of Southern literature that bloomed after the Civil War offered idealized pictures of plantation life before the war. These false depictions both defended the pre-war slave society and justified post-war practices of segregation that treated the freed slaves as second-class citizens.

Such abuses of language illustrate a problem first described over four hundred years ago by the Renaissance scholar Francis Bacon. Bacon suggested that the glass in the windows of depiction can be "enchanted": the perspective may be distorted. Words can color or alter things, thus disguising or obscuring reality. This ability to shape perceptions can then become a serious ethical problem.

Arousing Feelings

Language can also arouse powerful feelings, touching listeners and changing attitudes. This power of words is used ethically when it *strengthens* sound reasoning and credible evidence. It is abused if speakers *substitute* appeals to feelings for evidence or reasoning.

To arouse emotions, language must overcome barriers of time, distance, and apathy.

Overcoming Time.   Listeners live in the present. This makes it hard to awaken feelings about events that lie in the past or distant future. But skillful speakers can use words to make the past and future come alive. Stories that recapture feelings from the past are often told at company meetings to re-create the human dimension of the business and to re-establish corporate heritage and culture. In the following story, the speaker reminds listeners of the legend of Federal Express, a pioneer in overnight delivery:

It's hard to remember that Federal Express was once just a fly-by-night dream, a crazy idea in which a few people had invested—not just their time and their money but their lives and futures. I remember one time early on when things weren't going so well. Couldn't even make the payroll that week and looked like we were going to crash. Fred [Smith, founder of the company] was in a deep funk. "What the hell," he said, and flew off to Las Vegas. The next day he flew back and his face was shining. "We're going to make it," he said. He had just won $27,000 at the blackjack table! And we made it. We met the payroll. And then things began to turn around, and Federal Express grew eventually into the giant it is today.[7]

This story enlivens the past by emphasizing the contrast of emotions—the "deep funk" versus the "shining" face. The use of lively, colloquial dialogue—"What the hell," and "We're going to make it"—re-creates the excitement and brings those feelings into the present. It would not have been as effective had the speaker simply said, "Fred was depressed, but after he got back from Las Vegas he was confident." Such a bare summary would have distanced the listener and diminished the emotional power of the scene.

Language can also make the future seem close to listeners. Because words can cross the barrier of time, both tradition and a vision of tomorrow can guide us through the present.

Overcoming Distance.   The closer anything is to us, the easier it is to develop feelings about it. But what if speakers must discuss faraway people, places, and objects? Words can act like the zoom on your computer to bring such subjects closer to your audience.

Beth Tidmore, our student who won the U.S. Junior Olympics air rifle event at Colorado Springs, demonstrated a special gift for overcoming distance between herself and her listeners. When she wanted to share her feelings about her shooting experiences, she concentrated on sensory details of touch and smell. "My friends," she said, "don't know what it's like to feel the cold, smooth wood of the cheekpiece against your face. And they don't know the rich smell of Hoppe's No. 9 [oil] when you're cleaning your rifle." Through such sensory descriptions, she was able to communicate with listeners who themselves were far removed from such experiences.

Beth was even more effective when she appealed to her listeners to become involved in Special Olympics events. To move their feelings, Beth used a technique that—when successful—collapses the distance between listeners and subjects. This technique, the vicarious experience narrative, *invites listeners to imagine themselves participating in the action advocated by the speaker.*

> I've had so many great experiences, but these are hard to describe without overworking words like "fulfilling" and "rewarding." So I'm going to let you experience it for yourself. I want everybody to pack your bags—we're going to the Special Olympics summer games in Georgia!

Beth then became a tour guide for this imaginary trip, walking listeners through the moments that would move them in dramatic ways. Again, she had effectively bridged the distance between her subject and her audience.

Overcoming Apathy.   Modern audiences are beset with an endless barrage of information, persuasion, and entertainment. As a result, many of us become jaded—we may even develop a *resistance* to communication and turn away from appeals to our feelings.

Sally Duncan found an especially poignant way to overcome such apathy. Interestingly, it worked because of incompetent language usage. Sally began her informative speech by projecting a picture of her grandmother on the screen behind the lectern. She described her as a cultured, elegant woman who had a master's degree, had taught English for years, and had taken Sally to art museums and the theater. "Now," she said, "let me read my last letter from Nanny."

> Dear Sally. I am finally around to answer your last. You have to look over me. Ha. I am so sorry to when you called Sunday why didn't you remind me. Steph had us all so upset leaving and not telling no she was going back but we have a good snow ha and Kathy can't drive on ice so I never get a pretty card but they have a thing to see through an envelope. I haven't got any in the bank until I get my homestead check so I'm just sending this. Ha. When you was talking on the phone Cathy had Ben and got my groceries and I had to unlock the door. I forgot to say hold and I don't have Claudette's number so forgive me for being

so silly. Ha. Nara said to tell you she isn't doing no good well one is doing
pretty good and my eyes. Love, Nanny.

Sally paused for a long moment, and then said, "My Nanny has Alzheimer's." We
were riveted as she went on to describe the disease and how to cope with loved ones
who have it.

The role of words in arousing feeling is also underscored by the contrast between
denotative and connotative forms of meaning. The **denotative meaning** of a word
is its dictionary definition or generally agreed-on objective usage. For example, the
denotative definition of *alcohol* is "a colorless, volatile, flammable liquid, obtained
by the fermentation of sugars or starches, which is widely used as a solvent, drug
base, explosive, or intoxicating beverage."[8] How different this definition is from the
two connotative definitions offered in this chapter's opening example! **Connotative
meaning** invests a subject with the speaker's personal associations and emotions.
Thus, the "intoxicating beverage" is no longer just a chemical substance but rather is
"the poison scourge" or "the oil of conversation." Connotative language intensifies
feelings; denotative language encourages detachment.

Bringing Listeners Together

In many situations, individual action is not enough. It may take many people working together to get things done, and language can bring them together. Barack
Obama's campaign for the presidency depended very much on his ability to bring
together many diverse audiences in support of his bid. Thus in his celebrated
Speech on Race, delivered at a critical time in the campaign, he appealed directly for
this togetherness:

> I believe deeply that we cannot solve the challenges of
> our time unless we solve them together—unless we per-
> fect our union by understanding that we may have dif-
> ferent stories, but we hold common hopes; that we may
> not look the same and we may not have come from
> the same place, but we all want to move in the same
> direction—towards a better future for our children
> and our grandchildren.[9]

AP Wide World Photos

Note the emphasis on "we" and "our." Words can also
bring people together in times of grief. On April 16, 2007,
a lone gunman killed 32 people at Virginia Tech University
before turning his gun on himself. At a memorial ceremony the next day, the faculty and student body met to
find what comfort they could during those tragic days. The
honor of closing the ceremony fell to Nikki Giovanni, an
acclaimed poet who was also a University Distinguished
Professor. In her remarks, Giovanni combined the power
of poetry and prose to bring her listeners together:

Poet and professor Nikki Giovanni's eloquent language brought listeners together.

> We are Virginia Tech.
> We are strong enough to stand tall tearlessly;
> We are brave enough to bend to cry

▶ **denotative meaning** The dictionary
definition or objective meaning of a word.

▶ **connotative meaning** The emotional,
subjective, personal meaning that certain words
can evoke in listeners.

And sad enough to know we must laugh again.
We are Virginia Tech.
. . . We will continue to invent the future through our blood and tears,
through all this sadness. . . . We will prevail![10]

Note again the emphasis on "We," the great pronoun of inclusion. Note also how Giovanni combines opposites to create a sense of unity: sadness and laughter, "stand tall tearlessly" and "bend to cry," proposing that a promising future will grow out of the tragic past—that the past and future will come together just as her listeners are brought together by her words.

Although words can unite people, they can also drive them apart. Name calling, exclusionary language, and unsupported accusations can be notorious dividers.

Prompting Listeners to Take Action

Even when your listeners share an identity, they still may not be ready to act. What barriers might stand in their way? For one thing, they may not be convinced of the soundness of your proposal. They may not trust you, or they may not think they can do anything about a problem. They may also not be ready to invest the energy or take the risk that action demands.

Your language must convince listeners that action is necessary, that your ideas are sound, and that success is possible. In her speech urging students to act to improve off-campus housing conditions, Anna Aley painted vivid word-pictures of deplorable off-campus housing. She supported these descriptions with both factual examples and her personal experiences. She also reminded listeners that if they acted together, they could bring about change:

> What can one student do to change the practices of numerous Manhattan landlords? Nothing, if that student is alone. But just think of what we could accomplish if we got all 13,600 off-campus students involved in this issue! Think what we could accomplish if we got even a fraction of those students involved!

Anna then proposed specific actions that did not call for great effort or risk. In short, she made commitment as easy as possible. She concluded with an appeal to action:

> Kansas State students have been putting up with substandard living conditions for too long. It's time we finally got together to do something about this problem. Join the Off-Campus Association. Sign my petition. Let's send a message to these slumlords that we're not going to put up with this any more. We don't have to live in slums.

Anna's words expressed both her indignation and the urgency of the problem. Her references to time—"too long" and "it's time"—called for immediate action. Her final appeals to join the association and sign the petition were expressed in short sentences that packed a lot of punch. Her repetition of "slumlords" and "slums" motivated her listeners to transform their indignation into action.

Anna also illustrated another language strategy that is important when you want to move people to action: the ability to depict dramas showing what is at stake and what roles listeners should take.[11] Such scenarios draw clear lines between right and wrong. Be careful, however, not to go overboard with such techniques. Ethical communication requires that you maintain respect for all involved in conflict. As both speaker and listener, be wary of melodramas that offer stark contrasts between good and evil. Such depictions often distort reality.

Celebrating Shared Values

It is important for people to remind themselves occasionally of the values that tie them together. To celebrate these values is to strengthen them and the communities that share them. Often these celebrations take place during ceremonies such as those that celebrate Memorial Day, Martin Luther King's birthday, or presidential inaugurals.

Aristotle noted over two thousand years ago that spoken communication serving this vital function emphasizes the *image*. When images work well, they paint vivid word-pictures that show us our values in action. They often tell stories that teach us to treasure our traditions. Such language is colorful, concrete, and graphic—it appeals to the senses. Note how President Reagan used such language in his second inaugural address to call up memories of heroes and to strengthen the image of the American heritage:

> Hear again the echoes of our past. A general falls to his knees in the harsh snow of Valley Forge; a lonely President paces the darkened halls and ponders his struggle to preserve the Union; the men of the Alamo call out encouragement to each other; a settler pushes West and sings a song, and the song echoes out forever and fills the unknowing air.
> It is the American Sound. It is hopeful, big-hearted, idealistic—daring, decent and fair. That's our heritage. That's our song.[12]

You too can use the power of words to evoke the past as you find your own voice. The right words and phrases, used in the right places, can create a lasting picture.

The power of language is great, ranging from shaping perceptions to revitalizing group culture. How can you use words in ways that will help you both find your voice and express it in powerful ways? We turn now to the standards you must apply as you seek the answers to that question.

YOUR ethical VOICE   Managing Powerful Language

To use the power of words in ethical ways, follow these guidelines:

1. Avoid depictions that distort reality: Let your words illuminate the subject, not blind the listener.

2. Use words to support sound reasoning, not substitute for it.

3. Use language to empower both past traditions and visions of the future.

4. Use images to renew appreciation of shared values.

5. Use language to strengthen the ties of community, not divide people.

6. Use language to overcome inertia and inspire listeners to action.

7. Be careful about melodramatic language that reduces complex issues and the people in disputes into good versus evil.

8. Avoid language that degrades people, especially animal metaphors.

The Six C's of Language Use

For words to work for you, they must meet certain standards: clarity, color, concreteness, correctness, conciseness, and cultural sensitivity. We call these the six C's of oral language usage.

Clarity

Clarity is the first standard, because if your words are not clear, listeners cannot understand your meaning. To be clear, you must yourself understand what you want to say. Next, you must find words that convey your ideas as precisely and as simply as possible. The standard of clarity is met when something closely approximating the idea you intend is reproduced in the minds of listeners.

One factor that impairs clarity is the use of **jargon**, the technical language that is specific to a profession. If you use jargon before an audience that doesn't share that technical vocabulary, you may not be understood. For example, as he forecasted an event in 2008 that would devastate so much of Iowa, Brian Pierce, a meteorologist with the National Weather Service in Davenport, used the following words: "We are seeing a historic hydrological event taking place with unprecedented river levels occurring."[13] Mr. Pierce would have communicated a lot more clearly to a lot more people had he simply said, "We are in for one heckuva flood."

Speakers who fall into the jargon trap are so used to using technical language that they forget that others may not grasp it. It does not occur to them that they must translate the jargon into lay language to be understood by general audiences.

A similar problem is using words that are needlessly overblown and pretentious. A notorious example occurred when signmakers wanted to tell tourists how to leave the Barnum museum. Rather than drawing an arrow with the word Exit above it, they wrote "To the Egress." There's no telling how many visitors left the museum by mistake, thinking that they were going to see that rare creature—a living, breathing "Egress."

Sometimes speakers may deliberately avoid clarity—because the truth may hurt. Such efforts to soften and obscure the truth are called **euphemisms**. At moments, these efforts may be rather lighthearted, as when a sports commentator, speaking of the quarterback on a football team, said, "He has ball security issues" when he really meant, "This guy fumbles a lot." On a slightly more serious note, politicians in Tennessee agreed to pass a new hospital tax, as long as it wasn't called a "tax." Instead, it would have to be called a "coverage fee."[14]

At its worst, such language degenerates into **doublespeak**, the use of words to deliberately befuddle listeners and hide unpleasant truths. The language of doublespeak points listeners in a direction opposite from the reality of a situation. The *New York Times* charged that the Bush administration developed what they call *ecospeak* (an apparent variation of *doublespeak*) to disguise pro-business and anti-environmental initiatives:

> Mr. Bush . . . may fairly be said to have become the master of the ostensibly ecofriendly sound bite. . . . "Healthy Forests," for instance, describes an initiative aimed mainly at benefiting the timber industry rather than the communities threatened by fire. [In another case] Mr. Bush's purpose was to defend his controversial decision in August to rewrite the Clean Air Act in ways that spared power companies the expense of making investments in pollution controls. . . . His basic argument was that the rules thwarted modernization and economic growth . . . and that his own initiative—dubbed "Clear Skies,"

▶ **jargon** Technical language related to a specific field that may be incomprehensible to a general audience.

▶ **euphemism** Words that soften or evade the truth of a situation.

▶ **doublespeak** Words that point in the direction opposite from the reality they supposedly describe.

When they say:	What they often mean is:
Marital discord	Spouse beating
Downsizing	Firing
Making a salary adjustment	Cutting your pay
Failed to fulfill wellness potential	Died
Chronologically experienced citizen	Old codger
Initial and pass on	Let's spread the blame
Friendly fire	We killed our own people
Collateral damage	We killed innocent people

FIGURE 1
Doublespeak

in the come-hither nomenclature favored by the White House—would achieve equal results at lower cost.[15]

How can you avoid such violations of clarity and ethics? One way is through **amplification**, which extends the time listeners have for contemplating an idea and helps them bring it into sharper focus. You amplify an idea by defining it, repeating it, rephrasing it, offering examples of it, and contrasting it with more familiar and concrete subjects. In effect, you tell listeners something and then expand what you have just said. Bill Gates used amplification effectively in a speech on reforming high school education, illustrating how definition and contrast especially can clarify an idea:

> America's high schools are obsolete. By obsolete, I don't just mean that our high schools are broken, flawed, and underfunded—though a case could be made for every one of those points.
>
> By obsolete, I mean that our high schools—even when they're working exactly as designed—cannot teach our kids what they need to know today.
>
> Training the workforce of tomorrow with the high schools of today is like trying to teach kids about today's computers on a 50-year-old mainframe. It's the wrong tool for the times.[16]

Color

Color refers to the emotional intensity or vividness of language. Colorful words are memorable because they stand out in our minds, along with the ideas they convey. Colorful language paints striking pictures for listeners that linger in the mind. In her speech urging the purchase of hybrid cars, Davidson student Alexandra McArthur framed a colorful conclusion based on a **neologism**, an invented word that combines previous words in a striking new expression. In this case, Alexandra created her new word by combining "hybrid" and "hubris":

> If you do end up buying a hybrid, as you drive around town looking trendy, cruising past the gas stations, you may start feeling pretty good about yourself

Colorful language and a lively presentation bring speeches to life.

Amana productions inc\Getty Images Inc. RF

▶ **amplification**   The art of developing ideas by restating them in a speech.

▶ **neologism**   An invented word that combines previous words in a striking new expression.

and talking about your car any chance you get. This new form of pride, commonly called *hybris*, may be annoying to your friends but is nothing incurable. I'm sure they will forgive you when they get their first hybrid.

One very special type of colorful language is **slang**, expressions that arise out of common, ordinary, everyday usage. You may have been advised not to use slang, that it is coarse, even vulgar, and that it epitomizes "bad" English. But according to general semanticist S. I. Hayakawa, slang can also be "the poetry of everyday life." Or, as the poet Carl Sandburg noted, slang is "language that rolls up its sleeves, spits on its hands, and goes to work."

Slang has its use in speeches: It can add vigor to your message and be a source of identification between you and listeners. But use it with caution. Slang is inappropriate on formal occasions when a high level of decorum is called for. Moreover, you must be certain that your audience will understand your slang expressions. You should also avoid using ethnic slang or other words that your audience might find offensive. Finally, slang should be used sparingly—to emphasize a point or add a dash of humor and color. It should supplement standard English usage in your speech, not replace it.

Using colorful language makes a speech interesting and can enhance your ethos, adding to the impression that you are a competent, likable person.

Concreteness

It is almost impossible to discuss any significant topic without using some abstract words. However, if you use language that is overly abstract, your audience may lose interest. Moreover, because abstract language is more ambiguous than concrete language, a speech full of abstractions invites misunderstanding. Consider Figure 2, which illustrates movement along a continuum from abstract to concrete terms.

The more concrete your language, the more pictorial and precise the information you convey. Concrete words are also easier for listeners to remember. Your language should be as concrete as the subject permits.

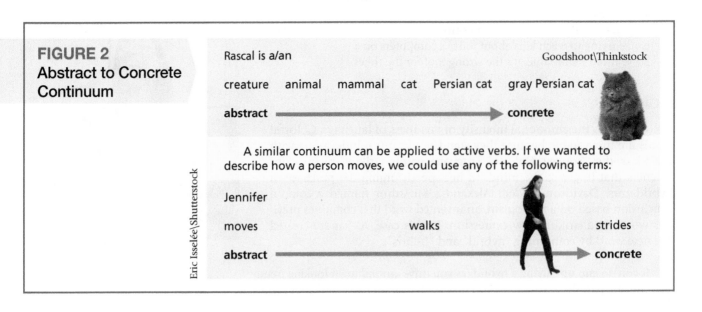

**FIGURE 2
Abstract to Concrete Continuum**

Rascal is a/an   Goodshoot\Thinkstock

creature   animal   mammal   cat   Persian cat   gray Persian cat

abstract ⟶ **concrete**

A similar continuum can be applied to active verbs. If we wanted to describe how a person moves, we could use any of the following terms:

Jennifer

moves   walks   strides

abstract ⟶ **concrete**

Eric Isselée\Shutterstock

▸ **slang** The language of the street.

Correctness

Nothing can damage your credibility more than the misuse of language. Glaring mistakes in grammar can make you seem uneducated and even ignorant. While touting his education plan, one prominent politician told listeners that the most important consideration should be, "Is your children learning?" Hopefully they would not miss the lesson on subject-verb agreement! Other common grammatical errors that make listeners cringe are listed in Figure 3.

Mistakes in word selection can be as damaging as mistakes in grammar. Occasionally, beginning speakers, wanting to impress people with the size of their vocabulary, get caught up in what we call the "thesaurus syndrome." They will look up a simple word to find a synonym that sounds more impressive. What they may not realize is that the words shown as synonyms often have slightly different meanings. For example, the words *disorganize* and *derange* are sometimes listed as synonyms. But if you refer to a disorganized person as "deranged," that person's reaction could be interesting.

People often err when using words that sound similar. Such confusions are called **malapropisms**, after Mrs. Malaprop, a character in an eighteenth-century play by Richard Sheridan. She would say, "He is the very *pineapple* of politeness," when she

---

FIGURE 3 Correcting Grammatical Errors

1. Using the wrong tense or verb form:
   Wrong: He *done* us a big favor.
   Right: He *did* us a big favor.

2. Lack of agreement between subject and verb:
   Wrong: *Is* your students giving speeches?
   Right: *Are* your students giving speeches?

3. Using the wrong word
   Wrong: *Caricature* is the most important factor in choosing a mate.
   Right: *Character* is the most important factor in choosing a mate.

4. Lack of agreement between a pronoun and its antecedent:
   Wrong: A hyperactive *person* will work *themselves* to death.
   Right: Hyperactive *people* will work *themselves* to death.

   or

   A hyperactive *woman* will work *herself* to death.

5. Improper type of pronoun used as subject:
   Wrong: *Him* and *me* decided to go to the library.
   Right: *He* and *I* decided to go to the library.

6. Improper type of pronoun used as object:
   Wrong: The speaker's lack of information dismayed my students and *I*.
   Right: The speaker's lack of information dismayed my students and *me*.

7. Double negative:
   Wrong: I *don't never* get bad grades on my speeches.
   Right: I *never* get bad grades on my speeches.

▶ **malapropisms** Language errors that occur when a word is confused with another word that sounds like it.

meant *pinnacle*. A prominent baseball player, trying to explain why he had forgotten an appointment for an interview, said "I must have had *ambrosia*" (which probably caused his *amnesia*, which is what he apparently meant). Archie Bunker, in the classic TV show *All in the Family*, was prone to malapropisms, such as "Don't let your imagination run *rancid*" when he meant *rampant*. William J. Crocker of Armidale College in New South Wales, Australia, collected the following malapropisms from his students:

A speaker can add interest to his talk with an *antidote*. [anecdote]

Disagreements can arise from an unintended *conception*. [Indeed they can! Inference would work better]

The speaker hopes to arouse *apathy* in his audience. [sympathy? empathy?]

Good language can be reinforced by good *gestation*. [gestures]

The speaker can use either an inductive or a *seductive* approach. [deductive][17]

Students, ballplayers, and fictional characters are not the only ones who make such blunders. Elected officials are also not above an occasional malapropism. One former United States senator declared that he would oppose to his last ounce of energy any effort to build a "nuclear waste *suppository*" [repository] in his state (sounds like an incredible new cure for constipation!). A long-gone but not forgotten Chicago mayor once commented that he did not believe "in casting *asparagus* [aspersions] on his opponents." And the Speaker of the Texas legislature once acknowledged an award by saying, "I am filled with *humidity*" (perhaps he meant moist hot air as well as humility).

The lesson is clear. To avoid being unintentionally humorous, use a current dictionary to check the meaning of any word you feel uncertain about. For additional help, refer to the Web site developed by Professor Paul Brians of Washington State University to help students avoid common errors of usage (www.wsu.edu/~brians/errors/index.html).

Conciseness

In discussing clarity, we talked about the importance of amplification in speeches to expand understanding. Although it may seem contradictory, you must also be concise, even while you are amplifying your ideas. You must make your points quickly and efficiently.

Simplicity and directness help you be concise. Thomas Jefferson once said, "The most valuable of all talents is that of never using two words when one will do." Abraham Lincoln was similarly concise as he criticized the verbosity of another speaker: "He can compress the most words into the smallest idea of any man I know."

One way you can achieve conciseness is by using **maxims**, compact sayings that encapsulate beliefs. To reinforce his point that we need to actively (and audibly) confront the problems of racism, sexism, and homophobia, Haven Cockerham, vice president of human resources for Detroit Edison, came up with this striking maxim: "Sometimes silence isn't golden—just yellow."[18]

Maxims attract mass-media attention during demonstrations. When used on signs, they can be picked up as signature statements for movements or campaigns. Their brevity and dramatic impact make them well suited to display on television's evening news.

A caution is in order about using maxims: They should not be substituted for a carefully designed and well-supported argument. However, once you have developed

▶ **maxims** Brief and particularly apt sayings.

a responsible and substantive speech, consider whether you might use maxims to reinforce your message.

Cultural Sensitivity

Because words can either lift and unite or wound and hurt your audience, you must exercise **cultural sensitivity** in your choice of language. Looking back into the history of human communication, you will find little about cultural sensitivity. The ancient Greeks, for example, worried only about speaking to other male Athenians who were "free men" and citizens. Today, with our increasing emphasis on lifestyles, racial diversity, and the pursuit of gender equity, cultural sensitivity becomes an important standard for effective language usage.

PhotoEdit Inc.

Cultural sensitivity requires adaptation and respect.

John Duesler, president of the Valley Swim Club in Philadelphia, might have profited from this advice. In the summer of 2009, Duesler's club accepted money from an inner-city day camp so that its children could swim once a week at the club. When the mostly minority group of children showed up, however, some club members apparently objected and the swimming privileges were revoked. Duesler's explanation? "There was concern that a lot of kids would change the complexion . . . and the atmosphere of the club." Later he admitted, "That was a terrible choice of words."[19]

A lack of cultural sensitivity almost always has negative consequences. At best, audience members may be mildly offended; at worst, they will be irate enough to reject both you and your message. Cultural sensitivity begins with being attuned to the diversity of your audience and careful about the words you choose. Don't be like the politician who singled out some audience members in wheelchairs for special praise. After lauding their accomplishments, he said, "Now, will you all stand and be recognized?"

Although you must make some generalizations about your audience, avoid getting caught up in stereotypes that suggest that one group is inferior in any way to another. Stay away from racial, ethnic, religious, or gender-based humor, and avoid any expressions that might be interpreted as racist or sexist.

How Special Techniques Can Magnify Your Voice

There are critical moments in a speech—often at the beginning, ending, or as arguments reach their conclusions—when you want your words to be most effective. At these moments, you can sometimes call on special techniques to magnify the power of your emerging voice.

The branch of communication study that deals with identifying, understanding, and utilizing these techniques is called *rhetorical style*. Over the centuries, many such techniques have been identified; they seem to be grounded in our nature and to have evolved perhaps to meet basic human needs for effective communication. Here we discuss three broad categories of techniques that are especially useful for public speaking: *figurative language*; techniques that alter the customary *order* of words; and techniques that exploit the *sounds* of words for special effects.

▶ **cultural sensitivity** The respectful appreciation of diversity within an audience.

359

Using Figurative Language

Figurative language uses words in unusual ways to create fresh understandings of the subjects of communication. We focus here on seven forms of figurative language that may be especially useful for public speakers: metaphor, enduring metaphor, simile, synecdoche, personification, culturetype, and ideograph.

Metaphor.   Drawing comparisons is a fundamental way in which our minds work to understand unfamiliar or abstract ideas. A **metaphor** offers a brief, concentrated form of comparison that is implied, unexpected, and sometimes even startling. It connects elements of experience that are not usually related. When you use a metaphor, you pull a rabbit out of a hat. Having read that, your first reaction might be, "Wait a minute, words are not rabbits and language is not a hat!" But when a metaphor works, the listener's next reaction is, "Oooh, I see what you mean!" Good metaphors reveal unexpected similarities in striking ways. They also can add color and concreteness to your message.

Metaphors, as Aristotle once noted, may be our most useful and versatile stylistic tool. They can be especially helpful in introductions and conclusions. At the beginnings of speeches, metaphors can offer an overall frame of understanding in which a topic can develop. Note how Antoinette M. Bailey, president of the Boeing-McDonnell Foundation, used a wave metaphor to open a speech presented to the International Women in Aviation Conference:

> Suppose we have gone down to the beach on a quiet day. We are standing in the water, admiring the view. Suddenly, a speedboat zooms by at full throttle. Seconds later, we are struck by a powerful wave. This is a bow wave, and it can knock you off your feet if you aren't prepared for it. A very large and fast-moving bow wave is just now beginning to hit the aerospace industry. This morning I want to talk about what we, as an industry, and we, as women, should do to prepare for it.[20]

Eloquent language can intensify our feelings about subjects.

In a similar vein, concluding metaphors can offer a final frame of understanding that interprets the meaning of a speech for its listeners. Student speaker Alexandra McArthur used the following metaphor as she concluded a speech warning her audience not to accept at face value the pictures of foreign countries painted in travel brochures: "Tourism may be an economic Band-Aid for the gaping wound of poverty." When Martin Luther King Jr. spoke to striking sanitation workers in Memphis the night before he was assassinated, he talked of the "spiritual journey" that his listeners had traveled. He ended his speech by saying that he had climbed the mountain ahead of them—that he had "seen the Promised Land." These metaphors of the journey and the mountain lifted his listeners and allowed them to share his vision, just as he had earlier shared his "dream" with them in his famous "I Have a Dream" oration. More than just communicating in a superficial way, such metaphors may reveal and share how the speaker perceives the world.

Because metaphors can be so powerful, you should select them carefully and use them with restraint. First, *the gravity of the metaphor must match the seriousness of your subject.* Just as you would not typically wear formal attire to a basketball game, you should not use certain metaphors to express certain subjects. If you used Dr. King's mountaintop image to express your overview of the can recycling industry in a speech to a general audience, the effect might be more ludicrous than persuasive.

▶ **figurative language**   Words used in surprising and unusual ways that magnify the power of their meaning.

▶ **metaphor**   Brief, concentrated form of implied comparison. Often connects subjects that are not usually related in order to create a surprising perspective.

Second, *mixing metaphors by combining images that don't fit together can confuse listeners and lower their estimation of your competence.* The politician who attacked an opponent saying, "You can't take the high horse and then claim the low road," mixed his metaphors.

Third, *you also should avoid trite metaphors,* such as "that person [or idea or practice] is so cool" or "I was on an emotional roller coaster." Overuse has turned these metaphors into clichés that no longer have any impact. Not only are they ineffective, but using them may again damage your ethos. Tired comparisons suggest a dull mind.

As useful and powerful as metaphor may be, it can also be quite dangerous. Certain animal metaphors, for example, can project and justify dehumanizing, scornful attitudes about groups of people. Consider this recent statement from the lieutenant governor of South Carolina about government assistance to the poor:

> My grandmother was not a highly educated woman, but she told me as a small child to quit feeding stray animals. You know why? Because they breed! You're facilitating the problem if you give an animal or a person ample food supply. They will reproduce, especially ones that don't think too much further than that.[21]

Enduring Metaphor. One special group of metaphors taps into shared experience that persists across time and that crosses many cultural boundaries. These **enduring metaphors**—or "archetypal metaphors" as they are sometimes called—are especially popular in speeches, perhaps because they invoke experience that has great meaning and that can bring people together. They connect their particular, timebound subjects with timeless themes, such as light and darkness, storms, the sea, disease, and the family. A brief look at three of these metaphors demonstrates their potential power to magnify meaning.[22]

Light and Darkness. From the beginning of time, people have made negative associations with darkness. The dark is cold, unfriendly, and dangerous. On the other hand, light brings warmth and safety. It restores control. When speakers use the light–darkness metaphor, they usually equate problems or bad times with darkness and solutions or recovery with light. The speaker's proposal may offer the "dawn," a "candle to light our way," or a "beacon of hope."

Storms and the Sea. The storm metaphor can be used to describe serious problems. Often the storm occurs at sea—a dangerous place under the best of conditions. When political problems are the focus of the speech, the "captain" who "steers the ship of state" can reassure us with his programs or principles—and make them seem very attractive in the process. In his first inaugural address, George W. Bush said that "through much of the last century, America's faith in freedom and democracy was a rock in a raging sea."[23]

The Family. Family metaphors express the dream of a close, loving relationship among people through such images as "the family of humanity."[24] As he asked listeners to transcend race, Barack Obama appealed to such images: "Let us be our brother's keeper, Scripture tells us. Let us be our sister's keeper."[25] Such metaphors can be especially useful when listeners may feel alienated from each

Petra Wegner\Alamy Images

Light and darkensss and storms and the sea are enduring metaphors.

▶ **enduring metaphors** Metaphors of unusual power and popularity that are based on experience that lasts across time and that crosses many cultural boundaries.

other and from their surroundings. In such situations, family metaphors can be a powerful force to bring listeners together and to effect identification. Wade Steck demonstrated the potential of such metaphors as he was describing his experiences at the University of Memphis Frosh Camp Program, his introduction to college life:

> When I got to Frosh Camp, they made me feel at home. First thing they did was to break us into "families" of ten to twelve people who would share the same cabin for those few days. Each "family" had its counselors, carefully selected juniors and seniors who were really called your "mom" and "dad." . . . The thing I liked most were the Fireside Chats. At night under the stars, watching the logs burn . . ., people would just relax and talk. I discovered that many of those in my family shared my concerns and anxieties.

Similarly, the *disease* metaphor pictures our problems as illness and offers solutions in the form of cures.[26] Metaphors of *war and peace* can frame conflict situations and our quest for their resolution.[27] The *building* metaphor, as when we talk about "laying the foundation" for the future, emphasizes our impulse to shape and control the conditions of our lives. And *spatial* metaphors often reflect striving upward and moving forward toward goals.[28]

Similes. A **simile** is a variation of metaphor that warns listeners that a comparison is coming. Words such as *like* or *as* function as signals that soften the impact of the expression. The result is to offer a more controlled form of figurative language in which the speaker guides the comparison in order to create certain planned effects. One such effect is to help listeners imagine things that are far removed from their experience. Remember Scott Champlin's words, "a force that spun me around *like* a twisted yo-yo at the end of a string"? Most of us, we hope, will never be hit by a tracer bullet while parachuting, but we may well have played with a yo-yo as children. Helped by the simile, we can imagine the experience.

A second intended effect is to heighten interest in and familiarize such experience. A particularly engaging example occurred in a speech by Davidson student Jessica Bradshaw concerning how Dr. Seuss composed the children's classic, *The Cat in the Hat*. Jess quoted Dr. Seuss as follows:

> The method I used is [like] the method you see when you sit down to make apple strudel without the strudel. . . . You take your limited, uninteresting ingredients and day and night, month after month, you mix them up into

FINDING YOUR
voice Enduring Metaphors in Contemporary Communication

Look for examples of enduring metaphors as used in contemporary public communication (speeches, editorials, advertising, visual, and televisual communication). Why do you think they are used in these ways? Are they effective? Might they connect with motivation? How so?

▶ **simile** A language tool that clarifies something abstract by comparing it with something concrete; usually introduced by "as" or "like."

thousands of combinations. You bake a batch. You taste it. Then you hurl it out the window. Until finally one night, when it is darkest just before dawn, a plausible strudel-less strudel begins to take shape before your eyes![29]

Simile can also be used to express feelings. Notice how one critic used it to focus her feelings about a proposal to send astronauts on an expedition to Mars: "Spending billions in outer space is *like* buying a new Lexus when the fridge is empty and the roof is leaking."[30]

Synecdoche. One of the great classic forms of figuration, **synecdoche** (sin-eck'-duh-key), is grounded in an ancient tendency of our nature: representing a subject by focusing on a vivid part of it or on something closely associated with it. Thus, the nautical expression "all hands on deck" represents a group of people by focusing on a useful part of them. "The pen is mightier than the sword" compares two great human activities, communication and warfare, by focusing on instruments traditionally associated with them.

Memphis student Sandra Baltz explained how three cultures interact harmoniously in her life by focusing on a food synecdoche that offered a simple, colorful, and concrete illustration of her point:

> In all, I must say that being exposed to three very different cultures—Latin, Arabic, and American—has been rewarding for me and has made a difference even in the music I enjoy and the food I eat. It is not unusual in my house to sit down to a meal made up of stuffed grape leaves and refried beans and all topped off with apple pie for dessert.

Synecdoche can be easily abused. If we focus on one feature of a subject and ignore others, we may distort the picture we present about the subject and cause listeners to draw warped or incomplete conclusions. Thus "all hands on deck" may cause us to miss a larger picture—that these are human beings who also have hearts and heads, thoughts and feelings, and who deserve to be treated as such.

Personification. One kind of figurative speech, **personification**, treats inanimate subjects, such as ideas or institutions, as though they had human form or feeling. The Chinese students who demonstrated for freedom in Tiananmen Square carried a statue they called the "Goddess of Liberty." They were borrowing a personification that has long been used in the Western world: the representation of liberty as a woman.[31] When those students then had to confront tanks, and their oppressors destroyed the symbol of liberty, it was easy for many, living thousands of miles away in another culture, to feel even more angry over their fate. Personification makes it easier to arouse feelings about people and values that might otherwise seem abstract and distant.

Culturetypes. **Culturetypes**, sometimes stated in the form of metaphor, express the values, identity, and goals of a particular group and time.[32] In 1960, John F. Kennedy dramatized his presidential campaign by inviting Americans to explore with him "new frontiers" of national possibility. That metaphor worked well in American culture, but it probably would not have made much sense in other countries. For Americans, the frontier is a unique symbol that stands for freedom, challenge, and opportunity.

▶ **synecdoche** Represents a subject by focusing on a vivid part of it or on something clearly associated with it.

▶ **personification** A figure of speech in which nonhuman or abstract subjects are given human qualities.

▶ **culturetypes** Terms that express the values and goals of a group's culture.

Some culturetypes include what rhetorical critic Richard Weaver once described as "god and devil terms."[33] Weaver suggested that *progress* has been a primary "god term" of American culture. People often seem willing to follow that word as though it were some kind of divine summons. Tell us to do something in the name of "progress," and many will feel prompted to respond. Other terms, such as *science, modern,* and *efficient,* are similarly powerful, Weaver argued, because they seem rooted in American values. If something is "scientific," we are apt to listen respectfully. If something is "modern," many of us think it is better, probably because it has benefited from "progress." If something is "efficient," many Americans will more often select it over options that are perhaps more ethical or beautiful. On the other hand, words like *terrorist* and *terrorism* are "devil terms." They can make a person, group, or action seem repulsive and threatening.

Culturetypes can change over time: In recent years, words like *natural, communication,* and *environment* have become more compelling; *liberalism* and *pollution,* if not devil terms, seem increasingly undesirable to many people.

Ideographs. Communication scholar Michael Calvin McGee identified an especially potent group of culturetypes that he called **ideographs**. These words express in a concentrated way a country's basic political values.[34] McGee suggested that words like *freedom, liberty,* and *democracy* are important because they are shorthand expressions of political identity. It is inconceivable to us that other nations might not wish to have a "democratic" form of government or that they might not prize "liberty" over every other value. Expressions such as "*freedom* fighters" and "*democracy* in action" have unusual power for us because they utilize ideographs.

As an audience, we can be especially vulnerable to such language, and it can be dangerous. After all, one person's "freedom fighter" can be another person's "terrorist." We must look behind such glittering generalities to inspect the agendas they may hide. "Trigger words" can trigger our emotional responses and short-circuit reflection. Ideographs and culturetypes can function as widely shared, cultural trigger words. They are capable of honorable work: They can magnify the appeal of sound arguments, remind us of our heritage, and suggest that we must be true to our values. But the potential for abusing such words in unethical communication is considerable. You must prove that they apply legitimately to your topic. As a speaker, use them sparingly, and as a listener, inspect them carefully.

To develop a healthy resistance to such words, we should respond to them with a series of critical questions:

1. *Is this really what it claims to be?* For example, does the development of increasingly more powerful weapons of mass destruction really represent "progress"? Are "freedom fighters" actually thugs?

FINDING YOUR

voice The Culturetypes of Our Time

What words would you nominate as culturetypes in contemporary society? Remember to look for "devil" as well as "god" terms. Find examples of how these words are actually used in public communication. What work do they do? Are there any ethical problems with these uses?

▶ **ideographs** Compact expressions of a group's basic political faith.

2. *Are those who make these claims legitimate sources of information?* For example, are those who advance the "science" of cryonics, the preservation of bodies by freezing them in hopes of discovering how to restore life to them on some future occasion, really "scientists"? Or are they simply exploiters?

3. *Do these claims reflect a proper hierarchy of values?* For example, lopping off the top of a mountain to strip-mine coal may be a highly "efficient" form of mining, but should we be featuring efficiency here? Could protection of the environment be a more important consideration?

4. *What kinds of actions are these words urging me to endorse or undertake?* For example, should I be asked to support and even die for "democracy" in a nation whose citizens may prefer some other form of government?

Changing the Order of Words

We grow accustomed to words falling into certain patterns in sentences. Strategic changes in this customary order of words violate these expectations and call attention to themselves. Why, we ask ourselves, has the speaker made these changes? What do they signify?

Antithesis, inversion, and *parallel construction* are techniques that change the way words are ordered in messages. Their primary functions are to magnify the speaker as a leader and to enhance appeals to action.

Antithesis. **Antithesis** arranges different or opposing ideas in the same or adjoining sentences to create a striking contrast. Beth Tidmore used the technique well in her speech on Special Olympics: "With the proper instruction, environment, and encouragement, Special Olympians can learn not only sport skills but life skills."

Antithesis can suggest that the speaker has a clear, decisive grasp of options. It magnifies the speaker as a person of vision, leadership, and action. Consider, for example, how President John F. Kennedy used antithesis in his Inaugural Address:

Ask not what your country can do for you—ask what you can do for your country.

Kennedy said essentially the same thing during a campaign speech in September 1960:

The new frontier is not what I promise I am going to do for you. The new frontier is what I ask you to do for your country.

Same message, different words. The first is memorable; the second is not. The difference is effective antithesis (as well as effective inversion and parallel construction).[35] In its entirety, the passage from the inaugural developed as follows:

And so, my fellow Americans: Ask not what your country can do for you—ask what you can do for your country.
My fellow citizens of the world: Ask not what America will do for you, but what together we can do for the freedom of man.

Inversion. **Inversion** reverses the expected order of words in a phrase or sentence to make a statement more memorable and emphatic. Consider how the impact of Kennedy's statement would have diminished had he used "Do not ask" instead of "Ask not."

Paul El-Amin concluded his criticism of internment practices after the 9/11 disaster by adapting the same passage from a meditation by the great theologian John

---

▶ **antithesis** A language technique that combines opposing elements in the same sentence or adjoining sentences.

▶ **inversion** Changing the normal order of words to make statements memorable.

Donne: "Ask not for whom the bell tolls. It tolls for thee. And it tolls for me. For all of us who love the Bill of Rights, it tolls." The "ask not" that begins this statement and the final sentence are both inverted from their usual order. The unusual order of the words gains attention and makes the statement impressive. Moreover, the "thee" adds to the impression that this is old, authentic wisdom. Used in student speeches, inversion works best as a beginning or ending technique, where it can gain attention, add dignity to the effort, and/or frame a memorable conclusion.

At times, inversion goes beyond reversing the expected order of words. In a baccalaureate address presented at Hamilton College, Bill Moyers commented on the many confusions of contemporary life and concluded: "Life is where you get your answers questioned."[36] Here the inversion of the conventional order of thoughts, in which answers usually follow questions rather than the other way around, makes for a witty, striking observation.

Parallel Construction. **Parallel construction** repeats the same pattern of words in a sequence of phrases or sentences for the sake of impact. Parallel construction can occur at any critical moment in a speech. As the Kennedy example illustrates, the repetition of the pattern of words can stamp its message into the mind and make its statement memorable. Perhaps the most famous examples in American public address are Martin Luther King's repeated phrase "I have a dream . . ." in his classic March on Washington speech and Lincoln's "of the people, by the people, and for the people . . ." near the end of the Gettysburg Address.

Using the Sounds of Words to Reinforce Their Sense

As they are pronounced, words have distinctive sounds. Part of the appeal of parallel construction is that it repeats these sounds, adding a sense of importance to the thoughts it conveys. At least two other techniques, alliteration and onomatopoeia, also arrange these sounds in distinctive ways. Both techniques magnify the language of feeling.

Alliteration. **Alliteration** repeats the initial sounds in a closely connected pattern of words. One student speaker who criticized the lowering of educational standards paused near the end of her speech to draw the following conclusion: "We don't need the doctrine of dumbing down." Her repetition of the *d* sound was distinctive and helped listeners remember her point. It expressed her strong feelings about practices she condemned.

Onomatopoeia. **Onomatopoeia** (on' uh mah' uh pay'uh) is the tendency of certain words to imitate the sounds of what they represent. For example, suppose you were trying to describe the scene of refugees fleeing from war and starvation. How could you bring that scene into focus for listeners who are far removed from it? One way would be to describe an old woman and her grandson as they *trudge* down a road to nowhere. The very sound of the word "trudge" suggests the weary, discouraged walk of the refugees. Memphis student Hannah Johnston also used the technique when she described packinghouse workers as "literally drenched in a river of blood." By its very sound, *drenched* suggests the unpleasant idea of being soaked with blood as you work. Combined with the "river of blood" metaphor, the technique draws listeners close to what the language describes. Onomatopoeia has this quality of conveying listeners into a scene by allowing them to hear its noises, smell its odors, taste its flavors, or touch its surfaces. The technique awakens sensory experience.

▶ **parallel construction** Wording points in the same way to emphasize their importance and to help the audience remember them.

▶ **alliteration** The repetition of initial consonant sounds in closely connected words.

▶ **onomatopoeia** Words that sound like the subjects they signify.

These various ways to magnify the power of language are summarized in Figure 4. As you consider how you might use them, remember that your words must not seem forced or artificial. For these techniques to work, they must seem to arise naturally and spontaneously in your speaking, and they must seem to fit both you and your subject. Use them sparingly so that they stand out from the rest of what you say. Employed artfully, and in accord with the six standards discussed earlier, they can both increase and harness the power of words so that they reinforce your message and help make your voice significant.

FIGURE 4 Magnifying the Power of Language

Using Figurative Language

Technique	Definition	Example
Metaphors	Unexpected figurative comparisons	An *iron curtain* has descended across the continent.
Enduring metaphors	Metaphors that transcend time and cultural boundaries	The development of the Internet marked the *dawn* of a new way of learning.
Similes	Figurative comparisons using *like* or *as*	The jellyfish is *like a living lava lamp.*
Synecdoche	Focusing on part to represent the whole	All *hands* on deck.
Personifications	Attributing human characteristics to things or events	Liberty *raises her flame* as a beacon.
Culturetypes	Words that express the values, identity, and goals of a group	This company is devoted to the ideals of *modern, efficient, progressive science.*
Ideographs	Words that express a country's basic political beliefs	All we ask is *liberty* and *justice.*

Manipulating the Order of Words

Technique	Definition	Example
Antithesis	Presenting contrasting ideas in parallel phrases	There is a *time to sow* and a *time to reap.*
Inversion	Changing the expected word order	This insult *we did not deserve,* and this result *we will not accept.*
Parallel construction	Repetition of words/phrases at beginning or end of sentences	*It's a program that ... It's a program that ... It's a program that ...*

Exploiting the Sounds of Words

Technique	Definition	Example
Alliteration	Repetition of initial sounds in closely connected words	Beware the *nattering nabobs* of *negativism.*
Onomatopoeia	Words that imitate natural sounds	The creek *gurgled* and *babbled* down to the river.

367

FINDING YOUR voice   Do Words Work for You?

Analyze how you used the power of language in your last speech. Did you have to overcome any barriers to perception or feeling among your listeners? Did you measure up to the standards suggested by the six C's? Did listeners respond to your message? What special techniques did you use? Could you have done better? How?

FINAL reflections   Give Me the Right Word

It may be helpful to end this chapter where we began it, reflecting on Joseph Conrad's eloquent "Give me the right word and the right accent, and I will move the world." Words, we now see, can also enlighten us or blind us, enflame us or benumb us, bring us together or drive us apart, inspire us to act or discourage action, and define who we are and are not. Words can heal us or injure us: There is no greater lie than the nursery maxim you may have chanted as a child, "Sticks and stones may break my bones but words can never harm me."

At their best, words can help us experience that "ah-hah" moment of illumination when we suddenly can see more clearly the world in which we live, who we are or must become in that world, and what we must do and say through our actions and our words. In short, words can help us come to focus, find our voice, and give it power.

A SAMPLE SPEECH

*In her self-introduction presented at Vanderbilt University, Ashley Smith used three contrasting photographs—each representing a different lifestyle—to structure her speech. This device also illustrates the cooperation of the visual and the verbal—pictures and words—to complete a very effective **synecdoche**. The photographs offer the surface details, but the words explain how they are representative of ways of life and what she learned from these exposures. In effect, they bring the photographs into focus for her speech.*

Three Photographs

ASHLEY SMITH

Photographs often tell stories that only a few can hear. I would like to tell you the story told to me by three snapshots that hang in my room in suburban Jacksonville, Florida. If you saw them, you might think them totally unrelated; together, they tell a powerful tale.

"Ashley, *levantete!*" I heard each morning for the month that I spent in Costa Rica as an exchange student. I would wake up at 5:30 to get ready for school and would stumble off to the one shower that the family of five shared. I had to wash myself in cold water because there was no warm water—that usually woke me up pretty fast! I then got dressed and breakfast would be waiting on the table. Predictably it would be fruit, coffee, and gallo pinto, a black bean and rice dish usually served at every meal.

We would then walk to school and begin the day with an hour and a half of shop class. After shop we would have about 15- to 20-minute classes in what you and I might call "regular" academic subjects: math and Spanish, for example. Those classes had frequent interruptions and were not taken very seriously. The socialization process was quite clear: These children were being prepared for jobs in the labor force instead of for higher education. Each afternoon as we walked home we passed the elite school where students were still busy working and studying. The picture in my room of my Costa Rican classmates painting picnic tables in the schoolyard reminds me of their narrow opportunities.

The second photograph on my wall is of a little girl in Botswana. She's nearing the end of her education and has finished up to the equivalent of the sixth grade. She will now return to a rural setting because her family cannot afford to continue her schooling. To add to the problem, the family goat was eaten by a lion, so she had to return to help them over this crisis.

But she didn't miss out on much—most likely, she would have gone on into the city and ended up in one of the shantytowns, one more victim of the unemployment, poverty, even starvation endured by the people. Her lack of opportunity is due not so much to class inequalities as in Costa Rica, but more to the cultural tradition of several hundred years of European exploitation. Recently there has been extensive growth there, but the natives have been left far behind.

The third photograph in my room is of four high school students, taken where I went to school in Jacksonville, Florida. We're all sitting on the lawn outside school, overlooking the parking lot full of new cars that will take us home to warm dinners and comfortable beds and large homes and privileged lives. Many of us—including myself for most of my life—took this world for granted. But now, for me, no more. I may have gained a lot in my travels, but I lost my political innocence.

One thing I gained is an intense desire to become an educator. I want to teach people to succeed on their merits despite the social and economic inequalities that they're faced with. And I want to learn from them as well. I want to teach the boy who never mastered welding that he could own the factory. And I want him to teach me how to use a rice cooker. I want to teach the girl who is exhausted each afternoon after walking to the river with a jar on her head to gather water that she could design an irrigation system. But I also want her to teach me how to weave a thatched roof. I want to travel and teach and learn.

Three photographs, hanging on my wall. They are silent, mute, and the photographer was not very skillful. But together they tell a powerful story in my life.

◀ Ashley's sharp, clear use of images helps shape listener **perceptions** and arouses **feelings** by overcoming barriers of distance. The touch of dialogue adds action to the picture.

◀ The Botswana picture personifies the cultural deprivation Ashley criticizes. Again, the combination of picture and words magnifies and explains her feelings and invites **identification** from her listeners.

◀ The third photograph offers a transition into Ashley's personal plan of action. We see that for her it reflects a way of life that hides the reality she had found elsewhere that now calls her into a life commitment.

◀ Again, Ashley uses synecdoche and personification to focus sharply on her life goals and to represent them to her listeners.

Notes

1. William Raspberry, "Any Candidate Will Drink to That," *Austin American Statesman*, 11 May 1984, p. A–10.
2. Ollie Reed, "Corsicans, Navajo Weave Ties," Scripps Howard News Service, 3 July 2001. *Commercial Appeal (Memphis)*, www.gomemphis.com (accessed 5 July 2001).
3. Among the most recent of these studies is that reported by Peter A. Andersen and Tammy R. Blackburn, "An Experimental Study of Language Intensity and Response Rate in E-Mail Surveys," *Communication Reports* 17 (no. 2) Summer 2004, pp. 73–82.
4. Jerry Tarver, "Words in Time: Some Reflections on the Language of Speech," *Vital Speeches of the Day*, 15 Apr. 1988, p. 410.
5. These powers of language were first explored in Michael Osborn, *Orientations to Rhetorical Style* (Chicago: Science Research Associates, 1976), and are developed further in Michael Osborn, "Rhetorical Depiction," in *Form, Genre, and the Study of Political Discourse*, eds. Herbert W. Simons and Aram A. Aghazarian (Columbia: University of South Carolina Press, 1986), pp. 79–107.
6. 5 Apr. 1996, http://www.v-j-enterprises.com/astro2.html (accessed 17 June 2008).
7. Based on the account in Claire Perkins, "The Many Symbolic Faces of Fred Smith: Charismatic Leadership in the Bureaucracy," *Journal of the Tennessee Speech Communication Association* 11 (1985): 22.
8. Adapted from *The American Heritage Dictionary*, 2nd ed. (Boston: Houghton Mifflin, 1985), p. 92.
9. Speech on Race, presented March 18, 2008, in Philadelphia, PA, http://www.nytimes.com/ 2008/03/18/us/politics/18text-obama.html?ei=5087&em=&en=ee.
10. Nikki Giovanni, "We Are Virginia Tech," 17 April 2007, www.americanrhetoric.com/speeches/nikkigiovannivatech-memorial.htm (accessed 14 May 2007). © 2007 Nikki Giovanni. Reprinted by permission.
11. Listeners whose lives seem dull and unrewarding are especially susceptible to such dramas. See the discussion in Eric Hoffer, *The True Believer: Thoughts on the Nature of Mass Movements* (New York: Harper, 1951).
12. Ronald Reagan, "Second Inaugural Address," *Vital Speeches of the Day*, 51 (1 Feb. 1985): 226–228.
13. AOL News, 13 June 2008, http://news.aol.com/story/_a/flood-puts-city-at-gods-mercy/ 20080612191009990001.
14. "TennCare Offset Fee Gets Backing," *The Memphis Commercial Appeal*, 12 March 2010, p. C1.
15. "Presidential Ecospeak," *New York Times*, Editorials/Op-Ed, 18 Oct. 2003, www.truthout.org/cgi-bin/artman/exec/view.cgi/15/2355 (accessed 29 Oct. 2003).

16. Bill Gates, "High Schools Are Obsolete: Teaching Kids What They Need to Know," *Vital Speeches of the Day* 71 (15 April 2005): 396–397.

17. "Malapropisms Live!" *Spectra,* May 1986, p. 6.

18. Haven E. Cockerham, "Conquer the Isms That Stand in Our Way," *Vital Speeches of the Day,* 1 Feb. 1998, p. 240.

19. "Swim Club President Apologizes, NBC Philadelphia, 10 July 2009 http://www.nbcphiladelphia.com/news/local-beat/Swim-Club-President-Apologizes-About-Pool (accessed 15 March 2010).

20. Antoinette M. Bailey, "Bow Wave," *Vital Speeches of the Day,* 1 June 2001, p. 502.

21. Memphis *Commercial Appeal,* 26 January 2010, p. A9.

22. For additional discussion of such metaphors, see Michael Osborn, "Archetypal Metaphor in Rhetoric: The Light-Dark Family," *Quarterly Journal of Speech* 53 (1967): 115–126, and "The Evolution of the Archetypal Sea in Rhetoric and Poetic," *Quarterly Journal of Speech* 63 (1977): 347–363.

23. George W. Bush, "Inaugural Address," *Vital Speeches of the Day,* 1 Feb. 2001, p. 226.

24. See another side of this image in J. Vernon Jensen, "British Voices on the Eve of the American Revolution: Trapped by the Family Metaphor," *Quarterly Journal of Speech* 63 (1977): 43–50.

25. Barack Obama's Speech on Race, http://www.npr.org/templates/story/story.php?storyId=8847867

26. For an insightful discussion of the metaphors we use to construct our ideas about illness, see Susan Sontag, *Illness as Metaphor* (New York: Vintage Books, 1979), and *AIDS and Its Metaphors* (New York: Farrar, Straus and Giroux, 1988).

27. See Robert Ivie, "Images of Savagery in American Justifications for War," *Communication Monographs* 47 (1980): 279–294.

28. Michael Osborn, "Patterns of Metaphor Among Early Feminist Orators," in *Rhetoric and Community: Studies in Unity and Fragmentation,* ed. J. Michael Hogan (Columbia: University of South Carolina Press, 1998), pp. 10–11.

29. Quoted from Dr. Seuss [Theodore Seuss Geisel], "How Orlo Got His Book," *The New York Times Book Review,* 17 Nov. 1957.

30. Wendi C. Thomas, "Spaced Out on Budget Priorities," *The Memphis Commercial Appeal,* 1 Jan. 2004, A1. (accessed 22 Jan. 2004).

31. Michael Calvin McGee, "The Origins of Liberty: A Feminization of Power," *Communication Monographs* 47 (1980): 27–45.

32. Osborn, *Orientations to Rhetorical Style,* p. 16.

33. Richard Weaver, "Ultimate Terms in Contemporary Rhetoric," in *The Ethics of Rhetoric* (Chicago: Henry Regnery, 1953), pp. 211–232.

34. Michael Calvin McGee, "The Ideograph: A Link Between Rhetoric and Ideology," *Quarterly Journal of Speech* 66 (1980): 1–16.

35. This example is adapted from Ronald H. Carpenter, *Choosing Powerful Words: Eloquence That Works* (Boston: Allyn & Bacon, 1999), pp. 14–15.

36. Bill Moyers, "Pass the Bread," a baccalaureate address presented at Hamilton College, May 20, 2006.

Ethical Responsibility in Human Communication

Values can be viewed as conceptions of The Good or The Desirable that motivate human behavior and that function as criteria in our making of choices and judgments. Concepts such as material success, individualism, efficiency, thrift, freedom, courage, hard work, competition, patriotism, compromise, and punctuality are value standards that have varying degrees of potency in contemporary North American culture. But we probably would not view them primarily as *ethical* standards of right and wrong. Ethical judgments focus more precisely on degrees of rightness and wrongness, virtue and vice, and obligation in human behavior. In condemning someone for being inefficient, conformist, extravagant, lazy, or late, we probably would not also be claiming they are unethical. However, standards such as honesty, promise-keeping, truthfulness, fairness, and humaneness usually *are* used in making ethical judgments of rightness and wrongness in human behavior.

Ethical issues may arise in human behavior whenever that behavior could have significant impact on other persons, when the behavior involves conscious choice of means and ends, and when the behavior can be judged by standards of right and wrong.[1] If there is little possible significant, immediate, or long-term impact of our actions (physical or symbolic) on other humans, matters of ethics normally are viewed as minimally relevant. If we have little or no opportunity for conscious free choice in our behavior, if we feel compelled to do or say something because we are forced or coerced, matters of ethics usually are seen as minimally relevant to *our* actions.

Some philosophers draw distinctions between ethics and morals as concepts. Ethics denotes the general and systematic study of what ought to be the grounds and principles for right and wrong human behavior. Morals (or morality) denotes the practical, specific, generally agreed-upon, culturally transmitted standards of right and wrong. Other philosophers, however, use the terms ethics and morals more or less interchangeably—as will be the case in this book.

INHERENCY OF POTENTIAL ETHICAL ISSUES

Potential ethical issues are inherent in any instance of communication between humans to the degree that the communication can be judged on a right–wrong dimension, that it involves possible significant influence on other humans, and that the communicator

---

[1]See, for example, Carl Wellman, *Morals and Ethics*, 2d ed. (Englewood Cliffs, NJ: Prentice-Hall, 1988), pp. xiii–xviii, 267.

Reprinted from *Ethics in Human Communication* edited by Richard Johannesen, Kathleen Valde, and Karen Whedbee (2007), by permission of Waveland Press, Inc.

consciously chooses specific ends sought and communicative means to achieve those ends. Whether a communicator seeks to present information, increase someone's level of understanding, facilitate independent decision making in another person, persuade about important values, demonstrate the existence and relevance of a societal problem, advocate a solution or program of action, or stimulate conflict—potential ethical issues inhere in the communicator's symbolic efforts. Such is the case for most human communication whether it is between two people; in small groups; in the rhetoric of a social movement; in communication from government to citizen; or in an advertising, public relations, or political campaign.

"Human beings always have a sense of the self, in the sense that they situate themselves somewhere in ethical space," contends philosopher Charles Taylor. "A human being exists inescapably in a space of ethical questions; she cannot avoid assessing herself in relation to some standards. To escape all standards would not be liberation but a terrifying lapse into total disorientation."[2] But some people ask, why worry at all about ethics in human communication? Indeed, to avoid consideration of ethics in communication, such persons may resort to various justifications: (1) everyone knows that this particular communication technique is unethical, so there is nothing to discuss; (2) since only success matters in communication, ethicality is irrelevant; (3) after all, ethical judgments are simply matters of individual personal opinion anyway, so there are no final answers; and (4) it is presumptuous, perhaps even unethical, to judge the ethics of others.[3]

Tension potentially exists between *"is"* and *"ought,"* between the actual and the ideal. What everyone is doing and what we judge they ought to do, what the majority says is ethical and what a few argue ought to be ethical, may differ. There may be a conflict between a communication technique we know is successful and the judgment that the technique ought not to be used because it is ethically suspect. We may overemphasize our understanding of the nature and effectiveness of communication techniques, processes, and methods at the expense of concern for the ethical use of such techniques. We should examine not only *how to*, but also *whether we ethically ought to*, employ methods and appeals. The question of "whether to" clearly is one not only of audience adaptation but also one of ethics. We may feel that ethical ideals are not realistically achievable and thus are of little usefulness. But Thomas Nilsen reminds us that "we must always expect a gap between ideals and their attainment, between principles and their application." Nevertheless, he feels that "ideals reflect genuine beliefs, intentions, and aspirations. They reflect what we in our more calm and thoughtful moments think ought to be, however aware we may be of our actual . . . level of achievement . . . . Our ideals provide an ultimate goal, a sense of direction, a general orientation, by which to guide conduct."[4]

How participants in a human communication transaction evaluate the ethics of that transaction, or how outside observers evaluate its ethics, will differ depending

---

[2]Charles Taylor, "The Dialogical Self," in *Rethinking Knowledge*, Robert F. Goodman and Walter R. Fisher, eds. (Albany: State University of New York Press, 1995), pp. 57–66.

[3]For one attempt to side-step ethical issues, see Theodore Levitt, "Are Advertising and Marketing Corrupting Society? It's Not Your Worry," *Advertising Age* (October 6, 1958): 89–92; a rebuttal to this position is Clyde Bedell, "To the Extent Advertising and Marketing are Corrupting Society—You'd Better Worry!" *Advertising Age* (October 27, 1958): 101–102.

[4]Thomas R. Nilsen, *Ethics of Speech Communication*, 2d ed. (Indianapolis: Bobbs-Merrill, 1974), p. 15.

on the ethical standards they employ. Some even may choose to ignore ethical judgments entirely. Nevertheless, *potential* ethical questions are there regardless of how they are resolved or answered.

Whether a communicator wishes it or not, communicatees generally will judge, formally or informally, the communicator's effort in part by those communicatees' relevant ethical standards. If for none other than the pragmatic reason of enhancing chances of success, the communicator would do well to consider the ethical criteria held by his or her audience.

ADAPTATION TO THE AUDIENCE

What are the ethics of audience adaptation? Most human communicators seek to secure some kind of response from receivers. To what degree is it ethical for communicators to alter their ideas and proposals in order to adapt to the needs, capacities, desires, and expectations of an audience? To secure acceptance, some communicators adapt to an audience to the extent of so changing their ideas that the idea is no longer really theirs. These communicators merely say what the audience wants them to say regardless of their *own* convictions. For example, in the words of one journalist, Bill Clinton "has been criticized throughout his career for trying to be all things to all people and saying whatever the person he is talking to wants to hear."[5] Other communicators, in contrast, go to the opposite extreme of making little or no adaptation to their audience. They do not take serious account of their audience. Their audience thus perceives the speaker, writer, or advertisement as unconnected to them or unconcerned about them. Some measure of adaptation in language choice, supporting materials, organization, and message transmission to reflect the specific nature of the audience is a crucial part of successful communication. No ironclad rule can be set down here.

The search is for an appropriate point between two undesirable extremes—the extreme of saying only what the audience desires and will approve and the extreme of complete lack of concern for and understanding of the audience. The search is for an appropriate point between too much adaptation to the audience and not enough. Both extremes are ethically irresponsible. This tension, this search for balance in audience adaptation, can be viewed as an example of Aristotle's Doctrine of the Mean (termed by others as the Golden Mean). For Aristotle, moral virtue usually represents a mean or intermediate point between two vices—the vice of excess and the vice of deficiency. For example, courage is a mean between foolhardiness and cowardice. Generosity is a mean between wastefulness and stinginess. Aristotle denies that the mean is a mathematically precise average or midpoint between extremes. Rather, the mean combines the right amount at the right time toward the right people in a right manner for the right motives. The mean is also relative to the person's status, specific situation, and strengths and weaknesses of character. A person generally disposed toward one extreme in an appropriate instance ought to tend toward the other extreme to redress the imbalance.[6] In this era of heightened awareness of ethnic,

---

[5]David Maraniss, "The Comeback Kid's Last Return," *Washington Post National Weekly Edition*, September 2–8, 1996, pp. 8–9. For further discussion of the audience adaptation ethical issue, see Wayne C. Booth, *The Rhetoric of RHETORIC* (Malden, MA: Blackwell, 2004), pp. 50–54.

[6]This explanation of the Golden Mean is indebted to Clifford G. Christians et al., *Media Ethics: Cases and Moral Reasoning*, 6th ed. (New York: Addison Wesley Longman, 2001), pp. 12–13. Also see Aristotle, *Nicomachean Ethics*, in *The Basic Works of Aristotle*, ed. Richard McKeon (New York: Random House, 1941), pp. 952–964 (1103a–1109b).

racial, religious, and sexual diversity, communicators face significant practical and ethical choices concerning the appropriate degree of audience adaptation.

THE IMPORTANCE OF ETHICS

Persons enrolled in communication courses frequently are preparing for careers in advertising, sales, law, journalism, business, or politics. But those interested in such careers may be surprised by the extremely negative perceptions that citizens have of the ethics and honesty of persons in those careers. The 2006 Gallup Poll of perceived honesty and ethics of 23 professions ranked the following 11, in descending order, as lowest in perceived ethicality: journalists, state governors, business executives, lawyers, stockbrokers, senators, congressmen, insurance salesmen, HMO managers, advertising practitioners, and, at the bottom, car salesmen (www.gallup.com; released December 14, 2006).

Evidence abounds that supports public concern over the decline of ethical behavior. A 2006 Gallup Poll of public perceptions of moral values in the United States found that 85 percent of respondents rated the current state of moral values as only fair/poor and 81 percent thought the level of moral values was getting worse (www.gallup.com; released May 25, 2006). A national firm that conducts background checks reviewed 2.6 million job applications in 2002 and found that 44 percent contained some lies (*New York Times*, December 28, 2002, p. C8). The Josephson Institute of Ethics conducted a 2006 national survey of over 33,000 high school students. The results show a puzzling contradiction. On the one hand, over 90 percent of those surveyed say that it is "important to me to be a person of good character," that "honesty and trust are essential in personal relationships," and that they are "satisfied with my own ethics and character." On the other hand, in stark contrast, 82 percent admitted they had lied to a parent (57 percent two or more times) and 62 percent lied to a teacher (35 percent two or more times) about something significant in the past year. Sixty percent admitted they cheated during a test at school this past year—35 percent cheated two or more times (www.josephsoninstitute.org; released October 15, 2006).

In his book, *The Cheating Culture* (2004), David Callahan documents a "pattern of widespread cheating throughout U.S. society," observes that people "not only are cheating in more areas but are feeling less guilty about it," and concludes that most of the cheating "is by people who, on the whole, view themselves as upstanding members of society." *The New Ethics: A Tour of the 21st Century Moral Landscape* (2004) is a wide-ranging analysis by Anita L. Allen. Her overview summary is one of pessimism and puzzlement: "Our contemporary ethical landscape is marked by ... widespread ethical failure against the background of a culture rich with moral resources. We seem to have everything we need for exemplary character and conduct, and yet wrongdoing flourishes in every sector. Why are we not better? How can we become better?"[7]

"A society without ethics is a society doomed to extinction," argues philosopher S. Jack Odell. According to Odell, the "basic concepts and theories of ethics provide the framework necessary for working out one's own moral or ethical code." Odell

---

[7]David Callahan, *The Cheating Culture: Why More Americans Are Doing Wrong to Get Ahead* (New York: Harcourt, 2004), pp. 12–14; Anita L. Allen, *The New Ethics: A Tour of the 21st-Century Moral Landscape* (New York: Miramax, 2004), p. xii.

believes that "ethical principles are necessary preconditions for the existence of a social community. Without ethical principles it would be impossible for human beings to live in harmony and without fear, despair, hopelessness, anxiety, apprehension, and uncertainty."[8]

A societal or personal system of ethics is not a magic or automatic cure-all for individual or collective ills. What can ethical theory and systematic reflection on ethics contribute? One answer is suggested by philosopher Carl Wellman:

> An ethical system does not solve all one's practical problems, but one cannot choose and act rationally without some explicit or implicit ethical system. An ethical theory does not tell a person what to do in any given situation, but neither is it completely silent; it tells one what to consider in making up one's mind what to do. The practical function of an ethical system is primarily to direct our attention to the relevant considerations, the reasons that determine the rightness or wrongness of any act.[9]

FREEDOM AND RESPONSIBILITY

American culture emphasizes dual concerns for maximizing latitude of freedom of communication and for promoting responsible exercise of such freedom. The current and future boundaries of freedom of communication in the United States are explored in such works as: *The System of Freedom of Expression, Freedom of Speech in the United States*, and *Speech and Law in a Free Society*.[10] Psychiatrist Thomas Szasz succinctly describes the interrelated and intertwined nature of freedom and responsibility.

> The crucial moral characteristic of the human condition is the dual experience of freedom of the will and personal responsibility. Since freedom and responsibility are two aspects of the same phenomenon, they invite comparison with the proverbial knife that cuts both ways. One of its edges implies options: we call it freedom. The other implies obligations: we call it responsibility. People like freedom because it gives them mastery over things and people. They dislike responsibility because it constrains them from satisfying their wants. That is why one of the things that characterizes history is the unceasing human effort to maximize freedom and minimize responsibility. But to no avail, for each real increase in human freedom ... brings with it a proportionate increase in responsibility. Each exhilaration with the power to do good is soon eclipsed by the guilt for having used it to do evil.[11]

---

[8]Odell in John C. Merrill and S. Jack Odell, *Philosophy and Journalism* (New York: Longman, 1983), pp. 2, 95.

[9]Wellman, *Morals and Ethics*, p. 305.

[10]See, for example: Thomas I. Emerson, *The System of Freedom of Expression* (New York: Random House, 1970); Franklyn S. Haiman, *Speech and Law in a Free Society* (Chicago: University of Chicago Press, 1981); Thomas L. Tedford and Dale Herbeck, *Freedom of Speech in the United States*, 5th ed. (State College, PA: Strata, 2004).

[11]Thomas Szasz, *The Theology of Medicine* (Baton Rouge: Louisiana State University Press, 1977), p. xiii. Also see J. Vernon Jensen, *Ethical Issues in the Communication Process* (Mahwah, NJ: Erlbaum, 1997), pp. 9–10.

African American legal scholar and social critic Stephen Carter describes the tension this way.

> On the one hand, freedom unrestrained by clear moral norms begets anarchy. On the other hand, moral norms that have the force of law often stifle freedom. This tension is inevitable in a nation that wishes to be both moral and free. But nobody can (or should want to) sustain the tension indefinitely; sooner or later, on every question on which we might disagree, the side of freedom or the side of restraint will have its way.[12]

The freedom versus responsibility tension can appear when we, as individuals, carry to an extreme the now traditional view that the best test of the worth of our ideas is their ability to survive in the free and open public "marketplace" of ideas. We might take the mistaken view that, as individuals, we have no responsibility to test the ethicality of our communication means and ends before we present them. Rather we incorrectly assume that the logical and ethical soundness of our ideas need only be evaluated through their ability to survive in competition with other ideas and differing viewpoints in the marketplace. Such a view could lead each of us to ignore our ethical responsibilities as communicators because the marketplace will ultimately render the necessary judgments. However, we must remember that while we do have First Amendment protection of freedom of speech and press, each of us also has the responsibility to exercise that freedom in an ethical manner.[13]

We now turn to an actual example of freedom and responsibility in tension. In the early morning of April 16, 2007, a student at Virginia Tech University, armed with two handguns, shot and killed two students in a dormitory. A little over two hours later, the killer murdered 30 students and faculty in a classroom building before committing suicide. In the time between the murders, the killer mailed to NBC News a self-produced package of 27 video clips, 43 photos, and an 18,000-word hate-filled manifesto of his beliefs and complaints. After receiving the package two days later, NBC made copies for its own use and promptly turned over the multi-media diatribe to the FBI (*Chicago Tribune*, April 19, 2007, sec. 1, pp. 1, 10).

Quickly NBC, MSNBC, and, later, CNN broadcasted (and continually rebroadcasted) excerpts from the written document, some of the hate and profanity-filled video clips, and photos showing the killer brandishing two handguns, holding a gun to his head, and holding a knife to his throat. The multi-media materials seemed intended by the killer to depict himself as a victim of societal forces beyond his control and as a hero, even a martyr, for the downtrodden. Very soon, controversy arose in the public press about whether NBC (and other media) had acted responsibly and ethically in giving such prominence to the killer's self-serving material. (For a chronology of events, see *Newsweek*, April 30, 2007, pp. 22–29.)

Don Wycliff, a well-respected Chicago journalist, approved of NBC's decisions. No "secondhand account" could have captured the killer's "mental and emotional" mind-set "as well as his writing, those photographs, and that frightful, appalling

---

[12]Stephen L. Carter, *Civility: Manners, Morals, and the Etiquette of Democracy* (New York: Basic Books, 1998), p. 207.

[13]Adapted from Alexander Meiklejohn, *Political Freedom* (New York: Harper & Brothers, 1948, 1960), pp. 73–74.

videotape." NBC, he felt, was justified, even obligated, to broadcast the material. Wycliff concluded: "They did the right thing. They did what a good news organization is supposed to do: responsibly inform the people about matters of genuine public importance" (*Chicago Tribune*, April 22, 2007, sec. 2, p. 7).

In contrast, a number of writers of letters-to-the-editor in the *Chicago Tribune* (April 21, 2007, sec. 1, pp. 24–25; April 28, 2007, p. 29) represent the viewpoint that while NBC has the right to freedom of the press, in this case it was ethically irresponsible in the way it exercised that right. Here, in summary form, are just four of their arguments. First, NBC's airing of the killer's own material gave him exactly the widespread publicity he sought. Second, broadcasting the material could encourage others to emulate the killer. Third, NBC's coverage should have centered more on the victims' lives and the impact of their deaths on others. Fourth, NBC's coverage caused unnecessary trauma and pain for the relatives and friends of those massacred. One letter writer believed that NBC's irresponsible coverage "proves that ratings trump ethics." Another writer concluded: "Yes there is free speech in the United States, but along with that, the media have a responsibility to exercise good judgment in their reporting and maintain some sense of decorum."

Consider, now, your own viewpoint on the freedom versus responsibility tension as manifested in this case. From your own memory of network television coverage of the Virginia Tech shootings, to what degree were the national broadcast media, especially NBC, MSNBC, and CNN, acting ethically or irresponsibly in exercising their press freedom? Why?

As communicators, our ethical responsibilities may stem from a position or role we have earned or been granted, from commitments (promises, pledges, agreements) we have made, from established ethical principles, from relationships we have formed, or from consequences (effects, impacts) of our communication on others. Responsibility includes the elements of fulfilling duties and obligations, of being held accountable as evaluated by agreed-upon standards, and of being accountable to our own conscience. But an essential element of responsible communication, for both sender and receiver, is the exercise of thoughtful and caring judgment. That is, the responsible communicator reflectively analyzes claims, soundly assesses probable consequences, and conscientiously considers relevant values (both abstract principles and personal relationships). In a sense a responsible communicator is *response-able*. She or he exercises the ability to respond (is responsive) to the needs and communication of others in sensitive, thoughtful, fitting ways.[14]

Feminist philosopher Margaret Urban Walker provides an apt summary:

> We can be responsible for specific tasks or goals, roles with discretionary powers, acts and failures to act, outcomes and upshots of actions (not always

---

[14]This discussion of responsibility is based on: J. Roland Pennock, "The Problem of Responsibility," in *Nomos III, Responsibility*, Carl J. Friedrich, ed. (New York: Liberal Arts Press, 1960), pp. 3–27; Ludwig Freund, "Responsibility—Definitions, Distinctions, and Applications in Various Contexts," in Ibid., pp. 28–42; H. Richard Niebuhr, *The Responsible Self* (New York: Harper and Row, 1963), pp. 47–89, 151–154; Edmund L. Pincoffs, "On Being Responsible for What One Says," paper presented at Speech Communication Association convention, Houston, December 1975; Kurt Baier, "Responsibility and Freedom," in *Ethics and Society*, Richard T. DeGeorge, ed. (Garden City, NY: Anchor Books, 1966), pp. 49–84. Also see Michael S. Pritchard, *On Becoming Responsible* (Lawrence: University Press of Kansas, 1991); John Martin Fischer, "Recent Work on Moral Responsibility," *Ethics*, 110 (October 1999): 93–139.

controllable or foreseen), contributions to outcomes that are not ours alone, and attitudes, habits, and traits. Specific distributions of responsibility roughly map out this complex terrain of who must account, how far and for what, to whom.[15]

From time to time, however, we or others attempt to evade ethical responsibility or accountability by using one or more excuses such as: (1) I was just following orders; I was told to do it; (2) it was part of my job to do it; (3) everyone else is doing it; (4) what I did won't make any difference anyhow; (5) it's not my problem or my responsibility; or (6) nobody else knew about it.[16]

The concern for ethically responsible communication finds apt expression in the words of Dag Hammarskjöld, a former Secretary General of the United Nations:

> Respect for the word—to employ it with scrupulous care and an incorruptible heartfelt love of truth—is essential if there is to be any growth in a society or in the human race.
>
> To misuse the word is to show contempt for man. It undermines the bridges and poisons the wells. It causes Man to regress down the long path of his evolution.[17]

THE INTENTIONAL AND THE SINCERE

Whether communicators seem *intentionally* and *knowingly* to use particular content or techniques is a factor that most of us take into account in judging degree of communication ethicality. If a dubious communication behavior seems to stem more from accident, from an unintentional slip of the tongue, or even from ignorance, often we are less harsh in our ethical assessment. For most of us, it is the intentional use of ethically questionable tactics that merits our harshest condemnation. As an example, Nicholas Rescher believes that there is no moral or ethical issue when persons unintentionally or accidentally use unsound evidence or illogical reasoning. But he sees the intentional use of faulty reasoning as quite different. "Undoubtedly, the person who sets out *deliberately to deceive* others by means of improper reasoning is morally culpable."[18]

In contrast, it might be contended that in argumentative and persuasive situations, communicators have an ethical obligation to double-check the soundness of their evidence and reasoning before they present it to others; sloppy preparation is

[15]Margaret Urban Walker, *Moral Understandings: A Feminist Study in Ethics* (New York: Routledge, 1998), pp. 93–100, espec. 94.

[16]Thomas A. Biyins, "Responsibility and Accountability," in *Ethics in Public Relations: Responsible Advocacy*, Kathy Fitzpatrick and Carolyn Bronstein, eds. (Thousand Oaks, CA: Sage, 2006), pp. 31–35. Also see Tamera B. Murdock and Jason M. Stephens, "Is Cheating Wrong? Students' Reasoning about Academic Dishonesty," in *The Psychology of Academic Cheating*, Eric M. Anderman and Tamera B. Murdock, eds. (Burlington, MA: Elsevier Academic Press, 2007), pp. 229–251.

[17]Dag Hammarskjöld, *Markings* (New York: Alfred A. Knopf, 1964), p. 112.

[18]Nicholas Rescher, *Dialectics: A Controversy-Oriented Approach to the Theory of Knowledge* (Albany: State University of New York Press, 1977), pp. 78–82; also see Glen H. Stamp and Mark L. Knapp, "The Construct of Intent in Interpersonal Communication," *Quarterly Journal of Speech*, 76 (August 1990): 282–299.

not an adequate excuse to lessen the harshness of our ethical judgment. A similar view might be advanced concerning elected or appointed government officials. If they use obscure or jargon-laden language that clouds the accurate and clear representation of ideas, even if that use is not intended to deceive or hide, they are ethically irresponsible. Such officials, according to this view, should be obligated to communicate clearly and accurately with citizens in fulfillment of their governmental duties.

In *Moralities of Everyday Life*, the authors note that usually "there is a close relationship between responsibility and intent—we are responsible for what we intend to do, what we are trying to do." Nevertheless they argue the position that "people are responsible for all that they cause so long as they can see that they cause it and can do otherwise. We may feel responsible only for what we intend; we are responsible for all that we do."[19]

As a related question we can ask, does *sincerity* of intent release a communicator from ethical responsibility concerning means and effects? Could we say that *if* Adolf Hitler's fellow Germans judged him to be sincere, they should not assess the ethics of his persuasion? In such cases, evaluations are probably best carried out if we appraise sincerity and ethicality separately. For example, a communicator sincere in intent may be found to utilize an unethical strategy. Or communication techniques generally considered ethical might be used by an insincere person. Wayne Booth reminds us that "sincerity is more difficult to check and easier to fake than logicality or consistency, and its presence does not, after all, guarantee very much about the speaker's case."[20] And Peter Drucker describes the different meanings of sincerity in Western and Eastern cultures. Westerners view sincerity as "words that are true to convictions and feelings" whereas people from Eastern cultures define sincerity as "actions that are appropriate to a specific relationship and make it harmonious and of optimum mutual benefit."[21]

COMPONENTS OF MORALITY AND INTEGRITY

The research program of James Rest and his colleagues on moral development suggests that moral action typically is the outcome of four complex and interrelated psychological processes.[22] They may occur in varying sequences and varying degrees of strength but all must be present in significant strength for the moral act to occur. *Moral sensitivity* involves interpreting the situation, recognizing it as one embodying ethical issues, using empathy and role-taking to understand how the act might affect all concerned, and imagining cause-effect sequences of events.

---

[19]John Sabini and Maury Silver. *Moralities of Everyday Life* (New York: Oxford University Press, 1982), pp. 65–66.

[20]Wayne C. Booth, *Modern Dogma and the Rhetoric of Assent* (Notre Dame: University of Notre Dame Press, 1974); also see Arnold M. Ludwig, *The Importance of Lying* (Springfield, IL: Charles C. Thomas, 1965), p. 227.

[21]Peter Drucker, *The Changing World of the Executive* (New York: Times Books, 1982), p. 249.

[22]The following summary is paraphrased from James Rest et al., *Postconventional Moral Thinking* (Mahwah, NJ: Erlbaum, 1999), pp. 100–103; James Rest and Darcia Narvaez, eds., *Moral Development in the Professions* (Hillsdale, NJ: Erlbaum, 1994), pp. 22–25; James Rest, *Moral Development: Advances in Theory and Research* (New York: Praeger, 1986), pp. 3–18. Also see Rushworth M. Kidder, *Moral Courage* (New York: Wm. Morrow, 2005), pp. 7, 35–38, 72.

Moral judgment involves deciding, after reflection and in light of relevant ethical standards, which act would be most morally justifiable. *Moral motivation* involves a degree of commitment to doing the moral act, preferring ethical standards when in conflict with other values (selfish gain, immediate self-satisfaction, etc.), and taking personal moral responsibility for consequences of the act. *Moral character* involves persistence, backbone, courage, toughness, energy, focus, and strength of conviction necessary for actually performing the behaviors necessary to accomplish the act. A person may possess the first three components in a situation, but if that person's character is weak rather than strong, the ethical act probably will not occur. Of course lack of sufficient strength for any one of the four components can result in moral failure in a situation.

In some senses, Rest's components leading to a moral act harmonize with the elements of "integrity" defined by Stephen Carter. For him, a person of integrity takes time and effort to deliberate about the right thing to do, actually does the right thing despite personal hardship, and is willing to explain what was done and to justify it.[23] Margaret Urban Walker elaborates her view of integrity as a "morally admirable quality."[24] She sees "integrity as a kind of *reliability*: reliability in the accounts we are prepared to give, act by, and stand by, in moral terms, and dependable responsiveness to the ongoing fit among our accounts, the ways we have acted, and the consequences and costs our actions have in fact incurred." Integrity as reliability, she believes, includes engaging in actions that are reasonably consistent and coherent ethically, providing sensible ethical justifications for these actions, keeping short-term and long-term promises, recognizing that sometimes we may be expected to account for consequences we did not control, and being willing to try to restore reliability after an action of dubious or failed ethicality.

ETHICS AND PERSONAL CHARACTER

An emphasis on duties, obligations, rules, principles, and the resolution of complex ethical dilemmas has dominated the contemporary philosophy of ethics. This dominant emphasis has been true whether as variations on Immanuel Kant's Categorical Imperative, on John Rawls's depersonalized veil of ignorance to determine justice, on statements of intrinsic ultimate goods, or on Jeremy Bentham's or John Stuart Mill's utilitarian views. The past several decades, however, have witnessed a growing interest among ethicists in a largely ignored tradition that goes back at least as far as Plato's and Aristotle's philosophies of ethics. This largely bypassed tradition typically is called virtue ethics or character ethics. Most ethicists of virtue or character see that perspective as a crucial complement to the current dominant ethical theories. Ethicists describe virtues variously as deep-rooted dispositions, habits, skills, or traits of character that incline persons to perceive, feel, and act in ethically right and sensitive ways. Also, they describe virtues as learned, acquired, cultivated, reinforced, capable of modification, capable of conflicting, and ideally coalesced into a harmonious cluster.

Ethical communication is not simply a series of careful and reflective decisions, instance by instance, to communicate in ethically responsible ways. Deliberate application of ethical rules sometimes is not possible. Pressure may be so great or a

---

[23]Carter, *Civility*, p. 274; Stephen L. Carter, *Integrity* (New York: Basic Books, 1996), pp. 7–12.
[24]Walker, *Moral Understandings*, pp. 115–120.

five principles summarized here: *Truthfulness* of the message (honesty, trustworthiness, nondeceptiveness). *Authenticity* of the persuader (genuineness, integrity, ethical character, appropriate loyalty). *Respect* for the persuadee (regard for dignity, rights, well-being). *Equity* of the content and execution of the appeal (fairness, justice, nonexploitation of vulnerability). *Social responsibility* for the common good (concern for the broad public interest and welfare more than simply selfish self-interest, profit, or career).

FORECAST

Throughout this book we present a variety of starting points and materials to aid in analyzing ethics in human communication. Certainly they are not to be viewed as the "last word" on the subject or as the only possible ones. Rather they should stimulate our thinking and encourage reflective judgment.

We explore seven perspectives for ethical assessment of human communication. Each perspective represents a major ethical viewpoint or conceptual "lens" that scholars intentionally, and others often unknowingly, use to analyze specific issues and instances. As categories, these perspectives are not mutually exclusive of each other and they are not in any priority. These perspectives should not be taken as exhaustive of possible stances; probably each of us could think of others. For each perspective, the essential elements—the sources of grounding—for that general perspective are briefly explained. Examples—versions—of each perspective are then analyzed. Versions simply are illustrative, not exhaustive.

Through examination of various perspectives, issues, problems, examples, and case studies, this book seeks to aid students and teachers of human communication. The goal is exploration of ethical responsibilities in contermporary communication—whether that communication is oral or written, whether it is labeled informative, persuasive, or rhetorical, whether it is labeled interpersonal, public, or mass.

Index